IFIP Advances in Information and Communication Technology 403

IFIP – The International Federation for Information Processing

IFIP was founded in 1960 under the auspices of UNESCO, following the First World Computer Congress held in Paris the previous year. An umbrella organization for societies working in information processing, IFIP's aim is two-fold: to support information processing within its member countries and to encourage technology transfer to developing nations. As its mission statement clearly states,

> IFIP's mission is to be the leading, truly international, apolitical organization which encourages and assists in the development, exploitation and application of information technology for the benefit of all people.

IFIP is a non-profitmaking organization, run almost solely by 2500 volunteers. It operates through a number of technical committees, which organize events and publications. IFIP's events range from an international congress to local seminars, but the most important are:

- The IFIP World Computer Congress, held every second year;
- Open conferences;
- Working conferences.

The flagship event is the IFIP World Computer Congress, at which both invited and contributed papers are presented. Contributed papers are rigorously refereed and the rejection rate is high.

As with the Congress, participation in the open conferences is open to all and papers may be invited or submitted. Again, submitted papers are stringently refereed.

The working conferences are structured differently. They are usually run by a working group and attendance is small and by invitation only. Their purpose is to create an atmosphere conducive to innovation and development. Refereeing is also rigorous and papers are subjected to extensive group discussion.

Publications arising from IFIP events vary. The papers presented at the IFIP World Computer Congress and at open conferences are published as conference proceedings, while the results of the working conferences are often published as collections of selected and edited papers.

Any national society whose primary activity is about information processing may apply to become a full member of IFIP, although full membership is restricted to one society per country. Full members are entitled to vote at the annual General Assembly, National societies preferring a less committed involvement may apply for associate or corresponding membership. Associate members enjoy the same benefits as full members, but without voting rights. Corresponding members are not represented in IFIP bodies. Affiliated membership is open to non-national societies, and individual and honorary membership schemes are also offered.

Gunar Schirner   Marcelo Götz
Achim Rettberg   Mauro C. Zanella
Franz J. Rammig (Eds.)

Embedded Systems: Design, Analysis and Verification

4th IFIP TC 10 International
Embedded Systems Symposium, IESS 2013
Paderborn, Germany, June 17-19, 2013
Proceedings

 Springer

Volume Editors

Gunar Schirner
Northeastern University
Boston, MA, USA
E-mail: schirner@ece.neu.edu

Achim Rettberg
Carl von Ossietzky University
Oldenburg, Germany
E-mail: achim.rettberg@iess.org

Franz J. Rammig
Paderborn University
Paderborn, Germany
E-mail: franz@upb.de

Marcelo Götz
Fed. University of Rio Grande do Sul
Porto Alegre, RS, Brazil
E-mail: mgoetz@ece.ufrgs.br

Mauro C. Zanella
ZF Friedrichshafen AG
Friedrichshafen, Germany
E-mail: mauro.zanella@zf.com

ISSN 1868-4238
ISBN 978-3-642-43028-2
DOI 10.1007/978-3-642-38853-8
Springer Heidelberg Dordrecht London New York

ISSN 1868-422X (electronic)
ISBN 978-3-642-38853-8 (eBook)

CR Subject Classification (1998): C.3, C.4, D.2.4, C.2, D.2.11, D.4.7, J.2, J.6, C.0, C.1, B.3, B.8

Typesetting: Camera-ready by author, data conversion by Scientific Publishing Services, Chennai, India

Printed on acid-free paper

Springer is part of Springer Science+Business Media (www.springer.com)

Preface

This book presents the technical program of the International Embedded Systems Symposium (IESS) 2013. The design, analysis, and verification of embedded systems are discussed from complementary views in chapters of this book, including design methodologies, dealing with nonfunctional aspects, verification, performance analysis, real-time systems design, and applications examples. The book includes a special chapter dedicated to the BMBF-funded ARAMIS project on Automotive, Railway and Avionics Multicore Systems. In addition, real-world application case studies are presented discussing challenges and realizations of embedded systems.

Over recent years, *embedded systems* have gained an enormous amount of processing power and functionality and have entered several application areas, owing to the fact that many of the formerly external components can now be integrated into a single System-on-Chip. This tendency has resulted in a dramatic reduction in the size and cost of embedded systems. As a unique technology, the design of embedded systems is an essential element of many innovations.

Embedded system smeet their performance goals, including real-time constraints, through a combination of special-purpose hardware and software components tailored to the system requirements. Both the development of new features and the reuse of existing intellectual property components are essential to keeping up with ever-demanding customer requirements. Furthermore, design complexities are steadily growing with an increasing number of components that have to cooperate properly. Embedded system designers have to cope with multiple goals and constraints simultaneously, including timing, power, reliability, dependability, maintenance, packaging and, last but not least, price.

The significance of these constraints varies depending on the application area a system is targeted for. Typical embedded applications include consumer electronic, automotive, medical, and communication devices.

The *International Embedded Systems Symposium (IESS)* is a unique forum to present novel ideas, exchange timely research results, and discuss the state of the art and future trends in the field of embedded systems. Contributors and participants from both industry and academia take active part in this symposium. The IESS conference is organized by the Computer Systems Technology committee (TC10) of the International Federation for Information Processing (IFIP), especially the working group 3.2 "Embedded Systems."

IESS is a true interdisciplinary conference on the design of embedded systems. Computer Science and Electrical Engineering are the predominant academic disciplines concerned with the topics covered in IESS, but many applications also involve civil, mechanical, aerospace, and automotive engineering, as well as various medical disciplines.

In 2005, IESS was held for the first time in Manaus, Brazil. In this initial instalment, IESS 2005 was very successful with 30 accepted papers ranging from specification to embedded systems application. IESS 2007 was the second edition of the symposium held in Irvine (CA), USA, with 35 accepted papers and two tutorials ranging from analysis, design methodologies to case studies from automotive and medical applications. IESS 2009 took place at the wonderful Schloss Montfort in Langenargen, Germany, with 28 accepted papers and two tutorials ranging from efficient modeling toward challenges for designers of fault-tolerant embedded systems.

IESS 2013 was held in Paderborn, Germany, at the Heinz Nixdorf Museums-Forum (HNF), which hosts the world largest computer museum.

The articles presented in this book are the result of a thorough review process implemented by the Technical Program Committee. Out of 42 valid submissions, 22 full papers were accepted yielding an acceptance rate of 52%. In addition, eight short papers are included yielding an overall acceptance rate of 74%.

First and foremost, we thank our sponsors dSPACE, ZF Friedrichshafen AG, the Carl von Ossietzky University Oldenburg, and the Paderborn University for their generous financial support of this conference. Without these contributions, IESS 2013 would not have been possible in its current form. Very special thanks to the Heinz Nixdorf Museums-Forum (HNF) for hosting the event. Especially, we thank Gabriele Himmelsbach from HNF for her outstanding organizational support in arranging the facilities and venue.

We would also like to thank IFIP as the organizational body for the promotion and support of the IESS conference.

Last but not least, we thank the authors for their interesting research contributions and the members of the Technical Program Committee for their valuable time and effort in reviewing the articles.

June 2013

Gunar Schirner
Marcelo Götz
Achim Rettberg
Mauro C. Zanella
Franz J. Rammig

IFIP TC10 Working Conference: International Embedded Systems Symposium (IESS) June 17–19, 2013 Heinz Nixdorf Muesums-Forum, Paderborn, Germany

General Chairs

Achim Rettberg   Carl v. Ossietzky University, Oldenburg, Germany
Mauro C. Zanella   ZF Friedrichshafen AG, Friedrichshafen, Germany

General Co-chair

Franz J. Rammig   University of Paderborn, Germany

Program Co-chair

Marcelo Götz   Federal University of Rio Grande do Sul, Brazil
Gunar Schirner   Northeastern University Boston, USA

Local Arrangements Chair

Achim Rettberg   Carl von Ossietzky University, Oldenburg, Germany

Publicity Chair

Marco Wehrmeister   Santa Catarina State University, Brazil

Web Chair

Tayfun Gezgin OFFIS   Insitute for Information Technology, Oldenburg, Germany

Finance Chair

Achim Rettberg   Carl von Ossietzky University, Oldenburg,
          Germany

Technical Program Committee

Samar Abdi   Concordia University Montreal, Canada
Christian Allmann   Audi Electronics Venture, Germany
Michael Amann   ZF Friedrichshafen, Germany
Richard Anthony   The University of Greenwich, UK
Jürgen Becker   University of Karlsruhe, Germany
Alecio Binotto   UFRGS, Brazil and LBNL, USA
Christophe Bobda   University of Potsdam, Germany
Luigi Carro   UFRGS, Brazil
Florian Dittmann   TWT, Germany
Rainer Doemer   University of California at Irvine, USA
Cecilia Ekelin   Volvo Technology Corporation, Sweden
Rolf Ernst   Technical University Braunschweig, Germany
Danubia B. Espindola   FURG, Brazil
Masahiro Fujita   University of Tokyo, Japan
Andreas Gerstlauer   University of Texas Austin, USA
Marcelo Götz   UFRGS, Brazil
Kim Grüttner   OFFIS, Germany
Andreas Hein   Carl von Ossietzky University, Oldenburg,
          Germany
Joerg Henkel   University of Karlsruhe, Germany
Stefan Henkler   OFFIS, Germany
Carsten Homburg   dSPACE, Germany
Uwe Honekamp   Vector Informatik, Germany
Michael Huebner   Ruhr University Bochum, Germany
Marcel Jackowski   USP, Brazil
Ricardo Jacobi   University of Brasilia, Brazil
Michael Keckeisen   ZF Friedrichshafen, Germany
Timo Kerstan   dSPACE, Germany
Amin Khajeh   Intel, USA
Doo-Hyun Kim   Konkuk University, Korea
Bernd Kleinjohann   C-LAB, Germany
Hermann Kopetz   Technical University Vienna, Austria
Marcio Kreutz   UFRN, Brazil
Horst Krimmel   ZF Friedrichshafen, Germany
Thomas Lehmann   HAW Hamburg, Germany
Armin Lichtblau   Mentor Graphics, Germany
Patrick Lysaght   Xilinx Research Labs, USA
Roger May   Altera, UK

Adam Morawiec	ECSI, France
Wolfgang Nebel	Carl von Ossietzky University, Oldenburg, Germany
Mike Olivarez	Freescale Semiconductor, USA
Carlos Pereira	UFRGS, Brazil
Edison Pignaton de Freitas	IME, Brazil
Franz Rammig	University of Paderborn, Germany
Achim Rettberg	Carl von Ossietzky University, Oldenburg, Germany
Carsten Rust	Sagem Orga, Germany
Stefan Schimpf	ETAS, Germany
Juergen Schirmer	Robert Bosch GmbH, Stuttgart, Germany
Gunar Schirner	Northeastern University Boston, USA
Aviral Shrivastava	Arizona State University, USA
Joachim Stroop	dSPACE, Germany
Hiroyuki Tomiyama	Ritsumeikan University, Japan
Flavio R. Wagner	UFRGS, Brazil
Marco Wehrmeister	UDESC, Brazil
Marilyn Wolf	Georgia Institute of Technology, USA
Mauro Zanella	ZF Friedrichshafen, Germany
Jianwen Zhu	University of Toronto, Canada

Co-organizing Institution

IFIP TC 10, WG 10.2 and WG 10.5

Sponsors

dSPACE GmbH
ZF Lemförder GmbH
Carl von Ossietzky University, Oldenburg
University of Paderborn

Table of Contents

Design Methodologies

Non-functional Aspects of Embedded Systems

Verification

Performance Analysis

ARAMIS Special Session

Real-Time Systems

Embedded System Applications

Real-Time Aspects in Distributed Systems

TECSCE: HW/SW Codesign Framework for Data Parallelism Based on Software Component

Takuya Azumi[1], Yasaman Samei Syahkal[2], Yuko Hara-Azumi[3],
Hiroshi Oyama[4], and Rainer Dömer[2]

[1] College of Information Science and Engineering, Ritsumeikan University
takuya@cs.ritsumei.ac.jp
[2] Center for Embedded Computer Systems, University of California, Irvine
{ysameisy,doemer}@uci.edu
[3] Graduate School of Information Science, Nara Institute of Science and Technology
yuko-ha@is.naist.jp
[4] OKUMA Corporation
hi-ooyama@okuma.co.jp

Abstract. This paper presents a hardware/software (HW/SW) codesign framework (TECSCE) which enables software developers to easily design complex embedded systems such as massive data-parallel systems. TECSCE is implemented by integrating TECS and SCE: TECS is a component technology for embedded software, and SCE provides an environment for system-on-a-chip designs. Since TECS is based on standard C language, it allows the developers to start the design process easily and fast. SCE is a rapid design exploration tool capable of efficient MPSoC implementation. TECSCE utilizes all these advantages since it supports transformation from component descriptions and component sources to SpecC specification, and lets the developers decide data partitioning and parallelization at a software component level. Moreover, TECSCE effectively duplicates software components, depending on their degree of data parallelizing, to generate multiple SpecC specification models. An application for creating a panoramic image removing objects, such as people, is illustrated as a case study. The evaluation of the case study demonstrates the effectiveness of the proposed framework.

1 Introduction

Increasing complexities of embedded system and strict schedules in time-to-market are critical issues in the today's system-level design. Currently, various embedded systems incorporate multimedia applications, which are required more and more complex functionalities. Meanwhile, the semiconductor technology progress has placed a great amount of hardware resources on one chip, enabling to implement more functionalities as hardware in order to realize efficient systems. This widens design space to be explored and makes system-level designs further complicated - to improve the design productivity, designing systems at a higher abstraction level is necessary [1].

G. Schirner et al. (Eds.): IESS 2013, IFIP AICT 403, pp. 1–13, 2013.

Hardware/software (HW/SW) codesign of these systems mainly relies on the following challenging issues: (1) data parallelism to improve performance, (2) support for software developers to implement such complicated systems without knowing system-level languages such as SystemC and SpecC, (3) implementation to directly use existing code without modification, and (4) management of communication between functionalities. To the best of our knowledge, there is no work addressing all of the above issues.

This paper presents a system-level framework (TECSCE) to cope with the preceding issues. This framework aims at enabling even software developers to easily design complicated systems such as multimedia applications which are rich in data parallelism. For this, we integrate a component technology for embedded software, TECS (TOPPERS Embedded Component System [2]), and the system-on-a-chip environment SCE [3], which is based on SpecC language. Since TECS is based on conventional C language, it allows the developers to start the design process easily and fast. SCE is a rapid design exploration tool capable of efficient MPSoC implementation.

The contribution of this work is to present a system-level design method for software developers to deal with massively parallel embedded systems using TECS. In existing HW/SW codesign technologies, a designer needs to manually add or modify HW/SW communication sources (e.g., their size, direction, and allocator) in input behavioral descriptions, which is complex to specify and error-prone. In contrast, in the proposed framework, the developer can design the overall system at a software component level and has no need to specify the HW/SW communication in the input description because TECS defines the interface between components, and the communication sources are automatically generated. Moreover, a new mechanism of duplicating components realizes data partitioning at the software component level for an effective speedup of the applications.

The rest of this paper is organized as follows. Section 2 explains TECS, SCE, and the overview of the proposed framework. Section 3 depicts a case study of adapting the proposed framework. The evaluation of the case study is shown in Section 4. Related work is described in Section 5. Finally, Section 6 concludes this paper.

2   TECSCE

In this section, the overviews of TECS, SCE, and a system-level design framework (TECSCE) integrating TECS and SCE are presented.

2.1   TECS

In embedded software domains, software component technologies have become popular to improve the productivity [2,4,5]. It has many advantages such as increasing reusability, reducing time-to-market, reducing software production cost, and hence, improving productivity [6].

TECS adopts a static model that statically instantiates and connects components. The attributes of the components and interface sources for connecting

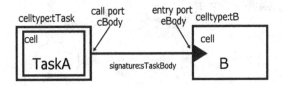

Fig. 1. Component diagram

the components are statically generated by the interface generator. Furthermore, TECS optimizes the interface sources. Hence, no instantiation overhead is introduced at runtime, and the runtime overhead of the interface code is minimized [7]. Therefore, these attributes of TECS are suitable for system-level designs.

Furthermore, in system-level designs, parallelism and pipeline processing should be considered. TECS supports parallelism and pipeline processing on a real-time OS for multi-processors in embedded software [8]. The *oneway* calling is provided to support the parallelism. It means that a caller component does not need to wait until a callee component finishes executing. At a software level for multiprocessors environment, the parallelism has been already supported in TECS. Therefore, it is possible to adapt the feature for system-level designs.

Component Model in TECS. A *cell* is an instance of component in TECS. *Cells* are properly connected in order to develop an appropriate application. A *cell* has *entry port* and *call port* interfaces. The *entry port* is an interface to provide services (functions) to other *cells*. Each service of the *entry port* called the *entry function* is implemented in C language. The *call port* is an interface to use the services of other *cells*. A *cell* communicates in this environment through these interfaces. To distinguish *call ports* of caller *cells*, an *entry port array* is used. A subscript is utilized to identify the *entry port array*. A developer decides the size of an *entry port array*. The *entry port* and the *call port* have *signatures* (sets of services). A *signature* is the definition of interfaces in a *cell*. A *celltype* is the definition of a *cell*, as well as the *Class* of an object-oriented language. A *cell* is an entity of a *celltype*.

Figure 1 shows an example of a component diagram. Each rectangle represents a *cell*. The dual rectangle depicts a active *cell* that is the entry point of a program such as a task and an interrupt handler. The left *cell* is a TaskA *cell*, and the right *cell* is a B *cell*. Here, each of tTask and tB represents the *celltype* name. The triangle in the B *cell* depicts an *entry port*. The connection of the *entry port* in the *cells* describes a *call port*.

Component Description in TECS. The description of a component in TECS can be classified into three descriptions: a *signature* description, a *celltype* description, and a *build* description. An example for component descriptions is presented in Section 3 to briefly explain these three descriptions [1] .

---

[1] Please refer [2] for the more detailed explanations.

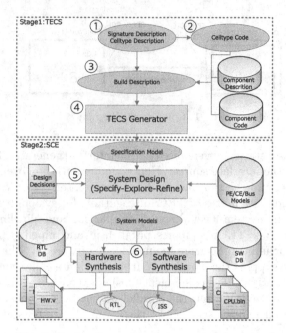

Fig. 2. Design flow using the proposed framework

2.2   SCE

SCE implements a top-down system design flow based on a specify-explore-refine paradigm with support for heterogeneous target platforms consisting of custom hardware components, embedded software processors, dedicated IP blocks, and complex communication bus architectures. The rest of features and design flow is explained in the next subsection.

2.3   Overview of TECSCE

Figure 2 represents the design flow using the proposed framework. The circled numbers in Figure 2 represent the order of design steps.

- Step1: A framework user (hereafter, a developer) defines *signatures* (interface definitions) and *celltype* (component definitions).
- Step2: The developer implements *celltype* source (component source code) in C language. They can use the template code based on *signatures* and *celltype* descriptions.
- Step3: The developer describes an application structure including definitions of *cells* (instances of component) and the connection between *cells*. In this step, the developer decides the degree of data partitioning. If it is possible to use existing source code (i.e., legacy code), the developer can start from Step3.
- Step4: The SpecC specification model based on the component description, including definitions of *behaviors* and *channels*, is generated by a TECS

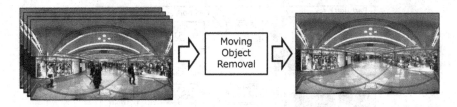

Fig. 3. Target application. Left images are input images. Right image is a result image.

generator. The specification model is a functional and abstract model that is free of any implementation details.

- Step5: The designer can automatically generate system models (Transaction-level models) based on design decisions (i.e. mapping the behaviors of the specification model onto the allocated PEs).
- Step6: The hardware and software parts in the system model are implemented by hardware and software synthesis phases, respectively.

SCE supports generating a new model by integrating the design decisions into the previous model.

3 Case Study for Proposed Framework

In this section, the proposed framework is explained through a case study. First, a target application is described. Then, two kinds of mechanism to generate specification models (Step4 in Figure 2) are depicted.

3.1 Target Application

The target application named MovingObjectRemoral for a case study of the framework is an application for generating a panoramic image removing objects, such as people. In the panoramic image view system, such as Google Street View, a user can see images from the street using omnidirectional images. Figure 3 illustrates the target application. The application creates the image without people as shown in the right image of Figure 3 based on the algorithm [9] by using a set of panoramic images which are taken at the same position.

Since creating an image by removing obstacles needs a number of original images, each of which has too many pixels, the original program is designed only for off-line use. Because the output image depends on the place and environment, we do not know how many source images are needed to create the output image. Therefore, currently, we need enormously long time to take images at each place. Our final goal is to create the output image *in real-time* by using our framework.

3.2 TECS Components for the Target Application

Figure 4 shows a TECS component diagram for the target application. Each rectangle represents a *cell* which is a component in TECS. The left, middle, and

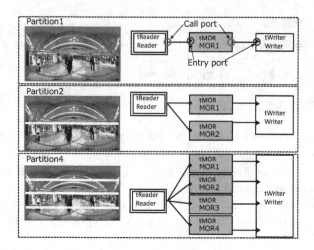

Fig. 4. Component diagram for target application

```
1  signature sSliceImage {
2   [ oneway ] void  sendBlock([ in ]const slice *slice_image);
3  };
```

Fig. 5. Signature description for the target application

```
1 [ singleton,  active]            8  celltype tMOR{
2 celltype tReader {               9    entry sSliceImage eSliceImage;
3    call sSliceImage cSliceImage[]; 10   call sSliceImage cSliceImage;
4 };                               11   attr{
5 celltype tWriter {               12     float32_t rate = 0.75;
6    entry sSliceImage eSliceImage[]; 13  };
7 };                               14   var{
                                   15     int32_t count = 0;
                                   16     slice out_slice_image;
                                   17     slice slice_images[MAX_COUNT];
                                   18   };
                                   19 };
```

Fig. 6. Celltype description for the target application

right *cells* are a Reader *cell*, an MOR (MovingObjectRemoral) *cell*, and a Writer *cell*, respectively. The Reader *cell* reads image files, slices the image, and sends the sliced image data to the MOR *cells*. The MOR *cell* collects background colors (RGB) of each pixel based on the input images. The Writer *cell* creates the final image based on the data collected by the MOR *cell*. Here, tReader, tMOR, and tWriter represent the *celltype* name.

Figure 5 shows a *signature* description between tReader and tMOR, and between tMOR and tWriter.

The *signature* description is used to define a set of function heads. A *signature* name, such as sSliceImage, follows a *signature* keyword to define the *signature*. The initial character ("s") of the *signature name* sSliceImage represents the

```
 1  const int32_t SliceCount = 2;
 2  [ generate(RepeatJoinPlugin," count=SliceCount")]
 3  cell tReader Reader {
 4    cSliceImage[0] = MOR_000.eSliceImage;
 5  };
 6  [ generate(RepeatCellPlugin," count=SliceCount")]
 7  cell tMOR MOR_000 {
 8    cSliceImage = Writer.eSliceImage[0];
 9  };
10  cell tWriter Writer{
11  };
```

Fig. 7. Build description for the target application

signature. A set of function heads is enumerated in the body of this keyword. TECS provides the *in, out,* and *inout* keywords to distinguish whether a parameter is an input and/or an output. The *in* keyword is used to transfer data from a caller *cell* to a callee *cell.* The *oneway* keyword means that a caller *cell* does not need to wait for finishing a callee *cell.* Namely, the *oneway* keyword is useful when a caller *cell* and a callee *cell* are executed in parallel.

Figure 6 describes a *celltype* description. The *celltype description* is used to define the *entry ports, call ports, attributes,* and *variables* of each *celltype.* The *singleton* keyword (Line 1 in Figure 6) represents that a singleton *celltype* is a particular *cell,* only one of which exists in a system to reduce the overhead. The *active* keyword (Line 1 in Figure 6) represents the entry point of a program such as a task and an interrupt handler. A *celltype* name, such as tReader, follows a *celltype* keyword to define *celltype.* The initial character ("t") of the *celltype* name tReader represents the *celltype.* To declare an *entry port,* an *entry* keyword is used (Line 6 and 9 in Figure 6). Two words follow the *entry* keyword: a *signature* name, such as sSliceImage, and an *entry port* name, such as eSliceImage. The initial character ("e") of the *entry port* name eSliceImage represents an *entry port.* Likewise, to declare a *call port,* a *call* keyword is used (Line 3 and 10 in Figure 6). The initial character ("c") of the *call port* name cSliceImage represents a *call port.*

The *attr* and *var* keywords that are used to increase the number of different *cells* are attached to the *celltype* and are initialized when each *cell* is created. The set of attributes or variables is enumerated in the body of these keywords. These keywords can be omitted when a *celltype* does not have an attribute and/or a variable.

Figure 7 shows a *build* description. The *build* description is used to declare *cells* and to connect between *cells* for constructing an application. To declare a *cell,* the *cell* keyword is used. Two words follow the *cell* keyword: a *celltype* name, such as tReader, and a *cell* name, such as Reader (Lines 3-5, Lines 7-9, and Lines 10-11 in Figure 7). In this case, eSliceImage (*entry port* name) of MOR_000 (*cell* name) is connected to cSliceImage (*call port* name) of Reader (*cell* name). The *signatures* of the *call port* and the *entry port* must be the same in order to connect the *cells.*

3.3 *cellPlugin*

At the component level (Step 3 in Figure 2), the proposed framework realizes data partitioning. A new plugin named *cellPlugin* is proposed to duplicate *cells* for data partitioning and connect the *cells*. There are two types of *cellPlugin*: RepeatCellPlugin and RepeatJoinPlugin.

RepeatCellPlugin supports duplication of *cells* depending on the *slice count* i.e. the number of data partitions. and connection between the *call port* of the duplicated *cells* and the *entry ports* of the connected *cell* in the original *build* description (Line 6 in Figure 7). RepeatJoinPlugin provides connection between the *call port* of the duplicated *cells* generated by RepeatCellPlugin (Line 2 in Figure 7). Note that it is easy to duplicate MOR *cells* for realizing data partitioning and parallelization as shown in Figure 4.

3.4 *cd2specc*

In this subsection, policies of transformation from a component description to a specification model in SpecC language are described. A basic policy of transformation is that a *cell* and an argument of function of *signature* correspond to a *behavior* and a *channel* in SpecC language, respectively. The tReader, tMOR, and tWriter *celltypes* correspond to tReader, tMOR, tWriter behaviors generated by *cd2specc*, respectively. The following pseudo code describes the examples of generated SpecC code.

Pseudo Code 1. tMOR behavior

```
 1  behavior tMOR(channel definitions){  11  void main(){
 2  void eSliceImage_sendBlock             12    while true do
                    (slice_image){         13      receive slice_image data
 3    for i to HIGHT / SliceCount do       14      call eSliceImage_sendBlock
 4     for j to WIDTH do                   15    end while
 5      store pixel color                  16  }
 6      sort                               17  }
 7     end for
 8    end for
 9    send new image to Writer
10  }
```

Pseudo Code 1 shows a tMOR behavior. If a behavior has an *entry function*, the behavior receives parameters to call the *entry function*. In this case, tMOR behavior receives sliced images by using channels to call *entry function* (eSliceImage_sendBlock) in Pseudo Code 1. Although there are several ways to realize tMOR, here we show in the pseudo code an algorithm to do so easily. This is often used for sorting algorithm based on brightness of each pixel to find the background color for each pixel. In this case, the brighter color depending on the rate value (Line 12 in Figure 6) is selected.

Pseudo Code 2. Main behavior

```
1  behavior Main(channel definitions){      9   int main(){
2    // declaration of channels            10     par{
3    // declaration of behaviors           11       Reader.main();
4    tReader Reader(...);                   12       MOR_000.main();
5    tMOR    MOR_000(...);                  13       MOR_001.main();
6    tMOR    MOR_001(...);                  14       //...
7    //...                                  15       Writer.main();
8    Writer  Writer(...);                   16     }
                                            17   }
                                            18 }
```

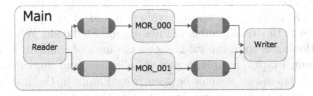

Fig. 8. Specification model of SpecC language when *slice count* is two

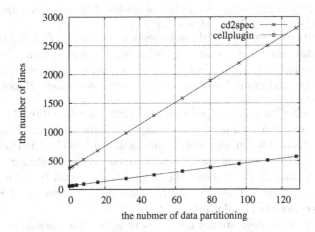

Fig. 9. Size of generated code in SpecC language

A SpecC program starts with execution of the main function of the root behavior which is named Main as shown in Pseudo Code 2. The roles of the main behavior are instantiation of behaviors, initialization of channels, connection of channels between behaviors, and management of execution of the other behaviors.

All behavioral synthesis tools typically do not support all possible C language constructs, such as recursion, dynamic memory allocation. Thus, TECS component source obeying these restrictions can be synthesized. Since recursion and dynamic memory allocation are not usually used for embedded software, these restrictions are not critical.

Figure 8 shows a specification model of SpecC language when *slice count* is two. The model consists of four behaviors and four communication channels. The numbers of channels and MOR instances are depended on the number of *slice count*.

4   Evaluation

For the experimental evaluation of the TECSCE design flow, we used the application described in Section 3 to show effectiveness of *cellPlugin* and *cd2specc* for improving design productivity.

First, we measured the number of lines of each component description generated by *cellPlugin* and each SpecC code generated by *cd2specc*. The values in Figure 9 represent the total number of lines of generated code. When the number of data partitioning is zero, the value shows the lines of common code, e.g., definitions of channel types, template code of behaviors, and implementation code based on *entry functions*. As can be seen from Figure 9, the lines of the code proportionally grow to *slice count*. In TECSCE, the developers only change the parameter for *slice count* in order to manage the data partitioning. The results indicate that the communication code between behaviors have a significant impact on productivity. Therefore, it can be concluded that *cellPlugin* and *cd2specc* are useful, particularly for large *slice count*.

Next, we evaluated four algorithms to realize the MOR: *Bubble*, *Insert*, *Average*, and *Bucket*. *Bubble* is a basic algorithm for MOR based on a bubble sort to decide the background color. *Insert* is based on an insertion sort. *Average* is assumed that the background color is the average color value. *Bucket* is based on a bucket sort.

Each MOR behavior was mapped onto different cores based on ARM7TDMI (100MHz). The execution time of processing 50 images with 128x128 pixels on every core is measured when *slice count* was eight. An ISS (Instruction Set Simulator) supported by SCE was used to measure the cycle counts for estimation of the execution time. Table 1 shows the results of execution time for each core when *slice count* is eight. These results indicate that the generated SpecC descriptions are accurately simulatable.

All of the series of images are not necessary to collect the background color for the target application because the series of images are almost the same. Therefore, if a few input images can be obtained per second, it is enough to generate the output image. In our experiments, two images per second were enough to generate an

Table 1. Results of Execution Time (ms) (*slice count* is Eight)

Algorithm	CPU1	CPU2	CPU3	CPU4	CPU5	CPU6	CPU7	CPU8
Bubble	16465.0	16343.0	16215.2	16162.5	16276.9	16325.0	16372.7	16396.3
Insert	2261.3	2360.5	2423.9	2425.4	2423.2	2384.4	2345.2	2317.8
Average	942.1	973.4	997.9	997.7	997.6	997.8	997.8	997.5
Bucket	944.9	973.2	987.7	980.8	998.8	999.3	999.4	999.2

output one. It is possible to use this application in real-time when each input image with 256x512 is used on this configuration (eight cores, ARM 100MHz, and *Bucket* algorithm). If the developers want to deal with bigger images in real-time, there are several options: to use higher clock frequency, to increase the number of data partitioning, to use hardware IPs, and so forth.

5   Related Work

HW/SW codesign frameworks have been studied for more than a decade.

Daedalus [10] framework supports a codesign for multimedia systems. It starts from a sequential program in C, and converts the sequential program into a parallel KPN (Kahn Process Network) specification through a KPNgen tool.

SystemBuilder [11] is a codsign tool which automatically synthesizes target implementation of a system from a functional description. It starts with system specification in C language, in which a designer manually specifies the system functionalities as a set of concurrent processes communicating with each other through channels.

SystemCoDesigner [12] supports a fast design space exploration and rapid prototyping of behavioral SystemC models by using an actor-oriented approach.

The system-on-chip environment (SCE) [3] is based on the influential SpecC language and methodology. SCE implements a top-down system design flow based on a specify-explore-refine paradigm with support for heterogeneous target platforms consisting of custom hardware components, embedded software processors, dedicated IP blocks, and complex communication bus architectures.

System-level designs based UML [13,14] are proposed to improve the productivity. One [13] is for exploring partial and dynamic reconfiguration of modern FPGAs. The other [14] is for closing the gap between UML-based modeling and SystemC-based simulation.

To the best of our knowledge, there is no work addressing all of the issues mentioned in Section 1. TECSCE solve all of the issues since *cd2specc*, which a part of TECSCE, makes the overall system at a software component level in order to hide the many implementation details such as communication between functionalities. The framework users do not need to specify the HW/SW communication in the input description because the communication sources are automatically generated from component descriptions TECS specifically defines the interface between components. Therefore, TECSCE realizes that existing code can be used without modification and without knowing system-level languages such as SystemC and SpecC. Moreover, *cellPlugin*, which is a part of TECSCE, supports that duplication of components realizes data partitioning at a component level for an effective speedup of the applications.

6   Conclusions

This paper proposed a new codesign framework integrating TECS and SCE, which enables software developers to deal with massive parallel computing for multimedia embedded systems. The advantage of our framework is that developers can directly exploit software components for system-level design without modifying input C sources (component sources). Moreover, since TECS supports data partitioning and SCE supports MPSoCs as target architectures, our framework can deal with more complex applications (such as MOR) and can help parallelize them for efficient implementation. The evaluation demonstrated the effectiveness of the proposed framework including *cellPlugin* and *cd2specc* and the capability of operating the MOR application in real-time. Furthermore, almost all multimedia applications can be adapted to the same model of our framework. *cellPlugin* and *cd2specc* are open-source software, and will be avaibale to download from the website at [15].

Acknowledgments. This work was partially supported by JSPS KAKENHI Grant Number 40582036. We would like to thank Maiya Hori, Ismail Arai, and Nobuhiko Nishio for providing the MOR application.

References

1. Sangiovanni-Vincentelli, A.: Quo vadis, SLD? Reasoning about the Trends and Challenges of System Level Design. IEEE 95(3), 467–506 (2007)
2. Azumi, T., Yamamoto, M., Kominami, Y., Takagi, N., Oyama, H., Takada, H.: A new specification of software components for embedded systems. In: Proc. 10th IEEE International Symposium on Object/Component/Service-Oriented Real-Time Distributed Computing, pp. 46–50 (May 2007)
3. Dömer, R., Gerstlauer, A., Peng, J., Shin, D., Cai, L., Yu, H., Abdi, S., Gajski, D.D.: System-on-Chip Environment: A SpecC-Based Framework for Heterogeneous MPSoC Design. EURASIP Journal on Embedded Systems 2008, 1–13 (2008)
4. AUTOSAR: AUTOSAR Specification, http://www.autosar.org/
5. Åkerholm, M., Carlson, J., Fredriksson, J., Hansson, H., Håkansson, J., Möller, A., Pettersson, P., Tivoli, M.: The SAVE approach to component-based development of vehicular systems. Journal of Systems and Software 80(5), 655–667 (2007)
6. Lau, K.K., Wang, Z.: Software component models. IEEE Transactions on Software Engineering 33(10), 709–724 (2007)
7. Azumi, T., Oyama, H., Takada, H.: Optimization of component connections for an embedded component system. In: Proc. IEEE/IFIP 7th International Conference on Embedded and Uniquitous Computing, pp. 182–188 (August 2009)
8. Azumi, T., Oyama, H., Takada, H.: Memory allocator for efficient task communications by using RPC channels in an embedded component system. In: Proc. the 12th IASTED International Conference on Software Engineering and Applications, pp. 204–209 (November 2008)
9. Hori, M., Takahashi, H., Kanbara, M., Yokoya, N.: Removal of moving objects and inconsistencies in color tone for an omnidirectional image database. In: Koch, R., Huang, F. (eds.) ACCV 2010 Workshops, Part II. LNCS, vol. 6469, pp. 62–71. Springer, Heidelberg (2011)
10. Nikolov, H., Thompson, M., Stefanov, T., Pimentel, A.D., Polstra, S., Bose, R., Zissulescu, C., Deprettere, E.F.: Daedalus: Toward composable multimedia mp-soc design. In: Proc. International 45th Design Automation Conference, pp. 574–579 (July 2008)

11. Honda, S., Tomiyama, H., Takada, H.: RTOS and codesign toolkit for multipro-
    cessor systems-on-chip. In: Proc. 12th Asia and South Pacific Design Automation
    Conference, pp. 336–341 (January 2007)
12. Keinert, J., Streübrbar, M., Schlichter, T., Falk, J., Gladigau, J., Haubelt, C.,
    Teich, J., Meredith, M.: Systemcodesigner an automatic esl synthesis approach by
    design space exploration and behavioral synthesis for streaming applications. ACM
    Trans. Des. Autom. Electron. Syst. 14(1), 1:1–1:23 (2009)
13. Vidal, J., de Lamotte, F., Gogniat, G., Diguet, J.P., Soulard, P.: UML design for
    dynamically reconfigurable multiprocessor embedded systems. In: Proceedings of
    the Conference on Design, Automation and Test in Europe, pp. 1195–1200 (March
    2010)
14. Mischkalla, F., He, D., Mueller, W.: Closing the gap between UML-based modeling,
    simulation and synthesis of combined HW/SW systems. In: Proceedings of the
    Conference on Design, Automation and Test in Europe, pp. 1201–1206 (March
    2010)
15. TECS, http://www.toppers.jp/tecs

Programming Robots with Events

Truong-Giang Le[1], Dmitriy Fedosov[2], Olivier Hermant[3],
Matthieu Manceny[1], Renaud Pawlak[4], and Renaud Rioboo[5]

[1] LISITE - ISEP, 28 rue Notre-Dame des Champs, 75006 Paris, France
[2] Saint-Petersbourg University of Aerospace Instrumentation, 67 Bolshaya Morskaya
street, 190000, Saint Petersburg, Russia
[3] CRI - MINES ParisTech, 35 rue ST-Honoré, 77300 Fontainebleau, France
[4] IDCapture, 2 rue Duphot, 75001 Paris, France
[5] ENSIIE, 1 square de la Résistance, F-91025 Évry CEDEX, France
{le-truong.giang,matthieu.manceny}@isep.fr,
{dvfdsv,renaud.pawlak}@gmail.com,
olivier.hermant@mines-paristech.fr,
renaud.rioboo@ensiie.fr

Abstract. We introduce how to use event-based style to program robots
through the INI programming language. INI features both built-in and
user-defined events, a mechanism to handle various kinds of changes
happening in the environment. Event handlers run in parallel either synchronously or asynchronously, and events can be reconfigured at runtime
to modify their behavior when needed. We apply INI to the humanoid
robot called Nao, for which we develop an object tracking program.

Keywords: robotics, event-based programming, context-aware reactive
systems, parallel programming.

1 Introduction

The word "robot" was coined by the Czech novelist Karel Capek in a 1920 play
titled Rassum's Universal Robots. In Czech, "robot" means worker or servant.
According to the definition of the Robot Institute of America dating back to
1979, robot is:

A reprogrammable, multifunctional manipulator designed to move material, parts, tools or specialized devices through variable programmed
motions for the performance of a variety of tasks.

At present, people require more from the robots, since they are considered as a
subset of "smart structures" - engineered constructs equipped with sensors to
"think" and to adapt to the environment [28]. Generally, robots can be put into
three main categories: manipulators, mobile robots and humanoid robots [26].

Robots now play an important role in many domains. In manufacturing,
robots are used to replace humans in remote, hard, unhealthy or dangerous
work. They will change the industry by replacing the CNC (Computer(ized)

G. Schirner et al. (Eds.): IESS 2013, IFIP AICT 403, pp. 14–25, 2013.

Numerical(ly) Control(led)) machines. In hospitals, they are employed to take care of the patients, and even do complex work like performing surgery. In education, robots may be good assistants for the children. They maybe also good friends for old people at home for talking and sharing housework. The global service robotics market in 2011 was worth $18.39 billion. This market is valued at $20.73 billion in 2012 and expected to reach $46.18 billion by 2017 at an estimated CAGR (Compound Annual Growth Rate) of 17.4% from 2012 to 2017 [20]. As a result, research on robot gets an increasing interests from governments, companies, and researchers [2,3].

Building a robot program is a complex task since a robot needs to quickly react to variabilities in the execution environment. In other words, a robot should be indeed autonomous. Besides, it should be able to do several things at one time. Consequently, using a programming language or development framework dedicated to robots is essential. The ultimate goal is to help programmers develop robot programs more efficiently and straightforwardly.

We give an overview of such robot programming languages and frameworks in Section 2. Next, in Section 3, we discuss how to define and apply events in our novel programming language called INI, especially its advanced features like events synchronization and reconfiguration. Then, we present a case study of using INI to control the humanoid robot Nao to track an object (Section 4). Finally, some conclusions and future work are discussed in Section 5.

2   Related Work

Classical languages like Java, C/C++, .Net are usually used for programming robot [1,17,22]. However, developing robot's applications using these languages require more time and effort since they are not fully dedicated to this purpose. For example, to support interaction between robots and environment when something happens, programmers have to construct a mechanism for event detection and handling. In order to do this, programmers need to write a lot of code or may use some extensions like [16,23] although they are not easy to adapt.

Additionally, several robotic development platforms and DSLs (Domain Specific Languages) have been designed to assist programmers. Urbiscript is a scripting language primarily designed for robotics. It's a dynamic, prototype-based, and object-oriented scripting language. It supports and emphasizes parallel and event-based programming, which are very popular paradigms in robotics, by providing core primitives and language constructs [12]. UrbiScript has some limitations. First, it is an untyped language. Besides, it lacks support for synchronization among events, which is essential in some scenarios. Moreover, events in UrbiScript cannot be reconfigured at runtime to change their behavior.

The KUKA Robot Programming Language is developed by KUKA, one of the world's leading manufacturers of industrial robots [6]. KUKA is simple, Pascal-like and lacks many features. A Matlab abstraction layer has been introduced to extend its capabilities [4]. RoboLogix is a scripting language that utilizes common commands, or instruction sets among major robot manufacturers. RoboLogix programs consist of data objects and a program flow [15]. The data objects reside in registers and the program flow represents the list of instructions, or instruction set, that is used to program the robot. However, RoboLogix still does not supply a well-defined mechanism for the robots to interact and react to environment.

In recent years, event-driven programming has emerged as an efficient method for interacting and collaborating with the environment in ubiquitous computing. Using event-driven style requires less effort and may lead to more robust software [8]. This style is used to write many kinds of applications: robotics, context-aware reactive applications, self-adaptive systems, interactive systems, etc. In consequence, several event-based programming languages have been developed so far [5,14]. However, in these languages, events still cannot be defined intuitively and straightforwardly, and their features are still limited. For example, events cannot run in parallel to take advantage of multiple processors. Besides, programmers may not dynamically customize events' behavior to deal with changes in the environment.

Considering limitations of current event-based programming language, we have developed a novel programming language called INI. With INI, developers may define and use events easily. Along with several built-in events, they also can write their own events in Java or in C/C++, and then integrate to INI programs. Events in INI may run concurrently either asynchronously or synchronously. Moreover, events may be reconfigured at run time to handle different scenarios happening in the context.

3   Event-Based Programming with INI

3.1   Overview

Events are used to monitor changes happening in the environment or for time scheduling. In other words, any form of monitoring can be considered to be compatible with event-based style. Generally, there are three types of events [21]:

- A timer event to express the passing of time.
- An arbitrary detectable state change in the system, e.g. the change of the value of a variable during execution.
- A physical event such as the appearance of a person detected by cameras.

For example, programmers may define an event to monitor the power level of their systems or to observe users' behavior in order to react. They can also specify an event to schedule a desired action at preferable time. To understand more about event-based programming, please refer to [9,10].

INI is a programming language developed by ourselves, which runs on Java Virtual Machine (JVM) but INI's syntax and semantics are not Java's ones. INI is developed aiming at supporting the development of concurrent and context-aware reactive systems, which need a well-defined mechanism for capturing and handling events. As shown later, INI supports all those kinds of event. Event callback handlers (or events instances) are declared in the body of functions and are raised, by default asynchronously, every time the event occurs. By convention, an event instance in INI starts with @ and takes input and output parameters. Input parameters are configuration parameters to tune the event execution. Output parameters are variable names that are filled in with values when then the event callback is called, and executed in a new thread. They can be considered as the measured characteristic of the event instance. It has to be noticed that those variables, as well as any INI variable, enjoy a global scope in the function's body. Both kinds of parameters are optional. Moreover, an event can also be optionally bound to an id, so that other parts of the program can refer to it. The syntax of event instances is shown below:

```
id:@eventKind[inputParam1=value1, inputParam2=value2, ...]
  (outputParam1, outputParam2, ...)
    { <action> }
```

Table 1. Some built-in events in INI

Built-in event kind	Meaning
@init()	used to initialize variables, when a function starts.
@end()	triggered when no event handler runs, and when the function is about to return.
@every[time:Integer]()	occurs periodically, as specified by its input parameter (in milliseconds).
@update[variable:T] (oldValue:T, newValue:T)	invoked when the given variable's value changes during execution.
@cron[pattern:String]()	used to trigger an action, based on the UNIX CRON pattern indicated by its input parameter.

Programmers may use built-in events (listed in Table 1), or write user-defined events (in Java or in C/C++), and then integrate them to their INI programs through bindings. By developing custom events, one can process data which are captured by sensors. To illustrate events in INI, let's consider a program which uses sensors to capture and collect weather and climate data like humidity, temperature, wind speed, rainfall, etc. In our program, we can define separate events to handle these tasks as shown in Figure 1. For instance, we can define an event @humidityMonitor to observe the humidity level periodically. This event has one input parameter named humPeriod that sets the periodicity of the checks (time unit is in hours). Besides, it has one output parameter named humidity to indicate the current humidity. Inside this event, depending on the value of the current humidity, we can define several corresponding actions such as warning when the humidity is too high. Other events can be defined in a similar structure. The last event is a built-in @cron event, which is employed to send these data to a server at 3:00 AM, 11:00 AM, and 7:00 PM every day (to learn more about UNIX CRON pattern, please refer to [7]). All events in our program run in parallel so that it can handle multiple tasks at one time.

```
1 function main() {
2 h:@humidityMonitor[humPeriod = 1](humidity) {
3   case {
4     humidity > ... {...}
5     default {...}
6   }
7 }
8 t:@temperatureMonitor[tempPeriod = 2](temperature) { ... }
9 ...
10 @cron[pattern = "0␣3-11-19␣*␣*␣*"]() {
11   //Send data to a server for tracking purpose ...
12 }
13 }
```

Fig. 1. A sample INI program used for collecting climate data

3.2 Advanced Use of Events

By default, except for the @init and @end events (see Table 1), all INI events are executed asynchronously. However, in some scenarios, a given event e0 may want to synchronize on other events e1,..., eN. It means that the synchronizing event e0 must wait for all running threads corresponding to the target events to be terminated before running. For instance, when e0 may affect the actions defined inside other events, we need to apply the synchronization mechanism. The syntax corresponding to the above discussion is:

```
$(e1,e2,...,eN) e0:@eventKind[...](...) { <action> }
```

Events in INI may be reconfigured at runtime in order to adjust their behavior when necessary to adapt to changes happening in the environment. Programmers may use the built-in function reconfigure_event(eventId, [inputParam1= value1, inputParam2=value2,...]) in order to modify the values of input parameters of the event referred to by eventId. For instance, in the example of Figure 1, we can call reconfigure_event(h, [humPeriod=0.5]) to set the humidity data collection period to 30 minutes. Now our event will gather data every 30 minutes instead of one hour as before. Besides, we also allow programmers to stop and restart events with two built-in functions: stop_event([eventId1, eventId2,...]) and restart_event([eventId1, eventId2,...]). For example, we can stop all data collection processes when the energy level of the system is too low, and restart them later when the energy is restored.

Last but not least, events in INI may be used in combination with a boolean expression to express the requirement that need to be satisfied before they can be executed. Programmers may use the syntax below:

```
<event_expression> <logical_expression> { <action> }
```

For example, if we want the event @humidityMonitor to be executed only when the temperature is higher than some threshold:

```
@humidityMonitor [humPeriod=1](humidity) temperature>... {...}
```

To understand more about the above mechanisms and other aspects of INI (e.g. developing user-defined events, rules, type system, type checking, and built-in functions), the readers may have a look at [19,27].

4 A Case Study with the Humanoid Robot Nao

In this section, we briefly present the humanoid robot Nao, especially its features related to the moving mechanism. Then we show an INI tracking program running on Nao. The purpose of our INI program is controlling the Nao to detect a ball in the space and then walk to reach it.

4.1 Introduction to Nao and Its Moving Mechanism

Nao is the humanoid robot that is built by the French company Aldebaran-Robotics [13,25]. It is equipped with many sensor devices to obtain robot's close environment information (see Figure 2). Nao has for instance become a standard platform for RoboCup, an international initiative that fosters research in robotics and artificial intelligence [11].

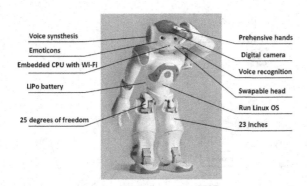

Fig. 2. Nao's features [25]

NAOqi is the middleware running on Nao that helps prepare modules to be run either on Nao or on a remote PC. Code can be developed on Windows, Mac or Linux, and be called from many languages including C++, Java, Python and .Net. The company Aldebaran Robotics developed many modules built on top of this framework that offer rich APIs for interacting with Nao, including functionalities related to audio, vision, motion, communication or several low-level accesses. They also provide a well-organized documentation, particularly on how to control the robot effectively [24].

Nao is able to walk on multiple floor surfaces such as carpet, tiles and wooden floors. Each step is composed of a double leg and a single leg support phase. With Nao, the basic foot step planner is used by the walk process [24], provided by three possible walk control APIs: `ALMotionProxy::setWalkTarget`

Velocity() (applied in our later case study), `ALMotionProxy :: walkTo()` or `ALMotionProxy::setFootSteps()`. The foot's position is specified by three parameters: x, y and θ (see Figure 3). x is the distance along the X axis in meters (forwards and backwards). y is the distance along the Y axis in meters (lateral motion). θ is the robot orientation relative to the current orientation (i.e. the rotation around the Z axis) in radians [-3.1415 to 3.1415]. The movement is composed of a translation by x and y, then a rotation around the vertical Z axis θ. It is possible to define custom gait parameters for the walk of Nao so that we can control the direction and speed to adjust to different scenarios. To learn more about these parameters (e.g. `MaxStepX`, `MaxStepY`, `MaxStepTheta`, `MaxStepFrequency`, etc.) along with their value ranges and default values, please refer to Nao's documentation [24]. In INI, we abstract over many of those parameters through user-defined events and functions in order to facilitate programming.

4.2   An INI Tracking Program Running on Nao

In this part, we show how INI can be applied for programming robot through the example of building a ball tracking program. Figure 3 displays the possible relative positions between the robot and the ball. There are three distinguished

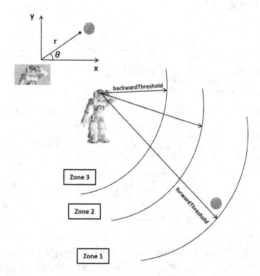

Fig. 3. Possible relative positions among the robot and the ball

zones that are specified based on the distance from the robot to the detected ball. And then according to which zone the ball belongs to, we can control the robot with the desired behavior:

- Zone 1: When the distance from the robot to the detected ball is larger than the `forwardThreshold` (unit is in meters and its range is 0.0 - 1.0 meters), the ball is considered as far from the robot and it needs to move in order to reach the ball.

- Zone 2: When the distance from the robot to the detected ball is between backwardThreshold (its unit and range are the same as forwardThreshold) and forwardThreshold, the robot does not move since its place can be considered as a good position to observe the ball. However, the robot's head still can turn to continue to follow the ball.
- Zone 3: When the distance from the robot to the detected ball is shorter than backwardThreshold, the ball is considered as too close and moving towards the robot. As a result, the robot will go backward in order to avoid the collision and keep its eyes on the ball.

The activity diagram of the strategy is shown in Figure 4. Our program is shown

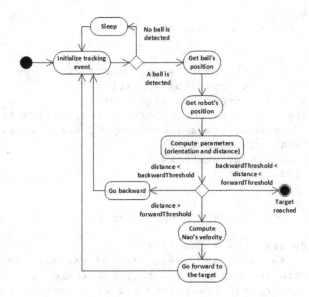

Fig. 4. The activity diagram for our program

in Figure 5. In our program, we employ three events. The event @init (lines 2-16) is applied to initialize the variables used later in our program. The purpose of using two variables forwardThreshold and backwardThreshold has been explained above. The variable interval (unit is in milliseconds) sets the delay after which, if no ball is detected, the robot temporarily stops tracking. The variable stepFrequency (normalized between 0.0 and 1.0, see more in [24]) is applied to set how often the robot will move and the variable defaultStepFrequency is applied to set the default value for step frequency. The two variables ip and port are used to indicate the parameters for Nao's network address. The boolean variable useSensors is used to indicate whether the program uses the direct returned values from sensors or the values after adjustments by the robot itself (please refer to Nao's documentation [24] to understand more). The variable targetTheta is the robot orientation relative to the ball's orientation. The variable robotPosition points out the robot's position when it detects the ball so

```
 1 function main() {
 2   @init() {
 3     forwardThreshold = 0.5
 4     backwardThreshold = 0.3
 5     interval = 1000
 6     stepFrequency = 0.0
 7     defaultStepFrequency = 1.0
 8     ip = "nao.local"
 9     port = 9559
10     useSensors = false
11     targetTheta = 0.0
12     robotPosition = [0.0,0.0,0.0]
13     stepX = 0.0
14     needAdjustDirection = false
15     i = 0
16   }
17   $(e) d:@detectBall[robotIP = ip, robotPort = port,
18     checkingTime = interval](ballPosition){
19     //Compute necessary parameters, and return in an array
20     parameters = process_position(ip, port, ballPosition,
21       forwardThreshold, backwardThreshold, useSensors)
22     targetTheta = parameters[0]
23     robotPosition = parameters[1]
24     stepX = parameters[2]
25     i = 0
26     needAdjustDirection = true
27     stepFrequency = defaultStepFrequency
28   }
29   $(d,e) e:@every[time = 200]() {
30     //Control the robot to go one step if the ball is detected
31     needAdjustDirection = reach_to_target(name, port,
32       stepFrequency, robotPosition, stepX, targetTheta,
33       needAdjustDirection, useSensors)
34     i++
35     case {
36     //Reset parameters after three consecutive walking steps
37       i>3 {
38         stepX = 0.0
39         targetTheta = 0.0
40         stepFrequency = 0.0
41       }
42     }
43   }
44 }
```

Fig. 5. An object tracking program written in INI

that then we can calculate appropriate needed direction and speed for its movement. stepX is the fraction (between 0.0 and 1.0) of MaxStepX (the maximum translation along the X axis for one step, see [24]). The sign of stepX also indicates the moving direction (forward or backward) of the Nao. The boolean variable needAdjustDirection is used to indicate whether we need to adjust the direction when the robot moves towards the ball. The intention of using the temporary variable i will be explained later.

The event @detectBall (lines 17-28) is a user-defined event written in Java, which uses image processing techniques to detect a ball with the help of video cameras located in the forehead of Nao. This event has three input parameters: robotIP , robotPort and checkingTime have the same meanings that the corresponding variables ip, port and interval described before own. Inside this event, when a ball is detected, we call the function process_position to process positions of the ball and the robot, and also specify the appropriate direction and velocity for the robot's movement.

The event @every (lines 29-43) is applied to control the robot to move towards the target every 200 milliseconds. The function reach_to_target is used to determine a suitable velocity for the robot and to control the robot moving towards the ball. The robot only moves when all needed parameters related to orientation, velocity and frequency are specified. Each call of that function makes one walking step. During execution, the robot may adjust the direction and velocity to make them more well-suited since the ball may change its position. As a result, after each step when the robot comes to the new location, we calculate the direction error. If the error for θ exceeds the allowed threshold (e.g. 10 degrees), the variable needAdjustDirection becomes true and some adjustments will be applied so that the robot walks in the correct way. We use the temporary variable i to reset some parameters. When i > 3, this means that the robot already walked for three successful steps without checking again the position of the ball. In this case, by resetting some parameters, the robot will stop temporarily. Then it waits to detect the ball again to check whether during its displacement, the ball has moved to another place or not. If yes, Nao gets the updated position of the ball, then continues to walk and reach it.

In our program, we synchronize the two events @detectBall and @every in order to avoid data access conflicts and unwanted behavior. For example, the robot is controlled to walk to the ball only when all needed parameters are calculated. Besides, we want to ensure that during the calculation of parameters, the robot is not moving so that the measured numbers are correct and stable. Consequently, we add the notation for synchronization, i.e. $(...)$ before each event (line 17 and line 29). Additionally, the event @every is also synchronized with itself so that each robot step does not overlap with others.

When running in experiment, our program completes well the desired requirements. The robot detects the orange ball in the space and then follows it. When the ball is moved to another position, Nao also changes the direction and speed to reach the ball if needed. A demonstration video can be watched on YouTube [18].

5   Conclusion and Future Work

In this paper, we presented how to write robot applications by using INI, a novel programming language that supports event-based paradigm. Programmers may use built-in events, or develop custom events in other languages like Java or C/C++ and then integrate them to INI programs. Moreover, events may run in parallel (asynchronously or synchronously) to speed up the execution and improve performance. Last but not least, in case of changes happening in the environment, events can be dynamically reconfigured to adapt to a new context.

For future work, we will extend our example by adding more features to our program such as detecting and avoiding obstacles on the way to the target and control robot's hands to catch the object. We also have a plan to develop more practical applications running on Nao. For example, we can build a program which may recognize the human voice commands, and then control the robot to act the desired behavior.

Acknowledgments. The work presented in this article is co-funded by the European Union. Europe is committed in Ile-de-France with the European Regional Development Fund.

References

1. Auyeung, T.: Robot programming in C (2006),
   http://www.drtak.org/teaches/ARC/cisp299_bot/book/book.pdf
2. Bar-Cohen, Y., Hanson, D.: The Coming Robot Revolution: Expectations and Fears About Emerging Intelligent, Humanlike Machines, 1st edn. Springer Publishing Company, Incorporated (2009)
3. Bekey, G.: Robotics: State of the Art and Future Challenges. World Scientific (2008)
4. Chinello, F., Scheggi, S., Morbidi, F., Prattichizzo, D.: Kuka control toolbox. IEEE Robot. Automat. Mag. 18(4), 69–79 (2011)
5. Cohen, N.H., Kalleberg, K.T.: EventScript: an event-processing language based on regular expressions with actions. In: Proceedings of the 2008 ACM SIGPLAN-SIGBED Conference on Languages, Compilers, and Tools for Embedded Systems, LCTES 2008, pp. 111–120. ACM, New York (2008)
6. KUKA Robotics Corporation: Kuka, http://www.kuka-robotics.com
7. Crontab, http://crontab.org/
8. Dabek, F., Zeldovich, N., Kaashoek, F., Mazières, D., Morris, R.: Event-driven programming for robust software. In: Proceedings of the 10th Workshop on ACM SIGOPS European Workshop, EW 10, pp. 186–189 (2002)
9. Etzion, O., Niblett, P.: Event Processing in Action. Manning Publications Co. (2010)
10. Faison, T.: Event-Based Programming: Taking Events to the Limit. Apress, Berkely (2006)
11. Federation, T.R.: Robocup's homepage, http://www.robocup.org/
12. Gostai: The Urbi Software Development Kit (July 2011)

13. Gouaillier, D., Hugel, V., Blazevic, P., Kilner, C., Monceaux, J., Lafourcade, P., Marnier, B., Serre, J., Maisonnier, B.: The Nao humanoid: A combination of performance and affordability. CoRR abs/0807.3223 (2008)
14. Holzer, A., Ziarek, L., Jayaram, K., Eugster, P.: Putting events in context: aspects for event-based distributed programming. In: Proceedings of the Tenth International Conference on Aspect-Oriented Software Development, AOSD 2011, pp. 241–252. ACM, New York (2011)
15. Logic Design Inc.: Robologix, http://www.robologix.com/programming_robologix.php
16. Jayaram, K.R., Eugster, P.: Context-oriented programming with EventJava. In: International Workshop on Context-Oriented Programming, COP 2009, pp. ·9:1–9:6. ACM, New York (2009)
17. Kang, S., Gu, K., Chang, W., Chi, H.: Robot Development Using Microsoft Robotics Developer Studio. Taylor & Francis (2011)
18. Le, T.G.: A demonstration video, http://www.youtube.com/watch?v=alKZ9gZa4AU
19. Le, T.G., Hermant, O., Manceny, M., Pawlak, R., Rioboo, R.: Unifying event-based and rule-based styles to develop concurrent and context-aware reactive applications - toward a convenient support for concurrent and reactive programming. In: Proceedings of the 7th International Conference on Software Paradigm Trends, Rome, Italy, July 24-27, pp. 347–350 (2012)
20. M&M: Service robotics market (personal & professional) global forecast & assessment by applications & geography (2012 - 2017) (2012), http://www.marketsandmarkets.com/
21. Mühl, G., Fiege, L., Pietzuch, P.: Distributed Event-Based Systems. Springer-Verlag New York, Inc., Secaucus (2006)
22. Preston, S.: The Definitive Guide to Building Java Robots (The Definitive Guide to). Apress, Berkely (2005)
23. Robomatter: Robotc, http://www.robotc.net/
24. Aldebaran Robotics: Nao software documentation, http://www.aldebaran-robotics.com/documentation/
25. Aldebaran Robotics: Nao's homepage, http://www.aldebaran-robotics.com
26. Russell, S., Norvig, P.: Artificial Intelligence: A Modern Approach, 3rd edn. Prentice Hall Press, Upper Saddle River (2009)
27. Truong-Giang, L.: INI Online (2012), https://sites.google.com/site/inilanguage/
28. Wadhawan, V.: Robots of the future. Resonance 12, 61–78 (2007)

Joint Algorithm Developing and System-Level Design: Case Study on Video Encoding

Jiaxing Zhang and Gunar Schirner

Department of Electrical and Computer Engineering
Northeastern University
Boston, MA, 02115
{jxzhang,schirner}@ece.neu.edu

Abstract. System-Level Design Environments (SLDEs) are often utilized for tackling the design complexity of modern embedded systems. SLDEs typically start with a specification capturing core algorithms. Algorithm development itself largely occurs in Algorithm Design Environments (ADE) with little or no hardware concern. Currently, algorithm and system design environments are disjoint; system level specifications are manually implemented which leads to the specification gap.

In this paper, we bridge algorithm and system design environments creating a unified design flow facilitating algorithm and system co-design. It enables algorithm realizations over heterogeneous platforms, while still tuning the algorithm according to platform needs. Our design flow starts with algorithm design in Simulink, out of which a System Level Design Language (SLDL)-based specification is synthesized. This specification then is used for design space exploration across heterogeneous target platforms and abstraction levels, and, after identifying a suitable platform, synthesized to HW/SW implementations. It realizes a unified development cycle across algorithm modeling and system-level design with quick responses to design decisions on algorithm-, specification- and system exploration level. It empowers the designer to combine analysis results across environments, apply cross layer optimizations, which will yield an overall optimized design through rapid design iterations.

We demonstrate the benefits on a MJPEG video encoder case study, showing early computation/communication estimation and rapid prototyping from Simulink models. Results from Virtual Platform performance analysis enable the algorithm designer to improve model structure to better match the heterogeneous platform in an efficient and fast design cycle. Through applying our unified design flow, an improved HW/SW is found yielding 50% performance gain compared to a pure software solution.

1 Introduction

The increasing complexity of Multi-Processor System-On-Chip (MPSoC) designs has become a major challenge. Designers combine components with diverse and distinct architecture characteristics heterogeneously to achieve efficient and flexible platform solutions, which however, dramatically increases design complexity.

G. Schirner et al. (Eds.): IESS 2013, IFIP AICT 403, pp. 26–38, 2013.

In order to tame the complexity, System-Level Design (SLD) has emerged with methodologies, tools and environments for a systematic design at higher levels of abstraction. System-Level Design Environments (SLDE), such as PeaCE [5] and SoC Environment (SCE) [2] operate on an input specification captured in an System-Level Design Language (SLDL), such as SystemC[15] and SpecC[3]. Based on an input specification, SLDEs provide design space exploration through early performance estimation, automated refinement into Transaction Level Models (TLM), and detailed analysis capabilities. Designers can use their synthesis to generate target implementations. A typical SLD environment is shown at the lower half of Fig. 1.

An Algorithm Design Environment (ADE), currently separated from the system-level design, is shown at the top half of Fig. 1. Algorithm development environments mainly concentrate on modeling algorithms. They simplify prototyping of algorithms by providing toolboxes of algorithm components, detailed (graphical) analysis and functional validation tools. Often, at this level of design, little or no hardware knowledge is concerned. ADE examples include TargetLink[13], LabView[7] and Simulink[18]. These ADEs also offer some generation capabilities, however focus on homogeneous solutions and do not offer exploration facilities comparable to SLDEs.

However, there is no direct connection between ADEs and SLDEs. Algorithms captured in environments like Simulink are abundantly available through various toolboxes (e.g. computer visions, signal processing), but they need to be converted manually into an SLDL specification for system designed exploration. The manual conversion is time-consuming, tedious and error-prone, which defines the *Specification Gap* (Fig. 1, middle). The specification gap lowers design productivity and hinders efficient co-design of algorithm and architecture.

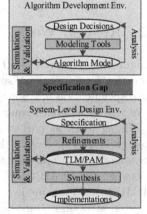

Fig. 1. Specification Gap

In this paper, we present a unified design flow that integrates both algorithm and system design environments by bridging the specification gap through *Algo2Spec*. In this paper, we focus on Simulink as an ADE, which offers modeling, simulating, debugging and analyzing multi-domain dynamic systems. We propose *Algo2Spec* to close the specification gap by synthesizing Simulink models into SLDL specifications. This enables rapid heterogeneous design space exploration, e.g. through automatically generated VPs at varying abstraction levels. Simultaneously, by extending an existing system design flow to the algorithm level, algorithm designers in Simulink are provided with rapid, dynamic and accurate feedback from heterogeneous VP analysis. Combining the environments creates a seamless unified design flow reaching from Simulink models, via specification, and VPs to target implementations. The unified flow simplifies model analysis and instant propagation up in the design flow, empowering designers to make strategic decisions for globally optimized designs.

We demonstrate the gained flexibility and efficiency of our unified flow using a video encoder design. We show multiple iterations of design decisions to highlight feedback across the environments. Within three design iterations, models with varying granularity are examined in heterogeneous platform explorations. Through applying the unified flow, a software/hardware co-design solution was identified that yields 50% performance gain compare to pure a software solution.

The remainder of this paper is structured as following: Section 2 introduces relevant related work. Section 3 overviews the design flow. Section 4 shows the cross-layer decisions. Section 5 demonstrates the flow benefits on the video encoder case study. Finally, section 6 concludes the paper.

2   Related Work

Significant research effort has been invested into system-level design usually starting from functional specifications. Conversely, the challenge of how to obtain the specification has not gained much attention and consequently specifications are mostly written manually.

Using UML as part of SoC design methodologies has been intensively studied [8,12,20,17]. Several language conversions to translate UML models into SystemC are proposed [20], [17]. Furthermore, a framework for co-simulation between MATLAB and UML under a co-design flow with application specific UML customizations is provided in [14]. However, these approaches mostly focus on structural conversion and behavior translation (with exception of state machines) is less explored.

A top-down refinement flow from Simulink to SystemC TLM in presented in [6,16]. Refinement and component exploration in their work happens in Simulink, requiring direct annotation, rewriting and modifications of Simulink models. This can be seen as contrary to abstraction separation as the top level of abstraction should not involve hardware concerns [9]. Moreover, no system exploration tools or profiling facilities are instantly applied in their approach to SystemC models. On the implementation side, the Simulink conversion is realized as external tools (ie. yacc/lex), which cannot be integrated to Simulink directly while increasing the overall design tool complexity.

Meanwhile, a re-coding approach [1] is proposed to transform flat C code into a structured SLDL specification. The effort similarly aims to close the specification gap, but directly targets C as an input language. Our approach, on the other hand, starts from a higher abstraction by using Simulink as input models.

Also some generation facilities are present within Simulink. The Simulink Embedded Coder (SEC) [10] directly generates target-specific embedded C code, however does not enable heterogeneous exploration. A co-simulation solution [11] is introduced between Simulink and generated SystemC TLM, however with the focus of being used as testbench rather than the design itself.

3   Unified Algorithm-System Design Flow

Our unified design flow combining both algorithm- and system-level design is shown in Fig. 2. The figure jointly represents three essential aspects (a) the design flow on the left, (b) model examples on the right and (c) decisions at varying levels. *Algorithm Design Environment* (ADE), *Specification Generation Tool* (SGT), namely our proposed *Algo2Spec*, as well as *System-Level Design Environment* (SLDE) compose a top-down design methodology with SGT connecting the other two major design environments. For the work in this paper, we select Simulink [18] as an ADE and the System-on-Chip Environment (SCE) [2] as an SLDE. The latter uses SpecC [3] as an SLDL. The principles and concepts, however, apply to SystemC [15] equally.

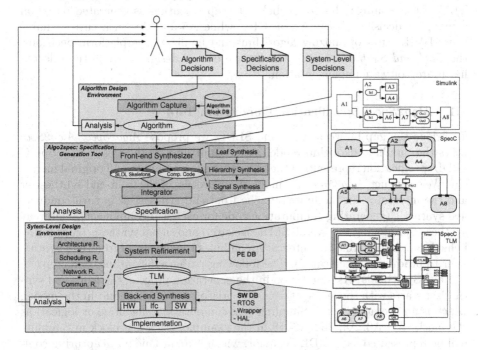

Fig. 2. Unified algorithm-system design flow with feedback/decision loop

The unified design flow, as depicted in Fig. 2, starts with designer capturing in ADE the algorithm with desired functionalities and structure. Available algorithms from the algorithm block database simplify and accelerate the development. The designer tunes and refines the algorithms in ADE as a cycle of modeling, simulation, debugging, validation and evaluation. The result of ADE is the captured algorithm in Simulink as for example shown on top right Fig. 2. The example consists of the top-level blocks A1, A2, A5, and A8, were A2 and A5 execute parallel and contain further sub-blocks.

After finishing the initial algorithm specification, the designer transitions to Specification Generation Tool (SGT), namely *Algo2Spec*, shown in the middle of the Fig. 2. *Algo2Spec* synthesizes the Simulink model into a specification in SpecC SLDL, following the designer's specification design decision. Different SLDL specification can be generated based on decisions of granularity, scheduling and optimization configurations. An SLDL specification example is shown next to the SGT, were leaf blocks are converted to leaf behaviors and hierarchical blocks are represented through hierarchical behaviors preserving the original hierarchy. Simulink signals are captured as variable in this example.

The generated specification is then the basis for detailed design space exploration in the SLDE. The designer can explore platform decisions: Processing Elements (PE) allocation, behavior to PE mapping, scheduling and communication refinement. In SLDE, depicted in the bottom of Fig. 2, *System Refinement* then realizes these decisions in form of Transaction-level Models (TLM). The TLM of the example, illustrated below the specification, is generated based on a mapping decision of A1, A2 on CPU while A5 and A8 on a custom hardware: HW1. After optimizing algorithms and finalizing the platform decisions, the *Back-end Synthesis* can synthesize the overall design down to the selected hardware/software implementation.

3.1 *Algo2Spec*: Specification Generation Tool

To bridge the gap between ADE and SLDE, we propose *Algo2Spec*. *Algo2Spec* takes the Similink algorithm model as an input and synthesizes it to a SpecC SLDL specification representing the algorithm's functionality and original hierarchy. We construct *Algo2Spec* as a multi-stage process of the front-end synthesizer and the integrator. In the first step, the front-end synthesizer in turn conducts leaf synthesis (generating computation code for each leaf component), hierarchy synthesis (producing the overall SLDL skeleton) and signal synthesis (connecting behaviors). Afterwards, the integrator combines the output of front-end synthesizer to produce a specification. The following paragraphs outline each step.

Leaf Synthesis. As a first step in the generation process, the front-end synthesizer starts with the leaf synthesis. It works on the smallest unit in the model, which is an atomic block in Simulink (e.g computation, algebraic or logical) as the blocks A1, A3, A4, and A6-A8 in the example. Each leaf block in Simulink will be represented as a SLDL behavior, which is an atomic unit capturing computational load. As SpecC SLDL is an extension over ANSI-C, C-code is needed for each behavior. To generate this, leaf synthesis iterates through the Simulink model and invokes Simulink Embedded Coder (SEC) as the back-end C code generator for each leaf. The result is a set of C files for each Simulink block expressing the computation.

Hierarchy Synthesis. The hierarchy synthesis is responsible for generating an overall SLDL skeleton for the Simulink model, capturing its structural and behavioral hierarchy. For this it creates an empty behavior for each identified leaf, and also creates hierarchical behaviors to represent the Simulink model structure. In our example A2 and A5 are hierarchical behaviors containing the child behaviors A3, A4 and A6, A7, respectively. During this stage, syntactical correctness and model functional validity are both enforced. Single rate models appear as a sequential composition. Multiple single-rate islands are represented as parallel behaviors communicating through channels. However, hierarchy flattening is necessary for multi-rate models to partition blocks running at different rates to different rate control behaviors in the SLDL specification. Scheduling is an important part of hierarchy synthesis, please see Sec. 4.

Signal Synthesis. Simulink uses signals for communicating between blocks by defining that each signal has to have at one simulation time interval the same value at every of its point. Signal synthesis recreates the same connectivity in SLDL communication primitives ensuring communication across behaviors. It mainly generates variables mapped through ports and routed through hierarchical behavior to enable communication. Signal synthesis becomes critical in multi-rate models, were buffers are needed. Buffers are generally represented as queues in the SLDL.

Integrator. After front-end synthesis, the integrator combines the computation code generated by leaf synthesis and the SLDL skeleton containing hierarchy, communication and scheduling generated by hierarchy/signal synthesis to output the final specification. The integrator localizes global variables and creates clean and well-defined communication interface adhering to the communication structure in original Simulink models. In addition, the integrator also inserts all initialization and termination routines to maintain proper model execution.

In result, all computation related procedures are merged into SLDL behaviors by the integrator. A specification that captures the model hierarchy, execution semantics, signal properties and valid results is generated. The SLDL specification serves as the fundamental element for detailed design space exploration. The SGT eliminates the need for manually writing the specification, thus avoid coding errors and significantly shortens the time to exploration.

Scope. As Simulink offers a wide range of modeling domains (e.g. continues time and discrete) and in order to achieve a feasible solution. The subset supported by *Algo2Spec* has to be limited. Most importantly, continues time models are out of scope for *Algo2Spec*. Restricting the scope of considered Simulink semantics for synthesis purpose has been shown effective in earlier approaches [19], which demonstrated tremendous benefits while targeting only a safe subset. For this paper, we target the following components: blocks under discrete and fixed step solver and SEC; special blocks in toolboxes (partially supported depending on configurations); multi-rate systems with limited rate-transition schemes.

4 Cross-Layer Decisions

With the tight integration, the unified design flow realizes a feedback/decision loop (see Fig. 2) where feedback by the analysis tools in ADE, SGT and SLDE respectively is propagated to the designer on the left-hand side. In result, on the right side, the designer enters new decisions into the flow for optimization and system-level exploration to identify a suitable algorithm / platform combination. Assisted by the multi-level analysis feedback, the designer can identify and eliminate bottlenecks at an appropriate level. The next paragraphs outline the decisions at each level as well as overall decision opportunities.

Algorithm Decisions. The decisions at the first level mostly stem from within the ADE. Through its simulation analysis, the designer improves the algorithm for optimizing functional performance. Examples include algorithm exploration to find the most suitable algorithm for a given task, the configuration or tuning of an algorithm. Functional performance in this context could refer to the detection accuracy of a vision algorithm.

However, algorithm composition also affects the later design. As a structural example, an S-Function block cannot be further decomposed into smaller blocks. Thus, it hinders finer granularity explorations. Higher dimensions and width of signals used between blocks may cause higher traffic if these blocks are mapped to different PEs. An additional degree of freedom is the exposed amount and type of parallelism. Different types of PEs (such as processor, GPU, custom hardware) efficiently operate on different types of parallelism (task-level, data-level, fine-grained, respectively). If the designer already has a PE type in mind, the algorithms with an appropriate parallelism can be chosen. Overall, algorithm decisions not only alter model functionality, but also impact the system-level explorability of the overall design and preferred PE-type mapping.

Specification Decisions. These decisions affect the generation of the specification in terms of granularity of SLDL blocks, scheduling of blocks and exposed parallelism. The granularity decision determines up to which level the Simulink's structure is exposed in SLDL, and conversely what is treated as a leaf component. At one extreme, the finest granularity exposes each atomic Simulink block as leaf in SLDL. This hinders Simulink to perform block fusion as all blocks are generated separately. Further, it may expose overly simplistic blocks, such as single stage combinatorial logic, to the SLDL. Overall, this may cause unnecessary communication overhead in the SLDL specification without offering impactful mapping alternatives. At the other extreme, the coarsest granularity treats the Simulink top model as one "big" leaf. It gives all cross-block optimization potential to Simulink, however, causes a loss of hierarchy which in turn removes the possibility of heterogeneous exploration. *Algo2Spec* therefore aims at at a granularity with a threshold balancing block fusion potential and exploration flexibility. In the current version, *Algo2Spec* relies on the designer to define the granularity (see Fig. 2). A heuristic and automatic decision making for deciding granularity is part of future work.

Simulink and the SLDL differ in execution semantics, which offers opportunities for scheduling exploration. One policy: *faithful scheduling* emulates the simulation semantics of Simulink. All Simulink blocks are statically scheduled in a sorted dependency list and executed sequentially. In result, all SLDL behaviors will be sequentially executed in the same order. A second scheduling policy: *pipelined scheduling* can be observed for example in the Simulink HDL Coder generated code. Blocks are executed in a pipeline fashion offering temporal parallelism. If selected, Simulink blocks are then synthesized into a pipelined SLDL model enabling parallelism exploring. For brevity and simplicity, this paper focuses on *faithful scheduling*.

It has to be noted that granularity and scheduling also affect the exposed parallelism. The desired parallelism depends on the targeted PE class as for example mapping to custom hardware component can benefit from much finer grained parallelism than a processor mapping.

System-Level Decisions. Once the specification is defined, a myriad of system-level decisions are required spanning architecture decisions (PE allocation and behavior mapping), scheduling decisions of behaviors within each PE (static, dynamic-priority, dynamic-FCFS), network decisions (interconnect and communication element allocation), and subsequent communication decisions (selecting interconnect specific communication and synchronization primitives). These decisions are for example discussed in [2]. The SLDE realizes these decisions by model refinement. It generates Transaction-Level Models (TLM) at varying levels of abstraction to implement these decisions. The generated TLMs are then used for performance/power/cost analysis driving new system-level design decisions.

Cross Layer Decisions. In addition to the decisions at each level, cross-layer decisions are needed. For example, we have observed in the past the need to change parallelism granularity and type depending on mapping decisions. Hence in result of system exploration, the algorithm definition needs to be changed. We also have experienced the necessity for platform specific algorithm tuning such as converting from floating to fixed point computation, or reducing memory bandwidth of a vision algorithm through parameter compression. Again, with automating the path from algorithm to specification and instant available performance feedback, the designer can easily try out various decision combinations that will yield better overall designs.

5   Case Study

We demonstrate the flexibility of the unified design flow by exploring a Motion JPEG (M-JPEG) video encoder. We have chosen this application for it is a real-life application that is not too complicated. M-JPEG is a video format that defines each frame of the video feed is compressed as a JPEG image separately, which is like MPEG [4] but without inter-frame predictive coding. It is primarily used in video-capturing equipment, such as digital cameras and webcams. We start with a Simulink model out of the vision toolbox. The model contains 294 blocks, 28 S-functions, 35 subsystems, 86 inports and 69 outputs. The model contains blocks with up to 8 levels in depth (which we will later simply refer to as depth). For our experiments, the design encodes a 910-frame QVGA (320x240) video stream.

In this case study, the designer performs three exploration steps of granularity identification (algorithm decisions/specification decisions), early estimations and platform explorations (system-level decisions). Based on simulation feedback, a new design iteration starts with new higher-level design decisions. Overall, we show three design iterations.

All iterations draw from the same database of processing element (PE) types. For simplicity, we restrict the exploration to one CPU (ARM7TDMI at 100MHz) that is assisted by up to two custom hardware components (HW1, HW2 at 100MHz). All PEs are connected to one processor bus of type AMBA AHB.

Initial Design Iteration. In the first iteration, the designer selects a coarse granularity which only exposes a minimum decomposition. This may potentially facilitate optimization of the generated computation code, such as block fusion by Simulink Embedded Coder (SEC) and reduce the overall traffic due to fewer components. With the selected granularity, *Algo2Spec* generates the coarse-grained specification as shown in Fig. 3. It only contains three leaf behaviors, PreProc, BlkProc and MatCon in behavior Encoder_DUT (Design Under Test) together with Stimulus and Monitor consisting the testbench.

After specification generation, the SLDE tools for early estimation can be used to identify allocation and mapping candidates. Fig. 5 shows the result of early estimations of both computation and communication demands on each generated leaf behavior in the specification. Computation expresses the

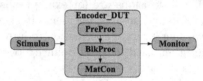

Fig. 3. Initial Specification

number of C-level operations executed in each leaf behavior. Communication demand shows number of bytes are transferred overall in a leaf behavior.

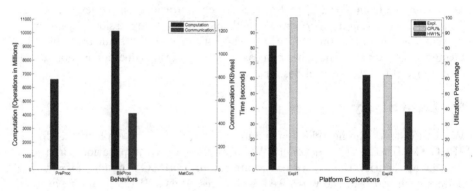

Fig. 4. Initial Early Estimation   **Fig. 5.** Initial Exploration Results

Due to the coarse granularity, not many blocks are available for PE mapping as they are all merged together into a few "super" blocks even though it has a fairly light overall traffic. BlkProc is the most computational and communicational expensive block. Thus the design is most suitable for SW-only mapping and one with a custom HW component for the most computation intense block BlkProc. Tabl. 1 summarize these explorations.

Fig. 5 plots the results of the platform explorations in terms of target execution time (in secs) and PE utilizations (in percentage). The leftmost bar indicates target execution time, while the right bars

Table 1. Initial Explorations

	Expl1	Expl2
CPU	All	All others
HW1		BlkProc

show PE utilizations. Expl1, the SW-only solution takes nearly 80s where Expl2, is faster with 60s. With dedicated HW for executing the most computational intensive behavior, both CPU and HW1 are load-balanced and the co-design solution offers some performance increase. However, the speedup is not too significant due to the coarse-grained model and limited parallelism. Hence, we start a new iteration for a finer-grained specification to increase mapping options.

Intermediate Design Iteration. A finer granularity with depth 3 (hierarchy levels) is chosen to generate a new specification. Fig. 6 illustrates the simplified fine-grained specification. The fine-grained specification decomposes all three levels of `PreProc` to 10 sub-behaviors; `BlkProc` to 4 sub-behaviors; `MatCon` to 1 sub-behavior (see Fig. 6). Two task-level parallelism within, `Spl_Par` and `ImgP_Par` are discovered while decomposing `Pre_proc` and scheduled in parallel in the generated SLDL specification.

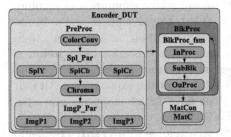

Fig. 6. Intermediate Specification

The estimation results in Fig. 7 omit two behaviors in `ImgP_Par` due to their low computation and communication demands. Also, it is inefficient to explore the task-level parallelism in `Spl_Par`, and `ImgP_Par` as these behaviors have low computation. Splitting `BlkProc` potentially introduces more traffic as `InProc` and `OuProc` have more data exchange with `SubBlk` within the original block. Consequently, Tabl. 2 shows selected explorations: Expl3, mapping `SubBlk` to HW1 and Expl4, mapping `SubBlk` and `Chroma` to HW1.

The results in Fig. 8 (with Expl1 for reference) show that Expl3 yields a similar performance gain as Expl2 in the previous iteration. Unexpectedly, Expl4 downgrades performance by incurring more traffic.

Table 2. Intermediate Explorations

	Expl3	Expl4
CPU	All others	All others
HW1	SubBlk	SubBlk, Chroma

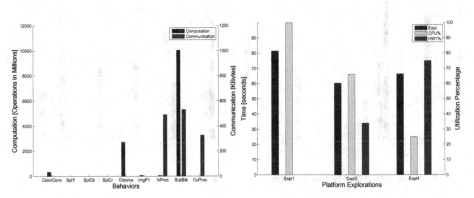

Fig. 7. Interm. Early Estimation   **Fig. 8.** Interm. Exploration Results

Even though this specification offers more mapping flexibility, it introduces too many oversimplified behaviors such as SplY, SplCb, SplCr and ImgP1/2/3. Hierarchy depth is imbalanced: BlkProc in Fig. 3 has depth of 8 while on the same level, PreProc and MatCon only have depths of 3 and 2. It is undesired to decompose computationally non-intense blocks unnecessarily while the computation heavy BlkProc is insufficiently split. Therefore, in the next iteration a custom granularity selectively splits BlkProc to an even finer granularity to expose potential parallelism without affecting other blocks with overheads.

Final Design Iteration. Fig. 9 shows the custom generated specification which has BlkProc with depths of 5, while PreProc and MatCon remains at level 1. BlkProc is decomposed now through 5 levels to Mot, along with three parallel behaviors: Tran1, Tran2 and Tran2.

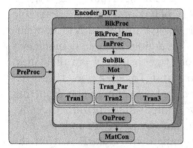

Fig. 9. Final Specification

Fig. 10 presents early estimation for behaviors with meaningful computation or communication. Tran1 has significant computation and low communication, making it a candidate for concurrent execution. This iteration now uses two custom hardware: HW1 and HW2. Tabl. 3 show the explorations. All four explorations have Tran1 mapped on a separated HW1, running concurrently with Tran2. The designer explores with Tran1, Tran2 and Tran3 to run in parallel by adding HW2 (Expl6, Expl7 and Expl8).

Fig. 11 shows that, mapping Tran2 does not boost the performance meaningfully as its low computation to communication ratio. Furthermore, Expl8, even though HW2 is load-balance, the overall performance still does not increase much due to additional traffic.

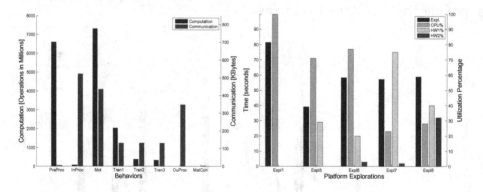

Fig. 10. Final Early Estimation   **Fig. 11.** Final Exploration Results

Expl5 achieves best performance splitting the two computational heavy blocks PreProc and Mot onto CPU and HW1 without much traffic. Meanwhile, it keeps Tran1 running in parallel with Tran2 and Tran3. Subsequently, Expl5 is selected for final implementation, which is generated by the back-end synthesis. Due to limitation of space, the details of the implementation are not further examined.

Table 3. Final Explorations

	Expl5	Expl6	Expl7	Expl8
CPU	All oth.	All oth.	All oth.	All oth.
HW1	PreProc Tran1 Mot	PreProc Tran1	PreProc Tran1 InProc	PreProc Tran1
HW2		Tran2	Tran2	Mot, Tran2

6 Conclusion

In this paper, we presented a unified algorithm and system design flow. We introduced *Algo2Spec* which closes the specification gap by generating SLDL specifications of Simulink algorithm models. Automating specification generation eliminates the error tedious manual implementation. Moreover, it enables algorithm designers to explore the platform implications of the chosen algorithms, and empowers a cross-layer decision process.

We demonstrated the unified flow using an MJPEG video encoder example and highlighted cross-layer design iterations. An improved HW/SW solution was identified yielding 50% performance gain compared to a pure software solution. All explorations are conducted in a few hours which yield a significant improvement on productivity and efficiency.

Acknowledgment. The work presented in this paper is in part supported by the National Science Foundation under Grant No. 1136027.

References

1. Chandraiah, P., Domer, R.: Code and data structure partitioning for parallel and flexible MPSoC specification using designer-controlled recoding. IEEE Transactions on Computer-Aided Design of Integrated Circuits and Systems 27(6), 1078–1090 (2008)
2. Dömer, R., Gerstlauer, A., Peng, J., Shin, D., Cai, L., Yu, H., Abdi, S., Gajski, D.D.: System-on-Chip Environment: A SpecC-based Framework for Heterogeneous MPSoC Design 2008(647953),13 (2008)
3. Gajski, D.D., Zhu, J., Dömer, R., Gerstlauer, A., Zhao, S.: SpecC: Specification Language and Design Methodology. Kluwer Academic Publishers (2000)
4. Gall, D.L.: MPEG: a video compression standard for multimedia applications. Communications of the ACM 34, 46–58 (1991)
5. Ha, S., Kim, S., Lee, C., Yi, Y., Kwon, S., Pyo Joo, Y.: PeaCE: A hardware-software codesign environment for multimedia embedded systems. ACM Transactions on Design Automation of Electronic Systems 12 (2007)
6. Jerraya, A.A., Bouchhima, A., Pétrot, F.: Programming models and HW-SW interfaces abstraction for multi-processor SoC. In: Design Automation Conference, pp. 280–285 (2006)

7. Johnson, G.: LabVIEW Graphical Programming: Practical Applications in Instrumentation and Control, 2nd edn. McGraw-Hill School Education Group (1997)
8. Martin, G., Mueller, W.: UML for SOC Design. Springer, Dordrecht (2005)
9. Marwedel, P.: Embedded Systems Design. Kluwer Academic Publishers (2003)
10. The Mathworks, Inc. Simulink Embedded Coder Reference R2011b (2011)
11. The Mathworks, Inc. Untimed SystemC/TLM Simulation (2012b)
12. Mellor, S.J., Balcer, M.J.: Executable UML: A Foundation for Model-Driven Architecture, 1st edn. Addison-Wesley Professional (May 2002)
13. MISRA. Misra ac tl: Modelling style guidelines for the application of targetlink in the context of automatic code generation (2007)
14. Mueller, W., Rosti, A., Bocchio, S., Riccobene, E., Scandurra, P., Dehaene, W., Vanderperren, Y.: UML for ESL design: basic principles, tools, and applications. In: International Conference on Computer Aided Design, pp. 73–80 (2006)
15. Open SystemC Initiative. Functional Specification for SystemC 2.0 (2000)
16. Popovici, K.M.: Multilevel Programming Envrionment for Heterogeneous MPSoC Architectures. PhD thesis, Grenoble Institute of Technology (2008)
17. Riccobene, E., Scandurra, P., Rosti, A., Bocchio, S.: A SoC design methodology involving a UML 2.0 profile for SystemC. In: Design, Automation, and Test in Europe, pp. 704–709 (2005)
18. The Mathworks Inc. MATLAB and Simulink (1993)
19. Tripakis, S., Sofronis, C., Caspi, P., Curic, A.: Translating discrete-time simulink to lustre. ACM Trans. Embed. Comput. Syst. 4(4), 779–818 (2005)
20. Vanderperren, Y., Dehaene, W.: From UML/SysML to MATLAB/Simulink: current state and future perspectives. In: Design, Automation, and Test in Europe (2006)

Automatic Execution of Test Cases on UML Models of Embedded Systems[*]

Marco A. Wehrmeister[1] and Gian R. Berkenbrock[2]

[1] Federal University of Technology – Paraná (UTFPR)
Av. Sete de Setembro, 3165, 80230-901 Curitiba, Brazil
wehrmeister@utfpr.edu.br
[2] Santa Catarina State University (UDESC)
Rua Paulo Malschitzki, s/n, 89219-710 Joinville, Brazil
gian@joinville.udesc.br

Abstract. During the design of an embedded system, fixing errors discovered only in later stages is a very expensive activity. In order to decrease such costs, the engineers have to identify and fix the introduced errors as soon as possible. Therefore, it makes sense to facilitate the errors detection during the whole the design cycle, including the initial specification stages. This work proposed a test-based approach to aid the early verification of embedded and real-time systems. The proposed approach applies test cases on the system behavior described in the high-level specifications. A tool to automate the execution of the test cases upon UML models has been created. Its initial goal is to improve the errors detection on the system behavior before the implementation phase, since test cases are based on the system requirements. Test cases are platform independent and describe: runtime scenarios; the behaviors to be tested along with their input; and the expected results. The tool executes automatically each test case, in which the specified behavior is simulated Thereafter, the obtained results are compared with the expected ones, indicating the success or failure of the test case. A case study was performed to validate the proposed approach. The achieved results demonstrate that it is feasible to test the system behavior even though when the implementation is still not available.

Keywords: Model-Driven Engineering, UML, testing, test cases execution, simulation.

1 Introduction

The design of embedded systems is a very complex task. The engineering team must cope with many distinct requirements and constraints (including timing constraints), whereas the project schedule shrinks due to the time-to-market pressure. Moreover, modern embedded and real-time systems are demanded to

---

[*] This work is being supported by National Council for Scientific and Technological Development (CNPq - Brazil) through the grant 480321/2011-6.

G. Schirner et al. (Eds.): IESS 2013, IFIP AICT 403, pp. 39–48, 2013.

deliver an increasing amount of services, affecting directly the complexity of their design. As the system size increases in terms of the number of functions, the number of potential errors or bugs also increases. As a consequence, additional resources (e.g. extra time, money and people) are needed to fix such problems before delivering the final system.

A common approach to deal with the system complexity is to decompose hierarchically a complex problem into smaller sub-problems, increasing the abstraction level [1]. *Model-Driven Engineering* (MDE) [2] has been seen as a suitable approach to cope with design complexity of embedded systems. It advocates that specifications with higher abstraction levels (i.e. models) are the main artifacts of the design. These models are successively refined up to achieve the system implementation using components (hardware and software) available in a target execution platform. Specifically, the engineers specify a *Platform Independent Model* (PIM) that is refined and mapped into a *Platform Specific Model* (PSM), from which source code can be generated automatically. CASE tools helps with such a transformation process.

As one can infer, the quality and correctness of the generated code is directly related with the information provided by the created models and their transformations. Thus, as the system implementation relies strongly on the created models, an undetected error in any model is easily propagated to latter design phases. An error introduced in early design stages and detected only in advanced stages leads to a higher repair cost. The total cost would be lower (from 10 to 100 times lower [3]) if the error had been detected and fixed in the phase in which it was introduced. Taking into account that MDE approaches strongly rely on the PIM and its transformation to a PSM, it is very important to provide techniques to test and verify the produced models. Consequently, the automation of these tasks (e.g. automatic execution of test cases on the system models) is requited.

Aspect-oriented Model-Driven Engineering for Real-Time systems (AMoDE-RT) [4][5] has been successfully applied to design embedded and real-time systems. The engineers specify the system's structure and behavior using UML[1] models annotated with stereotype of the MARTE profile[2]. In [6], AMoDE-RT was extended to include a verification activity in the specification phase, in order to enable the engineers to simulate the execution of the behavior specified in the UML model. However, such an approach was not adequate, since there is a considerable effort to create and run new tests.

This work extends that previous work by proposing the repeatable and automatic verification[3] of embedded and real-time systems based on their high-level specifications. The *Automated Testing for UML* (AT4U) approach proposes the automatic execution of test cases on the behavioral diagrams of an UML model. The set of test cases exercise parts of the system behavior (specified in an UML model) via simulation. The test results can be analyzed to check if the system has

---

[1] http://www.omg.org/spec/UML/2.4

[2] http://www.omg.org/spec/MARTE/1.1

[3] In this paper, "verification" means checking the specification using a finite set of test cases to exercise system behavior, instead of the exhaustive and formal verification.

behaved as expected. To support the proposed approach, the AT4U tool executes automatically the set of test cases on the UML model. Each test case describes a runtime scenario (on which the system is exercised) and the behavior selected to be tested. *Framework for UML Model Behavior Simulation* (FUMBeS) [6] simulates the indicated behavior, using the input arguments specified in the test case. The obtained result is compared with the expected result to indicate whether the test case succeeded or not.

It is important to highlight that this automated testing is done already in the specification phase, so that the UML model being created (or its parts) are verified as soon as possible, even if the model is still incomplete. The proposed approach has been validated with a real-world case study. The experiments show encouraging results on the use of AT4U and FUMBeS to simulate and test the system behavior in early design phase, without any concrete implementation.

This paper is organized as follows: section 2 discusses the related work; section 3 provides an overview the AT4U approach; section 4 presents the experiments performed to assess AT4U and their results; and finally, section 5 draws some the conclusions and discusses the future work.

2 Related Work

This section discusses some recent related work regarding Model-Based Test (MBT) and test automation. In [7], the authors discuss MBT and its automation. Several characteristics are evaluated, e.g. quality of MBT versus hand-crafted test in terms of coverage and number of detected failures. Among other conclusions, the authors state that MBT is worth using as it detects from two to six times more requirements errors.

In both [8] and [9], UML models annotated with stereotype of the *UML Testing Profile* (UTP) are used to generate tests using the language TTCN-3(*Testing and Test Control Notation,* version 3) in order to perform black-box testing on software components. The work presented in [8] uses sequence diagrams to generate the TTCN-3 code for the test cases behavior. Additionally, test case configuration code (written in TTCN-3) are generated from composite structure diagrams. Similarly, in [9], TTCN-3 code is generated from sequence and/or activity diagrams decorated with UTP stereotypes. However, that approach uses MDE concepts and created a mapping between the UML/UTP and TTCN-3 meta-model. A TTCN-3 model is obtained from UML model by using a model-to-model transformation.

In [10], MBT is applied in Resource-Constrained Real-Time Embedded Systems (RC-RTES). UML models are annotated with stereotype of the UTP to generate a test framework, comprising: a proxy test model, UTP artifacts (i.e. test drivers and test cases), and a communication interface. The tests cases are executed directly on the RC-RTES, however the produced results are mirrored to the design level. In that approach, the test cases are manually specified as sequence diagrams.

The automated generation of test cases is addressed in [11]. MDE techniques are use to generate test cases from sequence diagrams. The Eclipse Modeling

Framework (EMF) was used to create two PIM: the sequence of method calls (SMC) model and the xUnit models. By using the Tefkat engine, a model-to-model transformation translates a SMC model into a xUnit model. Thereafter, a model-to-text transformation combines the xUnit model, test data and code headers to generate test cases for a given target unit testing framework. The experiment conducted in [11] generated test cases for SUnit and JUnit.

Comparing the proposed verification approach with the cited works, the main difference is the possibility to execute the test cases directly on the high-level specification. This work proposes a PIM to represent test cases information likewise [11] and [9]. However, the proposed PIM seems to be more complete since it represents both the test case definitions and the results produced during testing. The test cases are manually specified (as in [10]) in XML files rather than using the UML diagrams as in [10], [8] and [9]. Finally, to the best of our knowledge, AT4U is the first approach that allows the automated execution of test cases on UML model.

3   Automated Testing for UML Models

The *Automated Testing for UML* (AT4U) approach have been created to aid the engineers to verify the behavior of embedded and real-time systems in earlier design stages. AMoDE-RT was extended to include a verification activity: the execution of a set of test cases upon the behavior described in the UML model. Therefore, the proposed approach relies on two techniques: (i) the automatic execution of many test cases, including test case scenario setup, execution of selected system behaviors, and the evaluation of the produced results; and (ii) the execution of the specified behavior via simulation.

The proposed approach is based on the ideas presented in the family of code-driven testing frameworks known as xUnit [12]. However, instead of executing the test cases on the system implementation, the test cases are executed on the UML model during the specification phase in an iterative fashion (i.e. a closed loop comprising specification and simulation/testing) until the specification is considered correct by the engineering team. For that, AT4U executes a set of test cases upon both individual elements (i.e. unit test) and groups of dependent elements (i.e. component test) that have been specified in the UML model. Further, as the execution of test cases is performed automatically by a software tool named *AT4U tool*, the testing process can be repeated at every round of changes on the UML model, allowing regression test. If inconsistencies are detected, the UML model can be fixed, and hence, the problem is not propagated to the next stages of the design. An overview of the AT4U approach is depicted in figure 1.

Usually, high-level specifications such as UML models are independent of any implementation technology or execution platform. The use of any platform specific testing technology is not desirable since engineers need to translate the high-level specification into code for the target execution platform before performing any kind of automated testing. In this situation, the testing results may be affected by both the errors introduced in the specification and the errors of this translation process.

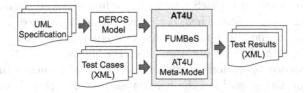

Fig. 1. Overview of AT4U verification approach

In order to to allow testing automation for platform independent specifications, AT4U provides: (i) a platform independent description of test cases, and (ii) a mechanism to execute these platform independent test cases. AT4U proposes a *test suite model*, whose meta-model is based on the concepts and ideas of the xUnit framework [12] and the UML Testing profile[4]. AT4U meta-model represents the following information: (i) the test cases used to exercise the system behavior; and (ii) test case results, which are produced during the execution of each test case. For details on AT4U meta-model, see [13]. It is important to note that this *test suite model* is platform independent, and thus, it could be used later in the design cycle to generate test cases in the chosen target platform.

The AT4U tool automates the execution of test cases on high-level specifications. It takes as input a DERCS model[5] (created from the UML model that represents the embedded real-time system under test) and an XML file containing the description of all test cases that must be executed. Once the system model and the test suite model are loaded, the test cases are executed on the model as follows. For each test case, the AT4U performs: (i) the setup of the initial scenario; (ii) the simulation of the selected methods; and (iii) the evaluation of the results obtained from the simulated execution of the methods set.

In the *scenario initialization phase*, the information provided by the AT4U meta-model is used to initialize the runtime state of DERCS' objects. Each object described in the input scenario provides the values to initialize the DERCS's objects, i.e. these values are directly assigned to runtime information of the corresponding attributes.

Thereafter, in the *method testing phase*, AT4U executes the methods specified within the test case, checking if the associated assertions are valid or not. This phase is divided in two parts: (i) method setup and execution; and (ii) the evaluation of the assertions associated with the method under test. Once all input arguments are set, FUMBeS simulates the execution of the behavior associated with the method under test. Each individual actions associated with the simulated behavior is executed and its outcomes eventually modify the runtime state of the DERCS model (for details see [6]).

---

[4] http://www.omg.org/spec/UTP/1.1/

[5] *Distributed Embedded Real-time Compact Specification* (DERCS) is a PIM suitable for code generation and simulation. Unfortunately, due to space constraints, a discussion on the reasons that led to the creation and use of DERCS is out-of-scope for this text. Interested readers should refer to [5] and [6].

After the simulation, FUMBeS returns the value produced during the execution of the method under test. Then, *evaluation phase* takes place. The assertions associated with the method under test are evaluated. AT4U tool compares the expected result with the one obtained after the method execution, using the specified comparison operation. In addition, AT4U tool evaluates the assertions related the expected scenario of the whole test case. For that, it compares the expected scenario described in the test case with the scenario obtained after executing the set of methods. Each object of the expected scenario is compared with its counterpart in the DERCS model. If the state of both objects is similar, the next object is evaluated until all objects described in the expected scenario are checked. The test case is marked as successful if all assertions are valid, i.e. those related to each individual method must be valid, along with those related to the whole test case. If any of these assertions is not valid, the test case failed and is marked accordingly.

It is worth noting that an important issue of any automated testing approach is to provide the feedback on the executed test cases. AT4U approach reports the outcomes of the test cases by means of an XML file. This file is generated from the output elements provided by the AT4U model.

The root of the XML document (*TestSuite*) is divided in various nodes, each one reporting the results of one test case. Each *TestCase* node has two subtrees. *Scenario* subtree reports the input, expected and result scenarios. Each of these scenarios reports the snapshot of the objects states in the following moments: *Input* describes the objects before the execution of any method; *Expected* indicates the objects specified in the expected scenario of the test case; and *Result* reveals the objects after the execution of all methods within the test case. *Methods* subtree presents information on the methods exercised during the test case. For each *Method*, the following information is reported: *InputParameters* describes the values used as input to simulate the execution of the method's behavior; *ReturnedValue* indicates the expected and the obtained value returned after the execution of the method; *Scenario* reports the input, expected and result scenarios (the snapshots are taken after the method execution).

However, although a comprehensive amount of data is provided by this report, the XML format is not appropriate for reading by human beings. This XML file could be processed (e.g. using XSLT - eXtensible Stylesheet Language Transformations[6]) to produce another document in a human readable format, such as HTML or RTF, so that the test cases results are better visualized. Such a feature is subject for our future work. However, it is important to highlight that, by generating an XML file containing the results of the execution of each test case, other software tools could process such information analyze the obtained results. For instance, test coverage could be evaluated, or software documentation could be generated based on such an information.

---

[6] http://www.w3.org/TR/xslt

4   AT4U Validation: UAV Case Study

This section presents a case study conducted to validate the AT4U approach. This case study has two main goals. The first one is to check if the proposed approach is practicable, i.e. if the engineers can specify a set of test cases and execute them automatically on the UML model of an embedded and real-time system. The second one is to evaluate the performance of the AT4U tool, in order to assess how much time AT4U tool takes to execute the set of test cases.

The AT4U approach was applied in the movement control system of an Unmanned Aerial Vehicle (UAV) presented in [5]. More precisely, 20 test cases have been created to test parts of the movement control system in 4 different situations: (i) the system operating under normal environmental conditions (4 test cases); (ii) the sensing subsystem is running, but the helicopter is powered down and it lies on the ground (4 test cases); (iii) the helicopter is powered on, but it lies on the ground (7 test cases); (iv) the system operating under hostile environmental conditions (5 test cases).

The set of test cases exercises a total of 31 distinct methods, including simple get/set methods and methods with more complex computations. Some of these methods have been simulated more than once (in different situations), and hence, 143 different simulations have been performed to execute the complete set of test cases. The normal and abnormal values have been chosen as input for the test cases. The complete set of test cases was executed and all assertions were evaluated as true, indicating that all test cases were successful.

Figure 2 shows a small fragment of the report generated by AT4U tool regarding the test case for the method *TemperatureSensorDriver.getValue()*. Lines 102-105 show that the expected and returned values are equal. Hence, the assertion on the behavior of this method was evaluated as true (*assertResult= "true"*). The set of test case has been repeated 10 times and their results remained the same. Thereafter, the behavior of the *TemperatureSensorDriver.getValue()* was modified in the UML model, in order to check if its test case would fail. Now, this method returns the value of *sTemperature.Value* plus one instead of returning directly this value. The complete set of test cases was executed again. As expected, this test case failed, since its assertion is not valid anymore.

The first goal of this case study was achieved as various test cases have been specified and executed repeatedly on the high-level specification of the embedded and real-time system. By using AT4U approach, it is possible to perform regression tests. Modifications on the UML model can be automatically evaluated by the test cases previously developed. An error introduced in the system's parts that are covered by the test cases is quickly detected; at least one of these parts is going to eventually fail, as it was illustrated in the previous paragraph.

As mentioned, the second goal of this case study is to evaluate the performance of the AT4U tool. The technologies reused were implemented in Java (i.e. DERCS, FUMBeS, and EMF), and thus, AT4U tool was developed using the JDK 1.6. The experiments have been conducted with a MacBook equipped with an Intel Core 2 Due processor running at 2.16 MHz, 2 GB of RAM, Snow Leopard as operating system, and Java SE Runtime Environment version 1.26.0_26

```
001  <?xml version="1.0" encoding="UTF-8"?>
002  <TestSuite>
003    <TestCase id="TC-1.3">
004      <Scenario assertResult="true">
     ...
099      </Scenario>
098      <Methods>
099        <Method name="getValue" obj="sTemperature"
100                assertResult="true">
101          <InputParameters></InputParameters>
102          <ReturnedValue assertResult="true">
103            <Expected>20</Expected>
104            <Result>20</Result>
105          </ReturnedValue>
106          <Scenario assertResult="true">
     ...
201          </Scenario>
202        </Method>
203      </Methods>
204    </TestCase>
205  </TestSuite>
```

Fig. 2. XML file reporting test case results

(build 1.6.0_26-b03-384-10M3425). To run the experiment, the system was rebooted, all background applications finished, and the experiments executed in a shell session.

The set of test cases was executed 100 times. The complete set was executed in 3712 ms on average, and the average execution time per test case was 185,6 ms (25,96 ms per method). It is important to note that this performance is highly dependent on the tested behaviors. In fact, depending on the complexity of the tested behaviors (e.g. the amount of loop iterations, branches, or executed actions), this execution time can be longer or shorter. Hence, the numbers presented in this case study show only that it is feasible to run test cases to simulate the behavior specified in an UML model.

Considering that there is no implementation available in the specification phase, the AT4U execution time would not be a problem, since engineers do not need to spend time implementing a functionality to verify a solution. Hence, the errors in the specification may be quickly detected without having any implementation or the complete UML model. This performance allows the execution of the whole set of test cases at every round of changes on the UML model to assess if errors were introduced in the specification.

5   Conclusions and Future Work

To decrease the overall cost, it is very important to provide methods and tools to check the created artifacts as soon as possible in the design cycle. The later an error is detected, the higher the cost and effort to fix it [3]. This works proposes an additional activity in the AMoDE-RT approach. Specifically, the AT4U approach supports the automation of the verification activities of system specifications, more precisely, UML models. The specification phase became an iterative process comprising modeling, model-to-model transformations, and model testing and simulation. By using the AT4U verification approach, engineers specify and execute a set of test case during the creation of the UML model.

AT4U tool supports the proposed approach by automating the execution of the test cases on the UML model. It uses the FUMBeS framework to simulate (parts of) the system behavior. In other words, AT4U executes (the parts of) the embedded and real-time system under controlled and specific situations that have been defined within the test cases. Test cases are represented in a platform independent fashion by means of a test suite model. Engineers write test cases in an XML file which is used to instantiate the mentioned testing model. Similarly, AT4U tool reports the results of the test cases execution in an XML file. This report provides information such as the initial, expected and resulting scenarios used in each test case, as well as the data produced by the executed behaviors and the results of the assertions evaluation.

Although this work is the initial step towards automatic execution of test cases in both models and system implementation, it already presented encouraging results. The proposed approach has been validated with a real-world application of embedded and real-time systems domain. The experiments show indications that AT4U approach is suitable for the purpose of an early assessment of system behavior. Engineers may verify the system specification, and also evaluate different solutions, while the specification is being created in early stages of design. It is worth pointing out that there is no need to implement any part of the system under design to check the suitability of a solution.

Moreover, AT4U enables the regression test of UML model. This helps the engineers to identify whether an error has been included in the specification in the latter refinement steps. Although the benefits already mentioned in this paper, AT4U is not intended to be the unique technique used to verify the system. It shall be used along with other verification methods and tools including code-driven testing automation frameworks, in order to improve the confidence on the design and also to decrease the number of specification errors.

Future work directions include the improvement of AT4U in order to support the use of the UML testing profile to specify the set of test cases, instead of using an XML file Two new tools are needed to support AT4U: one to facilitate the specification of the test cases XML file; and another to facilitate the visualization of the testing report. A test cases generation tool is also important. Such a tool would use the information provided by AT4U PIM to generate the corresponding test cases for a selected target platform. In addition, this tool could create the test cases automatically based on the execution flow of the system behavior. An UML virtual machine using FUMBeS is also envisaged. It should simulate the whole embedded and real-time system, i.e. the execution of its active objects and their concurrent execution, respecting the time constraints.

References

1. Parnas, D.L.: On the criteria to be used in decomposing systems into modules. Communications of the ACM 15(12), 1053–1058 (1972), doi:10.1145/361598.361623
2. Schmidt, D.C.: Guest editor's introduction: Model-driven engineering. Computer 39(2), 25–31 (2006)
3. Broekman, B.M., Notenboom, E.: Testing Embedded Software. Addison-Wesley, Boston (2002)
4. Wehrmeister, M.A., Freitas, E.P., Pereira, C.E., Wagner, F.R.: An aspect-oriented approach for dealing with non-functional requirements in a model-driven development of distributed embedded real-time systems. In: Proc. of 10th International Symposium on Object Oriented Real-Time Distributed Computing, pp. 428–432. IEEE Computer Society, Washington (2007)
5. Wehrmeister, M.A., Pereira, C.E., Rammig, F.: Aspect-oriented model-driven engineering for embedded systems applied to automation systems. IEEE Trans. on Industrial Informatics (2013), To appear in special issue on Software Engineering in Factory and Energy Automation, doi:10.1109/TII.2013.2240308
6. Wehrmeister, M.A., Packer, J.G., Ceron, L.M.: Support for early verification of embedded real-time systems through UML models simulation. SIGOPS Operating Systems Review 46(1), 73–81 (2012), doi:10.1145/2146382.2146396
7. Pretschner, A., et al.: One evaluation of model-based testing and its automation. In: Proc. 27th International Conference on Software Engineering, pp. 392–401. ACM, New York (2005)
8. Baker, P., Jervis, C.: Testing UML2.0 models using TTCN-3 and the UML2.0 testing profile. In: Gaudin, E., Najm, E., Reed, R. (eds.) SDL 2007. LNCS, vol. 4745, pp. 86–100. Springer, Heidelberg (2007)
9. Zander, J., Dai, Z.R., Schieferdecker, I., Din, G.: From U2TP models to executable tests with TTCN-3 - an approach to model driven testing. In: Khendek, F., Dssouli, R. (eds.) TestCom 2005. LNCS, vol. 3502, pp. 289–303. Springer, Heidelberg (2005)
10. Iyenghar, P., Pulvermueller, E., Westerkamp, C.: Towards model-based test automation for embedded systems using UML and UTP. In: Proc. of IEEE 16th Conference on Emerging Technologies Factory Automation, pp. 1–9 (September 2011)
11. Javed, A.Z., Strooper, P.A., Watson, G.N.: Automated generation of test cases using model-driven architecture. In: Proc. of the Intl. Workshop on Automation of Software Test. IEEE Computer Society (2007)
12. Beck, K.: Simple smalltalk testing. In: Beck, K. (ed.) Kent Beck's Guide to Better Smalltalk, pp. 277–288. Cambridge University Press, New York (1999)
13. Wehrmeister, M., Ceron, L., Silva, J.: Early verification of embedded systems: Testing automation for UML models. In: 2012 Brazilian Symposium on Computing System Engineering (SBESC), pp. 1–7. Brazilian Computer Society, Porto Alegre (2012)

Compiler Optimizations Do Impact the Reliability of Control-Flow Radiation Hardened Embedded Software

Rafael B. Parizi, Ronaldo R. Ferreira, Luigi Carro, and Álvaro F. Moreira

Instituto de Informática, Universidade Federal do Rio Grande do Sul, Porto Alegre, Brazil
{rbparizi,rrferreira,carro,afmoreira}@inf.ufrgs.br

Abstract. This paper characterizes how compiler optimizations impact software control-flow reliability when the optimized application is compiled with a technique to enable the software itself to detect and correct radiation induced soft-errors occurring in branches. Supported by a comprehensive fault injection campaign using an established benchmark suite in the embedded systems domain, we show that the careful selection of the available compiler optimizations is necessary to avoid a significant decrease of software reliability while sustaining the performance boost those optimizations provide.

Keywords: compiler optimization, compiler orchestration, embedded systems, fault tolerance, LLVM, radiation, reliability, soft errors, tuning.

1   Introduction

Compiler optimizations are taken for granted in modern software development, enabling applications to execute more efficiently in the target hardware architecture. Modern architectures have complex inner structures designed to boost performance, and if the software developer were to be aware of all those inner details, performance optimization would jeopardize the development processes. Compiler optimizations are transparent to the developer, who picks the appropriate ones to the results s/he wants to achieve, or, as it is more common, letting this task to the compiler itself by flagging if it should be less or more aggressive in terms of performance.

Industry already offers microprocessors built with 22 nm transistors, with a prediction that transistor's size will reach 7.4 nm by 2014 [1]. This aggressive technology scaling creates a big challenge concerning the reliability of microprocessors using newest technologies. Smaller transistors are more likely to be disrupted by transient sources of errors caused by radiation, known as *soft-errors* [2]. Radiation particles originated from cosmic rays when striking a circuit induce bit flips during software execution, and since transistors are becoming smaller there is a higher probability that transistors will be disrupted by a single radiation particle with smaller transistors requiring a smaller amount of charge to disrupt their stored logical value. The newest technologies are so sensitive to radiation that their usage will be compromised even at the sea level, as predicted in the literature [3]. In [4] it is shown that modern 22nm GPU cards are susceptible to such an error rate that makes their usage unfeasible in

G. Schirner et al. (Eds.): IESS 2013, IFIP AICT 403, pp. 49–60, 2013.
© IFIP International Federation for Information Processing 2013

critical embedded systems. However, industry is already investing in GPU architectures as the platform of choice for high performance and low power embedded computing, such as the ARM Mali® embedded GPU [5].

The classical solution to harden systems against radiation is the use of *spatial redundancy*, i.e. the replication of hardware modules. However, spatial redundancy is prohibitive for embedded systems which usually cannot afford extra costs of hardware area and power. The increase on power is a severe problem, because it is expected that 21% of the entire chip area must be turned off during its operation to meet the available power budget, and an impressive chip area of 50% at 8 nm [6]. This creates the *dark silicon* problem [6]: a huge area of the circuit cannot be used during its lifecycle. This problem gets worse when the microprocessor has redundant units, because system's reliability could be compromised if redundant units were turned off. The current solution to this problem is to use radiation hardened microprocessors, which are designed to endure radiation. The problem with this approach is the low availability and high pricing of those radiation hardened components. For instance, a 25 MHz microprocessor has a unitary price of U$ 200,000.00 [7]. This high pricing makes the use of radiation hardened microprocessors unfeasible for embedded systems used in aircrafts, not to say about cars and low-end medical devices such as pacemakers. For these critical embedded systems where cost is the major constraint a cheaper but yet effective approach for reliability against radiation is necessary.

Software-Implemented Hardware Fault-Tolerance (SIHFT) [8] is an approach for radiation reliability that adds redundancy in terms of extra instructions or data to the application, keeping the hardware unchanged. SIHFT techniques work by modifying the original program by adding *checking mechanisms* to it. SIHFT are classified either as *control-flow* or as *data-flow*. The former is designed to detect when an illegal jump has occurred during application execution to possibly proceed with the resolution of the correct jump address or at least signaling that such an error has occurred. The latter checks if a data variable being read is correct or not. While the effects of data-flow SIHFT methods are clear (usually the duplication of program variables or the addition of variable checksums solve the problem), the impacts of the control-flow ones is yet not well understood. Because control-flow methods modify the program's control-flow graph (CFG), which happens to be the same artifact used by compiler optimizations, the efficiency of control-flow reliability techniques might be influenced by the optimizations in an unpredictable way.

In this paper we evaluate how the cumulative usage of compiler optimizations influence reliability of applications hardened with the state-of-the-art *Automatic Correction of Control-flow Errors* (ACCE) [9] control-flow SIHFT technique, which was chosen because it is the current most efficient method in terms of reliability, attaining an error correction rate of ~70%. The application set we use in this paper is drawn from the MiBench [10] suite. For the sake of clarity, the ACCE technique is briefly reviewed in Section 2. Section 3 presents the fault model we assume and the methodology used in this paper. Finally, Section 4 presents the impact of individual and cumulative optimization passes using the LLVM [11] as the production compiler.

2   Automatic Correction of Control-flow Errors

ACCE [9] is a software technique for reliability that detects and corrects control-flow errors (CFE) due to random and arbitrary bit flips that might occur during software execution. The hardening of an application with ACCE is done at compilation, since it is implemented as a transformation pass in the compiler. ACCE modifies the applications' basic blocks with the insertion of extra instructions that perform the error detection and correction during software execution. In this section we briefly explain how ACCE works in two separate subsections, one dedicated to error detection and the other to error correction in the subsections 2.1 and 2.2, respectively. The reader should refer to the ACCE article for a detailed presentation and experimental evaluation [9]. The fault model that ACCE assumes is further described in Section 3.

2.1   Control-Flow Error Detection

ACCE performs online detection of CFEs by checking the signatures in the beginning and in the end of each basic block of the control-flow graph, thus, ACCE is classified as a *signature checking* SIHFT technique as termed in the literature. The basic block signatures are computed and generated during compilation; the signature generation is critical because it needs to compute non-aliased signatures between the basic block, i.e. each block must be unambiguously identified. In addition, for each basic block found in the CFG two additional code regions are added, the *header* and the *footer*. The signature checking during execution takes place inside these code regions. Fig. 1 shows two basic blocks (labeled as **N2** and **N6**) with the additional code regions. The top region corresponds to the header and the bottom to the footer. Still at compilation ACCE creates for each function in the application two additional blocks, the function entry block and the *Function Error Handler* (FEH). For instance, Fig. 1 depicts a portion of two functions, *f1* and *f2*, both owning *entry blocks* labeled as **F1** and **F2**, and function error handlers, labeled as **FEH_1** and **FEH_2**, respectively. Finally, ACCE creates a last extra block, the *Global Error Handler* (GEH), which can only be reached from a FEH block. The role of these blocks will be presented soon.

At runtime ACCE maintains a global *signature register* (represented as **S**), which is constantly updated to contain the signature of the basic block that the execution has reached. Therefore, during the execution of the *header* and *footer* code regions of each basic block, the value of the signature register is compared with the signatures generated during compilation for those code regions and, if those values do not match, a control flow error has just been detected and the control should be transferred to the corresponding FEH block of the function where execution currently is at. ACCE also maintains the *current function* register (represented as **F**), which stores the unique identifier of the function currently being executed. The current function register is only assigned at the extra entry function block. This process encompasses the *detection* of an illegal and erroneous due to a soft error.

Fig. 1 depicts an example of the checking and update of signatures performed in execution time that occurs in a basic block. In this example, the control-flow error occurs in the block **N2** of function **F1**, where an illegal jump incorrectly transfers the

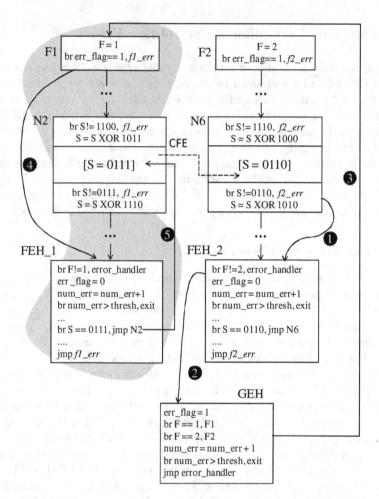

Fig. 1. Depiction of how the control is transferred from a function to the basic blocks that ACCE has created when a control-flow error occurs during software execution. In this figure, there is a control flow error (dashed arrow) causing the execution to jump from the block N2 of function F1 to the block N6 of function F2.

control flow to the basic block **N6** of function **F2**. When the execution reaches the footer of the block **N6** the signature register **S** is checked against the signature generated at compilation. In this case, **S** = 0111 (i.e. the previous value assigned in the header of the block **N2**). Thus, the branch test in the **N6** footer will detect that the expected signature does not match with the value of **S**, and, thus, the CFE error must signaled (step 1 in Fig. 1). In this example, the application branches to the address *f2_err*, making the application enter the **FEH_2** block (since the error was detected by a block owned by the function **F2**, the function error handler invoked is the **FEH_2**). At this point, the CFE was detected and ACCE can proceed with the correction of the detected CFE.

2.2 Control-Flow Error Correction

The correction process starts as soon as an illegal jump is detected by the procedure described in subsection 2.1, with the control flow transferred to the FEH corresponding to the function where the CFE was found. The FEH checks if the illegal jump was originated in the function it is responsible to handle its detected errors by comparing the value of the function's identifier (**F1** or **F2**, in the example of Fig. 1) with the current function register **F**. If the error happened in the function stored in the **F** register, FEH evaluates the current value of the signature register and then transfers the control to the basic block that is the origin of the illegal jump (this origin is stored in the **S** register). On the other hand, if the illegal jump was not originated in the function where the detection has occurred, the FEH then transfers the control flow to the GEH. In this case, the GEH is responsible for identifying the function where the CFE has occurred and to transfer the control flow back to this function, so that the error is correctly treated by the function's FEH. The GEH searches the function where the error has occurred and transfers the control to its entry block, which will then sends the control flow to the proper FEH so that the error can be corrected, i.e. branching the control to the basic block where the CFE has occurred.

Recalling the example depicted in Fig. 1, after the CFE is detected and the control is transferred to **FEH_2** (step 1) the **F** register is matched against the function identifier of the function from where the control came. However, since the CFE originated in the basic block **N2** of function **F1**, **F** = 1. Therefore, **FEH_2** is not capable of finding the basic block where the CFE originated, and then it transfers the control to the **GEH** so that the correct FEH can be found (step 2). The **GEH** searches for the function identifier stored in **F**, until it finds that it should branch to **F1** (step 3). Upon reaching the entry block **F1**, the variable *err_flag* = 1, because it was assigned to 1 in the **GEH**, meaning that there is an error that should be fixed, thus, the control branches to **FEH_1** (step 4). Now since **F** = 1, **FEH_1** knows that it is the FEH capable of handling the CFE and, as such, sets the variable *err_flag* to 0. Finally, it searches for the basic block that has the signature equals the register S. Upon finding it, the control branches to this basic block, i.e. **N2** in Fig. 1 (step 5). This last branch restores the control flow to the point of the program right before the occurrence of the CFE. Notice that inside all the FEH and the GEH there is the variable *num_error* counting how many times the control has passed through a FEH or GEH. This acts as a threshold for the number of how many times the correction must be attempted, which is necessary to avoid an infinite loop in case the registers **F** or **S** get corrupted for any reason. This process concludes the correction of a CFE with ACCE.

3 Fault Model and Experimental Methodology

The fault model we assume in the experiments is the *single bit flip*, i.e. only one bit of a word is changed when a fault is injected. ACCE is capable of handling multiple bit flip as long as the bits flipped is within a same word. Since the fault injection, as it will be discussed later, guarantees that the injected fault ultimately turned into a manifested error it does not matter how many bits are flipped, i.e. there is no silent data corruption: faults that cause a word to change its value that does not change the behavior of the program nor its output. This could happen in the case the fault flipped the bits of a dead variable.

The ACCE technique was implemented as a transformation pass in the LLVM [11] production compiler, which performs all the modifications in the control-flow graph described in section 2 using the LLVM Intermediate Representation (LLVM-IR). The ACCE transformation pass was applied *after* the set of compiler optimizations, since doing in the opposite order a compiler optimization could invalidate the ACCE generated code and semantics.

Since ACCE is a SIHFT technique to detect and correct control-flow errors, the adopted fault model simulates three distinct control flow disruptions that might occur due to a control flow error. Remind that a CFE is caused by the execution of an illegal branch to a possibly wrong address. The branch errors considered in this paper are:

1. *Branch creation*: the program counter is changed, transforming an arbitrary instruction (e.g. an addition) into an unconditional branch;
2. *Branch deletion*: the program counter is set to the next program instruction to execute independently if the current instruction is a branch;
3. *Branch disruption*: the program counter is disrupted to point to a distinct and possibly wrong destination instruction address.

We implemented a software fault injector using the GDB (GNU Debugger) in a similar fashion as [12], which is an accepted fault injection methodology in the embedded systems domain, in order to perform the fault injection campaigns. The steps of the fault injection process are the following:

1. The LLVM-IR program resulting from the compilation with a set of optimization and with ACCE is translated to the assembly language of the target machine;
2. The execution trace in assembly language is extracted from the program execution with GDB;
3. A branch error (branch creation, deletion or disruption) is randomly selected. In average each branch error accounts for 1/3 of the amount of injected errors;
4. One of the instructions from the trace obtained in step 2 is chosen at random for fault injection. In this step a histogram of each instruction is computed because instructions that execute more often have a higher probability to be disrupted;
5. If the chosen instruction in step 4 executes n times, choose at random an integer number k with $1 \le k \le n$;
6. Using GDB, a breakpoint is inserted right before the k-th execution of the instruction selected in step 4;
7. During program execution, upon reaching the breakpoint inserted in step 6, the program counter is intentionally corrupted by flipping one of its bits to reproduce the branch error chosen in step 3;
8. The program continues its execution until it finishes.

A fault is only considered valid if it has generated a CFE, i.e. silent data corruption and segmentation faults were not considered to measure the impacts of the compiler optimizations on reliability. All the experiments in this paper were performed in a 64-bit Intel Core i5 2.4 GHz desktop with 4 GB of RAM and the LLVM compiler version 2.9. For all programs versions, where each version corresponds to the program compiled with a set of optimizations plus the ACCE pass, 1,000 faults were injected using the aforementioned fault injection scheme. In the experiments we considered ten benchmark applications from the MiBench [10] embedded benchmark suite: *basicmath*, *bitcount*, *crc32*, *dijkstra*, *fft*, *patricia*, *quicksort*, *rijndael*, *string search*, and *susan* (comprising *susan* corners, edge, and smooth).

4 Impact of Compiler Optimizations on Control-Flow Reliability of Embedded Software

This section looks at the impacts on software reliability when an application is compiled with a set of compiler optimizations and further hardened with the ACCE method. Throughout this section the baseline for all comparisons is an application compiled with the ACCE method without any other compiler optimization. ACCE performs detection and correction of control-flow errors, thus all data discussed in this section considers the *correction rate* as the data to compute the efficiency metric. In this analysis we use 58 optimizations provided by the LLVM production compiler. Finally, the results were obtained using the fault model and fault injection methodology described in section 3.

The impact of the compiler optimizations when compiling for reliability is measured in this paper using the metric *Relative Improvement Percentage* (RIP) [13]. The RIP is presented in Eq. 1, where F_i is a compiler optimization, $E(F_i)$ is the error correction rate obtained for a hardened application compiled with F_i, and E_B is the error correction rate obtained for the baseline, i.e. the application compiled only with ACCE and without any optimization.

$$RIP_B(F_i) = \frac{E(F_i) - E_B}{E_B} \times 100\%$$

(1)

Fig. 2 shows a scatter plot of the obtained RIP for each application, with each of the 58 LLVM optimizations being a point in the y-axis. Each point represents the hardened application compiled with a single LLVM optimization at a time. Thus, for each application have 58 different versions (points in the chart). Fig. 2 shows that several optimizations increase the RIP considerably, sometimes reaching a RIP of ~10%. This is a great result, which shows that reliability can be increased for free just picking appropriate optimizations that facilitates for ACCE the process of error detection and correction. However, we also see that some optimizations totally jeopardize reliability, reaching a RIP of −73.27% (bottom filled red circle for *bitcount*).

It is also possible to gather evidence that the structure of the application also influences how an optimization impacts on the RIP of reliability. Let us consider the *block-placement* optimization, which is represented by the white diamond in Fig. 2. In

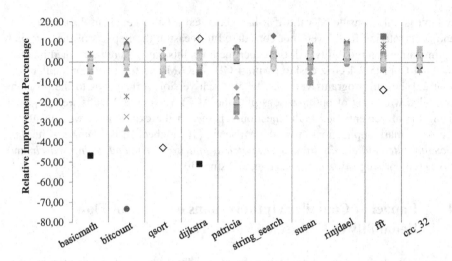

Fig. 2. Relative Improvement Percentage for the error correction rate of applications hardened with ACCE under further compiler optimization. Each hardened application was compiled with a single optimization at a time, but all applications were compiled with the 58 LLVM optimizations, thus, each hardened application has 58 versions. The baseline (RIP = 0%) is the error correction rate of the hardened application compiled without any LLVM optimization. Each point in the chart represents the application with one optimization protected with ACCE.

the case of the *qsort* application, *block-placement* has a RIP of −42.75% and a RIP of +11.68%. The reader can notice that other optimizations also have this behavior (increasing RIP for sovme applications and decreasing it for others). It also happens that some hardened applications are less sensitive to compiler optimizations, as it is the case of the *crc_32* one, where the RIP is within the ± 5% interval around the baseline.

Fig. 3 depicts the RIP of a selected subset of the 58 LLVM optimizations, making it clear that even within a small subset the variation in RIP for reliability is far from

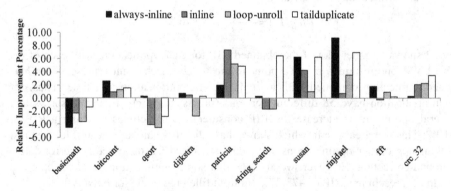

Fig. 3. Relative Improvement Percentage of a selected subset of the 58 LLVM optimizations. The baseline (RIP = 0%) is the error correction rate of the hardened application compiled without any LLVM optimization.

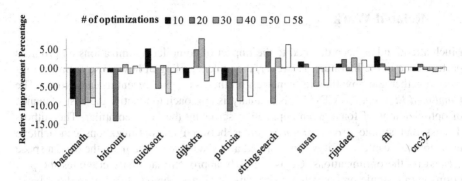

Fig. 4. Relative Improvement Percentage of random subsets of the 58 LLVM optimizations with a varying number of optimizations for each different subset: 10, 20, 30, 40, 50, 58 optimizations. The RIP for each subset was measured taking the average of 6 random subsets for each subset size. Hence, distinct possible optimizations subsets were considered. The baseline (RIP = 0%) is the error correction rate of the hardened application compiled without any LLVM optimization.

negligible. For instance, the *always-inline* LLVM optimization has an error correction RIP interval of [−4.55%, +9.24%].

Usually compiler optimizations are applied in bulk, using several of them during compilation. Therefore, it is important to also examine if successive optimization passes could compromise or increase software reliability of a hardened application. Fig. 4 presents the error correction rate RIP where the hardened application was compiled with a subset of the 58 LLVM optimizations. In this experiment we used six sizes of subsets: 10, 20, 30, 40, 50, and 58. The RIP shown in Fig. 4 is the average of five random subsets, i.e. it is an average of distinct subsets of the same size. Taking the average and picking the optimizations at random reproduces the effects of indiscriminately picking the compiler optimizations or, at least, choosing optimizations with the object of optimizing performance without previous knowledge of how the chosen optimizations influence together the software reliability.

It is possible to see that the cumulative effect of compiler optimizations in the error correction RIP is in most of the cases deleterious, but for a few exceptions. Fig. 4 confirms that some applications are less sensitive to the effects of compiler optimizations, e.g. the *crc32* has its RIP within the [−1.11%, 0.73%]. On the other hand, *basicmath*, *bitcount*, and *patricia* are jeopardized. Interesting to notice that the RIP in case of picking a subset of optimizations is not subject to the much severe reduction that was measured when only a single optimization was used (Fig. 2), evidencing that the composition of distinct optimization may be beneficial for reliability.

Based on the data and experiments discussed in this section it is clear that choosing of compiler optimizations requires the software designer to take into consideration that some optimizations may not be adequate in terms of reliability for a given application. Moreover, data shows that a given optimization is not only by itself a source of reliability reduction; reliability is also dependent of the application being hardened and how a given optimization facilitates or not the work of the ACCE technique.

5   Related Work

Much attention has been devoted to the impact of compiler optimizations on program performance in the literature. However, the understanding of how those optimizations work together and how they influence each other is a rather recent research topic. The *Combined Elimination* (CE) [13] is an analysis approach to identify the best sequence of optimizations of for a given application set using the GCC compiler. The authors discuss that simple *orchestration* schemes between the optimizations can achieve near-optimal results as if it was performed an exhaustive search in all the design space created by the optimizations. CE is a greedy approach that firstly compiles the programs with a single optimization, using this version as the baseline. From those baseline versions the set of *Relative Improvement Percentage* (RIP) is calculated, which is the percentage that the program's performance is reduced/increased (section 4 discussed RIP in details). With the RIP at hand for all baselines, the CE starts removing the optimizations with negative RIP, until the total RIP of all optimizations applied into a program do not reduce. CE was evaluated in different architectures, achieving an average RIP of 3% for the SPEC2000, and up to 10% in case of the Pentium IV for the floating point applications.

The *Compiler Optimization Level Exploration* (COLE) [14] is another approach to achieve performance increase by selecting a proper optimization sequence. COLE uses a population-based multi-objective optimization algorithm to construct a Paretto optimal set of optimizations for a given application using the GCC compiler. The data found with COLE give some insightful results about how the optimization. For instance, 25% of the GCC optimizations appear in at most one Paretto set, and some of them appear in all sets. Therefore, 75% of all optimizations do not contribute to improve the performance, meaning that they can be safely ignored! COLE also shows that the quality of an optimization is highly tied with the application set.

The *Architectural Vulnerability Factor* (AVF) [15] is a metric to estimate the probability that the bits in a given hardware structure will be corrupted by a soft-error when executing a certain application. The AVF is calculated as the total time the vulnerable bits remains in the hardware architecture. For example, the register file has a 100% AVF, because all of its bits are vulnerable in case of a soft-error. This metric is influence by the application due to liveness: for instance, a dead variable has a 0% AVF because it is not used in a computation. The authors in [16] evaluate the impact of the GCC optimizations in the AVF metric by trying to reduce the *AVF-delay-square-product* (ADS) introduced by the authors. The ADS relates considers a linear relation of the AVF between the square of the performance in cycles, clearly prioritizing performance over reliability. It is reported that the –O3 optimization level is detrimental both to the AVF and performance, because for the benchmarks considered (MiBench) have increased the number of loads executed. Again, the *patricia* application was the one with the highest reduction in the AVF at 13%.

In [17] the authors analyze the impact of compiler optimizations on data reliability in terms of variable liveness. *Liveness* of a variable is the time period between the variable is written and it is last read before a new write operation. The authors conclude that the liveness is not related only with the compiler optimization, but it also depends on the application being compiled, which is in accordance with the discussion we made in section 4. The paper shows that some optimizations tend to extend the time a variable is stored in a register instead of memory. The goal behind this is obvious: it is much faster to fetch the value of a variable when it is in the register than in memory. However, the memory is usually more protected than registers because of cheap and efficient Error Correction Code (ECC) schemes, and, thus, thinking about reliability it is not a good idea to expose a variable in a register for a longer time. The solution to that could be the application of ECC such as Huffman to the program variables itself. Decimal Hamming (DH) [18] is a software technique that does that for a class of programs where the program's output is a linear function of the input. The generalization of efficient data-flow SIHFT techniques such as DH (i.e. ECC of program variables) is still an open research problem.

6   Conclusions and Future Work

In this paper we characterized the problem of compiling embedded software for reliability, given that compiler optimizations do impact the coverage rate. The study presented in this paper makes clear that choosing optimizations indiscriminately can decrease software reliability to unacceptable levels, probably avoiding the software to be deployed as originally planned. Embedded software and systems deployed in space applications must always be certified evidencing that they support harsh radiation environments, and given the increasing technology scaling, other safety critical embedded systems might have to tolerate radiation induced errors in a near future. Therefore, the embedded software engineer must be very careful when compiling safety critical embedded software.

Design space exploration (DSE) for embedded systems usually considers "classical" non-functional requirements, such as energy consumption and performance. However, this paper has shown the need for automatic DSE methods to consider reliability when pruning the design space of feasible solutions. This could be realized with the support of compiler orchestration during the DSE step. As future work we are studying how to efficiently extend automatic DSE algorithms to implement compiler orchestration for reliability against radiation induced errors.

Acknowledgments. This work is supported by CAPES foundation of the Ministry of Education, CNPq research council of the Ministry of Science and Technology, and FAPERGS research agency of the State of Rio Grande do Sul, Brazil. R. Ferreira was supported with a doctoral research grant from the Deutscher Akademischer Austauschdienst (DAAD) and from the Fraunhofer-Gesellschaft, Germany.

References

1. ITRS. ITRS 2009 Roadmap. International Technology Roadmap for Semiconductors. Tech. Rep. (2009)

2. Borkar, S.: Designing reliable systems from unreliable components: the challenges of transistor variability and degradation. Micro 25(6), 10–16 (2005)
3. Normand, E.: Single event upset at ground level. IEEE Trans. on Nuclear Science 43(6), 2742–2750 (1996)
4. Rech, P., et al.: Neutron-induced soft-errors in graphic processing units. In: IEEE Radiation Effects Data Workshop (REDW 2012), 6 p. IEEE (2012)
5. ARM Mali Graphics Hardware, http://www.arm.com/products/multimedia/mali-graphics-hardware/index.php
6. Esmaeizadeh, H., et al.: Dark silicon and the end of multicore scaling. In: ISCA 2011: Proc. of the 38th Int. Symp. on Comp. Arch., pp. 365–376 (2011)
7. Mehlitz, P.C., Penix, J.: Expecting the unexpected – radiation hardened software. In: Infocom @ American Inst. of Aeronautics and Astronautics (2005)
8. Goloubeva, O., Rebaudengo, M., Reorda, M.S., Violante, M.: Software-Implemented Hardware Fault Tolerance. Springer, New York (2006)
9. Vemu, R., Gurumurthy, S., Abraham, J.: ACCE: Automatic correction of control-flow errors. In: ITC 2007: IEEE Int. Test Conf., pp. 1–10 (2007)
10. Guthaus, M.R., Ringenberg, J.S., Ernst, D., Austin, T.M., Mudge, T., Brown, R.B.: MiBench: A free, commercially representative embedded benchmark suite. In: WWC-4 2001: Proc. of the IEEE Int. Workshop of Workload Characterization, pp. 3–14. IEEE (2001)
11. Lattner, C., Adve, V.: LLVM: A compilation framework for lifelong program analysis & transformation. In: CGO 2004: Proc. of the Int. Symp. on Code Generation and Optimization, pp. 75–88. IEEE, Washington, DC (2004)
12. Krishnamurthy, N., Jhaveri, V., Abraham, J.A.: A design methodology for software fault injection in embedded systems. In: DCIA 1998: Proc. of the Workshop on Dependable Computing and its Applications. IFIP (1998)
13. Pan, Z., Eigenmann, R.: Fast and Effective Orchestration of Compiler Optimizations for Automatic Performance Tuning. In: Proceedings of the International Symposium on Code Generation and Optimization (CGO 2006), pp. 319–332. IEEE (2006)
14. Hoste, K., Eeckhout, L.: Cole: compiler optimization level exploration. In: Proceedings of the 6th Annual IEEE/ACM International Symposium on Code Generation and Optimization (CGO 2008), pp. 165–174. ACM (2008)
15. Mukherjee, S.S., Weaver, C., Emer, J., Reinhardt, S.K., Austin, T.: A systematic methodology to compute the architectural vulnerability factors for a high-performance microprocessor. In: Proc. of the 36th Annual IEEE/ACM Int. Symp. on Microarchitecture (MICRO 36), pp. 29–41. IEEE (2003)
16. Jones, T.M., O'Boyle, M.F.P., Ergin, O.: Evaluating the Effects of Compiler Optimisations on AVF. In: Workshop on Interaction Between Compilers and Computer Architecture, INTERACT-12 (2008)
17. Bergaoui, S., Leveugle, R.: Impact of Software Optimization on Variable Lifetimes in a Microprocessor-Based System. In: Proceedings of the 2011 Sixth IEEE International Symposium on Electronic Design, Test and Application (DELTA 2011), pp. 56–61 (2011)
18. Argyrides, C., Ferreira, R., Lisboa, C., Carro, L.: Decimal hamming: a novel software-implemented technique to cope with soft errors. In: Proc. of the 26th IEEE Int. Symp. on Defect and Fault Tolerance in VLSI and Nanotech. Sys., DFT 2011, pp. 11–17. IEEE (2011)

Power Reduction in Embedded Systems Using a Design Methodology Based on Synchronous Finite State Machines

Douglas P.B. Renaux and Fabiana Pöttker

Federal Technological University of Paraná, Department of Electronic Engineering,
Curitiba, Brazil
{douglasrenaux,fpottker}@utfpr.edu.br

Abstract. To achieve the highest levels of power reduction, embedded systems must be conceived as low-power devices, since the early stages of the design process. The proposed Model-Based-Development process uses Synchronous Finite State Machines (SFSM) to model the behavior of low-power devices. This methodology is aimed at devices at the lower-end of the complexity spectrum, as long as the device behavior can be modeled as SFSM. The implementation requires a single timer to provide the SFSM clock. The energy reduction is obtained by changing the state of the processor to a low-power state, such as deep-sleep.

The main contribution is the use of a methodology where energy consumption awareness is a concern from the early stages of the design cycle, and not an afterthought to the implementation phase.

Keywords: Synchronous finite state machine, energy consumption, ARM microcontroller, Tankless water heater, Model-Based-Development.

1 Introduction

The reduction of power consumption by embedded devices has become a major concern for designers for three main reasons: (1) Global electrical energy consumption is growing at a rate close to 40% per decade [1] and embedded devices, in the order of 100 billion, contribute to this consumption; (2) many embedded devices, mainly due to mobility requirements, are battery powered (using both rechargeable and non-rechargeable batteries) and lower consumption results in a longer usage time and less pollution to the environment; (3) in a futuristic view, embedded devices will harvest energy from the environment, thus disposing of a very limited energy budget.

Bohn [2] presents a futuristic scenario of Ambiental Intelligence where a large number of embedded devices will be present in our surroundings, including clothes, appliances, and most of the equipment that we use daily. This ubiquitous network of devices, many being of very small dimensions, will benefit from the approach of Energy Harvesting, i.e. the use of the energy sources in our surroundings, including moving objects, vibrating machine parts, changes in temperature, light and other

G. Schirner et al. (Eds.): IESS 2013, IFIP AICT 403, pp. 61–72, 2013.
© IFIP International Federation for Information Processing 2013

electromagnetic waves. Since the amount of energy obtainable by Energy Harvesting is usually very small, such devices will be required to have extremely low power consumption levels, in the order of tens to hundreds of μW [3].

To achieve the lowest possible levels of energy consumption, the low-power requirements must be a major concern since the early stages of development. The proposed methodology addresses this concern by the use of Synchronous Finite State Machines (SFSM) as it is a modeling approach that is prone to low-power implementation. A straightforward implementation of putting the processor in deep-sleep mode between clock ticks of the SFSM results in very low consumption levels combined with low resources usage: just a timer is required.

2   Problem Domain

2.1   Approaches for the Reduction of Energy Consumption in Embedded Systems

There are many approaches to achieve energy consumption reduction in Embedded Systems [4]. These can be categorized in four classes:

- **Hardware**: these are hardware design techniques including lower supply voltage, lower processor clock frequencies, low power functional blocks design and low power operating modes.
- **Computer Architecture and Compilers**: concerns the instruction-set design techniques and the appropriate use of the instruction-set by the compilers [5],[6].
- **RTOS**: the kernel can manage the system's energy consumption by changing to low-power modes or reducing the processing power [7],[10].
- **Application**: the applications can change state to low-power requirement modes whenever their processing needs allow so [4].

The methodology proposed in this paper falls into the Application class.

Our approach uses a very straightforward mechanism of changing the state of the processor to sleep-state, where power consumption is minimal and the CPU is not operating. Another approach is used in Chameleon [13], an application level power management system that controls DVFS settings.

2.2   Synchronous Finite State Machines

A Synchronous Finite State Machine performs state transitions only when its clock ticks. Hence, its transitions are synchronous, as opposed to Asynchronous Finite State Machines where transitions may occur as soon as an external event triggers them.

One important difference between SFSM and AFSM is depicted in Fig. 1 where a SFMS is presented. The initial state is A. The occurrence of the event *ev1* enables a transition to state B. This transition occurs only on the next clock tick. Between two consecutive clock ticks, more than one event may occur. This situation is illustrated by the transition from state B to state A. This transition is enabled if both events *ev1* and *ev2* occurred between two consecutive clock ticks.

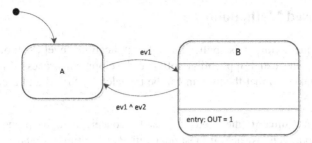

Fig. 1. Example of a State Diagram of a SFSM

3   Related Work

The reduction of energy consumption in embedded systems has been the research subject for several decades already. All the approaches listed in Section 2.1 have been analyzed. Ishihara [8] presents techniques for analysis and measurements in embedded systems, so that energy consumption reduction techniques can be evaluated. Tiwari [9] presents a methodology for embedded software energy consumption analysis.

Venkatachalam [5] presents a survey of the available techniques for energy consumption reduction in embedded systems. These techniques can be applied at several levels: circuit, systems, architecture and applications.

At circuit level, most of the power consumption is due to charging the intrinsic capacitances in digital circuits. Power is a function of the capacitance, clock frequency and the square of the supply voltage. The Dynamic Voltage Scaling (DVS) technique is frequently used to reduce power consumption. It consists of the reduction in the supply voltage and clock frequency whenever the system does not require its full processing speed.

Other circuit level techniques comprise the reduction of transistor sizes in the IC fabrication process, thus, diminishing the intrinsic capacitances, as well as logic gates restructuring to reduce the amount of switching needed. Concerning the buses, some of the applied techniques are the reduction of switching frequency, crosstalk, and signal amplitude, as well as bus segmentation and bus precharging.

At compiler level, energy consumption reduction is obtained by code optimization (less instruction to produce the same logical result) and by reducing the number of memory accesses.

At the applications level, the application and its runtime environment (e.g. RTOS) exchange information concerning opportunities for energy reduction, such as availability of resources and processing power requirements.

The proposed methodology is concerned with design techniques at the applications level. Future improvements in the proposed methodology will include the interactions with the RTOS and the required support to be implemented in the RTOS.

4   Proposed Methodology

The proposed methodology is applicable at the applications level (Section 2.1), therefore, it follows the usual application software development process. In each phase, decisions are taken so that the system can be modeled by SFSM and implemented as such.

1. **Operational Concept**: the product must be conceived to be prone to a SFSM modeling approach, as such, it must deal with discrete time events and actions. Inputs may represent continuous values, but they will be sampled synchronously to the SFSM clock. Outputs will be generated on every SFSM clock period, hence, with delays when compared to a system that operates continuously.
2. **Software Requirements**: the requirements must consider the discrete time operation of the system, hence, delays in input signal detection and output signal generation should be allowed. The larger the allowed delays, the higher the possibilities for reduction of energy consumption. At this phase, if functional and temporal requirements are too stringent then the solution space is reduced, as well as the attainable low-power requirements.
3. **Software Architecture**: The current version of our proposed methodology concerns lower-complexity devices that can be modeled as a single SFSM or as a collection of SFSM. If several SFSM are used, from an energy consumption point of view, it is preferable if all the SFSM clocks have the same period or are multiples of the same master period, thereby reducing the number of times that the processor has to switch from deep-sleep mode to operating mode.
   The selection of the SFSM clock period is of significance both for the reduction of consumption and also for the effect on the control algorithm of the embedded device. In the remainder of this section, several considerations regarding the determination of the SFSM clock period are presented.
4. **Software Design and Implementation**: to improve flexibility, reusability, and portability, the control algorithms design should be parameterized with respect to the SFSM clock periods such that changes to the clock period do not required code modifications except for a possible change in a defined constant.
   For the implementation either a hardware timer or an RTOS timer is required to tick at the end of each SFSM clock period. On each tick the processor is awakened from the deep-sleep mode and executes a simple procedure: (1) reading inputs, (2) identifying if a transition is enabled and firing it, (3) generating new outputs, and (4) returning to deep-sleep mode.
5. **Software Testing**: special care must be taken in the testing phase with respect to input detection delay and output delays due to the SFSM operation.

4.1   Considerations on the Proposed Technique

Applicability

The proposed technique is aimed at lower complexity embedded systems, particularly to reactive systems. It is feasible to apply this technique to systems composed of several SFSM, however, more significant reduction of energy consumption is achieved when all SFSM operate with the same clock period or on multiples of the same clock period.

SFSM Clock Period Selection

In general, most embedded applications allow for a range of the SFSM clock period. The higher the SFSM clock period, the higher the reduction in energy consumption, at the expense of a larger output delay.

The energy consumption (in Wh) over a given time of operation (much larger than the SFSM clock period) is given by (1). The same type of equation (2) is used to calculate the power consumption (in W). Equation 2 can be simplified to (3) when the computation time is considerably smaller than the SFSM clock period. Figure 2 shows the asymptotes of (3) and their crossing point T_m. As may be noticed, there is no benefit in increasing the SFSM clock period above T_m because the maximum consumption reduction has already been achieved. Hence, the optimal SFSM clock period to achieve the maximum reduction in power consumption is given by (4).

$$EC = EC_{ON}\frac{t_{ON}}{T_{clk}} + EC_{DS}\frac{(T_{clk}-t_{ON})}{T_{clk}} \qquad (1)$$

$$C = C_{ON}\frac{t_{ON}}{T_{clk}} + C_{DS}\frac{(T_{clk}-t_{ON})}{T_{clk}} \qquad (2)$$

$$C \cong C_{ON}\frac{t_{ON}}{T_{clk}} + C_{DS} \qquad (3)$$

$$T_m = \frac{C_{ON}}{C_{DS}} \times t_{ON} \qquad (4)$$

Where:

EC – energy consumption (in Wh)
C – power consumption (in W)
C_{ON} – power consumption with the processor operating
C_{DS} – power consumption with the processor in the deep sleep mode
t_{ON} – computation time
T_{clk} – SFSM clock period
T_m – optimal SFSM clock period

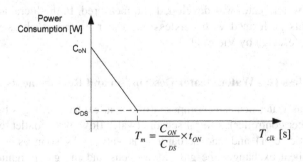

Fig. 2. Asymptotic behavior of equation (3) – power consumption versus SFSM clock period

Figure 3 presents the effect of the SFSM clock period increase on the power consumption of two embedded systems with different power consumptions when the processor is operating. The embedded system 1 (Consumption 1) has a power consumption (C_{ON}) five times lower than embedded system 2 (Consumption 2), while both have the same power consumption in deep sleep mode (C_{DS}). In both cases the reduction in power consumption is significant with the increase of the clock period, up to their T_m (0.021s for the system 1 and 0.1s for the system 2 – obtained from Equation 4). Higher SFSM clock periods than these would only lead to an increased delay in the response time of the system without significant reduction in power consumption.

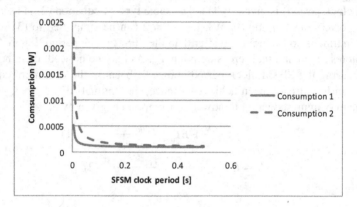

Fig. 3. Effect of the SFSM clock period on the energy consumption

Effects on Real-Time Systems
When a system is modeled as a SFSM a computational delay is added and this delay is dependent on the SFSM clock. The effect of the delay must be taken into account in the design process of the system as well as the maximum possible clock period.

5   Experimental Results

To illustrate the proposed methodology and validate the results the control unit of a tankless gas water heater was developed and measured. In the literature there are other experiments performed with tankless gas water heaters, such as the fuzzy logic control unit presented by Vieira [11].

5.1   Tankless Gas Water Heater Description and Requirements

A tankless gas water heater is composed of a heat exchanger, a gas burner, a control unit (gas heater controller), several sensors (water flow, water outlet temperature, and pilot flame detector) and one actuator (gas valve). As soon as water is flowing through the heat exchanger the gas valve opens and the gas is ignited by the pilot flame. Water is heated while it flows through the heat exchanger. There is no storage of hot water in this system. As soon as the usage of hot water stops the gas valve is closed and the flame extinguish.

The gas heater controller is the electronic module responsible for the control of the temperature at the water outlet by controlling the gas flow valve. The controller needs to sensor the water temperature (T_w), the water flow (W) and the presence of the pilot flame (P) as well as the desired temperature (T_s) selected by the user.

The functional requirements concern the opening of the gas valve to allow for the adequate gas flow to maintain the water temperature within 2 degrees Celsius from the desired temperature. The safety requirements are that the gas flow valve must be closed if the water flow is below the safety limit (0.5 liters per minute) or the pilot flame is off.

Figure 4 depicts the tankless gas water heater block diagram. The controller receives signals from the water flow sensor (W), the pilot light sensor (P) and the water temperature sensor (Tw). The first two sensors are digital (on/off) while the water temperature sensor is analog. The desired temperature (Ts) is given by a 10 position selector. Table 1 presents the desired temperature corresponding to each position of the selector switch. The water outlet temperature sensor is connected to a 4 bit analog-to-digital converter. The temperatures corresponding to each value of the ADC are also presented in Table 1. The controller output V controls the gas flow valve in the range from 0% (valve totally closed) up to 100% (valve totally open).

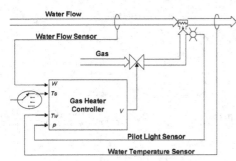

Fig. 4. Tankless gas water heater block diagram

Table 1. Desired and Measured Temperature Ranges

	Desired Temperature (°C) - T_s	Measured Temperature (°C) - T_w
0		below 38°
1	40°	38° to 42°
2	44°	42° to 46°
3	48°	46° to 50°
4	52°	50° to 54°
5	56°	54° to 58°
6	60°	58° to 62°
7	64°	62° to 66°
8	68°	66° to 70°
9	72°	70° to 74°
10	76°	74° to 78°
11		78° to 82°
12		82° to 86°
13		86° to 90°
14		90° to 94°
15		94° to 98°

5.2   Control Algorithm Design

The control algorithm is implemented by the SFSM presented in Fig 5. In the *Idle* state, no water is flowing and the gas flow valve is closed. When the water flow is above the minimum level of 0.5 liters/min and the pilot flame is on, then the SFSM transitions to the *Init Delay* state and, after 3 seconds, it transitions to the T state with the gas flow valve at 50%. The control algorithm consists of making no corrections to the gas flow valve output whenever the measured temperature is within 2 degrees of the desired temperature; to do small corrections (2% per 350 ms control cycle) when the temperature difference is small (up to one setting of the temperature selector) and doing larger corrections (10% per 350 ms control cycle) when the temperature difference is larger.

Due to the safety requirement, whenever the water flow is below the minimum level or the pilot flame is off, the SFSM transitions to the *Idle* state.

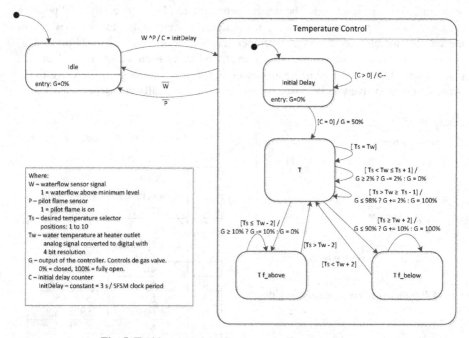

Fig. 5. Tankless gas water heater controller state diagram

5.3   Control Algorithm Simulation

The tankless gas heater was simulated in Matlab/Simulink. The block diagram of the simulation model is depicted in Fig 6. The thermal transfer is modeled as a second order system with a time constant of 1 second. This block models the thermal transfer from the flame to the heat exchanger followed by the thermal transfer from the heat exchanger to the water flow. The change in temperature is given by (derived from the formulae presented by Henze [12]):

$$dT = P\ [kW] \times \frac{1}{flow\ [\frac{kg}{s}]} \times \frac{1}{c_{pw}} \qquad (5)$$

where:
P is the power (in kW) generated due to gas burning
$flow$ is the water flow (in kg/s) through the heat exchanger
c_{pw} is the specific heat capacity of water (4.18 kJ/kg.K)

The gas heater controller has an input for the timer tick and two parameterized inputs to accommodate for the changes in the SFSM clock period. The simulation evaluates the desired temperature step-response (desired temperature changed to 40 degrees). Fig 7 shows the response of the simulation: after 12 seconds the system stabilizes within ± 1 degree of the desired temperature.

The simulations were performed with SFSM clock periods ranging from 25 ms to 350 ms. Due to the parameterization of the correction values the responses are nearly identical for all values of the SFSM clock periods.

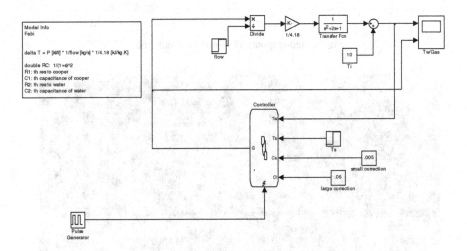

Fig. 6. Tankless gas heater simulation model

5.4   Implementation

For the implementation an ARM Cortex-M processor was used: the NXP LPC 1343, a Cortex-M3 processor running at 72 MHz (Fig 8). The SFSM was implemented in C using the EWARM compiler from IAR. The SFSM clock ticks were generated by the SYSTICK timer, a standard timer available in all Cortex-M3 processors. On every tick the processor wakes up, executes the SFSM and returns to deep-sleep mode (Section 4). On this processor, the required supply current is of 21 mA in the operating mode and of 100 uA in deep-sleep mode.

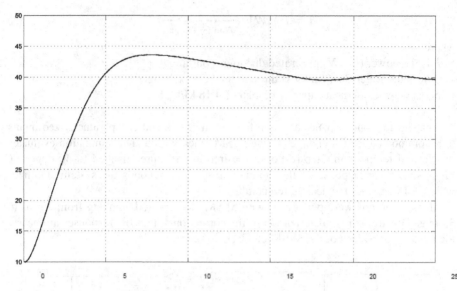

Fig. 7. Step-response obtained by simulation

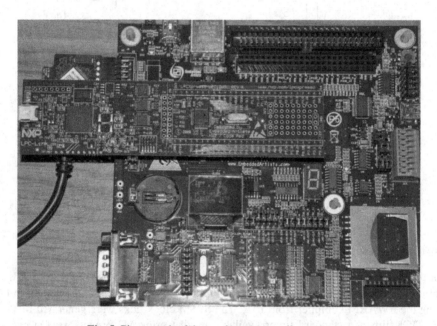

Fig. 8. Photograph of the gas heater controller prototype

Energy consumption was evaluated at three scenarios: (1) processor operating continuously; (2) SFSM clock period of 25 ms and (3) SFSM clock period of 350 ms. For scenarios (2) and (3), deep-sleep mode is used. The measured values of the supply current and supply power are presented in Table 2. The supply voltage is of 3.3 V.

The optimal SFSM clock period (Section 4.1) for this implementation is 21 ms. One can observe that changing the SFSM clock period from 25 ms to 350 ms (a 14 fold increase) results in a power reduction from 606 uW to 350 uW, a reduction of only 42%.

The effects of the changes in the SFSM clock period on the water temperature are not noticeable, as predicted by the simulation results. This is mainly due to the time constants of the physical system (heat transfer from flame to heat exchanger and then to water flow) being larger than the maximum SFSM clock periods used in this evaluation.

Table 2. Measured Power Consumption

Scenario	Supply Current	Power Consumption
Continuously in operating mode	21 mA	69 mW
SFSM clock period of 25 ms.	184 uA	606 uW
SFSM clock period of 350 ms	106 uA	350 uW

6   Conclusion

The proposed methodology advocates the use of Synchronous Finite State Machine models since the early phases of development as well as a concern, during requirements elicitation, for delay tolerances. In this way, a straightforward implementation technique of short execution bursts followed by periods of low-power deep-sleep results in significant reduction of energy consumption.

A tankless gas water heater controller was implemented with the proposed methodology. This controller is powered from a 4000 mAh non-rechargeable battery whose life is extended from 190 hours (if the processor is in continuous operating mode) to 2.25 years (using deep-sleep mode).

One could argue that the total amount of energy consumed by a gas water heater renders useless the small amount of energy that is saved in the given example. However, there are two important considerations: (1) currently the gas water heater has two energy sources – gas and electricity; the potential for significant reduction in energy consumption from the battery will extend battery life, reducing cost and environmental waste. (2) Since gas water heaters produce waste heat, one could apply energy harvesting to power the electronics, provided a start-up mechanism is available.

The proposed methodology is currently aimed at devices of lower complexity. A future research direction is broadening the scope to include more complex devices; these are likely to require the use of an RTOS that should manage the entry into deep-sleep mode. Another research direction is the application of the technique to Asynchronous Finite State Machines, aiming at the devices whose functionality is not adequately modeled by SFSM.

References

1. International Energy Agency – 2012 Key World Energy Statistics (2012), http://www.iea.org/publications/freepublications/publication/name,31287,en.html
2. Bohn, J., Coroama, V., Langheinrich, M., Mattern, F., Rohs, M.: Social, Economic and Ethical Implications of Ambient Intelligence and Ubiquitous Computing. In: Weber, W., Rabaey, J.M., Aarts, E. (eds.) Ambient Intelligence, pp. 5–29. Springer (2005)
3. Strba, A.: Embedded Systems with Limited Power Resources, Enocean (2009), http://www.enocean.com/fileadmin/redaktion/pdf/white_paper/wp_embedded_systems_en.pdf
4. Inführ, J., Jahrmann, P.: Hard- and Software Strategies for Reducing Energy Consumption in Embedded Systems. Seminar-Thesis, Vienna University of Technology (2009)
5. Venkatachalam, V., Franz, M.: Power Reduction Techniques for Microprocessor Systems. ACM Computing Surveys 37(3), 195–237 (2005)
6. Ortiz, D.A., Santiago, N.G.: Highl Level Optimization for Low Power Consumption on Microprocessor-Based Systems. In: 50th Midwest Symposium on Circuits and Systems, Montreal, pp. 1265–1268 (2007)
7. Wiedenhoft, G.R., Hoeller Jr., A., Fröhlich, A.A.: Um Gerente de Energia para Sistemas Profundamente Embarcados. In: Workshop de Sistemas Operacionais, Rio de Janeiro, pp. 796–804 (2007)
8. Ishihara, T., Goudarzi, M.: System-Level Techniques for Estimating and Reducing Energy Consumption in Real-Time Embedded Systems. In: International SoC Design Conference, Seoul, pp. 67–72 (2007)
9. Tiwari, V., Malik, S., Wolfe, A.: Power Analysis of Embedded Software: A First Step Towards Software Power Minimization. IEEE Transactions on VLSI Systems, 437–445 (1994)
10. Huang, K., Santinelli, L., Chen, J., Thiele, L., Buttazzo, G.C.: Adaptive Dynamic Power Management for Hard Real-Time Systems. In: 30th IEEE Real-Time Systems Symposium, Washington, pp. 23–32 (2009)
11. Vieira, J.A.B., Mota, A.M.: Modeling and Control of a Water Gas Heater with Neuro Fuzzy Techniques. In: 3rd WSEAS International Conference, Switzerland, pp. 3571–3576 (2002)
12. Henze, G.P., Yuill, D.P., Coward, A.H.: Development of a Model Predictive Controller for Tankless Water Heaters. HVAC&R Research 15(1), 3–23 (2009)
13. Liu, X., Shenoy, P., Corner, M.D.: Chameleon: Application-Level Power Management. IEEE Transactions on Mobile Computing 7(8) (August 2008)

Low-Power Processors Require Effective Memory Partitioning

Leonardo Steinfeld[1], Marcus Ritt[2], Fernando Silveira[1], and Luigi Carro[2]

[1] Instituto de Ingenieria Electrica, Facultad de Ingenieria, Universidad de la
Republica, Uruguay
[2] Instituto de Informatica, Universidade Federal do Rio Grande do Sul, Brasil

Abstract. The ever increasing complexity of embedded systems demands for rising memory size, and larger memories increase the power drain. In this work, we exploit banked memories with independent low-leakage retention mode in event-driven applications. The resulting energy saving for a given number of banks is close to the maximum achievable value, since the memory banks access pattern of event-driven applications presents a high temporal locality, leading to a low saving loss due to wake-up transitions. Results show an energy reduction up to 77.4% for a memory of ten banks with a partition overhead of 1%.

Keywords: banked memory, event-driven applications, power management, wireless sensor network.

1 Introduction

In the last years, there has been a lot of research dealing with processing power optimization resulting in a variety of ultra-low power processors. These processors pose a primary energy limitation for SRAM, where the embedded SRAM consumes most of the total processor power [1]. Partitioning a SRAM memory into multiple banks that can be independently accessed reduces the dynamic power consumption, and since only one bank is active per access, the remaining idle banks can be put into a low-leakage sleep state to also reduce the static power [2]. However, the power and area overhead due to the extra wiring and duplication of address and control logic prohibits an arbitrary fine partitioning into a large number of small banks. Therefore, the final number of banks should be carefully chosen at design time, taking into account this partitioning overhead. The memory organization may be limited to equally-sized banks, or it can allow any bank size. Moreover, the strategy for the bank states management may range from a greedy policy (as soon as a bank memory is not being accessed it is put into low leakage state) to the use of more sophisticated prediction algorithms [3].

Memory banking has been applied for code and data using scratch-pad and cache memories in applications with high performance requirements (e.g. [2],[4]). We follow the methodology employed in [4], in which a memory access trace is used to solve an optimization problem for allocating the application memory

G. Schirner et al. (Eds.): IESS 2013, IFIP AICT 403, pp. 73–81, 2013.

divided in blocks to memory banks. However, to the best of our knowledge, this is the first time SRAM banked memories are considered for event-driven applications code, and the use of such characteristics leads to meaningful power savings, as it will be shown.

The main contribution of this work is to show that, thanks to our new problem formulation, one can find the optimum partitioning of memory banks in the very common event-driven applications. We derive expressions for energy savings in the case of equally sized banks based on a detailed model for different power management strategies. The maximum achievable energy saving is found, and the limiting factors are clearly determined. We show that it is possible to find a near optimum number of banks at design time, irrespective of the application and the access pattern to memory, provided that the energy memory parameters are given, such as energy consumption characteristics and the partition overhead as a function of the number of banks. We show that using our approach in a banked memory leads to aggressive (close to 80%) energy reduction in event-driven applications.

The remainder of this paper is organized as follows. In Section 2, we present a memory energy model, and in Section 3 we derive expressions for the energy savings of a banked memory. The experiments are presented in Section 4 and in Section 5 we discuss the results. Finally Section 6 contains concluding remarks.

2   Banked Memory Energy Model

In this section we present a memory energy model for deriving expressions for the energy consumption of an equally-sized banked memory with different power management strategies.

2.1   Memory Energy Model

The static power consumed by a SRAM memory depends on its actual state: ready or sleep. During the ready state read or write cycles can be performed, but not in the sleep state. Since the memory remains in one of these states for a certain amount of cycles, the static energy consumed can be expressed in terms of energy per cycle (E_{rdy} and E_{slp}) and number of cycles in each state. Each memory access, performed during the ready state, consumes a certain amount of energy (E_{acc}). The ready period during which memory is accessed is usually called the active period, and the total energy spent corresponds to the sum of the access and the ready energy ($E_{act} = E_{acc} + E_{rdy}$), i.e. the dynamic and static energy. On the other hand, the ready cycles without access are called idle cycles, consuming only static energy ($E_{idl} = E_{rdy}$). Each state transition from sleep to active (i.e. the wake-up transition) has an associated energy cost (E_{wkp}) and a latency, considered later. Based on the parameters defined above, the total energy consumption of a memory can be defined as

$$E = E_{act}n_{act} + E_{idl}n_{idl} + E_{slp}n_{slp} + E_{wkp}n_{wkp}, \tag{1}$$

Table 1. Memory energy consumption coefficients

E_{act}	E_{idl}	E_{slp}	E_{wkp}
1.78×10^{-6}	3.28×10^{-7}	3.28×10^{-8}	7.95×10^{-6}

where n_{act}, n_{idl} and n_{slp} are the sum of the cycles in which the memory is in active, idle and in sleep state respectively, and n_{wkp} is the number of times the memory switches from sleep to active state.

The energy values in Eq. (1) depend on the size of the memory, and generally energy is considered proportional to it [2]. Using the CACTI tool [5], we simulated a pure RAM memory, one read/write port, 65 nm technology and a high performance ITRS transistor type, varying its size from 512 B to 256 KB. CACTI outputs the dynamic and leakage energy, corresponding to the access and idle of our model. The active energy is directly computed (dynamic plus leakage). The access, active, and idle energy were fitted to a linear function as a function of the memory size to determine the energy coefficients. The energy consumed per cycle in the sleep state is a fraction of the idle energy, since we suppose that a technique based on reducing the supply voltage is used to exponentially reduce the leakage [6]. We considered a reduction factor of leakage in sleep state of 0.1, which is generally accepted in the literature [7]. Finally, before a memory bank could be successfully accessed, the memory cells need to go back from the data retention voltage to the ready voltage, which involves the loading of internal capacitances. Since the involved currents in this process are similar to those in an access cycle, the associated wake-up energy cost is proportional to the access energy, ranging the proportionality constant from about 1 [8] to hundreds [9]. We adopt an intermediate value of 10. Table 1 shows the different coefficients used in the remainder of this work.

Finally, partitioning a memory in N equally sized banks reduce the energy by N,

$$E_k = \frac{\mathbf{E}_k}{N}. \tag{2}$$

for $k \in \{act, idl, slp, wkp\}$, where $\mathbf{E}_k$ is the corresponding energy consumption per cycle of the whole memory.

3 Energy Savings

In this section we derive expressions for the energy savings of a memory of equally sized banks for two different management schemes. The first general expression corresponds to any power management by means of which a bank may remain in idle state even if it is not accessed. The decision algorithm may range from a simple fixed time-out policy to dynamic and sophisticated prediction algorithms. The second expression correspond to the simplest policy, greedy, in which a bank is put into sleep state as soon as it is not being accessed, and is determined as a special case of the former.

The total energy consumption per cycle of the whole banked memory after n cycles have elapsed is

$$\bar{E}_N = E_{act} \sum_{i=1}^{N} \frac{n_{act_i}}{n} + E_{idl} \sum_{i=1}^{N} \frac{n_{idl_i}}{n} + E_{slp} \sum_{i=1}^{N} \frac{n_{slp_i}}{n} + E_{wkp} \sum_{i=1}^{N} \frac{n_{wkp_i}}{n}, \quad (3)$$

Since the total number of cycles is $n = n_{act_i} + n_{idl_i} + n_{slp_i}$ for all banks, and that there is only one bank active per cycle

$$\sum_{i=1}^{N} n_{act_i} = n \qquad (4)$$

then we obtain

$$\bar{E}_N = E_{act} + (N-1)E_{slp} + (E_{idl} - E_{slp}) \sum_{i=1}^{N} \frac{n_{idl_i}}{n} + E_{wkp} \sum_{i=1}^{N} \frac{n_{wkp_i}}{n}. \quad (5)$$

The first two terms of the sum are the consumption of having only one bank in active state and the remaining $N-1$ banks in sleep state. The third term, related to the idle energy, depends on the fraction of idle cycles performed by each bank i. The last term of the sum represents the wake-up energy as a function of the average wake-up rate of each memory bank, that is the average number of cycles elapsed between two consecutive bank transitions from sleep to active (for example, one transition in 1000 cycles).

We define the energy savings of a banked memory as the relative deviation of the energy consumption of a equivalent single bank memory ($E_1 = NE_{act}$, always active)

$$\delta E = \frac{NE_{act} - \bar{E}_N}{NE_{act}}. \qquad (6)$$

The energy saving of a banked memory of N uniform banks is

$$\delta E_N = \frac{N-1}{N}\left(1 - \frac{E_{slp}}{E_{act}}\right) - \frac{1}{N}\left(\frac{E_{idl} - E_{slp}}{E_{act}}\right) \sum_{i=1}^{N} \frac{n_{idl_i}}{n} -$$

$$-\frac{1}{N}\frac{E_{wkp}}{E_{act}} \sum_{i=1}^{N} \frac{n_{wkp_i}}{n}. \qquad (7)$$

If a greedy power management is considered a memory bank it is put into sleep state as soon as is not being accessed, hence there is no idle cycles and Eq. (7) simplifies to

$$\delta E_N^{grdy} = \frac{N-1}{N}\left(1 - \frac{E_{slp}}{E_{act}}\right) - \frac{1}{N}\frac{E_{wkp}}{E_{act}} \sum_{i=1}^{N} \frac{n_{wkp_i}}{n}. \qquad (8)$$

In this case, the application blocks allocation to memory banks must minimize the accumulated wake-up rate in order to maximize the energy saving. Note that the energy saving does not depend on the access profile among the banks, since the access to every bank costs the same as all banks have the same size. Still, the allocation of blocks to banks must consider the constraints of the banks size. Finally, the energy saving can be improved by increasing N and at the same time keeping the accumulated wake-up rate low. The maximum achievable saving corresponds to the sleep to active rate, which is equivalent to have the whole memory in sleep state. Even so, the partition overhead limits the maximum number of banks.

Compared to Eq. (8), the general expression Eq. (7) has an additional term, which is related to the energy increase caused by the idle cycles. This does not mean that the energy saving is reduced, since the accumulated wake-up ratio may decrease.

3.1   Effective Energy Saving

As mentioned previously, the wake-up transition from sleep to active state of a bank memory has an associated latency. This latency forces the microprocessor to stall until the bank is ready. The microprocessor may remain idle for a few cycles each time a new bank is waken up, incrementing the energy drain. This extra microprocessor energy can be included with the bank wake-up energy and for simplicity we will not consider it explicitly. Moreover, if the wake-up rate is small and the active power of the microprocessor is much higher than idle power, this overhead can be neglected. Additionally, the extra time due to the wake-up transition is not an issue in low duty-cycle applications, since simply slightly increases the duty-cycle.

On the other hand, the partitioning overhead must be considered to determine the effective energy saving. A previous work had characterized the partitioning overhead as a function of the number of banks for a partitioned memory of arbi-trary sizes [9]. In that case the hardware overhead is due to an additional decoder (to translate addresses and control signals into the multiple control and address signals), and the wiring to connect the decoder to the banks. As the number of memory banks increases, the complexity of the decoder is roughly constant, but the wiring overhead increases [9]. The partition overhead is proportional to the active energy of an equivalent monolithic memory and roughly linear with the number of banks, as can be clearly seen by inspecting the data of the aforemen-tioned work (3.5%, 5.6%, 7.3% and 9% for a 2-, 3-, 4-, and 5-bank partitions, resulting in an overhead factor of approximately 1.8% per bank). Consequently, the relative overhead energy can be modeled as:

$$\delta E_N^{ovhd} = k_{ovhd} N. \tag{9}$$

In this work, the memory is partitioned into equally-sized banks. As result the overhead is expected to decrease leading to a lower value for the overhead factor.

3.2   Energy Savings Limits

The energy savings in the limit, as the wake-up and idle contributions tend to zero, is

$$\delta E_N^{max} = \frac{N-1}{N}\left(1 - \frac{E_{slp}}{E_{act}}\right). \tag{10}$$

If the partition overhead is considered (Eq. 9), the maximum effective energy saving is

$$\delta E_{N,eff}^{max} = \frac{N-1}{N}\left(1 - \frac{E_{slp}}{E_{act}}\right) - k_{ovhd}N. \tag{11}$$

$\delta E_{N,eff}^{max}$ is maximized for

$$N_{opt} = \sqrt{\frac{1}{k_{ovhd}}\left(1 - \frac{E_{slp}}{E_{act}}\right)}. \tag{12}$$

4   Experiments

In this section we present experiments comparing the predicted energy savings by our model to the energy savings obtained by solving an integer linear program (ILP).

The criteria for selecting the case study application were: public availability of source files, realistic and ready-to-use application. We chose a wireless sensor network application (data-collection) from the standard distribution of TinyOS (version 2.1.0) [1]. The application, MultihopOscilloscope, was compiled for nodes based on a MSP430 microcontroller[2]. Each node of the network periodically samples a sensor and the readings are transmitted to a sink node using a network collection protocol.

We simulated a network composed of 25 nodes using COOJA[10] to obtain a memory access trace of one million cycles or time steps.

For the sake of simplicity, the block set was selected as those defined by the program functions and the compiler generated global symbols (user and library functions, plus those created by the compiler). The size of the blocks ranges from tens to hundreds of bytes, in accordance with the general guideline of writing short functions, considering the run-to-completion characteristic of TinyOS and any non-preemptive event-driven software architecture. The segments size of the application are 3205 bytes of text, 122 and 3534 bytes of zero-valued and initialized data respectively. The number of global symbols is 261.

The problem of allocating the code to equally sized banks was solved using an ILP solver for up eight banks, for the greedy power management using a segment trace of 5000 cycles. The total memory size was considered 10% larger than the

---

[1] www.tinyos.net
[2] www.ti.com/msp430

Table 2. Optimum number of banks as a function of partition overhead

$k_{ovhd}(\%)$	0	1	2	3	5
N_{opt}	∞	10	7	6	4
$\delta E_{N,eff}^{max}(\%)$	97.1	77.4	69.2	62.9	52.8

application size, to ensure the feasibility of the solution. The average energy consumption is calculated considering the whole trace using the memory energy model and the block-to-bank allocation map. The energy saving is determined comparing with a memory with a single bank with no power management.

5   Results and Discussion

The optimum number of banks estimated using Eq. (12) (after rounding) as a function of k_{ovhd} (1%, 2%, 3% and 5%) is shown in Table 2. The energy savings is limited by the partition overhead, reaching a value of 77.4% for an overhead of 1%. The energy saving limit, as the partition overhead tends to zero and N to infinity, is 97.1% (the corresponding value of $1 - E_{slp}/E_{act}$).

Table 3 compares the energy saving results as a function of the number of banks and the partition overhead. It can be observed that the maximum energy saving for greedy strategy with 2%, 3% and 5% of partition overhead is achieved for seven, six and five banks respectively (both marked with a gray background). The optimum number of banks for an overhead of 5% differs from what arises in the previous limit case (see Table 2). This means that the saving loss due to wake-up transitions shifts the optimum number of banks. For a given partition overhead, the energy saving for the estimated optimum number of banks is within about 4% of the saving limit (comparing saving values in Table 2 to the corresponding values in Table 3, number of banks: four, six and seven, and partition overhead: 5%, 3% and 2% respectively). This difference came from the wake-up transitions losses. In this case study, due to its even-driven nature, the code memory access patterns are caused by external events. Each event triggers a chain of function calls starting with the interrupt subroutine. This chain may include the execution of subsequent functions calls starting with a queued handler function called by a basic scheduler. The allocation of highly correlated functions to the same bank leads to a bank access pattern with a high temporal

Table 3. Energy saving for greedy power management

greedy	number of banks						
	2	3	4	5	6	7	8
k_{ovhd} 1	43.7	58.1	64.8	68.9	71.4	72.9	73.7
(%) 2	41.7	55.1	60.8	63.9	65.4	65.9	65.7
3	39.7	52.1	56.8	58.9	59.4	58.9	57.7
5	35.7	46.1	48.8	48.9	47.4	44.9	41.7

locality. Hence, the total wake-up fraction across the banks is very low. This explain the modest difference with the limit value.

6 Conclusions

We have found that aggressive energy savings can be obtained using a banked memory, up to 77.4% (estimated) for a partition overhead of 1% with a memory of ten banks, and 65.9% (simulated) for a partition overhead of 2% with a memory of seven banks. The energy saving is maximized by properly allocating the program memory to the banks in order to minimize the accumulated wake-up rate. The saving increases as a function of the number of banks, and is limited by the partition overhead. The derived model gives valuable insight into the particular factors (coming from the application and the technology) critical for reaching the maximum achievable energy saving. Moreover, at design time the optimum number of banks can be estimated, considering just energy memory parameters. The resulting energy saving for a given number of banks is close to the derived limit, since event-driven applications present access patterns to banks with a high temporal locality.

References

1. Verma, N.: Analysis Towards Minimization of Total SRAM Energy Over Active and Idle Operating Modes. IEEE Transactions on Very Large Scale Integration (VLSI) Systems 19(9), 1695–1703 (2011)
2. Golubeva, O., Loghi, M., Poncino, M., Macii, E.: Architectural leakage-aware management of partitioned scratchpad memories. In: DATE 2007: Proceedings of the Conference on Design, Automation and Test in Europe, pp. 1665–1670. EDA Consortium, San Jose(2007)
3. Calimera, A., Macii, A., Macii, E., Poncino, M.: Design Techniques and Architectures for Low-Leakage SRAMs. IEEE Transactions on Circuits and Systems I: Regular Papers 59(9), 1992–2007 (2012)
4. Ozturk, O., Kandemir, M.: ILP-Based energy minimization techniques for banked memories. ACM Trans. Des. Autom. Electron. Syst. 13(3), 1–40 (2008)
5. Thoziyoor, S., Ahn, J.H., Monchiero, M., Brockman, J.B., Jouppi, N.P.: A Comprehensive Memory Modeling Tool and Its Application to the Design and Analysis of Future Memory Hierarchies. In: 2008 International Symposium on Computer Architecture, pp. 51–62. IEEE, Washington, DC (2008)
6. Qin, H., Cao, Y., Markovic, D., Vladimirescu, A., Rabaey, J.: SRAM leakage suppression by minimizing standby supply voltage. In: SCS 2003: Proceedings of the International Symposium on Signals, Circuits and Systems, pp. 55–60. IEEE Comput. Soc., Los Alamitos (2004)
7. Rabaey, J.: Low power design essentials. Springer (2009)
8. Calimera, A., Benini, L., Macii, A., Macii, E., Poncino, M.: Design of a Flexible Reactivation Cell for Safe Power-Mode Transition in Power-Gated Circuits. IEEE Transactions on Circuits and Systems I: Regular Papers 56(9), 1979–1993 (2009)

9. Loghi, M., Golubeva, O., Macii, E., Poncino, M.: Architectural Leakage Power Minimization of Scratchpad Memories by Application-Driven Sub-Banking. IEEE Transactions on Computers (2010)

10. Eriksson, J., Österlind, F., Finne, N., Tsiftes, N., Dunkels, A., Voigt, T., Sauter, R., Marrón, P.J.: COOJA/MSPSim: interoperability testing for wireless sensor networks. In: Proceedings of the 2nd International Conference on Simulation Tools and Techniques, Simutools 2009, pp. 1–7. ICST (Institute for Computer Sciences, Social-Informatics and Telecommunications Engineering), Brussels (2009)

Enhancement of System-Lifetime by Alternating Module Activation

Frank Sill Torres

Dept. of Electronic Engineering, Federal University of Minas Gerais, Brazil
franksill@ufmg.br

Abstract. Reliability and robustness have been always important parameters of integrated systems. However, with the emergence of nanotechnologies reliability concerns are arising with an alarming pace. The consequence is an increasing demand of techniques that improve yield as well as lifetime reliability of to-day's complex integrated systems. It is requested though, that the solutions result in only minimum penalties on power dissipation and system performance. The approach Alternating Module Activation (AMA) offers both extension of system lifetime and low increase of power and delay. The essential contribution of this work is an analysis to which extent this technique can be improved even more. Thereby, components that enable partial concurrent error detection as well as Built-in self-test functionality are included. Further, a flow for comparison of system's lifetime on cell-level is presented. Final results indicate an improvement of the system's lifetime of up to 58 % for designs in which the expected instance lifetime differs by factor 2.

Keywords: Robustness, Redundancy, Sleep Transistor, Modeling, BIST.

1 Introduction

CMOS is still the predominating technology for digital designs with no identifiable concurrence in the near future. Driving forces of this leadership are the high miniaturization capability and the robustness of CMOS. The latter, though, is decreasing with an alarming pace against the background of technologies with sizes at the nanoscale. Such technologies, with device dimensions in the range of a few nanometers, suffer from an increased susceptibility to different kinds of failures during operation [1]. In contrast to previous technology generations, solutions within the manufacturing process are not sufficient anymore to deal with these kinds of issues. Accordingly, reliability concerns are not only an issue of manufacturing anymore, but also have to be considered in all abstraction layers of the design process. Thereby, three main strategies can be identified: (I) design techniques that detect errors [2], (II) techniques that detect and correct errors [3] and (III) those techniques that try to avoid or at least prolongate errors [4][5]. As those techniques of strategy (I) require another mechanism to cope with the detected error, they do not increase the expected lifetime of the designs as aimed at in this work.

We proposed in previous works [6][7] a design technique that relates to strategy (III) and combines Sleep Transistors with the idea of modular redundancy to extend

G. Schirner et al. (Eds.): IESS 2013, IFIP AICT 403, pp. 82–91, 2013.

lifetime reliability of integrated circuits. In this work, we propose how this approach can be combined with techniques of strategy (II) to cope with errors as they can finally still occur.

The remainder of this contribution is organized as follows: section 2 summarizes the initial approach while section 3 presents the proposed extensions of the design technique. The subsequent section 4 introduces an extended flow on cell-level in order to compare lifetime reliability of integrated circuits. The following section 5 presents and discusses simulation results before section 6 concludes this work.

2   Alternating Module Activation

This section describes the fundamentals of the previously developed approach Alternating Module Activation as well as requirements for the necessary control logic.

2.1   Basic Idea

An essential characteristic of power gating with Sleep Transistors [8] is its ability to dynamically disconnect the power supply during the runtime of integrated systems. Hence, during the disconnected state the gated logic is ideally without any inherent currents and voltages, and thus electromagnetic fields. Furthermore, local temperatures are reduced as there is no switching activity present. It should be noted that these are key parameters for several lifetime decreasing effects, like electromigration [9], gate-oxide breakdown [10], and negative bias temperature instability [11], of integrated circuits. Thus, during an idle phase of a gated logic these effects are eliminated or at least strongly reduced. As a consequence, the mean time to failure (MTTF), which is the average time that a system operates until it fails, is prolonged approximately by the time that the design is in the idle phase. This relation is applied by the proposed approach Alternating Module Activation (AMA). Hereby, each gated module (i.e. each logic block) is implemented at least two times (see also Fig. 1). During the runtime though, only one of these instances is active while the others are disconnected from the power supply. Consequently, the resulting ideal mean time to failure $MTTF'_{AMA}$ of a module realized with the proposed approach can be expressed by:

$$MTTF'_{AMA} = N \cdot MTTF_{min} \qquad (1)$$

where N is the number of redundant instances and $MTTF_{min}$ is the minimum MTTF over all module instances. Equation (3) refers to the ideal case where any additional logic is neglected and the gated modules are completely disconnected from the power supply.

It could be shown in previous works [7] that there is a moderate increase in dynamic power dissipation of ca. 6 %, while the leakage and area are roughly doubled.

2.2   Control Circuitry

In order to properly work, additional logic is required to multiplex the results from the currently active instance to the subsequent module. This is implemented by multiplexers that are placed behind the redundant instances as depicted in Fig. 1. Here, a simple 2:1 multiplexer is shown to forward the correct signals from the redundant instances of the module A to the subsequent module B.

Commonly, power gated logic requires additional clock cycles before the logic can be fully operated again (i.e. wake-up time [8]). Hence, it is not feasible to connect the signals controlling the Sleep Transistors (here /Sleep1 and /Sleep2) also directly to the multiplexers. Instead, a control signal scheme as shown in Fig. 1 should be applied to ensure data consistency. Thereby, it has to be assured that before a transition of the multiplexed outputs both instances are active (/Sleep1 and /Sleep2 are logically '1').

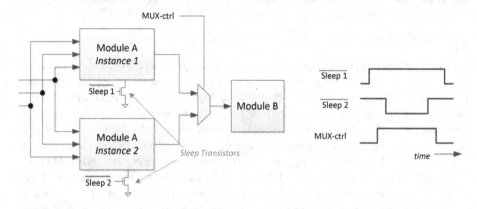

Fig. 1. The initial AMA approach with two redundant instances, whereas the results of the active instance are forwarded by the subsequent multiplexer, and related control signal scheme

Considering the transition time the mean time to failure MTTF″$_{AMA}$ results to:

$$MTTF''_{AMA} = N \cdot (1 - p_{trans,i}) \cdot MTTF_i \quad \text{with: } MTTF_i = MTTF_{min} \tag{2}$$

with p_{trans} is the probability that the instance i is in the transition phase but its output is still not forwarded by the multiplexer.

For a comprehensive investigation, it has to be considered that the lifetime of the system also depends on the MTTF of the multiplexers. The multiplexers though are realized as transmission gates [6], whereas only one path is active at a time. Thus, the impact of failure mechanisms, like gate-oxide breakdown or electromigration [12], is also correspondingly smaller. Nevertheless, it is reasonable to apply special design strategies for the multiplexers as well, like transistors with thicker gate oxide and wider wires.

3   Enhanced Alternating Module Activation

This section proposes extensions of the AMA approach that increase the lifetime in case of faultiness of one of the instances. Beside this, error detection capability and Built-in self-test (BIST) functionality are added.

3.1   Partial Concurrent Error Detection

A missing function of the initial version of the Alternating Module Activation approach is error detection capability. Hence, it is proposed to add comparators to each multiplexer. Its function is the verification that all multiplexer's inputs have the same value, and thus, whether all instances of a module produce equal results (comparator C-M in Fig. 2). However, only during the transition phase, i.e. when one instance is disconnected from supply while another is connected (see Fig. 1), more than one instance is active at the same time. This presents a limitation as only during this phase concurrent error detection (CED) is possible. The intention of this partial CED though, is not the identification of transient faults [13]. In contrast, its purpose is the detection of permanent faults.

It is recommended to modify the transition phase in the way that all instances are connected for a limited time. Thus, the probability of detection of an error can be increased. Considering this change, the mean time to failure $MTTF'_{EAMA}$ of a module results to:

$$MTTF'_{EAMA} = N \cdot (1 - p_{trans}) \cdot MTTF_{min} \tag{3}$$

where p_{trans} denotes the probability that the instances are in transition phase and its outputs are not forwarded by the multiplexer. Consequently, the increase of p_{trans} reduces the time between the occurrence of a permanent failure and its detections.

3.2   Selective Complete Deactivation of Instances

One major drawback of the initial version of the AMA approach is the complete function loss if one of the instances fails. Thus, it is proposed to utilize the existence of at least two instances of each module. The basic idea is the complete deactivation of an instance in case of failure, i.e. the control algorithm stops to consider the defective instance. This deactivation can pushed so far that the single instance configuration is reached. Thus, the expected life time of the circuit can be increased by the difference of the mean time to failure of the instances of each module. Considering exclusively the MTTF of the instances of the module the resulting $MTTF_{mod\_EAMA}$ can be estimated with:

$$\text{MTTF}_{\text{EAMA}} = \begin{bmatrix} N \cdot \text{MTTF}_1 + (N-1) \cdot (\text{MTTF}_2 - \text{MTTF}_1) + \\ \dots + (\text{MTTF}_N - \text{MTTF}_{(N-1)}) \end{bmatrix} \cdot (1 - p_{trans})$$

$$= (1 - p_{trans}) \cdot \sum_{i=1}^{N} \text{MTTF}_i \qquad \text{with: } \text{MTTF}_i > \text{MTTF}_{(i-1)}$$

(4)

Hence, in case of different mean time to failures of the instances the increase $\Delta\text{MTTF}_{\text{mod\_EAMA}}$ results to:

$$\Delta\text{MTTF}_{\text{EAMA}} = (1 - p_{trans}) \cdot \sum_{i=2}^{N} \text{MTTF}_i \quad \text{with: } \text{MTTF}_i > \text{MTTF}_{(i-1)} \; .$$

(5)

These differences of the MTTF result from variations of process parameters, aberrations of layout parameters, on-die temperature distribution, and effects through neighboring blocks.

3.3   Built-In Self-Test for Faulty Instance Identification

Another missing function of the initial approach is the identification of a faulty instance. Hence, it is proposed to add a memory based Built-In Self-Test (BIST) mode. Therefore, test input and output vectors for each module have to be generated and stored in a memory block whose inputs are multiplexed to the module inputs. Further, the outputs of the memory and the module are connected to comparators (see Fig. 2). Thus, in case of detection of an error by the partial CED the proposed BIST structure can be applied for successive tests of each instance for identification of the faulty one.

3.4   Final Architecture and Control Scheme

Fig. 2 shows the final architecture of the extended approach whereas the initial blocks are greyed out. For reasons of lifetime extension both kinds of comparators as well as the memory can be switched off by Sleep Transistors when it is not needed. Fig. 3 depicts the new control structure which is extended by two phases of error detection. As described in subsection 3.1 the partial CED is only active during the transition phase. Further, the design changes to the BIST mode only in case of the detection of an error. During that mode the system has to be halted as no correct functionality can be guaranteed. After detection of a faulty instance it is removed from the list of possible active instances and the system returns to normal operation.

4   Technique for MTTF Comparison on Cell-Level

This section proposes a new technique on cell-level for the comparison of mean time to failure of integrated designs.

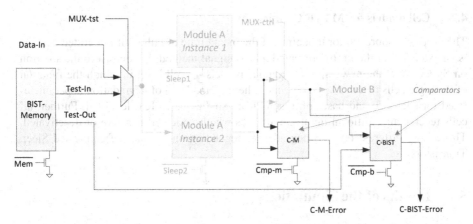

Fig. 2. Structure of Enhanced AMA (blocks of the initial AMA are greyed out)

4.1   Types of Modeling of Failure Mechanisms

Several models for individual failure mechanisms within integrated circuits can be found in the literature [8][9][12], whereas SPICE simulations are reported as the most accurate approach used by circuit designers. However, the accuracy comes together with major computational efforts and simulation times, which limits the maximum number of elements within an investigation. In contrast, approaches on higher levels decrease drastically the effort in computation, allowing the analysis of considerably more complex design [14][15]. However, this gain comes with the price of reduced accuracy.

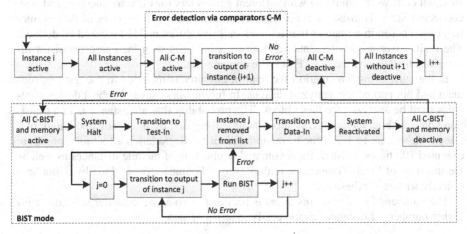

Fig. 3. Control flow for extended AMA approach, enhanced by an error detection phase during module transition and a BIST mode

4.2   Cell models for MTTF Comparison

The proposed approach for modeling of the meant time to failure of integrated designs is an extension of the in [6] presented mixed-signal method. In contrast to the solution on SPICE level the new approach applies models on cell-level in which the function of the logic cells deteriorates over time. Thereby, the level of degradation is parameterized for each cell and bases on results from studies on SPICE level [6]. Further, all cells receive an additional input that defines whether the cell is active or deactivated. This allows different level of degradation depending on the state of connected Sleep Transistors.

5   Results of the Simulations

In this section, the setup of the test environment is presented before the obtained simulation results are discussed.

5.1   Setup of the Test Environment

The presented simulation results are based on designs from the ISCAS benchmark suite (c1355 and c3450) [15], the ITC99 benchmark suite (b05, b15 and b21) [17], and two proprietary designs, i.e. a 32-bit multiplier (mult) and a simple 8-bit MIPS-like processor (MIPS). The applied library consists of 8 standard cells described as VERILOG modules with a hard degradation limit that takes the cell active time into consideration. The levels of cell degradation are based on simulation results obtained from the test environment presented in [7]. Thereby, all cells were realized in a predictive 16 nm technology [18] and simulated with the same error models as in [7]. Next, all cells were simulated with different parameters for the error models, and with connected Sleep Transistors in on- and off-mode. Thereby, the values of the parameters were chosen in a manner that for each cell five different MTTF could be defined. The multiplexer are implemented as transmission gates with increased transistor dimensions that elevate the MTTF of these components.

In the current implementation the control circuitry is included in the test environment and not part of the analyzed designs. In future works several robust design strategies shall be analyzed for these block. The probability that an instance is in a transition phase without having its outputs forwarded, defined by frequency and length of a transition, was set to 1 %. Due to random values for degradation all simulations were executed 100 times. Further, the automated duplication of module instances as well as the insertion of Sleep Transistors, multiplexer and comparators is done by a tool specifically written for these tasks.

The number of redundant instances is limited to two as we consider solutions with higher numbers of instances as too costly in terms of area.

5.2   Results and Discussion

In a first step it was verified whether the results of the initial AMA approach (see section 2) can be reproduced in the proposed test environment. Therefore, for each design the MTTF of the raw version without any redundant blocks was estimated. Subsequently, those designs were modified according to the AMA approach presented in section 2. Thus, each design was duplicated and complemented with the multiplexer, while the test environment was extended by the related control logic. Further, for both experiments the cell degradation models that lead to the longest MTTF were chosen. At these simulations, a design was considered as defective with the appearance of the first wrong result at the design outputs. The results presented in Fig. 4 show that the improvements of the initial approach could be reproduced whereas the MTTF could be increased by an average of factor 1.98.

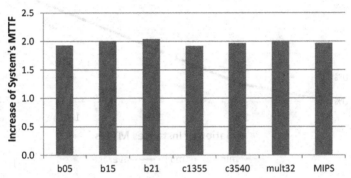

Fig. 4. Increase of Mean Time To Failure (MTTF) of designs realized with the initial AMA approach (each module with two instances) compared to the raw versions

In the next step the proposed extension of the AMA approach (see section 3) was analyzed. Initially, the designs were simulated with each module realized as single instance and for all five degradation classes of the cells. Next, comparators and a memory based BIST were added while the control logic was extended by error verification. Then, each modified design was simulated five times whereas the cell degradation models of one instance of each module were varied.

The results of this analysis are depicted in Fig. 5. Here, the increase of the mean time to failure of the extended approach compared to the initial one is shown for varying relation between the MTTFs of the instances. The depicted curves show the minimum, average, and maximum improvement of the system's MTTF compared to the initial approach. It follows that for equal distributed MTTFs of the instances the proposed extension leads only to a negligible increase of expected system lifetime (average: 1 %). In contrast, already with one group of instances having a 25 % lower mean time to failure the system's MTTF can be increased in average by 8 %. If one group of the instances has a MTTF this is by factor 2 shorter the improvement increases up to 51 % (average: 50 %). Hence, it could be shown that the presented approach can considerably increase the system lifetime.

It should be noted that these simulations cannot classify the increase of robustness against errors that are not based on temporary degradation but abrupt failures, e.g.

based on high temperature peaks, extreme overvoltage due to electro-static discharge, or infant mortality effects.

For this analysis we consider a comparison of the MTTF of raw designs with the extended version of the approach as not conclusive. This is due to fact that the choice for the cell degradation model for the raw versions would be only random.

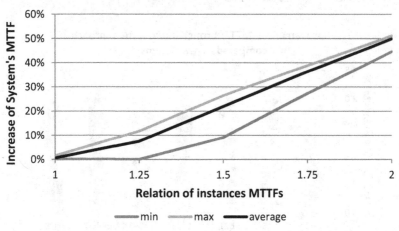

Fig. 5. Improvement of Mean Time To Failure (MTTF) of extended approach compared to the initial approach under variation of relation of instance's MTTFs (each module with 2 instances)

6   Conclusion

Integrated circuits realized in nanometer technology are continuously more suscepti-ble to severe failure mechanisms. This alarming development necessitates design techniques to improve the lifetime reliability. Hence, the presented work proposes an extension of an approach that combines the ideas of Sleep Transistors and modular redundancy in a beneficial way. Thereby, the approach aims at increased lifetime reliability while the impact on delay and power dissipation is kept to a minimum. Due to proposed extensions of this work it is possible to detect permanent errors. Further-more, the modifications lead to extension of the expected system's lifetime as faulty instances can be identified and disconnected. In order to compare system lifetime, we also proposed a modeling technique on cell-level. Finally, simulation results show that the proposed improvements of the design approach can extend the system's Mean Time To Failure (MTTF) in average by 52 % if the instance's MTTF differ by factor 2.

Acknowledgements. This work was supported by grants from CNPq, CNPq/DISSE, CAPES, FAPEMIG, and UFMG/PRPq.

References

1. Srinivasan, J., Adve, S., Bose, P., Rivers, J.: The impact of technology scaling on lifetime reliability. In: Proceedings of IEEE International Conference on Dependable Systems and Networks (2004)
2. Bernardi, P., Bolzani, L.M.V., Rebaudengo, M., Reorda, M.S., Vargas, F.L., Violante, M.: A new hybrid fault detection technique for Systems-on-a-Chip. IEEE Transaction on Computers 55(2), 185–198 (2006)
3. Mitra, S., Seifert, N., Zhang, M., Shi, Q., Kim, K.S.: Robust System Design with Built-In Soft-Error Resilience. Computer 38(2), 43–52 (2005)
4. Inukai, T., Hiramoto, T., Sakurai, T.: Variable threshold CMOS (VTCMOS) in series connected circuits. In: Proceedings of the International Symposium on Low Power Electronics and Design, pp. 201–206 (2001)
5. Tschanz, J., et al.: Adaptive body bias for reducing impacts of die-to-die and within-die parameter variations on microprocessor frequency and leakage. IEEE Journal of Solid-States Circuits 37, 1396–1402 (2002)
6. Sill Torres, F., Cornelius, C., Timmermann, D.: Reliability Enhancement via Sleep Transistors. In: Proceedings of 12th IEEE Latin-American Test Workshop, pp. 1–6 (2011)
7. Cornelius, C., Sill Torres, F., Timmermann, D.: Power-Efficient Application of Sleep Transistors to Enhance the Reliability of Integrated Circuits. Journal of Low Power Electronics 7(4), 552–561 (2011)
8. Powell, M., Yang, S.-H., Falsafi, B., Roy, K., Vijaykumar, T.N.: Gated-Vdd: A circuit technique to reduce leakage in deep-submicron cache memories. In: Proceedings of International Symposium on Low Power Electronics and Design, pp. 90–95 (2000)
9. Srinivasan, J., Adve, S.V., Bose, P., Rivers, J., Hu, C.-K.: RAMP: A Model for Reliability Aware Microprocessor Design. IBM Research Report, RC23048 (2003)
10. Stathis, J.: Reliability limits for the gate insulator in cmos technology. IBM Journal of Research & Develop 46(2/3), 265–286 (2002)
11. Maricau, E., Gielen, G.: NBTI model for analogue IC reliability simulation. Electronics Letters 46(18) (2010)
12. Failure Mechanisms and Models for Semiconductor Devices, JEDEC Publication JEP122-A, Jedec Solid State Technology Association (2002)
13. Possamai Bastos, R., Sill Torres, F., Di Natale, G., Flottes, M., Rouzeyre, B.: Novel transient-fault detection circuit featuring enhanced bulk built-in current sensor with low-power sleep-mode. Microelectronics Reliability 52(9-10), 1781–1786 (2012)
14. Lorenz, D., Barke, M., Schlichtmann, U.: Aging analysis at gate and macro cell level. In: Proceedings of Computer-Aided Design, pp. 77–84 (2010)
15. Xiao, J., Jiang, J., Zhu, X., Ouyang, C.: A Method of Gate-Level Circuit Reliability Estimation Based on Iterative PTM Model. In: Proceed. Dependable Computing, pp. 276–277 (2011)
16. Hansen, M., Yalcin, H., Hayes, J.P.: Unveiling the ISCAS-85 Benchmarks: A Case Study in Reverse Engineering. IEEE Design & Test 16(3), 72–80 (1999)
17. Basto, L.: First results of ITC'99 benchmark circuits. IEEE Design & Test of Computers 17(3), 54–59 (2000)
18. Zhao, W., Cao, Y.: New generation of Predictive Technology Model for sub-45nm early design exploration. IEEE Transactions on Electron Devices 53(11), 2816–2823 (2006)

Model Checking Memory-Related Properties
of Hardware/Software Co-designs

Marcel Pockrandt, Paula Herber, Verena Klös, and Sabine Glesner

Technische Universität Berlin
{marcel.pockrandt,paula.herber,verena.kloes,sabine.glesner}@tu-berlin.de

Abstract. Memory safety plays a crucial role in concurrent hardware/-software systems and must be guaranteed under all circumstances. Although there exist some approaches for complete verification that can cope with both hardware and software and their interplay, none of them supports pointers or memory. To overcome this problem, we present a novel approach for model checking memory-related properties of digital HW/SW systems designed in SystemC/TLM. The main idea is to formalize a clean subset of the SystemC memory model using UPPAAL timed automata. Then, we embed this formal memory model into our previously proposed automatic transformation from SystemC/TLM to UPPAAL timed automata. With that, we can fully automatically verify memory-related properties of a wide range of practical applications. We show the applicability of our approach by verifying memory safety of an industrial design that makes ample use of pointers and call-by-reference.

1 Introduction

Concurrent HW/SW systems are used in many safety critical applications, which imposes high quality requirements. At the same time, the demands on multi-functioning and flexibility are steadily increasing. To meet the high quality standards and to satisfy the rising quantitative demands, complete and automatic verification techniques such as model checking are needed. Existing techniques for HW/SW co-verification do not support pointers or memory. Thus, they cannot be used to verify memory-related properties and they are not applicable to a wide range of practical applications, as many HW/SW co-designs rely heavily on the use of pointers.

In this paper, we present a novel approach for model checking memory-related properties of digital HW/SW systems implemented in SystemC/TLM [15,20]. SystemC/TLM is a system level design language which is widely used for the design of concurrent HW/SW systems and has gained the status of a de facto standard during the last years. The main idea of our approach is to formalize a clean subset of the SystemC memory model using multiple typed arrays. We incorporate this formal memory model into our previously proposed SystemC to timed automata transformation [13,14,21]. With that, we enable the complete and automatic verification of safety and timing properties of SystemC/TLM designs, including memory safety, using the UPPAAL model checker. Our approach

G. Schirner et al. (Eds.): IESS 2013, IFIP AICT 403, pp. 92–103, 2013.

can handle all important elements of the SystemC/TLM language, including port and socket communication, dynamic sensitivity and timing. Thus, we can cope with both hardware and software and their interplay. We require our approach for model checking of memory-related properties of SystemC/TLM designs to fulfill the following criteria:

1. The SystemC memory model subset must be clearly defined.
2. The automatic transformation from SystemC/TLM to UPPAAL must cover the most important memory related constructs, at least the use of pointer variables and call-by-reference.
3. The resulting representation should produce as little overhead as possible on verification time and memory consumption for the UPPAAL model checker.
4. To ease debugging, the automatically generated UPPAAL model should be easy to read and understand.

Note that our main goal is to make the theoretical results from formal memory modeling applicable for practical applications, and in particular, to transfer the results from the verification of C programs (with pointers) to the verification of HW/SW co-designs written in SystemC. We do not aim at supporting the full C memory model, including inter-type aliasing and frame problems. Instead, we focus on a small, clean subset of the SystemC memory model that is sufficient for most practical examples and can be verified fully automatically.

The rest of this paper is structured as follows: In section 2, we briefly introduce the preliminaries. In section 3, we summarize related work. In section 4, we present our approach for the formalization of the SystemC memory model with UPPAAL timed automata. Then, we show how we incorporated the memory model into our previously proposed automatic transformation from SystemC/TLM to UPPAAL. In Section 5, we describe the verification of memory safety with our approach. Finally, we present the results of this transformation for our case study in Section 6 and conclude in Section 7.

2   Preliminaries

In this section, we briefly introduce the preliminaries that are necessary to understand the remainder of the paper. First, we give an overview over the system level design language SystemC/TLM and UPPAAL timed automata (UTA). Then we give a brief introduction into our transformation from SystemC to timed automata.

2.1   SystemC/TLM

SystemC [15] is a system level design language and a framework for HW/SW co-simulation. It allows modeling and executing of hardware and software on various levels of abstraction. It is implemented as a C++class library, which provides the language elements for the description of hardware and software, and an event-driven simulation kernel. A SystemC design is a set of communicating processes, triggered by events and interacting through channels. Modules and channels represent structural information. SystemC also introduces an integer-valued time model with arbitrary time resolution. The execution of the design is controlled by the SystemC scheduler. It controls the simulation time, the execution of processes, handles event notifications and updates primitive channels.

Transaction Level Modeling (TLM) is mainly used for early platform evaluation, performance analysis, and fast simulation of HW/SW systems. The general idea is to use *transactions* as an abstraction for all kind of data that is transmitted between different modules. This enables simulations on different abstraction levels, trading off accuracy and simulation speed. The TLM standard [20] and its implementation are an extension of SystemC, which provide interoperability between different transaction level models. The core of the TLM standard is the *interoperability layer*, which comprises standardized transport interfaces, sockets, and a generic payload.

2.2 Uppaal Timed Automata

Timed automata [1] are finite-state machines extended by clocks. Two types of clock constraints are used to model time-dependent behavior: *Invariants* are assigned to locations and restrict the time the automaton can stay in this location. *Guards* are assigned to edges and enable progress only if they evaluate to true. Networks of timed automata are used to model concurrent processes, which are executed with an interleaving semantics and synchronize on channels.

UPPAAL [2] is a tool suite for modeling, simulation, and verification of networks of timed automata. The UPPAAL modeling language extends timed automata by bounded integer variables, a template mechanism, binary and broadcast channels, and urgent and committed locations. Binary channels enable a blocking synchronization between two processes, whereas broadcast channels enable non-blocking synchronization between one sender and arbitrarily many receivers. Urgent and committed locations are used to model locations where no time may pass. Furthermore, leaving a committed location has priority over non-committed locations.

A small example UPPAAL timed automaton (UTA) is shown in Figure 1. The initial location is denoted by ◎, and `request?` and `ack!` denote sending and receiving on channels, respectively. The clock variable x is first set to zero and then used in two clock constraints: the invariant `x <= maxtime` denotes that the corresponding location must be left before x becomes greater than maxtime, and the guard `x >= mintime` enables the corresponding edge at `mintime`. The symbols ◎ and © depict urgent and committed locations.

2.3 Transformation from SystemC to UPPAAL

In previous work [13,14,21], we have presented an approach for the automatic transformation of the informally defined semantics of SystemC/TLM designs into the formal semantics of UTA. The transformation preserves the (informally defined) behavioral semantics and the structure of a given SystemC design and

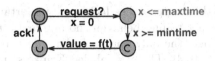

Fig. 1. Example Timed Automaton

can be applied fully automatically. It requires two major restrictions. First, we do not handle dynamic process or object creation. This hardly narrows the applicability of the approach, as dynamic object and process creation are rarely used in SystemC designs. Second, the approach only supports data types that can be mapped to (structs and arrays of) int and bool.

In our transformation, we use predefined templates for SystemC constructs such as events, processes and the scheduler. Then, each method is mapped to a single UTA template. Call-return semantics is modeled with binary channels. Process automata are used to encapsulate the method automata and care for the interactions with event objects, the scheduler, and primitive channels. Our transformation is compositional in the sense that we transform each module separately and compose the system in a final instantiation and binding phase. For detailed information on the transformation of SystemC/TLM designs to UTA we refer to [12].

3   Related Work

In the past ten years, there has been a lot of work on the development of formal memory models for C and C-like languages and in particular on the verification of pointer programs. Three main approaches to reason about memory in C (cf. [26]) exist: First, semantic approaches regard memory as a function from some kind of address to some kind of value. Second, there exist approaches that use multiple typed heaps in order to avoid the necessity of coping with inter-type aliasing. In these approaches, a separate heap is used for each language type that is present in a given program or design. In [5], Bornat describes under which restrictions such a memory model is semantically sound. Third, approaches based on separation logic (an extension of Hoare logic) [22] are able to cope with aliasing and frame problems. The main idea of separation logic is to provide inference rules that allow for the expression of aliasing conditions and local reasoning.

With our approach, we mainly adapt the idea of multiple typed heaps [5] by providing a separate memory array for each datatype used in a given design.

There also have been several approaches to provide a formal semantics for SystemC in order to enable automatic and complete verification techniques. However, many of them only cope with a synchronous subset of SystemC [18,23,24,10], cannot handle dynamic sensitivity or timing, and do not consider pointers or memory. Other approaches which are based on a transformation from SystemC into some kind of state machine formalism [11,25,27,19], process algebras [17,9] or sequential C programs [6,7] do not cope with pointers or memory as well.

Furthermore, most of these approaches lack some important features (e.g., no support for time, no exact timing behavior, no automatic transformation). To the best of our knowledge, the only approach that can cope with pointers and memory is the work of [16,4]. There, a labeled Kripke structure-based semantics for SystemC is proposed and predicate abstraction techniques are used for verification. However, the main idea of this approach is to abstract from the hardware by grouping it into combinational and clocked threads, which are then combined into a synchronous product for the overall system. They do neither address timing issues nor inter-process communication via sockets and channels. Thus, it remains unclear how they would cope with deeply integrated hardware and software components and their interplay. Several approaches exists for the verification of memory safety properties. However, these approaches focus on pure C (e.g., BLAST [3] and VCC/Z3 [8]) and cannot cope with the special semantics of SystemC/TLM.

4   Formalization and Transformation of the SystemC Memory Model

In this paper, we present a novel approach for model checking memory-related properties of HW/SW systems implemented in SystemC/TLM. The main idea of our approach is to formalize a clean subset of the SystemC memory model using separate memory arrays for each type present in a given design (cf. [5]). In order to enable model checking of memory-related properties, we incorporate this formal memory model into our SystemC to Timed Automata Transformation Engine (STATE) [13,14,21]. To this end, we define a set of transformation rules, which covers all memory-related constructs that are relevant for our subset of the SystemC memory model. For each memory-related construct, we define a UTA representation. With that, we can automatically transform a given SystemC/TLM design that makes use of pointers and memory into a UTA model.

In the following, we first state a set of assumptions that define a subset of the SystemC memory model. Then, we present our representation of the SystemC memory model within UPPAAL. Finally, we present the transformation itself.

4.1   Assumptions

Our memory model covers many memory related constructs like call-by-reference of methods, referencing of variables, derefencing of pointers and pointers to pointers in arbitrary depth. However, we require a given SystemC/TLM model to fulfill the following assumptions:

1. No typecasts are used.
2. No direct hardware access of memory addresses (e. g., *int *p; p = 0xFFFFFF;*).
3. Structs are only referenced by pointers of the same type as the struct. This also means that there are no direct references to struct members.
4. No pointer arithmetic is used.
5. No dynamic memory allocation.

6. No recursion is used.
7. No function pointers are used.

Assumptions 1, 5, and 6 are necessary as UPPAAL does not support typecasting, dynamic memory allocation or recursion. The second assumption is necessary because we do not model the memory bytewise and can only access it per variable. The third assumption is due to the fact that we do not flatten structs and therefore struct members do not have an own address. As we only model the data memory, assumption 7 is necessary. The Assumptions 1-4 can be considered as minor ones and hardly restrict the expressiveness of our memory model. As most SystemC/TLM models do neither make use of dynamic memory allocation nor of recursion, Assumptions 5 and 6 are acceptable as well.

With the assumptions above, we have a clear definition of the subset of the SystemC memory model that we want to support with our approach.

4.2 Representation

The main idea of our representation is to model the memory of the System-C/TLM design with multiple typed arrays. As UPPAAL does not support polymorphic datatypes, we create a separate array for each datatype used in the design. Pointers then can be modeled as integer variables, which point to a position in the array for the corresponding type. Array variables are interpreted as pointers to the first array element. All other variables are modeled as constant pointers if they are ever referenced (e.g., call-by-reference or direct referencing).

Figure 2 shows a small example of our UPPAAL representation for the SystemC memory model. While pointers, integers and struct variables are arbitrarily spread over the memory in the SystemC memory model, we group them together in our UPPAAL representation. In our example, there exist an integer variable i and two objects s and t of type data. Furthermore, there is an integer pointer p, pointing to i, and a pointer q of type data, pointing to t. In the resulting UPPAAL model, i is placed in the array intMem and s and t are placed in the array dataMem. The pointers are transformed from real addresses into the corresponding array indices. Note that the arrays have a finite and fixed size which cannot be altered during the execution of the model. However, the pointers can point to all existing data of their type.

4.3 Transformation

For the transformation of a given design, we sort all variables into three disjunct sets: *PTR*, containing all pointers, *REF* containing all referenced nonpointer variables and all arrays and *VAR* containing all other nonpointer variables.

The result can be used to extract the memory model of the SystemC/TLM model and to transform it into a UPPAAL memory model as proposed in 4.2. Figure 3 shows a small example for the transformation. Except for additional array accesses, the resulting UPPAAL model has the same structure and variable

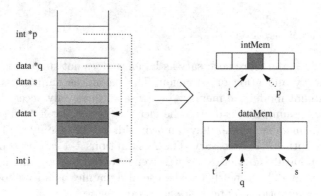

Fig. 2. Memory Representation in SystemC and UPPAAL

```
1
2   data arr [3];
3   data x;
4   data *p;
5
6   x.val = 23;
7   p = &x;
8   p->val = 42;
9   arr [2].val = 12;
10  *p = arr [1];
11  p = &arr [2];
```

```
1   int dataMEM[DATAMEMSIZE];
2   const int arr = 0;
3   const int x = 3;
4   int p;
5
6   dataMEM[x].val = 23;
7   p = x;
8   dataMEM[p].val = 42;
9   dataMEM[arr+2].val = 12;
10  dataMEM[p] = dataMEM[arr+1];
11  p = arr + 2;
```

(a) SystemC/TLM representation   **(b)** UPPAAL representation

Fig. 3. Memory Representation Examples

names as the original design. This eases manual matching with the corresponding
SystemC/TLM design to correct detected errors in SystemC/TLM designs.

Table 1 shows the transformation rules we use, with var ∈ *REF*, arr ∈ *REF* ∧
isArray(arr), p,q ∈ *PTR*, arbitrary data types T, U, V and W, and the arbitrary
expression E. In general, every referenced variable is converted into a typed array
index. While for nonpointer variables this index is constant, pointers can be
arbitrarily changed. Direct accesses to these variables and pointer dereferencing
operations can be modeled by typed array accesses. Direct pointer manipulation
and variable referencing can be performed without any typed array access.

For all variable types in the *REF* and *PTR* sets, we generate a typed array
representing the memory for this type. The size of each typed array is determined
by the total amount of referenced variables of this type. For all members of the
REF set, we reserve one field in the typed array per variable per module instance
and generate a constant integer with the name of the variable and the index
of the reserved field. For arrays, we reserve one field per element and set the
constant integer to the index of the first element in the array. We replace every

variable access with an array access to the typed array and every referencing of the variable by a direct access. If the variable is an array, the index is used as an offset. For all members of the *PTR* set we generate an integer variable with the initial value NULL (-1) or the index of the variable the pointer points to. As -1 is not a valid index of the typed array, all accesses to uninitialized pointers result in an array index error. Furthermore, we replace every dereferencing operation to the pointer with an array access to the corresponding typed array.

We implemented the transformation rules in our previously proposed transformation from SystemC to UPPAAL and thus can transform a given SystemC/TLM model with pointers fully automatically. Currently, our implementation does not support pointers to pointers and arrays of pointers, though both can be added with little effort.

Table 1. Transformation Rules

SystemC	UPPAAL
Declarations	
T var;	⇒ const int var = newIndex(T);
T var = E;	⇒ const int var = newIndex(T);
	TMEM[var] = E;
U arr[E];	⇒ const int arr = newIndex(U, E);
U arr[] = $\{v_0,...,v_{n-1}\}$;	⇒ const int arr = newIndex(U, n);
	UMEM[arr+0] = v_0; ...;
	UMEM[arr+(n-1)] = v_{n-1};
V *p;	⇒ int p = -1;
W *q = E;	⇒ int q = E;
Variable Access	
var	⇒ TMEM[var]
arr[E]	⇒ UMEM[arr+E]
&(E)	⇒ E
&arr[E]	⇒ arr+E
Pointer Access	
*(E)	⇒ TMEM[E] (with E of type T)
NULL	⇒ -1
Field Access	
var.field	⇒ TMEM[var].field
var.p→field	⇒ VMEM[TMEM[var].p].field
arr[E].field	⇒ UMEM[arr+E].field
arr[E].p→field	⇒ VMEM[UMEM[arr+E].p].field
p→field	⇒ VMEM[p].field
p→q→field	⇒ WMEM[VMEM[p].q].field

5   Verification of Memory Safety

As our transformation from SystemC to UPPAAL is able to cope with pointers and other memory-related constructs, the UPPAAL model checker can now be used to verify memory safety properties. In general, we can verify all properties that can be expressed within the subset of CTL supported by UPPAAL [2] (e.g., safety, liveness and timing properties as shown in [21]). For convenience, our verification framework generates two memory safety properties automatically:

(a) All pointers in the design are always either null, or they point to a valid part of the memory array corresponding to their type.
(b) The design never tries to access memory via a null pointer.

To verify the first property, it is necessary to check for all pointers $p_0...p_n$ that they are either null or have a value within the range of their typed array. If the function $u(p_i)$ yields the size of the typed array of the type of p_i, property (a) can be formalized as follows:

$$AG\ (p_0 = \text{null} \vee 0 \le p_0 \le u(p_0) - 1) \wedge\ ...\ \wedge\ (p_n = \text{null} \vee 0 \le p_n \le u(p_n) - 1)$$

The second property cannot be captured statically, as it needs the dynamic information where in the program a pointer is used to access memory. To solve this problem, we have developed an algorithm identifying all memory accesses in all processes $\text{Proc}_0...\text{Proc}_n$. For each transition comprising a memory access, a unique label l_i is assigned to its source location. With these labels, the property that a memory access ma_i that uses a pointer p_j is valid can be formalized as follows:

$$safe(ma_i) \equiv (\text{Proc}(ma_i).l_i \implies (p_j \ne \text{null}))$$

Using this abbreviation, the second property can be formalized as follows:

$$AG\ safe(ma_0) \wedge ... \wedge safe(ma_n)$$

Both memory safety properties described above are automatically generated for all pointers in a given design within our verification framework.

6   Evaluation

In this section we evaluate our approach with an industrial case study, namely a TLM implementation of the AMBA AHB, provided by Carbon Design Systems.

The original model consists of about 1500 LOC. To meet the assumptions of our approach, we performed the following modifications: (1) we changed the sockets to TLM standard sockets, (2) we replaced the generic payload type with a specific one, (3) we replaced operators for dynamic memory management (e.g., *new, delete*) by static memory allocation and (4) we only transfer constant data through the bus. The latter modification drastically simplifies the verification problem. However, our focus is on verifying the correct concurrent behavior, synchronization, timing, and memory safety which do not depend on the data that is transfered over the bus. The modified model consists of about 1600 LOC.

We also performed experiments on a pointer-free variant of the AMBA AHB design to evaluate the additional verification effort produced by our memory

Table 2. Results from the Amba AHB Design

| | Verification time ([h:]min:sec) | | | | | | | |
| | Pointer-free design | | | | Design with pointers | | | |
	1M1S	1M2S	2M1S	2M2S	1M1S	1M2S	2M1S	2M2S
transformation time	0:04	0:04	0:04	0:04	0:03	0:03	0:04	0:05
deadlock freedom	< 1	< 1	0:27	1:08	6:17	12:06	37:28	1:24:25
only one master	-	-	0:14	0:34	-	-	24:07	54:32
bus granted to M1	< 1	< 1	0:15	0:37	3:56	7:47	24:10	54:06
bus granted to M2	-	-	0:15	0:38	-	-	24:10	54:02
timing	< 1	< 1	0:22	0:54	11:37	22:24	1:09:15	2:32:04
memory safety (a)	-	-	-	-	4:36	9:16	27:57	1:04:07
memory safety (b)	-	-	-	-	6:36	13:19	39:12	1:27:29
# states	5K	9K	537K	1M	15M	26M	64M	127M
memory usage	< 1 mb	2 mb	61 mb	112 mb	873 mb	1.5 gb	2.2 gb	3.9 gb

model. Therefore, we manually removed all memory related constructs from the original design and tried to keep the resulting design completely side-effect free. In the following, we compare the results of two different experiments: transformation and verification of (1) the pointer-free design and (2) of a design featuring pointers and other memory-related constructs (like call-by-reference).

For both designs, we verified the following properties: (1) deadlock freedom, (2) a bus request is always eventually answered with a grant signal, (3) the bus is only granted to one master at a time, (4) a transaction through the bus is always finished within a given time limit. For the CTL formulae we refer to [21]. For the design with pointers and other memory-related constructs, we additionally verified memory safety, as described in Section 5. All experiments were run on a 64bit Linux system with a dual core 3.0 GHz CPU and 8 GB RAM. To evaluate the scalability of our approach we used different design sizes (from 1 master and 1 slave, 1M1S, to 2 master and 2 slaves, 2M2S). The results of the verification are shown in Table 2.

All properties have been proven to be satisfied at the end of the verification phase. During the verification, we detected a bug in the original design which led to a deadlock situation. When a transaction is split into several separate transfers, a counter variable is used to store the number of successful transfers before the split occurs. This variable was not reset in the original design. As a consequence, all split transactions besides the first one failed. This is a typical example which is both difficult to detect and to correct with simulation alone. With our approach, the generation of a counter example took only a few minutes. Due to the structure preservation of our transformation and the graphical visualization in UPPAAL, it was easy to understand the cause of the problem.

Our results show that the verification effort, in terms of CPU time and memory consumption, is drastically increased if pointers and other memory-related constructs are taken into account. This is due to the fact that the memory model introduces an additional integer variable for each variable in the design. However, formal verification via model checking, if successful, is only performed once during the whole development cycle. At the same time, the generation of counter examples only takes a few minutes. Most importantly, we are not aware of any other approach that can cope with the HW/SW interplay within SystemC/TLM models and at the same time facilitates the verification of memory-related properties, for example memory safety.

7   Conclusion and Future Work

We presented a novel approach for model checking of memory-related properties on HW/SW systems implemented in SystemC/TLM. We formalized a clean subset of the SystemC memory model with UTA. We use this formalization for a fully-automatic transformation of SystemC/TLM into equivalent UPPAAL timed automata. This enables the use of the UPPAAL model checker to verify memory-related properties. For convenience, we generate two memory safety properties, namely that all pointers only point to valid memory locations or null and that no null pointer accesses are used, automatically within our verification framework.

We implemented our approach and showed its applicability with an industrial design of the AMBA Advanced High Performance Bus (AHB). We were able to verify deadlock freedom, timing, and memory safety. We detected a deadlock situation in the AMBA AHB design, which could easily be resolved with the help of the counter-example generated by the UPPAAL model checker. Our memory model produces a significant overhead to verification time and memory consumption. However, this overhead is compensated with the possibility to verify memory-related properties and the drastically increased practical applicability of our approach.

In our case study, we manually modified the design such that only constant data is transfered over the bus. For future work, we plan to extend our approach with automatic data abstraction techniques to enable the verification of even larger SystemC/TLM designs without manual interaction.

References

1. Alur, R., Dill, D.L.: A Theory of Timed Automata. Theoretical Computer Science 126, 183–235 (1994)
2. Behrmann, G., David, A., Larsen, K.G.: A Tutorial on UPPAAL. In: Bernardo, M., Corradini, F. (eds.) SFM-RT 2004. LNCS, vol. 3185, pp. 200–236. Springer, Heidelberg (2004)
3. Beyer, D., Henzinger, T.A., Jhala, R., Majumdar, R.: Checking Memory Safety with Blast. In: Cerioli, M. (ed.) FASE 2005. LNCS, vol. 3442, pp. 2–18. Springer, Heidelberg (2005)
4. Blanc, N., Kroening, D., Sharygina, N.: Scoot: A Tool for the Analysis of SystemC Models. In: Ramakrishnan, C.R., Rehof, J. (eds.) TACAS 2008. LNCS, vol. 4963, pp. 467–470. Springer, Heidelberg (2008)
5. Bornat, R.: Proving pointer programs in Hoare Logic. In: Backhouse, R., Oliveira, J.N. (eds.) MPC 2000. LNCS, vol. 1837, pp. 102–126. Springer, Heidelberg (2000)

6. Cimatti, A., Micheli, A., Narasamdya, I., Roveri, M.: Verifying SystemC: A software model checking approach. In: FMCAD, pp. 51–59 (2010)
7. Cimatti, A., Griggio, A., Micheli, A., Narasamdya, I., Roveri, M.: KRATOS – A Software Model Checker for SystemC. In: Gopalakrishnan, G., Qadeer, S. (eds.) CAV 2011. LNCS, vol. 6806, pp. 310–316. Springer, Heidelberg (2011)
8. Cohen, E., Dahlweid, M., Hillebrand, M., Leinenbach, D., Moskal, M., Santen, T., Schulte, W., Tobies, S.: VCC: A Practical System for Verifying Concurrent C. In: Berghofer, S., Nipkow, T., Urban, C., Wenzel, M. (eds.) TPHOLs 2009. LNCS, vol. 5674, pp. 23–42. Springer, Heidelberg (2009)
9. Garavel, H., Helmstetter, C., Ponsini, O., Serwe, W.: Verification of an industrial SystemC/TLM model using LOTOS and CADP. In: MEMOCODE, pp. 46–55. IEEE (2009)
10. Große, D., Kühne, U., Drechsler, R.: HW/SW Co-Verification of Embedded Systems using Bounded Model Checking. In: Great Lakes Symposium on VLSI, pp. 43–48. ACM Press (2006)
11. Habibi, A., Moinudeen, H., Tahar, S.: Generating Finite State Machines from SystemC. In: DATE, pp. 76–81. IEEE (2006)
12. Herber, P.: A Framework for Automated HW/SW Co-Verification of SystemC Designs using Timed Automata. Logos (2010)
13. Herber, P., Fellmuth, J., Glesner, S.: Model Checking SystemC Designs Using Timed Automata. In: CODES+ISSS, pp. 131–136. ACM Press (2008)
14. Herber, P., Pockrandt, M., Glesner, S.: Transforming SystemC Transaction Level Models into UPPAAL Timed Automata. In: MEMOCODE, pp. 161–170. IEEE Computer Society (2011)
15. IEEE Standards Association: IEEE Std. 1666–2005, Open SystemC Language Reference Manual (2005)
16. Kroening, D., Sharygina, N.: Formal Verification of SystemC by Automatic Hardware/Software Partitioning. In: MEMOCODE, pp. 101–110. IEEE (2005)
17. Man, K.L.: An Overview of SystemCFL. In: Research in Microelectronics and Electronics, vol. 1, pp. 145–148 (2005)
18. Müller, W., Ruf, J., Rosenstiel, W.: An ASM based SystemC Simulation Semantics. In: Methodologies and Applications, pp. 97–126. Kluwer Academic Publishers (2003)
19. Niemann, B., Haubelt, C.: Formalizing TLM with Communicating State Machines. Forum on Specification and Design Languages (2006)
20. Open SystemC Initiative (OSCI): TLM 2.0 Reference Manual (2009)
21. Pockrandt, M., Herber, P., Glesner, S.: Model Checking a SystemC/TLM Design of the AMBA AHB Protocol. In: ESTIMedia, pp. 66–75. IEEE (2011)
22. Reynolds, J.C.: Separation logic: A logic for shared mutable data structures. In: LICS, pp. 55–74. IEEE Computer Society (2002)
23. Ruf, J., Hoffmann, D.W., Gerlach, J., Kropf, T., Rosenstiel, W., Müller, W.: The Simulation Semantics of SystemC. In: DATE, pp. 64–70. IEEE (2001)
24. Salem, A.: Formal Semantics of Synchronous SystemC. In: Design, Automation and Test in Europe (DATE), pp. 10376–10381. IEEE Computer Society (2003)
25. Traulsen, C., Cornet, J., Moy, M., Maraninchi, F.: A SystemC/TLM semantics in Promela and its possible applications. In: Bošnacki, D., Edelkamp, S. (eds.) SPIN 2007. LNCS, vol. 4595, pp. 204–222. Springer, Heidelberg (2007)
26. Tuch, H.: Formal Memory Models for Verifying C Systems Code (2008)
27. Zhang, Y., Vedrine, F., Monsuez, B.: SystemC Waiting-State Automata. In: Proceedings of VECoS 2007 (2007)

Reducing Re-verification Effort
by Requirement-Based Change Management*

Markus Oertel[1] and Achim Rettberg[2]

[1] OFFIS e.V., Escherweg2, D-26121 Oldenburg, Germany
markus.oertel@offis.de
[2] University of Oldenburg, Ammerländer Heerstraße 114-118, D-26111 Oldenburg,
Germany
achim.rettberg@informatik.uni-oldenburg.de

Abstract. Changes in parts of a safety critical system typically require
the re-verification of the whole system design. In this paper we present
a change management approach that contains the effects of a change
within a region of the system. The approach guarantees to maintain the
integrity of the system while performing changes. Our approach directly
integrates verification and validation activities in the process. Furthermore, the propagation of changes is not based on the interfaces of the
components and their interconnections, but exploits the knowledge of the
behavior described by the requirements. This approach creates a much
more precise set of affected system artifacts. In addition, we propose
techniques to analyze the propagation of changes automatically based
on formalized requirements and guide the selection of suitable compensation candidates.

Keywords: change management, system consistency, verification and
validation, formal methods, safety critical embedded systems, model-
based design.

1 Introduction

Today's safety critical embedded systems are subject to a strict quality assurance
process. Domain specific standards like the ISO 26262 [2] (automotive)or ARP
4761 [1] (aerospace) aim to reduce the risk of harming people by a systematic
hazard analysis and structured breakdown of safety requirements and system
design. Once having reached a consistent system state in which all verification
and validation (V&V) activities have been performed, changes can become extremely expensive since typically the whole system design needs to be verified
again.

Current change management tools used in a systems engineering context like
Reqtify [11], IBM Change [15] or Atego Workbench [4] focus on the traceability

---

* The research leading to these results has received funding from the ARTEMIS Joint
Undertaking under grant agreement n°269335 and the German Federal Ministry of
Education and Research (BMBF).

G. Schirner et al. (Eds.): IESS 2013, IFIP AICT 403, pp. 104–115, 2013.

[18][13] between requirements and/or system artifacts. If changes occur, these tools highlight the system artifacts directly connected by trace-links to a changed element. This approach has a couple of limitations: Changing a single component often requires changes in other components as well [12] to re-establish the consistency of the system. Based on the information available by the traceability links and the interconnections of components, it is not possible to contain the propagation of a change. This results again in very broad re-validation and re-certification activities. Furthermore, it is impossible to narrow down the set of system artifacts that are directly affected by the change. All linked elements are potential candidates and need to be checked for unwanted side-effects manually, although only a part of them are relevant to the change. Also the integration of configuration management features into the change management process needs to be improved: In contrast to current development guidelines like CMMI-DEV [8] baselines are set manually, not bound to consistency criteria, and the dependencies between updated system artifacts and verification results are not considered.

In literature change management and change impact analysis is basically approached from two different directions. Estimate the costs of a change before implementing it and identifying affected elements during the change process.

Most of the techniques to quantify the costs of a change do not consider a detailed analysis of the particular change but use knowledge about similar systems and engineering experience. Clarkson et al. [7] use a Design Structure Matrix in combination with a probabilistic approach to determine the likelihood and impact of changes on the different system components. Furthermore scenario based approaches[5] exist to determine quality metrics concerning modifyability for a given architecture. Change scenarios will be defined and for each of them the possible impact will be estimated. The average effort will be calculated based on all considered change-scenarios. This approach is suited to compare two architectures or determine the risk of expensive changes. It is not used in the development process itself to handle introduced changes. Verification and validation activities are not considered and difficult to integrate into the approach since only one unit of measure can be used for the calculations (Lines of code are used in the example).

Approaches for change management during the actual change process are typically based on graph structures [6] and are mostly related to software change management. Extensions exist to object oriented software [19] but the techniques are not applicable for system engineering since the implementation is too late available in the development process (which also might be physical and no code), therefore the requirements of the components are better suited to propagate changes.

In this paper we provide an approach for containing change effects and maintaining the consistency during the change process. Our technique ensures to identify all verification and validation activities that are affected by the change. The approach is based on the system requirements rather than the interconnections of components. Therefore we can limit the change propagation semantically without explicitly modeling it. Also the set of elements that are directly affected by a change is much smaller compared to other change management systems. I.e., from all connected elements only a subset needs to be checked for malfunctions through the change.

We currently cover the functional and timing aspects of the system within one design-perspective [10]. Perspectives represent the system at different structural stages, like a logical, technical or geometrical perspective. Aspects cover the properties within one perspective that are related to a particular topic like safety, timing or weight. Our approach allows the containment of changes within the mentioned aspects only. Nevertheless adding more aspects and perspectives is systematically possible. It is expected that for a given use case only a small subset of them needs to be added like weight, electromagnetic compatibility (EMC) or heat.

The base process is described in section 3. In section 4 the principles behind the containment of the change effects are explained. Section 5 provides an overview over the necessary formalization techniques and activities that can be checked automatically. Based on this formalization we introduce a concept of identifying system elements that can be modified to reach fast a consistent system again. The approach has been implemented in an OSLC based demonstrator. Section 7 introduces this prototype and first evaluation results. A conclusion and future development activities are outlined in the final section 8.

2   System Abstraction and Prerequisites

We analyzed many different meta-models and standards across various domains to identify a basic set of system artifacts and trace-links [17], that cover most of the currently used development artifacts. The change management process is described on these elements to be easy applicable to existing model-based development workflows.

The elements are:

- **Components**: Model-based representation of the interface of a system element. Depending upon the used perspective this can be logical components or concrete hardware or software parts [10].
- **Requirements**: Requirements represent functionality or properties that the component it is attached to shall fulfill.
- **Implementation**: Implementations represent the behavior of a component. This might be software (code or functional model) or a hardware implementation.
- **V&V Cases**: Representation of the activity and their results to prove a property of the system.

The trace-links are:

- **Satisfy**: Connects a requirement with a model component. It symbolizes a "shall satisfy" relation.

- **Derive**: A requirement is decomposed into multiple derived requirements.
- **Refine**: A requirement is formalized into another language or representation.
- **Implementation**: Connects an implementation to a component.

These links are verification target, i.e. that it needs to be proved that the claimed property holds. Therefore V&V cases can be connected to each link detailing the activity that needs to be performed to get the necessary evidence.

To establish a change management process that allows to encapsulate the change in a determined area of the development item, it is necessary that a few prerequisites by the development process itself are met. Still, the process shall be as less inversive to the common practice processes as possible.

The most important prerequisite is that the requirements are always linked to a component and formulated in a black box manner, meaning that the requirement specifies the intended behavior on the interface of this component. This is in line with the contract based design paradigms to ensure the composability of the specified elements [9].

There are also some assumptions on the technical setup for the later realisation: As stated in typical recommendations for configuration management [16] we require all system artifacts to be under version control. In addition we require also trace-links to be versioned and pointing to versioned elements. This is necessary since the semantics of a link may not be applied for a changed element, at least not without an analysis. E.g.: A component covers a special requirement, but after changing the requirement is has to be considered again whether the attached component is still the best to implement this requirement. The link is just valid for a special version of a requirement.

3   Change Management Process

During the processing of a change request verification results that are connected to modified elements need to be invalidated. Furthermore all modified elements, also the trace-links and verification results need to be versioned to point to the new targets. The consistency of these elements is necessary to allow a reject of the change request at any point in time. This might be necessary if it is foreseeable that the change is becoming too expensive. Furthermore the correct version of the verification targets is required to fulfill the traceability and documentation requirements from various safety standards.

The process to achieve these goals is depicted in figure 1 and consists of four basic steps that are executed in an iterative manner:

The system $(A, L)_v$ consists of the set of system artifacts $A = R \cup C \cup V \cup I$ (Requirements, Components, V&V cases and Implementations) and the set of links L. Each state of the system is identified by a version $v \in N^+$. In this description of the process a new version of the whole system is created in each step, this is a simplification in the notation, in the implementation, of course, each element is versioned for its own. A baseline $v \in B$ is a version in which all verification activities v of the system are executed successfully.

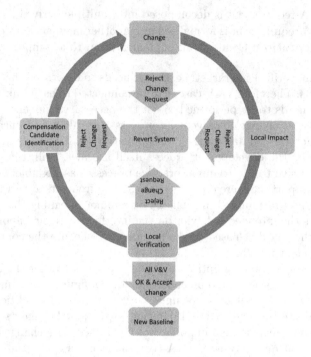

Fig. 1. Basic process for handling Change Requests

$$\mathfrak{v} \in B \rightarrow \forall v \in (A,L)_{\mathfrak{v}} : status(v) == success$$

In the i's execution of the *change* phase a set of elements of the system $(A,L)_{i-1}$ is modified, denoted as $E_{mod_i} \subseteq (A,L)_i$.

This modification alone results in an inconsistent system state, since the V&V cases connected to the system elements e that have not been changed are not valid anymore and need to be re-validated. In the *local impact* phase the connected V&V cases are reset:

$$\forall v \in (A,L)_i | e \in target(v) \wedge e \in E_{mod_i} : status(v) \rightarrow suspect$$

The set of elements evaluated by a V&V case v is expressed by $target(v)$

The suspect V&V cases $V_{suspect}$ need to be re-validated in the *local verification* phase:

$$v \in V_{suspect} \rightarrow \{failed, success\}$$

For the failed V&V cases it is necessary to adapt the system. The possible compensation candidates E_{comp} are the elements the V&V case is targeting.

$$E_{comp_i} = \bigcup_{v \in V_{suspect}} target(v)$$

The engineer needs to select one or more elements of this set and modify them so that the failed V&V activities are successful again. These modifications start the cycle again:

$$E_{mod_{i+1}} \subseteq E_{comp_{i+1}}$$

A new baseline can be created if all V&V activities are again successfully executed.

4 Consistency of the System

The described process uses the V&V activities to propagate changes across the system design. We claim to identify the parts of the system that are not affected by a change. In this paper we consider the functional aspect of the system within one perspective only. This means in particular, that "side-effects" over other aspects or perspectives are not considered. A typical example for these side-effects is change propagation through heat distribution. Due to a change on one part of the system other parts get that warm that they need additional cooling. The approach is designed in a way that these additional considerations can be added as needed by the system under development. The set of necessary perspectives can typically be limited in advance since the type of system often constitutes if e.g. EMC, weight or heat aspects have to be considered.

To be able to contain the change effects a defined set of V&V activities needs to be carried out. We use four different types of V&V cases that are necessary to comply with modern safety standards anyway (e.g. ISO 26262 [2] which basically evaluate each trace-link:

– The most important V&V activity is the verification of the correct derivation of requirements, i.e. that a requirement is correctly split up into sub-requirements. If changes in requirements cause this derive-relation between requirements to fail, other requirements need to be adapted as well. Using requirements for change propagation instead of connectors between components has the benefit that a criterion for stopping the change propagation is given. If the split-up is still (or again, after further modifications) correct, there is no further propagation in this part of the system. Therefore requirements build the backbone for change propagation. To prove the correct derivation of requirements a consistency check of these requirements is technically mandatory, since the split-up of inconsistent requirements is correct if the top-level and the sub-requirements result in a system that cannot be build.
– Also modifications in implementations or their components can result in change effect propagation. Therefore the implementation link between a component and an implementation needs to be verified. This check is limited to the interface, since the component itself does not contain any more information. This check is easily automatable.

- Similar to the implementation link, also the satisfy link (between requirement and component) needs to be checked. This analysis is also based in the interface.
- Due to the fact, that the structural system description in form of components is separated from the behavioral description in form of the implementations and requirements an additional V&V activity is needed that checks the relation of the requirement to the implementation. This is typically performed by testing.

The functional relations between the different components are extracted from the requirements. Whether one requirement change propagates towards other components is determined by the result of the test checking the correct derivation of the connected requirements. This step can be automated, see section 5. Therefore no explicit modeling of change propagation is necessary for the functional aspect. To be able to use the requirements for containing change effects they need to be stated in a blackbox manner, i.e. that they are just formulated on the interface of the attached component. This kind of requirements allows virtual integration [9] as needed by our approach. A formal prove that these prerequisites will contain any functional change effects will be published soon.

To guarantee that there is no influence by the change outside of the identified boundary it is assumed that all verification activities are accurate. Many of the mentioned verification activities can be automated using formal methods (see section 5) and therefore reach the desired accuracy. This especially applies for the analysis verifying the correct derivation of requirements which is responsible for the propagation of the changes using the requirements. To be able to get qualified or certified even the manually performed verification activities or test-cases need to have a reasonable level of confidence. The same level of confidence also applies for the propagation of the change.

5   Automating Change Impact Analysis

In the previous section we discussed how changes can propagate along the requirements through the system. Therefore, a reliable method of proving the requirements derivation is desired. This method can be realized using the formal requirements specification language (RSL) [10] and the entailment analysis [9].

The RSL is a formal but still human readable language to express requirements. It is based upon predefined patterns with attributes that can be filled by the requirements engineer and was designed to cover a whole range of different types of requirements.

A typical example of a pattern:

```
Whenever <EVENT> occurs <CONDITION> holds during [INTERVAL]
```

The formalization the the requirement "The emergency light shall provide illumination for at least 10 minutes after the emergency landing has been initiated" looks like:

```
Whenever EmergencyLandingInitiated occurs emergencyLight==ON holds
during [0s,600s]
```

The semantics of these patterns are described using timed automata.

The entailment analysis is a contract based virtual integration technique. Input are the specifications of the top-level component and a set of specifications of the direct sub-level components.

$$ent : r_{top} \times R_{sub} \to 0, 1 | R_{sub} \subseteq succ(r_{top})$$

The entailment relation is defined on the accepted traces T_a of the specifications [14]. Entailment is given, if the set of traces which are accepted by all sub-requirements is a subset of the set of accepted traces by the top-level requirement. In contrast, if there exists a trace that is accepted by all the sub-requirements but not from the top-level requirement the sub-requirements are not strict enough. These additional traces describe behavior which is forbidden by the specification of the top-level requirement and therefore the requirements breakdown is not correct.

$$ent(r, R) = \begin{cases} 1 & \text{iff } \bigcap_{r_s \in R} T_a(r_s) \subseteq T_a(r) \\ 0 & \text{iff } \bigcap_{r_s \in R} T_a(r_s) \nsubseteq T_a(r) \end{cases}$$

The entailment analysis fits the needs for the verification of derive links. It can be automatically proved that the behavior described by the derived requirements is in line with the top-level requirement. Consequently, if requirements are changed, but the derive-relation towards the top-level and towards the more refined requirements are still correct, the set of accepted traces is unchanged and a propagation of changes outside this boundary can be obviated.

6 Guided Compensation Candidate Selection by Shifting

Using the formalization and entailment analysis the change management process can be further automated. In some cases it is possible to identify a concrete element out of the set of compensation candidates which is a good choice to adapt to a change, because no implementation needs to be adapted but only requirements reformulated.

This guidance mechanism uses the fact that requirements are typically stated with some margins since the actual implementation might not be known at early phases of the development process. This typically includes timing or memory constraints as well as behavioral requirements. Furthermore, the usage of COTS (components-of-the-shelf) enforces this effect since externally purchased components commonly not match the requirements to 100% but are e.g. a little faster or provide additional features not needed at the time of component selection.

In terms of the entailment relation this means that the set of accepted traces by the top-level requirements which are not in the set of the sub-level requirements might be of significant size.

$$\Delta T_a(r_{top}, R) = T_a(r_{top}) - \bigcap_{r_s \in R} T_a(r_s) \neq \emptyset$$

If a requirement gets changed in the system, this buffer can be used to compensate the change not only locally but at a different location of the system. This can be achieved since ΔT_a can be shifted towards the upper level requirements and "collect more" traces that can be used at a chunk. This is realized by replacing the top-level requirement with the parallel composition of the sub-level requirements.

The parallel composition [20] of a set of requirements is also defined by the accepted traces. The composition includes only the traces that are compatible to all requirements.

$$T_a(r_1 \| r_2) = T_a(r_1) \cap T_a(r_2)$$

If entailment is given $(ent(r_{top}, R) = 1)$ it is obvious that the top-level requirement r_{top} can be replaced by the parallel composition $\|_{r \in R}$ without altering the result since entailment is always given this way:

$$ent(\|_{r_s \in R}, R) = 1$$
$$\Rightarrow \bigcap_{r_s \in R} T_a(r_s) \subseteq T_a(\|_{r_s \in R})$$
$$\Rightarrow \bigcap_{r_s \in R} T_a(r_s) \subseteq \bigcap_{r_s \in R} T_a(r_s)$$

While reducing the set of accepted traces for the top-level requirement by $\Delta T_a(r_{top}, R)$ a failed entailment relation using r_{top} as a sub-requirement might be successful again.

An example with timing requirements is depicted in figure 2. The requirements $R1$ to $R6$ represent time budgets, the arrows represent derive links. If requirement $R2$ is changed to $50ms$ because it was not possible to find an implementation that could fulfill this requirement the entailment relation $ent(R1, \{R2, R3, R4\})$ would fail (see figure 2(a)), causing additional changes in the system. In this case requirement $R4$ can be replaced by the parallel composition of $R5$ and $R6$, namely $30ms$, and the entailment relation $ent(R1, \{R2, R3, \{R5 \| R6\}\})$ is still valid (figure 2(b)).

Applying this technique over multiple levels and starting from more than one sub-requirement also non-trivial cases of shifting can be identified resulting only in requirement changes and no implementation changes. Furthermore, it is not necessary to re-validate the changed requirements.

7   Prototype

The tool landscape used for model-based development of safety-critical embedded systems is characterized by a high degree of distribution and heterogeneity [17]. Different development teams are working with different tools (for requirements management, verification, test, modeling, simulation, etc...) and different repositories on the final product. Therefore an integrated change management solution needs to overcome tool, supply-chain and data-format boundaries. Therefore, our prototype implementation "ReMain" uses an OSLC

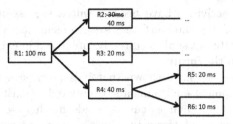

(a) Entailment fails because of changes in R2

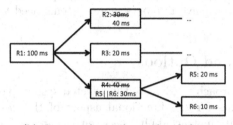

(b) Corrected entailment by shifting

Fig. 2. Simplified example using timing requirements

[3] based communication to access the different system artifacts across different repository locations. The tool consists of a server component handling the change requests and initiating the versioning of artifacts and a client that displays the affected system parts to the user and handles his input.

In the current demonstrator setup requirements can be stored in IBM DOORS or MS Excel, components are represented as EAST-ADL or AUTOSAR models and Implementations are read from Simulink models. The V&V cases are managed by the ReMain tool itself. Missing V&V cases which were necessary (see section 4) for our approach can be identified and generated. A dedicated V&V repository is planned for future versions.

The typical workflow should not be touched, so developers can automatically trigger the change management process by changing elements with their known modeling tool (e.g. Simulink or DOORS). The OSLC adapters of these tools will detect the change and send a modification event to the server part of the ReMain tool.

After receiving the modification event the ReMain server will perform the "local impact" activity. In particular, this includes the versioning of the connected links and V&V cases and setting their status to "suspect". The client will display only the part of the system that is currently affected by the change.

The status of the different V&V cases is represented by colored bubbles after the name of the element. The engineer gets a direct overview which activities still have to be performed and how much the change already propagated through the system. If formalized requirements are used the entailment analyzes can be executed automatically directly from the user interface of the ReMain client. If a verification activity fails, compensation candidates are highlighted.

If all verification activities have been executed successfully a new baseline can be created containing the consistent system elements. The baseline is currently stored externally but shall be directly integrated in existing configuration management tools in the future.

First evaluation results have shown that it is much easier to track changes in distributed development environments. Compared to existing approaches the decision how to react on changes can be made much faster. We use an ABS braking system as a test platform in which a saving in verification activities of more than 80% could be reached depending upon the artifacts that have been changed. For conclusive numbers more systems need to be analyzed in a systematic way.

8   Conclusion and Outlook

We presented an approach to identify the affected system parts during changes of system components for the functional aspect of the design. Using proper requirement formulation, traceability between system artifacts and a defined set of verification activities it is possible to reduce the re-certification effort of products since changes outside of the identified boundary have no effect on the system behavior.

In contrast to existing change management approaches the propagation of changes is not based on connected interfaces, but on the stated requirements of the system. This ensures semantically correct change effect propagation without the need of explicitly modeling the propagation. Furthermore, the set of system artifacts that need to be investigated during the process is reduced compared to approaches using the interconnections of components. Using formalized requirements the propagation process can be automated and even suggestions to possible good compensation candidates for failed V&V activities can be given. In the prototype implementation "ReMain" the process has been integrated in a highly distributed development environment consisting of commonly used development tools and formats like DOORS, Excel, Simulink, AUTOSAR and EAST-ADL.

Still, a couple of features are not yet discussed or implemented: Separating a requirement into an assumption and a promise (contract), the propagation of changes can even further reduced, also the compensation candidate selection is likely to benefit from this approach. Furthermore, the process needs to be extended to cover more than one perspective and more than the functional aspect. This includes the integration of allocation decisions. It is the aim to provide a change management solution where additional aspects (like EMC or heat distribution) can be added to cover the "side-effects" that are needed for the system under development. Also the accuracy of the approach needs to be investigated if the confidence in the executed V&V activities is low.

References

1. Arp-4761:aerospace recommended practice: Guidelines and methods for conducting the safety assessment process on civil airborne systems and equipment (1996)

2. Iso 26262: Road vehicles - functional safety (November 2011)
3. Oslc: Open services for lifecycle collaboration (December 2012),
   http://open-services.net/
4. atego: Atego workbench (November 2012),
   http://www.atego.com/products/atego-workbench/
5. Bengtsson, P., Bengtsson, P., Bengtsson, P.: Architecture-level modifiability analysis. Journal of Systems and Software 69 (2002)
6. Bohner, S.A.: Extending software change impact analysis into cots components. In: Proceedings of the 27th Annual NASA Goddard/IEEE Software Engineering Workshop, pp. 175–182 (December 2002)
7. Clarkson, P., Simons, C., Eckert, C.: Predicting change propagation in complex design. Journal of Mechanical Design(Transactions of the ASME) 126(5), 788–797 (2004)
8. CMMI Product Team: Cmmi for development, version 1.3: Improving processes for developing better products and services (November 2010), http://www.sei.cmu.edu/reports/10tr033.pdf
9. Damm, W., Hungar, H., Josko, B., Peikenkamp, T., Stierand, I.: Using contract-based component specifications for virtual integration testing and architecture design. In: Design, Automation Test in Europe Conference Exhibition (DATE), pp. 1–6 (March 2011)
10. Damm, W., Hungar, H., Henkler, S., Stierand, I., Josko, B., Reinkemeier, P., Baumgart, A., Büker, M., Gezgin, T., Ehmen, G., Weber, R.: SPES2020 Architecture Modeling. Tech. rep., OFFIS e.V. (2011)
11. Dassault Systems: Reqtify (November 2012),
    http://www.3ds.com/products/catia/portfolio/geensoft/reqtify/
12. Eckert, C., Clarkson, P., Zanker, W.: Change and customisation in complex engineering domains. Research in Engineering Design 15, 1–21 (2004), http://dx.doi.org/10.1007/s00163-003-0031-7
13. Gotel, O., Finkelstein, C.: An analysis of the requirements traceability problem. In: Proceedings of the First International Conference on Requirements Engineering, pp. 94–101 (April 1994)
14. Hungar, H.: Compositionality with strong assumptions. In: Nordic Workshop on Programming Theory, pp. 11–13. Mälardalen Real–Time Research Center (November 2011)
15. IBM: Rational change (November 2012),
    http://www-01.ibm.com/software/awdtools/change/
16. International Organization for Standardization: Iso 10007: Quality management systems guidelines for configuration management (June 2003)
17. Rajan, A., Wahl, T. (eds.): CESAR - Cost-efficient Methods and Processes for Safety-relevant Embedded Systems. Springer (2013) No. 978-3709113868
18. Ramesh, B., Powers, T., Stubbs, C., Edwards, M.: Implementing requirements traceability: a case study. In: Proceedings of the Second IEEE International Symposium on Requirements Engineering, pp. 89–95 (March 1995)
19. Ryder, B.G., Tip, F.: Change impact analysis for object-oriented programs. In: Proceedings of the 2001 ACM SIGPLAN-SIGSOFT Workshop on Program Analysis for Software Tools and Engineering, PASTE 2001, pp. 46–53. ACM, New York (2001), http://doi.acm.org/10.1145/379605.379661
20. SPEEDS: SPEEDS core meta-model syntax and draft semantics, SPEEDS D.2.1.c (2007)

Formal Deadlock Analysis of SpecC Models Using Satisfiability Modulo Theories

Che-Wei Chang and Rainer Dömer

Center for Embedded Computer Systems
University of California, Irvine
Irvine, CA 92697-2625, USA

Abstract. For a system-on-chip design which may be composed of multiple processing elements running in parallel, improper execution order and communication assignment may lead to problematic consequences, and one of the consequences could be deadlock. In this paper, we propose an approach to abstracting SpecC-based system models for formal analysis using satisfiability modulo theories (SMT). Based on the language execution semantics, our approach abstracts the timing relations between the time intervals of the behaviors in the design. We then use a SMT solver to check if there are any conflicts among those timing relations. If a conflict is detected, our tool will read the unsatisfiable model generated by the SMT solver and report the cause of the conflict to the user. We demonstrate our approach on a JPEG encoder design model.

1 Introduction

An embedded system design can be implemented in many ways, and a typical design usually consists of hardware and software components running on one or multiple processing elements. In such a design, the partitioned components on different processing elements are executed in parallel. To make sure the data dependency and the execution order is correct, communication between components synchronizes the execution of components on different processing elements. In system-level description languages (SLDLs), like SpecC and SystemC, the communication between components is implemented as channels, and multiple types of channel are provided in the SLDLs to satisfy different kinds of communication and synchronization requirements.

Channels provide a convenient way to communicate among multiple processing elements. However, misusing the type of channel or setting incorrect buffer size in a channel can lead to deadlock situations, and it is difficult to determine the cause of deadlocks when the design is complex. In this paper we propose a method to perform static analysis and detect deadlocks in the design automatically. Based on the SpecC execution semantics, our approach can extract the timing relations between behaviors in the design, and then analyse these with Satisfiability Modulo Theories (SMT) to detect any conflicts. To accelerate the debugging process, our approach also reports the causes of the deadlock to the user if a deadlock situation is found.

G. Schirner et al. (Eds.): IESS 2013, IFIP AICT 403, pp. 116–127, 2013.

This report is organized as follows: in Section 2 we list the related works in formal validation of SLDLs. In Section 3, we briefly introduce SpecC SLDL and Satisfiability Modulo Theories. In Section 4, we describe our proposed approach in detail, including the assumptions and limitations at this point. Also, we illustrate the conversion from SpecC model to SMT assertions. In the last two sections, we demonstrate our approach with a JPEG encoder model and sum up with a conclusion and future work.

2   Related Work

A lot of research has been conducted in the area of verification and validation of system-level designs. We can see that many researchers convert the semantics or behavioral model of the SLDL into another well-defined representation and make use of existing tools to validate the extracted properties. In [3] and [4], a method to generate a state machine from SystemC and using existing tools for test case generation is proposed; in [5] and [6], a SystemC design is mapped into semantics of UPPAAL time automata and the resulting model can be checked by using UPPAAL model checker; [7] proposed an approach to translate SystemC models into a Petri-net based representation for embedded systems(PRES+) which can then be used for model checking. In [8], a SystemC design is represented in the form of predictive synchronization dependency graph (PSDG) and extended Petri Net, and an approach combining simulation and static analysis to detect deadlocks is proposed. [9] focuses on translating a SystemC design into a state transition system, i.e. the Kripke structure, so that existing symbolic model checking techniques can be applied on SystemC.

3   Preliminaries

3.1   SpecC SLDL

SpecC [1] is a SLDL and is defined as extension of the ANSI-C programming language. It is a formal notation intended for the specification and design of digital embedded systems, including hardware and software portions. SpecC supports concepts essential for embedded systems design, including behavioral and structural hierarchy, concurrency, communication, synchronization, state transitions, exception handling, and timing. The execution semantics of the SpecC language are defined by use of a time interval formalism [2].

3.2   Satisfiability Modulo Theories

Satisfiability (SAT) is the problem of determining if an assignment of the Boolean variables exists, that makes the outcome of a given Boolean formula true. Satisfiability Modulo Theories (SMT) checks whether a given logic formula is satisfiable over one or more theories. Unlike the formulas in Boolean SAT which are built from Boolean variables and composed using logical operations, the satisfiability of formula like $(x + 2y \leq 7) \wedge (2x - y \leq 10)$ can be solved by combining a SAT solver with a theory solver for linear arithmetic. The problem to be solved by SMT can be described with richer language (arithmetic and inequality in the example above), and the meaning of the formula will be captured by the supporting theories.

Our proposed approach abstracts the timing relations among the behavior and channel activities in the SpecC model, and then describes the relations in the form of inequality expressed in SMT-LIB2 language. After the formulas are generated, a SMT solver is then used to solve the formula and check if it is satisfiable. In our implementation, we use Z3 theorem prover developed at Microsoft Research as our SMT solver. For more detailed information about SMT-LIB2 language and Z3 theorem prover, please refer to [11] and [10].

4   From SpecC to SMT Assertions

In this section, we first introduce the supported SpecC execution types in our approach and their execution semantics.

4.1   Execution

The basic structure of a SpecC behavior includes port declaration, a *main* method, local variable and function declaration (optional), and sub-behavior instantiation (optional). The supported SpecC behavior models in our tool can be categorized into the following two types:

Leaf Behavior: A behavior is called leaf-behavior if it is purely composed of local variable(s), local function(s) and a *main* method, and there is no sub-behavior instantiation in the behavior. In the example shown in *Figure* 4, behavior *ReadPic* and *Block*1 are leaf behaviors.

Non-Leaf Behavior: A behavior is called non-leaf behavior if it is purely composed of sub-behavior instance(s) and a main method. For non-leaf behaviors, all statements in the *main* method are limited to statements specifying the execution type of the behavior and function calls to sub-behavior instances. In the example shown in *Figure* 4, behavior *DUT*, *Read*, *JPEG_encoder* and *Pic2Blk* are non-leaf behaviors.

Note that for simplicity our tool does not support models which do not fit into these two categories, and the execution types we are going to describe in this section is for non-leaf behaviors only since sub-behavior instantiation can only occur in non-leaf behavior.

In SpecC, the sub-behavior or sub-channel instantiation is regarded as a statement of function call to a method of the sub-behavior or sub-channel. To specify the execution time of a statement, for each statement s in a SpecC program, a time interval $\langle T_{start}(s), T_{end}(s) \rangle$ is defined. $T_{start}(s)$ and $T_{end}(s)$ represent the start and end times of the statement execution respectively, and the following condition must hold: $T_{start}(s) < T_{end}(s)$

The execution time of an instantiated behavior s $T_{exe}(s)$ is defined as $T_{exe}(s)$ = $T_{end}(s)$ - $T_{start}(s)$. For a statement S consisting of a set of sub-behavior instances $\langle s_{sub\_1}, s_{sub\_2}, s_{sub\_3}, ... s_{sub\_n} \rangle$, the following condition holds:

$$\forall i \in \{1, 2, 3, ... n\}, T_{start}(S) \leq T_{start}(s_{sub\_i})$$
$$T_{end}(S) \geq T_{end}(s_{sub\_i})$$

The type of execution defines the relation between the T_{start} and T_{end} of the behavior instance under the current behavior, and it is specified in the *main* method of the behavior. In the following, four types of supported execution are described, which are *Sequential*, *Parallel*, *Pipelined*, and *Loop* execution. *Figure 1* shows an example of specifying *Sequential*, *Parallel* and *Pipelined* execution in a SpecC behavior. *Loop* execution is not a explicitly defined behavioral execution in SpecC, but we can regard it as a special case of *Pipelined* execution with only one instance inside.

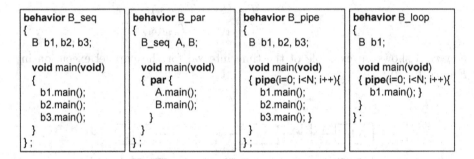

Fig. 1. Four Supported Execution Types

Sequential Execution. *Sequential* execution of statements is defined by ordered time intervals that do not overlap. Formally, for a statement S consisting of a sequence of sub-statements $\langle s_1, s_2, ... s_n \rangle$, the time interval of statement S includes all time intervals of the sub-statements, and the following conditions hold:

$$\forall i \in \{1, 2, ..., n\}, T_{start}(S) \leq T_{start}(s_i)$$
$$T_{start}(s_i) < T_{end}(s_i)$$
$$T_{end}(s_i) \leq T_{end}(S)$$
$$\forall i \in \{1, 2, ..., n-1\}, T_{end}(s_i) \leq T_{start}(s_{i+1})$$

Note that sequential statements are not necessarily executed continuously. Gaps may exist between T_{end} and T_{start} of two consecutive statements, as well as between the T_{start} (T_{end}) of the sub-statement and the T_{start} (T_{end}) of the statement in which the sub-statement is called. *Figure 2* shows an example of the time interval for the sequential execution in *Figure 1*.

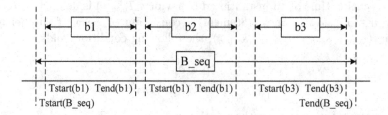

Fig. 2. Time interval for sequential execution

Parallel Execution. *Parallel* execution of statements can be specified by *par* or *pipe* statements. In particular, the time intervals of the sub-statements invoked by a *par* statement are the same. Formally, for a statement S consisting of concurrent sub-statements $\langle s_1, s_2, ... s_n \rangle$, the following conditions hold:

$$\forall i \in \{1, 2, ..., n\}, T_{start}(S) = T_{start}(s_i)$$
$$T_{end}(S) = T_{end}(s_i)$$
$$T_{start}(s_i) < T_{end}(s_i)$$

Figure 3 shows an example of the time interval for the parallel execution in *Figure* 1.

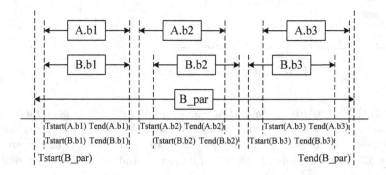

Fig. 3. Time interval for parallel execution

Pipelined and Loop Execution. *Pipelined* execution of statements is a special form of concurrent execution. The syntax of *pipe* statement in SpecC is illustrated in *Figure* 1, where N in the example specifies the number of iterations. Formally, for a statement S consisting of sub-statements $\langle s_1, s_2, ... s_n \rangle$ executed for m iterations in pipelined manner, let $s_{i.j}$ represents the j-th iteration of the execution of statement s_i. Then the following conditions hold:

$$\forall i, x \in \{1, 2, ..., n\}, \ j, y \in \{1, 2, ..., m\} :$$
$$T_{start}(s_{i \cdot j}) < T_{end}(s_{i \cdot j}),$$
$$T_{start}(s_{i \cdot j}) = T_{start}(s_{x \cdot y}), \quad if \ \ i + j = x + y$$
$$T_{end}(s_{i \cdot j}) = T_{end}(s_{x \cdot y}), \quad if \ \ i + j = x + y$$
$$T_{end}(s_{i \cdot j}) \leq T_{start}(s_{x \cdot y}), \quad if \ \ i + j < x + y$$

Loop execution is not defined explicitly in the behavioral execution semantics of SpecC, but it can be regarded as a special case of *Pipelined* execution with only one sub-statement.

Note that in the definition of *pipelined* statements the iteration number could be infinity if the number is not specified, i.e. no range specification after the statement *pipe*. However, to simplify the static analysis in this proposed method, at this point, the number of iterations has to be a finite integer and explicitly specified in the model.

Please be aware that for now our proposed method does not support all types of execution and communication defined in SpecC. Full support of SpecC is part of our future work.

4.2 Communication

In SpecC, the communication between two behaviors can be implemented by port variable, channel communication, or by accessing global variables. Since right now the goal of our approach is to detect deadlocks in the design, the communication implemented with port variables and global variables are not taken into consideration because they will not lead to deadlock situation in the design.

Multiple types of channels are defined in SpecC. These include semaphore, mutex, barrier, token, queue, handshake, and double handshake. In this paper, we use queue channel with different buffer sizes to model the supported channel communication in our approach. For example, to model the blocking characteristics of handshake channels, we use a queue channel with one element buffer and zero element buffer to implement the handshake and double handshake channel.

To clearly identify the communication between behaviors, we also impose some limitations on the communication between behaviors. First, to make the data dependency between behaviors clear, we limit the communication between behaviors to point-to-point, i.e. every instantiated channel in the design is dedicated to the communication between a pair of sender and receiver. Second, to abstract the channel activity without looking into too much detail of the behavior model, the function call of the sending (receiving) function to (from) a certain channel can only be executed once in the *main* method of a behavior, i.e. a function call to channel communication in any type of iteration (for or while loop) in the *main* method of a behavior model is not supported. For the case that the output of a behavior has to be separated into multiple parts and sent to another behavior, the sending (receiving) function calls have to be wrapped in a behavior and executed in loop execution by using *pipe* statements.

Figure 4 shows an example of the situation described above. In this example, a small picture of size 24-by-16 pixels is read and encoded into a JPEG file. Since the input image block size for a JPEG encoding process is eight-by-eight pixels, the picture has to be separated into 6 sub-blocks. The raw picture is read into the topmost behavior *DUT* by sub-behavior *Read*, then behavior *Pic2Blk* divides the picture into six 8-by-8-pixel blocks and sends the blocks to JPEG encoder model. Inside behavior *Pic2Blk*, behavior *Block1* is instantiated in a loop execution. Behavor *Block1* fetches the block from the raw picture according to the current iteration number, and calls the sending function to send the data to JPEG encoder through channel *Q*. In this example, channel *Q* is a queue channel with two buffers and each buffer is an integer array of size 64.

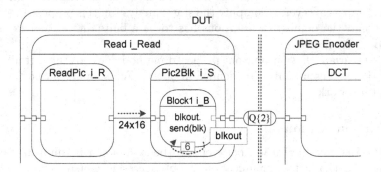

Fig. 4. Behavior *Read* in the JPEG encoder SpecC model

Similar to the time interval $\langle T_{start}, T_{end} \rangle$ defined for the execution of a statement, a time stamp set $\langle T_{sent}(Q), T_{rcvd}(Q) \rangle$ is also defined for each channel communication activity between behaviors, where T_{sent} represents the time stamp when the the execution of sending a data to the channel finishes, and T_{rcvd} represents the time stamp when the execution of receiving data from the channel finishes. Based on the definition of T_{sent} and T_{rcvd}, for a queue channel Q communication through which m data items are transferred, the relation between time stamps $T_{sent}(Q_i)$ and $T_{rcvd}(Q_i)$, where Q_i represents the i-th data transfer through channel Q, should hold:

$$\forall i \in \{0, 1, 2, ..., m - 1\}, T_{sent}(Q_i) \leq T_{rcvd}(Q_i)$$
$$\forall i \in \{0, 1, 2, ..., m - 2\}, T_{sent}(Q_i) < T_{sent}(Q_{i+1})$$
$$T_{rcvd}(Q_i) < T_{rcvd}(Q_{i+1})$$
$$\forall i \in \{0, 1, 2, ..., m - n - 1\}, T_{rcvd}(Q_i) \leq T_{sent}(Q_{i+n})$$

where n is the buffer depth of channel Q.

4.3   From Time Stamps to SMT Assertions

Figure 5 shows the flow of our proposed method. First, the SpecC model is converted into a design representation called SpecC internal representation(SIR).

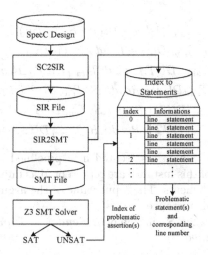

Fig. 5. The flow of converting a SpecC model into SMT assertions and deadlock analysis with the Z3 SMT solver

The next step is to traverse the internal representation structure and generate the assertions corresponding to the statements in the design. At the same time, an index-to-statement record is created which links the generated assertions to the statements in the design. After the assertions and records are generated, we use the Z3 theorem prover to check if there is any conflict in the set that makes the equations unsatisfiable. If there are any, Z3 will report the indices of assertions leading to the conflict, and our tool can use the indices to access the record and report the problem information to the user. In the following part of this section, we use the model shown in *Figure 4* as an example, and illustrate the corresponding assertions for the model.

Execution to SMT Assertions: In our proposed method, we use uninterpreted functions in SMT-LIB2 language to represent every time stamp in the model, and convert the timing relations between those stamps into assertions. For an uninterpreted function, the user can define the number of arguments, the data type of argument, the data type of the return value, and its interpretation. In our method, the return value of an uninterpreted function is seen as the value of a time stamp, and the argument(s) of the function is (are) used to specify the number of times a behavior instance is executed in a pipelined structure or a loop. For a behavior instance, which is not in a pipelined or loop execution, the time stamps of this instance are represented as uninterpreted functions with no argument since the behavior will only be executed once.

For example, for instance i_S in behavior *Read* in *Figure 4*, the following assertions will be generated:

$(declare - fun\ T_{start}DUT.i\_Read.i\_S\ ()\ Int)$

$(declare - fun\ T_{end}DUT.i\_Read.i\_S\ ()\ Int)$

$(assert\ (<=\ T_{start}DUT.i\_Read\ T_{start}DUT.i\_Read.i\_S))$

$(assert\ (<=\ T_{end}DUT.i\_Read.i\_S\ T_{end}DUT.i\_Read))$

$(assert\ (<\ T_{start}DUT.i\_Read.i\_S\ T_{end}DUT.i\_Read.i\_S))$

$(assert\ (<=\ T_{end}DUT.i\_Read.i\_R\ T_{start}DUT.i\_Read.i\_S))$

For a behavior instance, which is executed in a pipelined or loop for multiple times, the time stamps of this instance are represented as uninterpreted functions with one or multiple arguments. The input value of the argument is the number of execution times of this instance.

For example, for instance $S1$ in behavior *Sender* in *Figure* 4, the following assertions will be generated:

$(declare - fun\ T_{start}DUT.i\_Read.i\_S.i\_B\ (Int)\ Int)$

$(declare - fun\ T_{end}DUT.i\_Reae.i\_S.i\_B\ (Int)\ Int)$

$(assert\ (forall\ ((I0\ Int))\ (=>\ (and\ (>=\ I0\ 0)\ (<=\ I0\ 5))$

$\quad (<=\ T_{start}DUT.i\_Read.i\_S$

$\qquad (T_{start}DUT.i\_Read.i\_S.i\_B\ I0)))))$

$(assert\ (forall\ ((I0\ Int))\ (=>\ (and\ (>=\ I0\ 0)\ (<=\ I0\ 4))$

$\quad (<=\ (T_{end}DUT.i\_Read.i\_S.i\_B\ I0)$

$\qquad (T_{start}DUT.i\_Read.i\_S.i\_B\ (+\ I0\ 1))))))$

Communication to SMT Assertions: In our approach, the time stamp of every channel activity is represented as an uninterpreted function with one argument, and the input value of the argument is the number of execution times of channel activity. For example, for channel Q in behavior DUT in *Figure* 4, the following assertions will be generated:

$$\forall i \in \{0, 1, ..., 5\}, \quad T_{sent}DUT.Q(i) \leq T_{rcvd}DUT.Q(i)$$
$$\forall i \in \{0, 1, ..., 3\}, \quad T_{rcvd}DUT.Q(i) \leq T_{sent}DUT.Q(i+2)$$

Our tool will also generate the equality for the time stamp of the channel activity and the time stamp of the function call to the interface of the corresponding channel. For example, the following assertion will be generated for the channel accessing function call *blkout* in *Figure* 4:

$$\forall i \in \{0, 1, ..., 5\},$$
$$T_{sent}DUT.q(i) = T_{sent}DUT.i\_Read.i\_S.i\_B.blkout(i)$$
$$T_{start}DUT.i\_Read.i\_S.i\_B(i) \leq T_{sent}DUT.i\_Read.i\_S.i\_B.blkout(i)$$
$$T_{sent}DUT.i\_Read.i\_S.i\_B.blkout(i) \leq T_{end}DUT.i\_Read.i\_S.i\_B(i)$$

For space limitations, we can only list a portion of the assertions as examples. Other assertions are generated based on the timing relations we described in *Section* 4.1 and *Section* 4.2.

During the assertion creation, a table named *index-to-statement* will also be generated. For every assertion generated by our tool, an identical index is given to the assertion and the information about the corresponding statement that is stored in the entry addressed by that index. Take assertion $T_{rcvd}DUT.Q(i) \leq T_{sent}DUT.Q(i+2)$ listed above as an example. This assertion is generated because channel Q is instantiated in behavior DUT and its depth is set to two. Therefore, in the entry addressed by the index of this assertion, the information of the statement specifying the depth of the channel is stored.

5   Experiments

In this section, we demonstrate our proposed method with a JPEG encoder SpecC model. In this example, the JPEG encoder is asked to encode five subframes of size eight-by-eight pixels from a raw picture. *Figure* 6 shows two different implementations of the SpecC JPEG encoder model.

In the JPEG encoder, every subframe will be encoded in three steps, two-dimensional discrete cosine transform (DCT), quantization, and Huffman encoding. For every subframe, these three encoding steps have to be executed in order. In our SpecC model, three behaviors D, Q, and H are implemented to perform the discrete cosine transform, quantization, and Huffman coding of JPEG encoding, respectively.

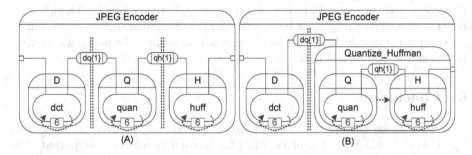

Fig. 6. Two examples of JPEG encoder SpecC model. Example(A) is a design without deadlock, while Example(B) will incur a deadlock situation.

As shown in *Figure* 6(A), behavior D, Q, and H are executed in parallel fashion. To make sure these three steps are executed in correct order, two queue channels are used to transfer the intermediate encoding data between these three behaviors, instead of using port variable connections. In model (B), sub-behavior Q and H are wrapped into a behavior *Quantize_Huff* and executed in sequential manner. The problem in model (B) is that behavior Q will halt forever after the first two iterations of its sub-behavior *quan*. In this composition, behavior *quan* will be executed six times before the execution of behavior Q finishes, but the execution will stop because the queue channel between behavior *quan* and behavior *huff* becomes full after the first two data sets are generated. Since behavior H can only be executed after the execution of behavior Q finishes, the sub-behavior *huff* cannot be executed to empty the queue channel *qh*.

We have used our tool to analyse both models. *Table* 1 shows the analysis results of the two models.

Table 1. Static SMT analysis results for model (A) and (B)

Design	*#of Assertions*	*Time*	*Satisfiability*	Error Report
Model-(A)	187	4.94s	SAT	N/A
Model-(B)	192	1.39s	UNSAT	Type: QUEUE Line[16]: Channel[qh] Type: SEQ Line[23]: Instance[Q] Line[24]: Instance[H] Type: LOOP Line[58]: Behavior[Q] Line[60]: Instance[quan] ...

In *Table* 1, the value in *Line* represents the line number of the statement in the SpecC model, and *Type* shows the type of information stored in the entry. For example, the *Type* : *SEQ* in this table shows that behavior instance Q and H are executed in sequential manner, and Q is executed before H. Though for now the error report might not be intuitive for the unfamiliar user to understand what led to the deadlock, the model designer who developed the model will easily recognize the deadlock situation.

6   Conclusion

In this paper we have proposed an approach to statically analyze deadlocks in SpecC models using a SMT solver. After the introduction of four supported execution types and queue channel communication in our tool, we have described our approach in detail by showing how to extract timing relations between time stamps according to SpecC execution semantics, and have illustrated the conversion from timing relations to SMT-LIB2 assertions. Finally we demonstrated our implementation with a JPEG encoder model, and showed that our approach is capable of detecting the deadlock in the model and reporting useful diagnostic information to the user.

At this point, this research is still far from complete and there is a lot of future work to do. Future work includes expanding the support for larger models, and extending our research to cover more design verification problems. For now our implementation only supports a confined set of SpecC models and leaves some important features of SpecC unsupported, such as FSM composition. In the future we will improve our tool so that it can extract the timing relations from a control-flow graph and represent the relations with SMT-LIB2 assertions. Except for the deadlock analysis, we also found that SMT solver might be suitable for time constraint analysis. We will keep exploring possible applications and make this approach more general in the future.

Acknowledgment. This work has been supported in part by funding from the National Science Foundation (NSF) under research grant NSF Award #0747523. The authors thank the NSF for the valuable support. Any opinions, findings, and conclusions or recommendations expressed in this material are those of the authors and do not necessarily reflect the views of the National Science Foundation.

References

1. Dömer, R., Gerstlauer, A., Gajski, D.: SpecC Language Reference Manual Version 2.0, http://www.cecs.uci.edu/~specc/reference/SpecC_LRM_20.pdf
2. Fujita, M., Nakamura, H.: The Standard SpecC Language. In: Proceedings of the International Symposium on System Synthesis, Montreal (October 2001)
3. Habibi, A., Moinudeen, H., Tahar, S.: Generating Finite State Machines from SystemC. In: Design, Automation and Test in Europe, pp. 76–81 (2006)
4. Habibi, A., Tahar, S.: An Approach for the Verification of SystemC Designs Using AsmL. In: Peled, D.A., Tsay, Y.-K. (eds.) ATVA 2005. LNCS, vol. 3707, pp. 69–83. Springer, Heidelberg (2005)
5. Herber, P., Fellmuth, J., Glesner, S.: Model Checking SystemC Designs Using Timed Automata. In: Int. Conf. on HW/SW Codesign and System Synthesis. ACM Press (2008)
6. Herber, P., Pockrandt, M., Glesner, S.: Transforming SystemC Transaction Level Models into UPPAAL timed automata. In: 2011 9th IEEE/ACM International Conference on Formal Methods and Models for Codesign (MEMOCODE), pp. 161–170 (2011)
7. Karlsson, D., Eles, P., Peng, Z.: Formal verification of SystemC Designs using a Petri-Net based Representation. In: DATE, pp. 1228–1233 (2006)
8. Chou, C.-N., Ho, Y.-S., Huan, C.H.C.-Y.: Formal Deadlock Checking on High-Level SystemC Designs. In: 2010 IEEE/ACM International Conference on Computer-Aided Design (ICCAD), pp. 794–799 (2010)
9. Chou, C.-N., Ho, Y.-S., Huan, C.H.C.-Y.: Symbolic Model Checking on SystemC Design. In: Proceedings of the 49th Annual Design Automation Conference, DAC 2012, pp. 327–333 (2012)
10. Z3 theorem prover, http://z3.codeplex.com/
11. Cok, D.R.: The SMT-LIB v2 Language and Tools: A Tutorial, http://www.grammatech.com/resources/smt/SMTLIBTutorial.pdf

Automated Functional Verification of Application Specific Instruction-set Processors*

Marcela Šimková, Zdeněk Přikryl, Zdeněk Kotásek, and Tomáš Hruška

Faculty of Information Technology, Brno University of Technology, Czech Republic
{isimkova,iprikryl,kotasek,hruska}@fit.vutbr.cz

Abstract. Nowadays highly competitive market of consumer electronics is very sensitive to the time it takes to introduce a new product. However, the ever-growing complexity of application specific instruction-set processors (ASIPs) which are inseparable parts of nowadays complex embedded systems makes this task even more challenging. In ASIPs, it is necessary to test and verify significantly bigger portion of logic, tricky timing behaviour or specific corner cases in a defined time schedule. As a consequence, the gap between the proposed verification plan and the quality of verification tasks is widening due to this time restriction. One way how to solve this issue is using faster, efficient and cost-effective methods of verification. The aim of this paper is to introduce an automated generation of SystemVerilog verification environments (testbenches) for verification of ASIPs. Results show that our approach reduces the time and effort needed for implementation of testbenches significantly and is robust enough to detect also well-hidden bugs.

1 Introduction

The core of current complex embedded systems is usually formed by one or more processors. The use of processors brings advantages of a programmable solution mainly the possibility of a software change after the product is shifted to the market.

The types of processors that are used within embedded systems are typically determined by an application itself. One can use *general purpose processors* (GPPs) or *application specific instruction-set processors* (ASIPs) or their combination. The advantages of GPPs are their availability on the market and an acceptable price because they are manufactured in millions or more. On the other hand, their performance, power consumption and area are worse in comparison to ASIPs that are highly optimised for a given task and therefore, have much better parameters.

However, one needs a powerful and easy-to-use tools for the ASIPs design, testing and verification as well as tools for their programming and simulation. These tools often use *architecture description languages* (ADLs) [6] for the description of a processor.

---

* This work was supported by the European Social Fund (ESF) in the project Excellent Young Researchers at BUT (CZ.1.07/2.3.00/30.0039), the IT4Innovations Centre of Excellence (CZ.1.05/1.1.00/02.0070), Brno Ph.D. Talent Scholarship Programme, the BUT FIT project FIT-S-11-1, research plan no. MSM0021630528, and the research funding MPO ČR no. FR-TI1/038.

G. Schirner et al. (Eds.): IESS 2013, IFIP AICT 403, pp. 128–138, 2013.

ADL allows automated generation of the programming tools such as C/C++ compiler or assembler, simulation tools such as *instruction-set simulator* (IIS) or profiler. Moreover, the representation of the processor in *hardware description language* (HDL) such as VHDL or Verilog is generated from this description. If the designer wants to change a design somehow (add a new feature, fix a bug), he or she just change the processor description and all tools as well as the hardware description are re-generated. This allows really fast design space exploration [4] within processor design phases. Examples of ADLs are LISA [2], ArchC [9], nML [1] or CodAL [3].

In some cases, when a special functional unit is added for instance a modular arithmetic unit (in cryptography processors) additional verification steps should be performed. The reason is that description of instructions can be different for simulation/hardware and for the C compiler (e.g. LISA language has separate sections describing the same feature for the simulator and for the C compiler). In this case, one should verify that the generated hardware can be programmed by the generated C compiler. In other words, the C compiler should be verified with respects to the features of a processor. Therefore, it is highly desirable to have a tool that automatically generates verification environments and allows checking all above mentioned properties.

In this paper we propose an innovative approach for automated generation of verification environments which is easily applicable in the development cycle of processors. As a development environment we utilise the Codasip framework [3] but the main principles are applicable in other environments as well. In order to verify a hardware representation of processors with respect to the generated C/C++ compiler we decided to apply functional verification approach as it offers perfect scalability and speed.

The following section shows the state of the art in the development of processors and description of verification techniques which are typically used in this field. Afterwards, the Codasip framework is described in Section 3. Our approach is introduced in Section 4, and Section 5 presents experimental results. In the end of this paper, the conclusions and our plans for future research are mentioned.

2 Verification in the Development Cycle of Processors

The following subsections introduce verification techniques used within processor design phases as well as research projects and companies dealing with processor design.

2.1 Verification Approaches

For verification of processors a variety of options exists: (*i*) formal verification, (*ii*) simulation and testing, and (*iii*) functional verification. However, their nature and preconditions for the speed, user expertise and complexity of the verification process are often a limiting factor.

Formal verification is an approach based on an exhaustive exploration of the state space of a system, hence it is potentially able to formally prove correctness of a system. The main disadvantages of this method are state space explosion for real-world systems and the need to provide formal specifications of behaviour of the system which makes this method often hard to use.

Simulation and testing, on the other hand, are based on observing the behaviour of the verified system in a limited number of situations, thus it provides only a partial guarantee of correctness of the system. However, because tests focus mainly on the typical use of the system and on corner cases, this is often sufficient. Moreover, writing tests is usually faster and easier than writing formal specifications.

Functional verification is a simulation-based method that does not prove correctness of a system but uses advanced verification techniques for reaching verification closure. Verification environments (or testbenches) are typically implemented in some hardware verification language, e.g. in SystemVerilog, OpenVera or *e*. During verification, a set of constrained-random test vectors is typically generated and the behaviour of the system for these vectors is compared with the behaviour specified by a provided *reference model* (which is called *scoreboarding*). In order to measure progress in functional verification (using coverage metrics), it is necessary to (*i*) find a way how to generate test vectors that cover critical parts of the state space, and (*ii*) maximise the number of vectors tested. To facilitate the process of verification and to formally express the intended behaviour, internal synchronisation, and expected operations of the system, *assertions* may be used.

All above mentioned features are effective in checking the correctness of the system and maximising the efficiency of the overall verification process. The popularity of functional verification is claimed by the existence of various verification methodologies, with OVM (*Open Verification Methodology*) [5] and UVM (*Universal Verification Methodology*) [5] being mostly used. They offer a free library of basic classes and examples implemented in SystemVerilog and define how to build easily reusable and scalable verification environments.

2.2 Design and Verification of Processors

There exist several research projects or companies dealing with processor design using ADLs. One of them is an open-source *ArchC* project [9]. A processor is described using ArchC language and the semantics of instructions is described using SystemC constructions [11]. All programming tools as well as IIS can be generated from the description in ArchC. The generation of a hardware representation is currently under development and there is no mention of verifying them so far.

Synopsys company offers *Processor Designer* [8] for designing processors. It uses LISA language. The programming tools, ISS as well as the HDL representation can be generated from the processor description. However, they do not provide any automatically generated verification environments. As mentioned in Section 1, instructions are described in two ways, the first one is used by the generator of the C compiler and the second one is used by ISS. Therefore, if the descriptions of instructions for ISS and the C compiler are not equivalent, then there is no automatic way how to detect it. In that case, C compiler cannot program the target processor properly.

Target company uses an enhanced version of nML language for the description of a processor microarchitecture [12]. The C compiler and ISS can be generated from the description of a processor as well as the HDL representation. According to the web presentation, the verification environment consists of a test program generator. It emits programs in assembly language (note that the assembly language is processor specific).

The generated test program is loaded by the ISS and a third party RTL simulator which evaluates the generated HDL representation. The program is executed and after the testing phase is completed, results are compared. If they are equal, then the test passed, otherwise an inconsistency is found and it needs to be investigated further. Nevertheless, a generator of test programs in some high-level language like C or C++ is missing. Therefore, the C compiler itself is not verified with respect to the processor.

When focusing on automated generation of verification environments in general (not necessary for processors), there already exist some commercial solutions which are quite close to our work. One example is *Pioneer NTB* from *Synopsys* [10] which enables to generate SystemVerilog and OpenVera testbenches for different hardware designs written in VHDL or Verilog with inbuilt support for third-party simulators, constrained-random stimulus generation, assertions and coverage. Another example is *SystemVerilog Frameworks Template Generator* (SVF-TG) [7] which assists in creating and maintaining verification environments in SystemVerilog according to the *Verification Methodology Manual* (VMM).

3 Codasip Framework

The Codasip Framework is a product of the Codasip company and represents a development environment for ASIPs. As the main description language it utilises ADL called CodAL [3]. It is based on the C language and has been developed by the Codasip company in cooperation with Brno University of Technology, Faculty of Information Technology. All mainstream types of processor architectures such as RISC, CISC or VLIW can be described.

The CodAL language allows two kinds of descriptions. In the early stage of the design space exploration a designer creates only the instruction-set (*the instruction-accurate description*). It contains information about instruction decoders, the semantics of instructions and resources of the processor. Using this description, programming tools such as a C/C++ compiler and simulation tools can be properly generated. The C/C++ compiler is based on LLVM platform [13].

As soon as the instruction-set is stabilised a designer can add information about processor microarchitecture (*cycle-accurate description*) which allows generating programming tools (without the C/C++ compiler), RTL simulators and the HDL representation of the processor (in VHDL or Verilog). As a result, two models of the same processor on different level of abstraction exist.

It is important to point out that in our generated verification environments the instruction-accurate description is taken as a golden (reference) model and the cycle-accurate description is verified against it.

The instruction-accurate description can be transformed into several formal models which are used for capturing particular features of a processor. Formal models which are used in our solution are *decoding trees* in case of instruction decoders and *abstract syntax trees* in case of semantics of instructions [14]. All formal models are optimised and then normalised into the abstract syntax tree representation that can be transformed automatically into different implementations (mainly in C/C++ languages). The generated code together with the additional code (it represents resources of processor such as registers or memories) forms ISS.

It should be noted that some parts of the generated code can be reused further in the golden model for verification purposes (more information in Section 4). At the same time as the golden model is generated, connections to the verification environment are established via the *direct programming interface* (DPI) in SystemVerilog. Automated generation of golden models reduces the time needed for implementation of verification environments significantly. Of course, a designer can always rewrite or complement the golden model manually.

The cycle-accurate description of a processor can be transformed into the same formal models as in case of the instruction-accurate description. Besides them, the processor microarchitecture is captured using *activation graphs*. In case of the cycle-accurate description, the formal models are normalised into the *component* representation. Each component represents either a construction in the CodAL language such as arithmetic operators or processor resources or it represents an entity at the higher level of abstraction such as the instruction decoder or a functional unit. Two fundamental ideas are present in this model, (*i*) components can communicate with each other using ports and (*ii*) components can exist within each other. In this way, component representation is closely related to HDLs and serves as an input for the HDL generator as well as for the generator of verification environments.

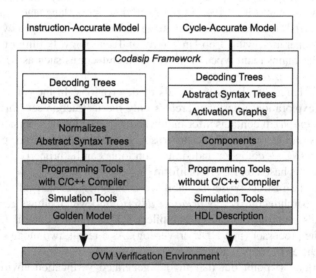

Fig. 1. Verification flow in the Codasip Framework

For better comprehension of the previous text, the idea is summarised once again in Figure 1. Codasip works with the instruction and the cycle-accurate description of a processor and specific tools are generated from these descriptions. The highlighted parts are used during the verification process. It should be noted that the presented idea is generally applicable and is not restricted only to the Codasip Framework.

Verification environments generated from formal models are thoroughly described in the following section.

4 Functional Verification Environments for Processors

The goal of functional verification is to establish the conformance of a design of processor to its specification. However, considerable time is consumed by designing and implementation of verification environments.

In order to comfortably debug and verify ASIPs designed in the Codasip framework as fast as possible and not waste time with implementation tasks we designed a special feature allowing automated pre-generation of OVM verification environment for every processor. In this way we can highly reuse the specification model provided in the CodAL language and all intermediate representations of the processor for comprehensive generation of all units.

Our main strategy for building robust verification environments is to comply with principles of OVM (they are depicted in Figure 2). We have fulfilled this task in the following way:

Fig. 2. Verification methodology

1. **OVM Testbench.** Codasip supports automated generation of object-oriented testbench environments created with compliance to open, standard and widely used OVM methodology.
2. **Program Generator.** During verification we need to trigger architectural and microarchitectural events defined in the verification plan and ensure that all corner cases and interesting scenarios are exercised and bugs hidden in them are exposed. For achieving the high level of coverage closure of every design of processor it is possible to utilise either a generator of simple C/C++ programs in some third-party tool or already prepared set of benchmark programs.
3. **Reference Methodology.** A significant benefit of our approach is gained by automated creation of golden models for functional verification purposes. We realised that it is possible to reuse formal models of the instruction-accurate description of the processor at the higher level of abstraction and generate C/C++ representation of these models in the form of reference functions which are prepared for every instruction of the processor. Moreover, we are able to generate SystemVerilog encapsulations, so the designer can write his/her own golden model with advantage of the pre-generated connection to other parts of the verification environment.
4. **Functional Coverage.** According to the high-level description of the processor and the low-level representation of the same processor in VHDL, we are able to automatically extract interesting coverage scenarios and pre-generate coverage points for comprehensive checking of functionality and complex behaviour of the processor. Of course, it is highly recommended to users to add some specific coverage

points manually. Nevertheless, the built-in coverage methodology allows measuring the progress towards the verification goals much faster.

In addition, interconnection with a third-party simulator e.g. ModelSim from Mentor Graphics allows us to implicitly support assertion analysis, code coverage analysis and signals visibility during all verification runs. A general architecture of generated OVM testbenches is depicted in Figure 3 and main components are described further.

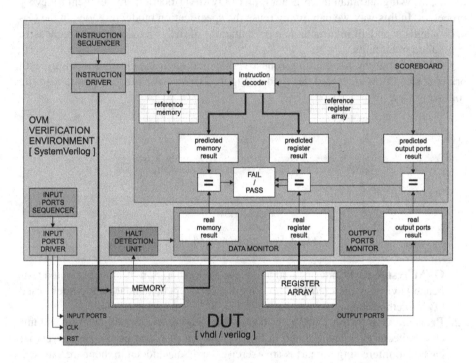

Fig. 3. OVM verification environments for user-defined processors in Codasip framework

- **DUT (Device Under Test)**. The verified hardware representation of the processor written in VHDL/Verilog. According to the type of the processor, different number of internal memories and register arrays is used. The processor typically contains a basic control interface with clock and reset signal, an input interface and an output interface.
- **OVM Verification Environment**. Basic classes/components of generated verification testbenches with compliance to OVM methodology:
  - **Input Ports Sequencer and Driver**. Generation of input sequences and supplying them to input ports of the DUT.
  - **Instruction Sequencer and Driver**. Generation of input test programs or reading already prepared benchmark programs from external resources. Afterwards, programs are loaded to the program memory of the processor as well as to the instruction decoder in Scoreboard.

- **Scoreboard**. This unit represents a self-checking mechanism for functional verification. In order to prepare expected responses of the verified processor to a particular program, Scoreboard uses a set of pre-generated reference functions created with respect to the specification described in the high-level Co-dAL language. For computational purposes a reference memory and a reference register array are used. As a result, predicted memory result, predicted register array result and predicted output ports result are prepared.
- **Halt Detection Unit**. It is necessary to define a specific time in simulation when images of memories and register arrays of processor are checked. Evidently, it should be done when a program is completely evaluated by the processor. This situation can be distinguished according to the detection of HALT instruction activity in the processor.
- **Data Monitor**. In case of the detection of HALT instruction activity, Data Monitor reads images of memories and register arrays of the processor and sends them to Scoreboard where they are compared with expected responses. If a discrepancy occurs, verification is stopped and a detailed report with description of an error is provided.
- **Output Ports Monitor**. Output ports of DUT are driven and their values are stored for later processing. In contrast with Data Monitor, this monitor works continuously not only in case of HALT instruction activity. Values generated by a reference model in Scoreboard are stored as well. Equivalence between stored values is checked by a function given by user or by default one.
- **Subscribers**. The aim of these units is to define functional coverage points, in other words interesting scenarios according to the verification plan which should be properly checked. These units are not present in Figure 3 although they are generated in every verification environment.

5   Experimental Results

In this section, the results of our solution are provided. We generated verification environments for two processors. The first one is the 16bits low-power DSP (Harward architecture) called Codea2. The second one is the 32bit high performance processor (Von Neumann architecture) called Codix. Detailed information about them can be found in [3]. We used Mentor Graphics' ModelSim SE-64 10.0b as the SystemVerilog interpreter and the DUT simulator. Testing programs from benchmarks such as *EEMBS* and *MiBench* or test-suites such as *full-retval-gcctestsuite* and *perrenial testsuite* were utilised during verification. The Xilinx WebPack ISE was used for synthesis. All experiments were performed using the *Intel Core 2 Quad* processor with 2.8 GHz, 1333 MHz FSB and 8GB of RAM running on 64-bit *Linux* based operating system.

Table 1 expresses the size of processors in terms of required *Look-Up Tables* (LUTs) and *Flip-Flops* (FFs) on the Xilinx *Virtex5* FPGA board. Other columns contain information about the number of tracked instructions and the time in seconds needed for generation of SystemVerilog verification environment and all reference functions inside the golden models (Generation Time). In addition, the number of lines of programming code for every verification environment is provided (Code Lines). A designer typically needs around *fourteen days* in order to create basics of the verification environment (without generation of proper stimuli, checking coverage results, etc.), so the automated generation saves the time significantly.

Table 1. Measured Results

Processor	LUTs/FF (Virtex5)	Tracked Instructions	Generation Time [s]	Code Lines
Codea2	1411/436	60	12	2871
Codix	1860/560	123	26	3586

Table 2 provides information about the verification runtime and results. As Codea2 is a low-power DSP processor some programs had to be omitted during experiments because of their size (e.g. programs using standard C library). Therefore, the number of programs is not the same as in case of Codix. Of course, the verification runtime depends on the number of tested programs and if the program is compiled with no optimisation the runtime is significantly longer.

Table 2. Runtime statistics

Processor	Programs	Runtime [min]
Codea2	636	28
Codix	1634	96

The coverage statistics in Table 3 can show which units of the processor have been appropriately checked. As one can see, the instruction-set functional coverage reaches only around fifty percent for both processors (i.e. a half of instructions were executed). The low percentage is caused by the fact that selected programs from benchmarks did not use specific C constructions which would invoke specific instructions. On the other hand, all processors registers files were fully tested (100% Register File coverage). This means that *read* and *write* instructions were performed from/to every single address in register files. The functional coverage of memories represents coverage of control signals in memory controllers. Besides functional coverage, ModelSim simulator provides also code coverage statistics like branch, statement, conditions and expression coverage. According to the code coverage analysis we were able to identify several parts of the source code which were not executed by our testing programs and therefore we must improve our testing set and explore all coverage holes carefully.

Table 3. Coverage statistics

Processor	Code Coverage [%]				Functional Coverage [%]		
	Branch	Statement	Conditions	Expression	Instruction-Set	Register File	Memories
Codea2	87.0	99.1	62.3	58.1	51.2	100	87.5
Codix	92.1	99.2	70.4	79.4	44.7	100	71.5

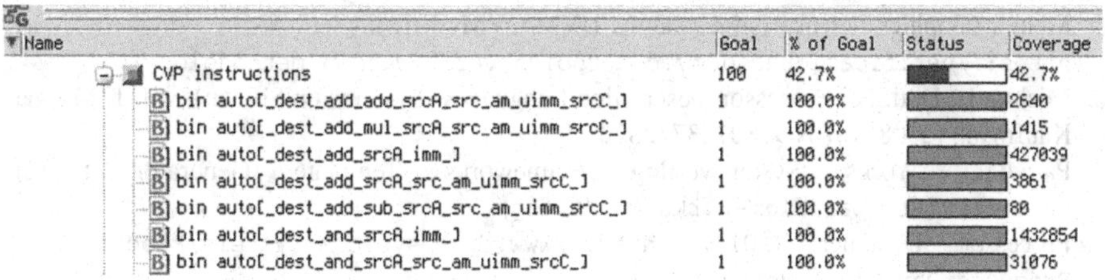

Name	Goal	% of Goal	Status	Coverage
⊟ 🔲 CVP instructions	100	42.7%	▭▬	42.7%
Ⓑ bin auto[_dest_add_add_srcA_src_am_uimm_srcC_]	1	100.0%	▬▬	2640
Ⓑ bin auto[_dest_add_mul_srcA_src_am_uimm_srcC_]	1	100.0%	▬▬	1415
Ⓑ bin auto[_dest_add_srcA_imm_]	1	100.0%	▬▬	427039
Ⓑ bin auto[_dest_add_srcA_src_am_uimm_srcC_]	1	100.0%	▬▬	3861
Ⓑ bin auto[_dest_add_sub_srcA_src_am_uimm_srcC_]	1	100.0%	▬▬	88
Ⓑ bin auto[_dest_and_srcA_imm_]	1	100.0%	▬▬	1432854
Ⓑ bin auto[_dest_and_srcA_src_am_uimm_srcC_]	1	100.0%	▬▬	31076

Fig. 4. Coverage Screenshot

Figure 4 demonstrates the status of instruction-set functional coverage for Codix processor after execution of 500 programs in ModelSim.

Of course, the main purpose of verification is to find bugs and thanks to our pre-generated verification environment we were able to target this issue successfully. We discovered several well-hidden bugs located mainly in the C/C++ compiler or in the description of a processor. One of them was present in the data hazard handling when the compiler did not respect a data hazard between read and write operation to the register file. Another bugs caused jumping to incorrectly stored addresses and one bug was introduced by adding a new instruction into the Codix processor description. The designer accidentally added a structural hazard into the execute stage of the pipeline.

6   Conclusion and Future Work

To summarise, implementation of functional verification environment is a manual and highly error prone process. As we wanted to accelerate creation and maintenance of advanced OVM verification environment for ASIPs we implemented a special feature which allows their automated generation. The experimental results show that the automatic generation is fast and robust and we were able to find several crucial bugs during the processors design.

In the future we plan to utilise a sophisticated generator of programs in order to achieve higher level of coverage of verified processors because during experiments we identified several holes in functional coverage and code coverage. Moreover, we want to discover the relation between test-templates and coverage points.

References

1. Fauth, A., Van Praet, J., Freericks, M.: Describing instruction set processors using nML. In: Proceedings of European Design and Test Conference, Paris, pp. 503–507 (1995) ISBN 0-8186-7039-8
2. Hoffmann, A., Meyr, H., Leupers, R.: Architecture Exploration for Embedded Processors with LISA. Springer (2002) ISBN 1402073380
3. Codasip Framework. Codasip (2012), http://www.codasip.com/
4. Martin, G., Bailey, B., Piziali, A.: ESL Design and Verification: A Prescription for Electronic System Level Methodology (Systems on Silicon). Morgan Kaufmann (2007) ISBN 0123735513

5. Mentor Graphics Verification Academy. UVM/OVM (2012), https://verificationacademy.com/topics/verification-methodology
6. Mishra, P., Dutt, N.: Processor Description Languages (Systems on Silicon), vol. 1. Morgan Kaufmann (2008) ISBN 9780123742872
7. Paradigm Works SystemVerilog Frameworks Template Generator (2012), http://svf-tg.paradigm-works.com/svftg/
8. Processor Designer (2012), http://www.synopsys.com/Systems/BlockDesign/ProcessorDev/Pages/default.aspx
9. Azevedo, R., et al.: The ArchC architecture description language and tools. International Journal of Parallel Program 33(5), 453–484 (2005) ISSN 0885-7458
10. Synopsys. Pioneer NTB (2012), http://www.synopsys.com/Tools/Verification/FunctionalVerification/Pages/Pioneer-NTB.aspx
11. SystemC Project (2012), http://www.systemc.org/home/
12. Target (2012), http://www.retarget.com/
13. The LLVM Compiler Infrastructure Project (2012), http://llvm.org/
14. Přikryl, Z.: Advanced Methods of Microprocessor Simulation. Information Sciences and Technologies, Bulletin of the ACM Slovakia 3(3), 1–13 (2011) ISSN 1338-1237

Compressing Microcontroller Execution Traces to Assist System Analysis

Azzeddine Amiar, Mickaël Delahaye, Yliès Falcone, and Lydie du Bousquet

Université Grenoble Alpes
Laboratoire d'Informatique de Grenoble
38041 Grenoble, France
FirstName.LastName@imag.fr

Abstract. Recent technological advances have made possible the retrieval of execution traces on microcontrollers. However, the huge amount of data in the collected trace makes the trace analysis extremely difficult and time-consuming. In this paper, by leveraging both cycles and repetitions present in an execution trace, we present an approach which offers a compact and accurate trace compression. This compression may be used during the trace analysis without decompression, notably for identifying repeated cycles or comparing different cycles. The evaluation demonstrates that our approach reaches high compression ratios on microcontroller execution traces.

1 Introduction

A microcontroller is an integrated circuit embedded in various kinds of equipment such as cars, washing machines or toys. Surprisingly, if microcontrollers are now affordable, the development of embedded software is still expensive. According to our industrial partners, this development cost is mainly due to the validation step, and especially debugging. Indeed, though there are several development environments for embedded applications, there exist few tools dedicated to their validation. Consequently, validation and debugging are carried out manually, and thus are tedious and time consuming tasks [12]. Recent microcontrollers allow trace recording. Using specialized probes it is possible to collect basic execution traces without input/output data. Due to the cyclic nature of most embedded programs, such traces consist in very long sequences of multiple repetitions of instructions.

In this paper, we aim to help automated or manual analysis of microcontroller traces by facilating the localization repetitions and by keeping the amount of data manageable. We propose a compression approach based on a grammar generation. Our algorithm, named Cyclitur, is based on our extension of the Sequitur algorithm [11]. Sequitur produces a grammar by leveraging *regularities* found in an input trace. The output grammar is an accurate but compact representation of the input trace. Compared with Sequitur, our extension, named ReSequitur, ensures an additional grammar property. Cyclitur is implemented in a tool named CoMET (see Figure 7). CoMET enables us to compress real traces recorded on embedded applications and network traffic simulations.

G. Schirner et al. (Eds.): IESS 2013, IFIP AICT 403, pp. 139–150, 2013.
© IFIP International Federation for Information Processing 2013

```
1  int main(void) {
2    while(1) {
3      static JOY_State_TypeDef JoyState = JOY_NONE;
4      static TS_STATE* TS_State;
5      JoyState = IOE_JoyStickGetState();
6      switch (JoyState) {
7        case JOY_NONE:
8          LCD_DisplayStringLine(Line5, "JOY: ---- "); break;
9        case JOY_UP:
10         LCD_DisplayStringLine(Line5, "JOY: UP "); break;
11       case JOY_DOWN:
12         LCD_DisplayStringLine(Line5, "JOY: DOWN "); break;
13       default:
14         LCD_DisplayStringLine(Line5, "JOY: ERROR "); break;
15     }
16     TS_State = IOE_TS_GetState();
17     Delay(1);
18     if (STM_EVAL_PBGetState(Button_KEY) == 0) {
19       STM_EVAL_LEDToggle(LED1);
20       LCD_DisplayStringLine(Line4, "Pol: KEY Pressed");
21     }
22     if (STM_EVAL_PBGetState(Button_TAMPER) == 0) {
23       STM_EVAL_LEDToggle(LED2);
24       LCD_DisplayStringLine(Line4, "Pol: TAMPER Pressed");
25   } } }
```

```
[...]
0x08000CA0," BL.W    LCD_WriteReg (0x08000D74)"
0x08000D74," PUSH    {r4-r6,lr}"
0x08000D76," MOV     r5,r0"
0x08000D78," MOV     r4,r1"
0x08000D7A," MOV     r0,r5"
0x08000D7C," BL.W    LCD_WriteRegIndex (0x08000DC8)"
0x08000DC8," PUSH    {r4,lr}"
0x08000DCA," MOV     r4,r0"
0x08000DCC," MOV     r0,#0x70"
[...]
```

Fig. 1. Example of C embedded software code and extract from execution trace

2   Motivation

Microcontrollers run software programs specially designed for embedded use. Embedded programs are most often written in the C programming language. A lot of those programs can be categorized as *cyclic*, i.e., they rely on a main loop that iterates indefinitely. In the following, we call the *loop header* the instruction that defines this main loop. Usually, at each iteration of the loop, sensors are read and actions are taken in response. Figure 1 gives a small example of embedded software in C. This program repetitively checks if the user moves a joystick or pushes a button, and displays some text on an LCD screen to describe the actions of the user. The cyclic aspect is represented by an infinite loop, which starts at line 2.

The cost of developing software for microcontrollers is still very high. The specificity of each use case and the very low-level programming render the development of such software error-prone. Consequently, a very large part of the development time is spent in debugging. However, the arrival of new microcontrollers has made possible the recording of execution traces. For instance, ARM Cortex-M microcontrollers include a module dedicated to trace recording, called Embedded Trace Macrocell. Using a specific probe, it is possible to record the execution trace of the program running on the microcontroller. Although race analysis seems pertinent to debug microcontroller programs, the collected traces usually contain a huge amount of data, due to the real-time and cyclic nature of the embedded programs. Figure 1 provides a small extract of the execution trace collected during the execution of the program. While the recorded trace was more than one million lines long, the chosen extract contains a few lines occurring during a call of the macro LCD_DisplayStringLine. This extract exemplifies what makes the trace analysis very difficult: a few lines of source code can give raise to a very large amount of data in the trace.

This paper proposes a method to assist the analysis process of microcontroller execution traces. In other words, we address the first two steps of the debug process, which are the comprehension and the analysis of execution traces. Indeed, we propose a method to compress the microcontroller execution traces [10,8,7], in order to have a high view to get a quick understanding of execution traces. Our tool CoMET (see Figure 7) implements our compression, and provides two visualizations. The engineer, by visualizing the compression generated by our approach, will be guided throughout the trace analysis, for instance, by identifying cycles that appears most often in the trace or by comparing cycles.

3   Cyclic Trace Compression

Given an input string, a grammar-based compression computes a small grammar that generates only one string, the input string. This grammar reveals the structure of the string and can often be used in further processing with no prior decompression, which is an opportunity for trace analysis.

Sequitur, proposed by Nevill-Manning and Witten [11], is a grammar-based compression algorithm. To generate a grammar, Sequitur takes a string as input, and finds repeated subsequences present in the string. Sequitur operates in linear time and in an online fashion. Each repetition gives rise to a rule in the grammar, and is replaced with a nonterminal symbol. The compression process is executed iteratively. For instance, for the string $cabcabcabcabcad$, Sequitur generates the following grammar:
$$S \to AABd, \quad A \to CC, \quad B \to ca, \quad C \to Bb$$
The original string contains 15 symbols and the Sequitur-generated grammar contains 14 symbols. The compression explicitly capture the repetitions of the subsequence cba.

In this paper we propose Cyclitur, an extension of Sequitur, to compress microcontroller execution traces. While keeping the same complexity as Sequitur, Cyclitur compresses consecutive repetitions and takes advantage of the cyclic nature of the trace. For instance, for the same string and if the loop header is a, Cyclitur computes this grammar:
$$S \to cA^4B, \quad A \to abc, \quad B \to ad$$
The grammar contains only 11 symbols and each of the cycles is represented by a single symbol (c as is, abc as A, and ad as B). This section first explains our formalism and details the improvements made to Sequitur to compress microcontroller execution traces.

3.1   Preliminaries

Given an alphabet Σ, an *r-string* α is a sequence of pairs $\langle symbol,\ number\ of$ *consecutive repetitions*$\rangle$. The set of *r-strings* over Σ is $\Sigma_r^* = (\Sigma \times \mathbb{N} \setminus \{0\})^*$. In an r-string α, $\alpha_{i,1}$ stands for the symbol of the i-th element of α and $\alpha_{i,2}$ for its number of repetitions. $|\alpha|$ denotes the number of elements in the r-string α. To lighten notations, repetition numbers are placed in superscript after symbols and they are omitted when equal to one. For instance, $ab^5 d^{10}$ is a shorthand for the sequence $\langle a, 1\rangle\langle b, 5\rangle\langle d, 10\rangle$. The *expansion* of the r-string $\alpha \in \Sigma_r^*$, noted $\widehat{\alpha}$, is a string in Σ^*, and is defined as follows:

$$\widehat{\alpha} = \underbrace{\alpha_{1,1} \cdots \alpha_{1,1}}_{\text{repeated } \alpha_{1,2} \text{ times}} \underbrace{\alpha_{2,1} \cdots \alpha_{2,1}}_{\alpha_{2,2} \text{ times}} \cdots \underbrace{\alpha_{|\alpha|,1} \cdots \alpha_{|\alpha|,1}}_{\alpha_{|\alpha|,2} \text{ times}} .$$

An *r-grammar* G is a 4-tuple $\langle \Sigma, \Gamma, S, \Delta \rangle$ where:

- Σ is a finite alphabet of *terminal* symbols,
- Γ is a disjoint finite alphabet of *nonterminal* symbols,
- $S \in \Gamma$ is a *start symbol*, i.e., a particular nonterminal,
- and $\Delta \subseteq \Gamma \times (\Sigma \cup \Gamma)_r^*$ is a set of *r-production rules*,

such that the following properties are verified:

- for every nonterminal A, there is a unique r-string α s.t. $\langle A, \alpha \rangle$ is in Δ,
- there is an ordering over Γ s.t., for each r-production rule $\langle A, \alpha \rangle$ in Δ, every nonterminal in α precedes A.

An r-production rule $\langle A, \alpha \rangle \in \Delta$ associates the nonterminal A and the r-string α, resp. called the *head* and the *body* of the rule. The *r-grammar body* is $\{\alpha \mid \exists A : \langle A, \alpha \rangle \in \Delta\}$, i.e., the set of rule bodies. Note that the additional properties ensure that an r-grammar contains one rule per nonterminal and is non recursive (cycle-free). In the following, we consider an r-grammar $G = \langle \Sigma, \Gamma, S, \Delta \rangle$.

3.2   Properties of Generated Grammars

ReSequitur is an algorithm that compresses a string to an r-grammar (see Figure 2). ReSequitur takes as inputs an alphabet Σ, a string to compress $\omega \in \Sigma^*$, a (possibly empty) initial set of symbols Γ_0, and an initial set of rules $\Delta_0 \subset (\Gamma_0 \times \Sigma_r^*)$. Like Sequitur, ReSequitur ensures that two properties called *digram uniqueness* and *rule utility* hold on the output r-grammar.

The digram uniqueness property states that an r-grammar should not contain two non-overlapping occurrences of the same digram in the r-grammar body.

Property 1 (Digram uniqueness). *The digram uniqueness property holds for G, noted $RUniqueness(G)$, if for all terminals $A, B \in \Gamma$, symbols $a, b, c, d \in \Sigma \cup \Gamma$, strictly positive integers $n, m, p, q \in \mathbb{N} \setminus \{0\}$, and r-strings $\alpha, \beta, \gamma, \delta \in (\Sigma \cup \Gamma)_r^*$, the two following statements hold:*

$$(A \neq B \wedge \{\langle A, \alpha\, a^n b^m\, \beta \rangle, \langle B, \gamma\, c^p d^q\, \delta \rangle\} \subset \Delta) \implies a^n b^m \neq c^p d^q$$

(in different rules)

$$(\langle A, \alpha\, a^n b^m\, \beta\, c^p d^q\, \gamma \rangle \in \Delta) \implies a^n b^m \neq c^p d^q$$

(in a same rule)

```
1  let S be a fresh nonterminal representing a rule (S ∉ Σ ∪ Γ₀)
2  G ← ⟨Σ, Γ₀ ∪ {S}, S, Δ₀ ∪ {⟨S, ε⟩}⟩
3  for i ← 1 to |ω| do
4  │    append (ωᵢ)¹ to the body of rule S
5  │    while ¬RUniqueness(G) ∨ ¬RUtility(G) ∨ ¬RConsecutive(G) do
6  │    │    if ¬RConsecutive(G) then
7  │    │    │    let a, n, m be s.t. aⁿaᵐ is a r-digram in G
8  │    │    │    replace every occurrence of aⁿaᵐ in G with aⁿ⁺ᵐ
9  │    │    else if ¬RUniqueness(G) then
10 │    │    │    let δ be a repeated r-digram in G
11 │    │    │    if ∃⟨A, α⟩ ∈ Δ : α = δ then
12 │    │    │    │    replace the other occurrence of δ in G with A
13 │    │    │    else
14 │    │    │    │    form new rule ⟨D, δ⟩ where D ∉ (Σ ∪ Γ)
15 │    │    │    │    replace both occurrences of δ in G with D
16 │    │    │    │    Δ ← Δ ∪ {⟨D, δ⟩}
17 │    │    │    │    Γ ← Γ ∪ {D}
18 │    │    │    end
19 │    │    else if ¬RUtility(G) then
20 │    │    │    let ⟨A, α⟩ ∈ Δ be a rule used once
21 │    │    │    replace the occurrence of A with α in G
22 │    │    │    Δ ← Δ ∖ {⟨A, α⟩}
23 │    │    │    Γ ← Γ ∖ {A}
24 │    │    end
25 │    end
26 end
27 return G
```

Fig. 2. Function ReSequitur($\Sigma, \omega, \Gamma_0, \Delta_0$)

The rule utility property ensures that every rule except the start rule is used more than once in the r-grammar body. This is formally defined as follows:

Property 2 (Rule utility). *The rule utility holds for G, noted RUtility(G), if:*

$$\forall A \in \Gamma \setminus \{S\} : \left(\sum_{\langle B,\beta \rangle \in \Delta} \sum_{i \in [1..|\beta|]} \begin{cases} \beta_{i,2} & \text{if } \beta_{i,1} = A \\ 0 & \text{if } \beta_{i,1} \neq A \end{cases} \right) \geq 2 .$$

In order to compress consecutive repetitions more efficiently, compared with Sequitur, ReSequitur ensures an additional property: any digram in an r-grammar body consists of different symbols.

Property 3 (No consecutive repetition). *G has no consecutive repetitions, which is noted RConsecutive(G), if the following statement holds:*

$$\forall a, b \in \Sigma \cup \Gamma, \forall n, m \in \mathbb{N} \setminus \{0\}, \forall \alpha, \beta \in (\Sigma \cup \Gamma)_r^*, \forall C \in \Gamma :$$
$$\langle C, \alpha \, a^n b^m \beta \rangle \in \Delta \Rightarrow a \neq b .$$

To ensure this property at each iteration of the outer loop, ReSequitur merges every digram of the form $a^n a^m$ into a single repeated symbol a^{n+m}.

```
1  Γ₀ ← ∅;  Δ₀ ← ∅;  ω' ← ε;  i ← 1
2  for  j ← 2 to |ω| do
3  │    if j = |ω| ∨ ωⱼ = lh then
4  │    │    ⟨Σ', Γ', S', Δ'⟩ ← ReSequitur(Σ, ωᵢ..ⱼ₋₁, Γ₀, Δ₀)
5  │    │    Γ₀ ← Γ';  Δ₀ ← Δ';  ω' ← ω' · S';  i ← j
6  │    end
7  end
8  ⟨Σ'', Γ'', S'', Δ''⟩ ← ReSequitur(Σ, ω', Γ₀, Δ₀)
9  return ⟨Σ'', Γ'', S'', Δ''⟩
```

Fig. 3. Function Cyclitur(Σ, ω, lh)

3.3 Exploiting Cycles with Cyclitur

Recall that our objective is to compress cyclic traces extracted from microcontrollers. Therefore, the first step in our approach is the *cycle detection*. A cycle is a subsequence of the execution trace that consists of one execution of the main loop of the embedded program. Cycle detection relies on the localization of a special event that represents the loop header. Detecting cycles using the loop header event consists in dividing the trace into blocks, where each block represents a specific cycle. Given a loop header lh, consider the set of cycles $C(\omega, lh)$ defined as a set of pairs of indexes over the execution trace ω as follows:

$$C(\omega, lh) = \{\langle i, j \rangle \in [1..|\omega|]^2 \mid i \leq j \wedge (i = 1 \vee \omega_i = lh) \wedge (j = |\omega| \vee \omega_{j+1} = lh)$$
$$\wedge \, \forall k \in [i+1..j] : \omega_k \neq lh\}.$$

Figure 3 presents the overall algorithm of the Cyclitur compression. ReSequitur is first applied on each cycle to detect repetitions (lines 2–7), while sharing the same set of rules. Then applying ReSequitur on the compression produced by the previous step allows to detect similar sequences of cycles in the trace (line 8).

4 Application Example

Cyclitur infers patterns in execution traces and can be used for many applications. As an example of such an application, we propose here to use the compression generated by Cyclitur to detect an abnormal behavior in the embedded context. As shown in Figure 4, in this example, a user equipped with a device (e.g. a smartphone) interacts with five sensors. The user turns from the right to the left, and whenever he is in front of a sensor, his device sends a message to the sensor. After receiving a notification from the device, the sensor sends a message to the user. Finally, when the user receives the message sent by the sensor, his device sends an acknowledgment to the sensor. If the user sends a message to a sensor, and he does not get a response from the sensor, within 15 seconds, he considers this behavior as abnormal behavior and he turns to the left and interacts with the next sensor. Figure 5 illustrates the execution trace generated using this example.

By using the word "*send*" as the loop header in the trace, the execution trace will be divided into blocks as shown in Figure 5. For example, the events that are related to the sending of a message from the device to a sensor will be compressed and represented by $C1$. Then the compression generated by Cyclitur will be of the form:

$$S \to A^{(n\ times)}, \quad A \to C1\ C2\ C3$$

Let us consider the following senario, the sensor 3 receives a message from the user, but it takes more than 15 seconds to answer. In this case, the user turns to the left and interacts with the sensor 4. While the user receives the message from the sensor 4, his device receives also the message from the sensor 3. Therefore, the device of the user sends an acknowledgment to sensor 3 and an acknowledgment to sensor 4. Using the trace compression illustrated in Figure 6, which is generated by Cyclitur and where the normal behavior is $C1\ C2\ C3$, it is intuitive to note that the abnormal behavior is $C1\ C1\ C2\ C2\ C3\ C3$.

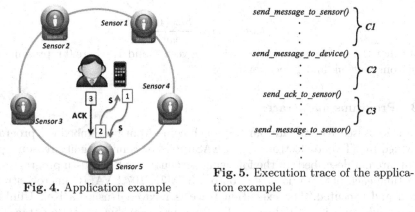

Fig. 4. Application example

Fig. 5. Execution trace of the application example

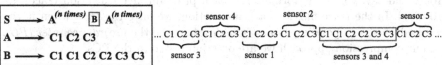

Fig. 6. Anomaly detection using trace compression

5   Implementation and Evaluation

The evaluation of our trace-compression approach is an experimental evaluation that consists in comparing grammars obtained by applying Sequitur and Cyclitur on various execution traces. The experimental evaluation was made possible thanks to our tool named CoMET.

5.1   CoMET

CoMET is a tool written in Java in 12,000 LOC that implements both Sequitur and Cyclitur algorithms. It takes as input an execution trace file. It extracts automatically a string of symbols, to finally output a grammar, either as text or as a Java object for programmatic use. As shown in Figure 7, CoMET provides two visualizations:

- *Cycle pie chart*: it provides the occurrence rates of cycles in the trace.
- *Cycle in time*: it emphasizes all occurrences of a specific cycle in the trace.

5.2   Metrics of Experimental Evaluation

In the following, we use a given string (trace) ω, and the output grammar (resp. r-grammar) generated with Sequitur (resp. Cyclitur), noted $G = \langle \Sigma, \Gamma, S, \Delta \rangle$. The *size* of the grammar G is the sum of the number of symbol occurrences in its body (both terminals and nonterminals) and the number of its rules. The *compression ratio*, noted $Comp(G)$, is used to compare the degree of compression of grammars generated using Sequitur and Cyclitur and is defined as follows:

$$Comp(G) = \frac{Size(G)}{|\omega|}$$

Note that the compression ratio varies between 0 and 1, where 0 represents the best compression, and 1 the worst.

5.3   Programs and Traces

The traces used to evaluate our approach come from five embedded programs provided by STMicroelectronics and EASii IC. For confidentiality reasons, programs are not described. In the following we denote by Pi the i-th program. One at a time each program is loaded onto a STM32F107 EVAL-C microcontroller board and executed. The execution trace is recovered using a Keil UlinkPro probe, and saved in *CSV* format. For each program, five execution traces are produced. In the trace file, for each instruction, we have the *time* when it was executed, the corresponding *assembly instruction* and the *program counter (PC)*. For our compression approach we are only interested in the PCs.

5.4   Results

Table 1 contains the results of the experimental evaluation, where each line represents a trace of a program. The columns #**Sym.** and #**Cycles** represent respectively the number of symbol occurrences and the number of cycles in a trace. For each generated grammar, Table 1 contains its size $Size()$ and its compression ratio $Comp()$. Figure 8 displays the arithmetic average of the compression ratios over the five collected traces of the program. Note that the use of other average measures give different values, but the same result: a clear difference of compression ratios between Sequitur and Cyclitur. The compression ratio varies between 0 and 1, where 0 represents the best compression, and 1 the worst. For example, for program P1, we observe that our approach produces better compression than Sequitur. The sizes of grammars generated by Sequitur for the execution traces of P1 vary from 1,051 up to 2,581.

Table 1. Evaluation results

Prog.	Trace	#Sym.	#Cycles	Sequitur		Cyclitur	
				$Size(G)$	$Comp(G)$	$Size(G')$	$Comp(G')$
P1	T1	1048575	7588	2581	0.002461436	1484	0.001415254
	T2	1048576	7274	1748	0.001667023	944	0.000900269
	T3	1048576	7109	1764	0.001682281	946	0.000902176
	T4	1048571	7586	1497	0.001427657	970	0.000925068
	T5	1048574	4448	1051	0.001002314	625	0.000596048
P2	T1	1048575	1515	21040	0.020160694	18102	0.017263429
	T2	1048575	1593	20324	0.019382495	16537	0.015770927
	T3	1048575	1591	18933	0.018055933	15970	0.015230193
	T4	1048576	1736	19658	0.01874733	16709	0.015934944
	T5	1048574	1789	19478	0.018575704	17335	0.016531976
P3	T1	1048572	1440	1918	0.001829154	1766	0.001684195
	T2	1048571	1442	1830	0.001745232	1407	0.001341826
	T3	1048573	1442	1813	0.001729016	1686	0.001607899
	T4	1048576	1441	1961	0.001870155	1661	0.001584053
	T5	1048576	1442	1842	0.001756668	1701	0.0016222
P4	T1	1048567	1277	1726	0.001646056	1407	0.001341831
	T2	1048571	1462	2199	0.00209714	1488	0.001419074
	T3	1048574	1276	1879	0.001791957	1325	0.001263621
	T4	1048575	1462	1706	0.00162697	1524	0.001453401
	T5	1048575	1462	1613	0.001538278	1416	0.001350404
P5	T1	1048573	16132	301	0.000287057	125	0.00011921
	T2	1048576	16132	295	0.000281334	132	0.000117302
	T3	1048570	7440	1599	0.001524934	1172	0.001117713
	T4	1048571	16131	309	0.000294687	137	0.000130654
	T5	1048576	16132	290	0.000276566	135	0.000128746

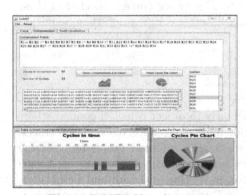

Fig. 7. CoMET Visualization

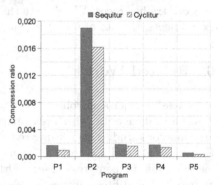

Fig. 8. Compared average compression ratios for each program

The sizes of original traces vary between 1,048,571 and 1,048,576, with 4,448 and 7,588 cycles. Therefore, the compression ratios vary between 0.0010 and 0.0025. Cyclitur produces grammars whose sizes vary from 625 to 1,484. The compression ratios vary between 0.0006 and 0.0014. Note that, for all considered programs, the use of Cyclitur leads to better compression than Sequitur. The compression ratios are better from 12% to 42%.

5.5   Cyclitur and Network Traces

We evaluate our trace-compression approach on four additional traces obtained from network simulations. The considered network is a Multi-Channel Multi-

Interface Wireless Mesh Network (WMN) with routers based on the IEEE 802.11 technology [4]. The loop header used to detect cycles is a specific event that refers to the emission of a request from client to server.

The *trace 1* consists in 6,011,850 events spread over 9,574 cycles. The compression ratio using Sequitur is 0.0027% for a generated grammar whose size is 16,531 (744 terminals, 12,375 nonterminals and 3,412 rules). The compression ratio for Cyclitur grammar reaches 0.0026% for a grammar of size 16,057 (373 terminals, 13,884 nonterminals and 4,182 rules). Cyclitur generates a grammar that contains more rules than the grammar generated by Sequitur, but is easier to understand and to analyze, because it is more compact and it facilitates cycle detection. The *trace 2* trace consists in 8,040,942 events spread over 9,574 cycles. Sequitur generates a grammar of size 18,639 while Cyclitur generates a grammar of size 18,439. The use of Sequitur and Cyclitur on the second trace gives respectively 0.00023% and 0.0022% compression ratios. The *trace 3* contains 13,883,977 events spread over 2,797 cycles. While Sequitur generates a grammar of size 28,181, Cyclitur generates a grammar of size 26,468. The compression ratios are respectively 0.0020% and 0.0019%. Finally, the *trace 4* contains 10,312,955 events spread over 33,834 cycles. While Sequitur reaches a 0.0016% compression ratio with a grammar of size 16,690. Cyclitur reaches a 0.0009% compression ratio with a grammar of size 10,145.

The previous results show that Cyclitur can be used likewise to compress network traffic traces. We observe that for all network traces collected in these experiments, the use of Cyclitur generates a better compression than Sequitur.

6   Related Work

Compressing microcontroller traces with the objective of analyzing them remains a challenge. In other areas, particularly in object oriented context, there are numerous studies concerning reduction and compression of execution traces. Hamou-Lhadj and Lethbridge [8] use an acyclic oriented graph representing method calls to compress traces. Other representations have been used such as trees [13] and finite automata [9]. Also, in [7] Hamou-Lhadj and Lethbridge, propose the removal of implementation and useless details to ease the analysis of execution traces. These object oriented approaches are not suitable for our purpose for multiple reasons. First, they discard the order of events, which is paramount to understand a program. Second, they use input/output data. In our context, this information is rarely available and raises important storage problems. Third, they reason about method calls. In optimized microcontroller code, function calls alone are inadequate to understand the program, since the core logic of a program is sometimes coded in a single function.

Generic data compression methods have been used for execution traces, e.g., Gzip [6]. However, almost no analysis can be performed on the compressed form of the execution trace. Larus [10] proposes to compress control flow paths using Sequitur. As Sequitur finds regularities in the path (e.g., repeated code), the output grammar can be used to detect hot subpaths, i.e., short acyclic paths that are costly. Our work consists in compressing traces by detecting and exploiting cycles. It allows us to reach better compression ratios than Sequitur. Burtscher et al. [2] also propose a value predictor-based compression algorithm for execution trace that obtain better compression ratios than Gzip or Sequitur. Zhang and Gupta [15] propose an improvement of value predictor-based compression for whole execution trace (WET), i.e., control flow and other information mixed together. Their method allows the user to extract partial information (e.g., the control flow path) from the compressed WET. If their method allows bidirectional decompression, such compression are usually not understandable by the engineer and automated analysis requires at least partial decompression. On the contrary, the simple structure offered by the grammar is well-suited for analysis. Moreover, these techniques may notably lose reference points (here, cycles). Like the run-length encoding, Cyclitur compresses consecutive repetitions but it also detects patterns and cycles. We believe that cycles revealed in the process of Cyclitur may assist automatic trace analysis, e.g., using cycle matching [1].

Grammar-based compression is the object of active research in information theory (cf. [3] for a survey). In particular, extensions of Sequitur are able to produce smaller grammars. For instance, Yang and Kiefer propose to generalize Sequitur to n-grams (rather than digram) [14]. If this leads to better compressions, it comes at a price: their algorithm does not share the time and space complexity of Sequitur, and as a result, is not usable on large amount of data.

7   Conclusion and Perspectives

In the microcontroller context, new microprocessors have enabled the recording of the execution of embedded software as a trace. Analyzing execution traces may help in embedded software debugging, which represents a large part of the cost of their development. However, collected traces contains a huge amount of data, making the analysis difficult and tedious. For both manual and automatic analysis of the trace, it seems opportune to have a compact and analyzable representation of the trace.

In this paper, we propose a trace compression method that aims at facilitating trace analysis. The method relies on a grammar-based compression named *Cyclitur* built upon the Sequitur algorithm [11]. Our approach starts by dividing a trace into cycles, where each cycle is an execution of the active main loop. The second step consists in discovering and compressing similarities in the trace.

Our approach is evaluated to compare its compression rate to the existing Sequitur algorithm. The experimental evaluation shows that our approach generates an equivalent or better compression than Sequitur on execution traces. On microcontroller execution traces, Cyclitur compression ratios were better than Sequitur compression ratios from 12% to 42%. In addition, Cyclitur may help in identifying and locating important details in an execution trace.

While Cyclitur is not aimed at competing with compression ratio of compression schemes in general, it would be interesting to compare Cyclitur with value predictor-based compressions [15,2]. Also, we intend to help locating faults in embedded software by analyzing compressed traces and adapting dynamic validation and data mining techniques [5].

Acknowledgment. This work has been funded by the French-government Single Inter-Ministry Fund (FUI) through the IO32 project (Instrumentation and Tools for 32-bit Microcontrollers). The authors would like to thank STMicroelectronics, AIM and ESAii IC for their help.

References

1. Aoe, J.: Computer Algorithms: String Pattern Matching Strategies. Wiley-IEEE Computer Society Press (1994)
2. Burtscher, M., Ganusov, I., Jackson, S., Ke, J., Ratanaworabhan, P., Sam, N.: The VPC trace-compression algorithms. IEEE Trans. on Computers 54(11), 1329–1344 (2005)
3. Charikar, M., Lehman, E., Liu, D., Panigrahy, R., Prabhakaran, M., Sahai, A., Shelat, A.: The smallest grammar problem. IEEE Trans. on Information Theory 51(7), 2554–2576 (2005)
4. De Oliveira, C., Theoleyre, F., Duda, A.: Connectivity in multi-channel multi-interface wireless mesh networks. In: International Wireless Communications and Mobile Computing Conference (IWCMC), pp. 35–40 (2011)
5. Fayyad, U., Piatetsky-shapiro, G., Smyth, P.: From data mining to knowledge discovery in databases. AI Magazine 17, 37–54 (1996)
6. Gailly, J.-L., Adler, M.: Gzip, http://www.gzip.org
7. Hamou-Lhadj, A., Lethbridge, T.: Summarizing the content of large traces to facilitate the understanding of the behaviour of a software system. In: International Conference on Program Comprehension (ICPC), pp. 181–190. IEEE Computer Society (2006)
8. Hamou-Lhadj, A., Lethbridge, T.C.: Compression techniques to simplify the analysis of large execution traces. In: International Workshop on Program Comprehension (IWPC), pp. 159–168. IEEE Computer Society (2002)
9. Heizmann, M., Hoenicke, J., Podelski, A.: Refinement of trace abstraction. In: Palsberg, J., Su, Z. (eds.) SAS 2009. LNCS, vol. 5673, pp. 69–85. Springer, Heidelberg (2009)
10. Larus, J.R.: Whole program paths. In: ACM SIGPLAN Conference on Programming Language Design and Implementation (PLDI), pp. 259–269. ACM (1999)
11. Nevill-Manning, C.G., Witten, I.H.: Identifying hierarchical strcture in sequences: A linear-time algorithm. Journal of Artificial Intellgence Research (JAIR) 7, 67–82 (1997)
12. Rohani, A., Zarandi, H.: An analysis of fault effects and propagations in AVR microcontroller ATmega103(L). In: International Conference on Availability, Reliability and Security (ARES), pp. 166–172 (2009)
13. Taniguchi, K., Ishio, T., Kamiya, T., Kusumoto, S., Inoue, K.: Extracting sequence diagram from execution trace of Java program. In: International Workshop on Principles of Software Evolution, pp. 148–154. IEEE Computer Society (2005)
14. Yang, E.-H., Kieffer, J.C.: Efficient universal lossless data compression algorithms based on a greedy sequential grammar transform—Part one: Without context models. IEEE Trans. on Information Theory 46(3), 755–777 (2000)
15. Zhang, X., Gupta, R.: Whole execution traces and their applications. ACM Trans. Archit. Code Optim. 2(3), 301–334 (2005)

Hardware and Software Implementations of Prim's Algorithm for Efficient Minimum Spanning Tree Computation

Artur Mariano[1,*], Dongwook Lee[2], Andreas Gerstlauer[2], and Derek Chiou[2]

[1] Institute for Scientific Computing
Technische Universität Darmstadt
Darmstadt, Germany
[2] Electrical and Computer Engineering
University of Texas, Austin, Texas, USA
artur.mariano@sc.tu-darmstadt.de,
{dongwook.lee@mail,gerstl@ece,derek@ece}.utexas.edu

Abstract. Minimum spanning tree (MST) problems play an important role in many networking applications, such as routing and network planning. In many cases, such as wireless ad-hoc networks, this requires efficient high-performance and low-power implementations that can run at regular intervals in real time on embedded platforms. In this paper, we study custom software and hardware realizations of one common algorithm for MST computations, Prim's algorithm. We specifically investigate a performance-optimized realization of this algorithm on reconfigurable hardware, which is increasingly present in such platforms.

Prim's algorithm is based on graph traversals, which are inherently hard to parallelize. We study two algorithmic variants and compare their performance against implementations on desktop-class and embedded CPUs. Results show that the raw execution time of an optimized implementation of Prim's algorithm on a Spartan-class Xilinx FPGA running at 24 MHz and utilizing less than 2.5% of its logic resources is 20% faster than an embedded ARM9 processor. When scaled to moderate clock frequencies of 150 and 250 MHz in more advanced FPGA technology, speedups of 7x and 12x are possible (at 56% and 94% of the ARM9 clock frequency, respectively).

Keywords: Prim's algorithm, FPGA, Hardware acceleration, MST.

1 Introduction

The minimum spanning tree (MST) problem is as an important application within the class of combinatorial optimizations. It has important applications in computer and communication networks, playing a major role in network reliability, classification and routing [1]. In many application domains, such as wireless and mobile ad-hoc networks (WANETS and MANETS), MST solvers

---

* This work was performed while Artur Mariano was at UT Austin.

G. Schirner et al. (Eds.): IESS 2013, IFIP AICT 403, pp. 151–158, 2013.

have to be run online, demanding efficient, low-power, real-time implementations on embedded platforms.

In this paper, we focus on hardware implementation of one particular, common MST solver: Prim's algorithm [2], which is used in several ad-hoc networks [3] for topology calculation and other maintenance tasks, such as broadcasts, at both initialization and run time. In particular, several maximum broadcast lifetime (MBL) algorithms have been proposed in the past, all as derivatives of Prim's algorithm, running on a general directed graph [4]. In such applications, Prim's algorithm is typically applied to medium to large network models with significant complexity, e.g. in terms of the number of nodes. In order to adapt to changing network conditions, the algorithm has to be executed in a distributed fashion at regular intervals on each node. In mobile and battery-operated nodes, cost, computational power and energy consumption are often critical resources, and high performance and low power realizations are required. For this purpose, platforms increasingly include reconfigurable logic to support hardware acceleration of (dynamically varying) tasks. This motivates an FPGA implementation of Prim's algorithm, where our primary focus is initially on improved real-time performance. To the best of our knowledge, there are currently no other studies of custom hardware realizations of this algorithm.

The rest of the paper is organized as follows: Section 2 provides a brief review of the theory behind Prim's algorithm including related work. Section 3 discusses the FPGA realization of the algorithm, and Sections 4 and 5 present the experimental setup and results. Finally, the paper concludes with a summary and outlook in Section 6.

2   Prim's Algorithm

Prim is a greedy algorithm that solves the MST problem for a connected and weighted undirected graph. A minimum spanning tree is a set of edges that connect every vertex contained in the original graph, such that the total weight of the edges in the tree is minimized.

The algorithm starts at a random node of the graph and, in each iteration, examines all available edges from visited to non-visited nodes in order to choose the one with the lowest cost. The destination of the chosen edge is then added to the visited nodes set and the edge added to the MST. The pseudo-code of the algorithm is presented as Algorithm 1.

2.1   Performance Analysis

As with a majority of graph traversals, Prim's algorithm has irregular memory access patterns. In CPUs, this limits cache use and thus overall performance. As such, the algorithm is memory-bound with low computational requirements, and its performance is highly dependent on the organization of memory storage and memory access patterns.

Algorithm 1: Standard Prim's algorithm.

Input: A non-empty connected weighted graph G composed of vertexes V_G and edges E_G, possibly with null weights;
Result: The minimal spanning tree in the $finalPath$ array;
Initialization: $V_T = \{r\}$, where r is a random starting node from V;

while $V_T \neq V_G$ **do**
    $minimum \leftarrow \infty$;
    for $Visited\ nodes\ s \in V_T$ **do**
        for $all\ edges\ E(s,v)\ and\ v \notin V_T$ **do**
            if $Weight(E) \leq minimum$ **then**
                $minimum \leftarrow Weight(E)$;
                $edge \leftarrow E$;
                $newVisited \leftarrow v$;

    $finalPath \leftarrow finalPath \cup \{edge\}$;
    $V_T \leftarrow V_T \cup \{newVisited\}$;

Depending on the used data structures, Prim's algorithm can have different asymptotic complexities. For common implementations using an adjacency matrix, Prim's complexity is $\mathcal{O}(V^2)$. For other implementations using adjacency lists with binary or Fibonacci heaps, the complexity reduces down to $\mathcal{O}((V+E)\ log\ V) = \mathcal{O}(E\ log\ V))$ and $\mathcal{O}(E+V\ log\ V)$, respectively. This comes at a higher fixed complexity per step with reduced regularity and exploitable parallelism. Hence, we focus in our work on the most common form using adjacency matrix based realizations.

2.2 Parallelism Analysis

Depending on the implementation of Prim's algorithm, it can exhibit some parallelism. For realizations that use an adjacency matrix to represent the graph, an improved implementation has been reported in [5], which is shown in Algorithm 2. This second version uses a supplemental array d to cache every value if it represents a cheaper solution than the ones seen so far, which allows lookups for minimum paths to be done in parallel.

In [5], the authors have pointed out that the outer while loop in this second implementation is hard to parallelize due to its inherent dependencies. However, the other operations in the body of the loop, namely minimum edge cost lookups (i.e. min-reduction steps) and updates of the candidate set can be processed in parallel over different elements of the supplementary array d. However, min-reduction operations have to take into account that values representing edges $E(s,d)$ in which $s \in V_T$ and $d \in V_T$ can not be considered.

Algorithm 2: Second implementation of Prim's algorithm.

Input: A non-empty connected weighted graph G composed of vertexes V_G and edges E_G, possibly with null weights;
Result: The minimal spanning tree in the d array;
Initialization: $V_T = \{r\}$ and $d[r] = 0$, where r is a random node from V;

for $v \in (V\text{-}V_T)$ do
   if $E(r,v)$ then
     | $d[v] \leftarrow Weight(E)$;
   else
     $\lfloor$ $d[v] \leftarrow \infty$

while $V_T \neq V_G$ do
   Find a vertex u such that:
     | $d[u] = \min\{d(v) \mid v \in (V - V_T)\}$
   $V_T \leftarrow V_T \cup \{u\}$;
   for $all \ v \in (V - V_T)$ do
     $\lfloor$ $d[v] \leftarrow \min\{d[v], Weight(u,v)\}$;

2.3 Related Work

There are a number of implementations of Prim's method on CPUs. Some work has been done on parallel realizations targeting SMP architectures with shared address space, growing multiple trees in parallel and achieving a reported speedup of 2.64x for dense graphs [6]. Additionally, in [7] a distributed memory implementation, which supports adding multiple vertexes per iteration was demonstrated using MPI. Next to CPU implementations, GPUs were also used to compute Prim's algorithm [8]. Such GPU implementations achieve only limited speedups of around 3x, highlighting the difficulties in implementing Prim's algorithm in an efficient and real-time manner. In [8], the authors argued that the difficulty in parallelizing Prim's algorithm is very similar to other SSSP (single source shortest path) problems, like Dijkstra's algorithm.

3 FPGA Implementation

We used high-level synthesis (HLS) to synthesize C code for the different Prim variants down to RTL. We employed Calypto Catapult-C [9] to generate RTL, which was further synthesized using Mentor Precision (for logic synthesis) and Xilinx ISE (for place & route). Table 1 summarizes LUT, CLB, DFF and BRAM utilizations over different graph sizes for both implementations. We have realized the algorithm for graph sizes up to $N = 160$ nodes, where graphs are stored as adjacency matrices with $N \times N$ float values representing edge weights (and with negative values indicating edge absence).

Within Catapult-C, we exploited loop unrolling and chaining only at a coarse granularity, i.e. for the bigger outer loops. This allows a fair comparison with

Table 1. FGPA synthesis results

Graphs size	40	70	100	130	160
Algorithm 1					
LUTs	1047	1044	1109	1425	1448
CLBs	523	522	554	712	724
DFFs	563	623	628	635	624
BRAMs	6	12	21	33	48
Algorithm 2					
LUTs	1029	1145	1198	1368	1425
CLBs	514	572	599	684	712
DFFs	592	622	635	658	653
BRAMs	7	13	22	34	49

Table 2. Test platform specifications

Device	CPUs		FPGA
Manufacturer	Intel	ARM	Xilinx
Brand	Pentium M	ARM 9	Spartan
Model	T2080	926EJ-S	3
Max clock	1.73 GHz	266 MHz	400 MHz
Cores	2	1	-
System mem	2 Gbytes	32 Mbytes	1.8 Mbit
L1 Cache	32kB	16kB	-
L2 Cache	4MB	-	-
Pipeline	12 stage	5 stage	-
Year	2006	2001	2003
Launch price	$134	$15.5	$3.5

CPUs, for which we did not realize manually optimized implementations. Exploited optimizations of the outer loops did not provide us with substantial performance gains, while unrolling of loops did increase total area. Area increases by 3 times for a 8x unrolling degree. We were not able to pipeline the loops due to dependencies. The middle inner loop in Algorithm 1 has shown some small performance improvements when unrolled, with no significant difference between unrolling by 2, 4 or 8 times. Overall, the code did not exhibit significant benefits when applying loop optimizations.

4   Experimental Setup

We tested the performance of Prim's algorithm on 3 devices: a desktop-class CPU, an embedded processor and a Xilinx FPGA. Characteristics of tested platforms are summarized in Table 2. We evaluated algorithm performance on all platforms in order to measure possible speedups when moving to the FPGA.

For FPGA prototyping, we utilized a development board that includes a Freescale i.MX21 applications processor (MCU), which communicates with a Xilinx Spartan 3 FPGA over Freescale's proprietary EIM bus. The MCU contains an integrated ARM9 processor running at 266 MHz, an AMBA AHB bus and an EIM module that bridges between the AHB and the EIM bus. The ARM9 runs an embedded Linux distribution with kernel version 2.6.16 on top of which we implemented a testbench that feeds the FPGA with data and reads its output. We utilized both polling and interrupt-based synchronization between the ARM9 and the FPGA. On the FPGA side, we manually integrated Catapult-generated RTL with a bus slave interface connection to the EIM bus, using a custom developed EIM slave RTL IP module to receive and send data from/to the CPU. Designs were synthesized to run at 24 MHz on the FPGA. The bus interface clock, on the other hand, was set to run at 65 MHz.

Measurements of FPGA execution times have been made both including and excluding communication overhead. To obtain total FPGA execution times, we measured the time stamps between sending the first data item and receiving the last result on the CPU side. This includes overhead for OS calls, interrupt handling and EIM bus communication. In addition, we developed a VHDL/Verilog testbench and performed simulations to determine the raw FPGA computation time without any such communication overhead.

For our experiments, the algorithm ran on all platforms with fully-connected[1] random graphs with orders (sizes) of up to 160 nodes (as determined by FPGA memory limitations). When compiling the code for the CPUs, we did not perform any manual tuning, solely relying on standard compiler optimizations using GCC 4.2.3 and GCC 4.5.2 for ARM9 and Pentium processors, respectively.

5   Results

Figure 1(a) shows total execution times of running Algorithm 1 for graphs with up to 160 nodes on the Intel Pentium, the ARM9 and the FPGA. We report execution times as the median of 5 measurements.

The Intel CPU clearly outperforms other devices. While a Pentium CPU is neither common in embedded domains nor comparable to other platforms in terms of price, we include its results as a baseline for reference.

Compared to the ARM9 processor, execution times on the FPGA are slightly larger across all graph orders. However, in this setup, measured execution times include communication overhead, which may limit overall FPGA performance. On the other hand, computation and communication are overlapped in the FPGA and computational complexities grow with the square of the graph size whereas communication overhead only grows linearly. Coupled with the fact that execution time differences between the ARM and the FPGA increase with growing graph sizes, this indicates that communication latencies are effectively hidden and clock frequency and/or hardware resources are limiting performance.

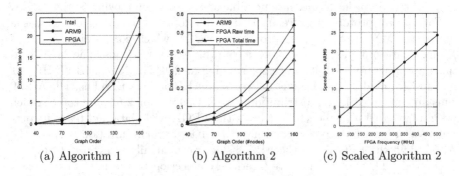

(a) Algorithm 1   (b) Algorithm 2   (c) Scaled Algorithm 2

Fig. 1. Total runtime and speedup of algorithms for graphs with up to 160 nodes

FPGA-internal storage sizes limit possible graph sizes to 160 nodes in our case. This limitation could be overcome by taking advantage of matrix symmetries: the same matrix could be represented with half of the data, enabling the study

---

[1] Graphs with $(k-1)$-connectivity with $k =$ order.

of bigger inputs, e.g. to see if FPGAs could overcome the ARM9. However, as previously mentioned, execution times are computation bound and relative differences of both devices are growing for larger inputs. As such, extrapolating would indicate that the FPGA will not be able to outperform the ARM9 even for larger inputs.

To take advantage of FPGA strengths with increasing benefits for any additional parallelism available in the algorithm [10,11], we have tested the second implementation of Prim's algorithm on dedicated hardware. Figure 1(b) shows the results of these experiments as measured on the FPGA and on the ARM9, where FPGA performance is reported both with and without communication overhead.

Algorithm 2 clearly performs better on both devices, with speedups of around 37.5x and 68.5x compared to Algorithm 1 for the ARM9 and FPGA, respectively. Even though the FPGA can take more advantage of the second implementation's parallelism than the single-core ARM9, the ARM9 still outperforms the FPGA in total execution time. However, when considering raw execution times without communication overhead, the FPGA performs better.

In addition, overall FPGA performance of designs on our board is limited to a maximum frequency of 24 MHz. To extrapolate possible performance, we scaled raw execution times for a graph with 160 nodes (requiring around 8.8 million clock cycles) to other clock frequencies, as shown in Figure 1(c). Assuming the bus interface is not a limiting factor, running the developed design on an ASIC or better FPGA in a more advanced technology would result in theoretical speedups of 5x and 10x for moderate clock frequencies of 100 MHz and 200 MHz, respectively, as also shown by Figure 1(c). However, this would most likely also come at increased cost, i.e. decreased price/efficiency ratios.

6   Summary and Conclusions

In this paper, we presented an FPGA implementation of Prim's algorithm for minimum spanning tree computation. To the best of our knowledge, this represents the first study of realizing this algorithm on reconfigurable hardware. Prim's algorithm plays a major role in embedded and mobile computing, such as wireless ad hoc networks, where FPGAs may be present to support hardware acceleration of performance-critical tasks. We followed a state-of-the-art C-to-RTL methodology using HLS tools to synthesize a high-level C description of two algorithmic variants down to the FPGA, with high performance being the primary goal. On our Spartan 3 FPGA with 66,560 LUTs, 33,280 CLB slices and 68,027 DFFs, our designs utilizes less than 2.5% of each type of logic resource.

Our results show that, considering total wall-time for any of the tried implementations, our unoptimized FPGA implementation running at a low clock frequency dictated by the bus interface reaches about the same performance as an implementation running on an embedded ARM core. However, in terms of raw computation cycles without any communication or OS overhead, the FPGA design achieves a speedup of ≈ 1.21. Using more advanced FPGA technology, with a different device, running at a moderate frequency of 150 MHz (55% of the ARM9's 266 MHz frequency), speedups of around 7.5x should be achievable. Compared to gains of 2.5-3x achieved on multi-core CPUs or GPUs, such an FPGA implementation can achieve better performance at lower cost and power consumption.

Prim's algorithm in its default implementations is limited in the available parallelism. In future work, we plan to investigate opportunities for further algorithmic enhancements specifically targeted at FPGA and hardware implementation, e.g. by speculative execution or by sacrificing optimality of results for better performance.

Acknowledgments. Authors want to thank UT Austin|Portugal 2011 for enabling this research collaboration (www.utaustinportugal.org).

References

1. Graham, R.L., Hell, P.: On the history of the minimum spanning tree problem. IEEE Ann. Hist. Comput. 7(1), 43–57 (1985)
2. Prim, R.C.: Shortest connection networks and some generalizations. Bell System Technology Journal 36, 1389–1401 (1957)
3. Benkic, K., Planinsic, P., Cucej, Z.: Custom wireless sensor network based on zigbee. In: 49th Elmar, Croatia, pp. 259–262 (September 2007)
4. Song, G., Yang, O.: Energy-aware multicasting in wireless ad hoc networks: A survey and discussion. Computer Communications 30(9), 2129–2148 (2007)
5. Grama, A., Karypis, G., Kumar, V., Gupta, A.: Introduction to parallel computing: design and analysis of algorithms, 2nd edn. Addison-Wesley (2003)
6. Setia, R., Nedunchezhian, A., Balachandran, S.: A new parallel algorithm for minimum spanning tree problem. In: International Conference on High Performance Computing (HiPC), pp. 1–5 (2009)
7. Gonina, E., Kale, L.: Parallel Prim's Algorithm with a novel extension. PPL Technical Report (October 2007)
8. Wang, W., Huang, Y., Guo, S.: Design and Implementation of GPU-Based Prim Algorithm. International Journal of Modern Education and Computer Science (IJMECS) 3(4), 55 (2011)
9. Bollaert, T.: Catapult Synthesis: A Practical Introduction to Interactive C Synthesis High-Level Synthesis. In: Coussy, P., Morawiec, A. (eds.) High-Level Synthesis, pp. 29–52. Springer Ned., Dordrecht (2008)
10. Singleterry, R., Sobieszczanski-Sobieski, J., Brown, S.: Field-Programmable Gate Array Computer in Structural Analysis: An Initial Exploration. In: 43rd AIAA/AMSE/ASCE/AHS Structures, Structural Dynamics, and Materials Conference, pp. 1–5 (April 2002)
11. Ornl, W.Y., Strenski, D., Maltby, J.: Performance Evaluation of FPGA-Based Biological Applications Olaf. Cray Users Group, Seattle (2007)

A Passive Monitoring Tool for Evaluation of Routing in *Wireless*HART Networks

Gustavo Kunzel[1], Jean Michel Winter[1], Ivan Muller[1], Carlos Eduardo Pereira[1], and João Cesar Netto[2]

[1] Federal University of Rio Grande do Sul, Electrical Engineering Dept., Porto Alegre, Brazil
{gustavo.kunzel,jean.winter,ivan.muller}@ufrgs.br,
cepereira@ece.ufrgs.br
[2] Federal University of Rio Grande do Sul, Informatics Dept., Porto Alegre, Brazil
netto@inf.ufrgs.br

Abstract. Wireless communication networks have received strong interest for applications in industrial environments. The use of wireless networks in automation systems introduces stringent requirements regarding real-time communication, reliability and security. The *Wireless*HART protocol aims to meet these requirements. In this protocol, a device known as Network Manager is responsible for the entire network configuration, including route definition and resource allocation for the communications. The route definition is a complex process, due to wireless networks characteristics, limited resources of devices and stringent application requirements. This work presents a tool that enables the evaluation of the topology and routes used in operational *Wireles-sHART* networks. By capturing packets at the physical layer, information of operating conditions is obtained, where anomalies in network topology and routes can be identified. In the case study, a *Wireless*HART network was deployed in a laboratory, and by the developed tool, important information about the network conditions was obtained, such as topology, routes, neighbors, superframes and links configured among devices.

Keywords: *Wireless*HART, Wireless industrial networks, Routing.

1 Introduction

The deployment of wireless networks in real-world control and monitoring applications can be a labor-intensive task [1]. Environmental effects often trigger bugs or degrade performance in a way that cannot be observed [2]. To track down such problems, it is necessary to inspect the conditions of network after devices deployment. The inspection can be complex when commercial equipment is used in applications. It can be difficult to gather specific information about the performance of the network, according to the limited visibility provided by the equipments.

Wireless networks has stringent requirements on reliable and real-time communication [3, 22] when used in industrial control applications. Missing or delaying the process data may severely degrade the control quality. Factors as signal strength variations, node mobility and power limitation may interfere on overall performance.

G. Schirner et al. (Eds.): IESS 2013, IFIP AICT 403, pp. 159–170, 2013.

Recently, the International Electrotechnical Commission certified the *Wireless*HART (WH) protocol as the first wireless communication standard for process control [4]. The good acceptance of the protocol by the industry has ensured the developing of different devices that meet the standard from several manufacturers. However, it can be seen that there is still a great lack of computational tools that allow a clearer examination of the behavior and characteristics of these networks and devices [5]. Many of these tools become essential as soon as the full operation of the network depends and varies according to the aspects of the environment as well as the distribution of devices.

The WH network enables mesh topologies, where all the devices have the task of forwarding packets to and from other devices. The Network Manager (NM) has the task of gather information about devices neighbors, network conditions and communication statistics. Based on this info, the NM defines the routes used for communication. The evaluation of the routes used may help user to improve network performance and identify problems, as well as device characteristics.

Several works address the collection of diagnosis information for wireless networks, utilizing active and passive mechanisms [2, 6-7, 17-24]. Active mechanisms involve instrumentation of the network devices with monitoring software. Passive mechanisms utilize sniffers that overhear the packets exchanged on the physical layer [6]. The passive method has advantages, as no interference is added to the network. However, related works do not address specific issues about the passive monitoring of WH packets. WH utilizes an authentication/encryption mechanism to provide secure communication, so the tool must keep track of information to correctly decode the packets and obtain decrypted data. Commercial tools provide means for collecting and decoding WH packets, but the results are shown in a spreadsheet format, making the analysis of data a labor-intensive task.

This work discusses the development of a passive monitoring software tool for evaluation of topology and routes used in WH networks, with a specific architecture to deal with the security information of the protocol. The user can input collected log files or implement a communication directly with sniffers, allowing online and offline analysis methods. Once received, the packets are decoded, an overview of the network is built and by means of statistics, charts, lists, graphs, and other information about the network is shown, helping the user on different evaluations of the network.

The paper is structured as follows. Diagnosis approaches for wireless sensor networks are presented in Section 2. Section 3 presents a short brief of WH and the protocol packet structure and routing mechanisms. Section 4 presents the tool structure. Section 5 presents a case study using the tool in a WH network. The conclusion and the future works are presented in Section 6.

2   Related Work

The diagnosis of wireless networks can be achieved in an active or passive fashion. The active mechanism involves the instrumentation of the nodes with monitoring software for capturing of diagnostic information. The active approaches require nodes to transmit specific messages to diagnosis tools using the communication channel or an alternative back channel [17-20]. This method may overload the normal network communication. A back channel is also not usually available on the devices and on the field. Scarce sensor resources (bandwidth, energy, constrained CPU and memory) may also affect the performance of this kind of diagnosis and change the behavior of the network [2]. The passive approaches in [2], [6], [21-24] utilize sniffers to overhear packets exchanged by the nodes, to form an overview of the network. This approach does not interfere on the network, as no additional bandwidth is required for diagnostic information transfer and no processing and energy power is used in the devices for diagnosis purposes [2]. On the other hand, the passive method is subjected to packet loss, caused by interference, collision and coverage of sniffers. Solutions for the sniffer's deployment problem are proposed in [22]. The hardware for the sniffers is not addressed in this work.

The software architectures for captured packets evaluation of IEEE 802.15.4 are proposed in [2], [6] and [24]. These works propose a generic architecture for collecting, merging, decoding, filtering and visualizing data. However, these approaches do not have mechanisms to deal with protocols that contain security and encryption like WH. Wi-Analys [7] is a commercial tool that provides means for collecting and decoding packets captured from WH networks, but the visualization of results is done in a spreadsheet format, what difficult the analysis of the information.

3   The *Wireless*HART Protocol

The WH standard is part of version 7 of the HART specification [8-9]. It features a secure network and operates on the 2.4 GHz ISM (Industrial, Scientific and Medical) radio band. The physical layer is based on the IEEE 802.15.4 standard in which direct sequence spread spectrum is employed [10]. A WH network supports a variety of devices, including field devices, adapters, portable devices, access points, network manager and a gateway to connect to a host application. The protocol allows multiple access and media arbitration by means of Time Division Multiple Access (TDMA) [11]. The links among devices are programmed and allocated in different time slots by the NM. The NM continuously adapts the routing and schedule due to changes in network topology and demand for communication [12]. The following subsections present the ISO/OSI layers of the protocol.

3.1 Data-Link Layer

The Data-Link Layer is responsible for secure, reliable, error free communication of data between WH devices [13]. The communications are performed in 10 ms timeslots, where two devices are assigned to communicate. A communication transaction within a slot supports the transmission of a Data-Link Protocol Data Unit (DLPDU) from a source, followed by an acknowledgment DLPDU by the addressed device. To enhance reliability, channel-hopping mechanism is combined with TDMA. DLPDU structure is presented in Fig. 1.

The CRC-16 ITU-T [14] is used for bit error detection and AES-CCM* [15] is used for message authentication. Authentication uses the WH Well-Known Key for advertisement DLPDUs and messages of joining devices. Other communications use the Network Key (provided by the NM when a device is joining the network). The Nonce used is a combination of the Absolute Slot Number (ASN) and the source address of the packet. ASN counts the total number of slots occurred since network's birth, and is known by devices through the advertise packets. Five types of DLPDU packets are defined: Advertisement, Acknowledge, Data, Keep-Alive and Disconnect.

Fig. 1. DLPDU structure

3.2 Network Layer

The Network Layer provides routing, end-to-end security and transport services. Data DLPDU packets contain in its payload a Network Layer Protocol Data Unit (NPDU), shown in Fig. 2. The NPDU contains three layers: Network Layer, with routing and packet time information, Security Layer that ensures private communication and enciphered payload, containing information being exchanged over network [16].

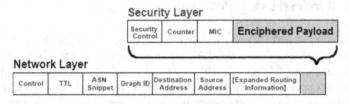

Fig. 2. NPDU structure

The AES-CCM* is also used for authentication of NPDU and decryption of the enciphered payload. The Join Key is used for devices joining the network. The Session Keys (provided by the NM when a device is joining the network) are used in other communications (between Device and Gateway, Device and NM). The Counter field of the Security Layer provides information for the Nonce reconstruction.

Three routing mechanisms are provided in the standard and are described below.

Graph Routing. A graph contains paths that connect different devices on the network. The NM is responsible for creating the graphs and configuring them on each device through transport layer commands [3]. A graph shows a set of direct links between source and final destination and can provide also redundant paths. To send a packet using this method, the source device of packet writes the specific Graph ID number in the NPDU header. All devices on the path must be preconfigured with graph information that specifies the neighbors to which packets may be forwarded.

Source Routing. The source routing provides one single directed path between source and destination device. A list of devices that the packet must travel is statically specified in the NPDU header of the packet [12]. This method does not require configuration of graphs and routes in the devices.

Superframe Routing. In this method, packets are assigned to a specific superframe and the device sends the message according to the identification of the superframe. The forwarding device selects the first available slot in the superframe, and sends the message. So, the superframe must have links that leads packet to its destination. Identification of the superframe routing is done in the NPDU header using the Graph ID field. If the field value is less than 255, then routing is done using superframe. If the value is 256 or more, then routing is done via graphs. A combination of superframe routing and the source routing is also allowed. In this case, the packet is forwarded through the source list with slots configured inside the specified superframe.

3.3 Transport Layer

The Transport Layer provides means to ensure end-end packet delivery, device status and one or more commands. Enciphered payload of the Security Layer contains a Transport Layer Protocol Data Unit (TPDU). Fig. 3 shows the structure of the TPDU packet.

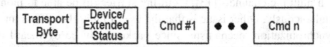

Fig. 3. TPDU structure

4   Routing Monitoring Tool Structure

The structure of the proposed tool is presented in Fig. 4. The tool provides meanings for capturing and decoding captured data, obtaining network information and visualizing routes configured in the devices.

4.1 Capture

The capture of the packets exchanged by nodes is carried out in a passive way by installing one or more sniffers within the area of network. The sniffers add also a timestamp to the captured packets. The deployed sniffers may not be able to hear all packets that occur in network. Reasons involve radio sensitivity, positioning and noise. A partial coverage of the network can meet the requirements of some types of analysis for the WH protocol. This approach has the advantage of limiting the amount of data processed in later steps. Further information about sniffers deployment can be

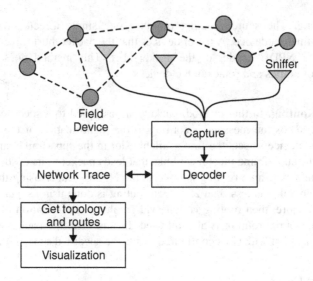

Fig. 4. Monitoring tool structure

found in [22]. For routing evaluation, sniffers may be deployed close to the Access Points, where all the management data to and from NM passes by.

An important factor to be observed in the diagnostic of WH protocol is the communication on multiple channels [13], requiring sniffers to be able to monitor the 16 channels simultaneously. Other issue is that the use of multiple sniffers introduces the need of a synchronization mechanism, since packets may be overheard in different sniffers who have a slightly different clock [2]. A merging process is necessary to combine several sniffers captures in a single trace, ordered according to the timestamp of packets. The merging methods can be found in [2], [6], and [21].

In order to keep the flexibility of the tool, the Capture Block has an interface for input of data from different sources, such as simulators, capture log files, or direct connection with sniffers. The received data is added in a queue to be processed.

4.2 Decoder

The Decoder Block aims to convert a packet from raw bytes to structured message description, according to the ISO/OSI model of WH. At the end of this process, the contents of the packets are interpreted to get information about network conditions. The decoding process is complex due the AES-CCM*, which requires that information about the keys and counters are obtained and stored. The main blocks of the decoder are shown in Fig. 5 and described below. Before execution, user must provide the system with the Network ID and Join Key to enable the decoder to obtain information needed for further authentication and decryption.

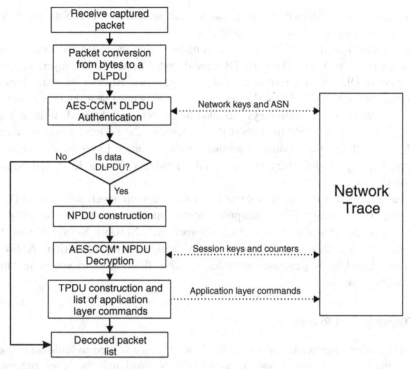

Fig. 5. Packet decoding sequence

Initially, the raw bytes of the packet are converted to its specific type of DLPDU. The packets with wrong CRC-16 and wrong header are identified. Once structured, the DLPDU packets that do not belong to the Network ID provided are identified.

Network Trace. The Network Trace Block provides the necessary information to the decoder for authentication and decryption of packets. It also holds information discovered of the network (e.g. devices, superframes and links). Depending on the coverage of the sniffers, the data stored in the Network Trace may be similar to the data stored in the NM, which have full information about the network operation. For each new message authenticated or decrypted, the Network Trace must be updated in order to maintain updated information of the keys, counters and network. Authentication and decryption of some packets may be compromised, as result of missing keys due to packet loss. The user should be aware of this issue when evaluating the network.

For authenticating the DLPDUs, the Network Trace must keep trace of the current ASN of the network, using an advertise packet captured. While the ASN of the network is not provided, authentication and further processes are compromised. The DLPDU must be authenticated in order to verify its integrity. The Message Integrity Code (MIC) field of the DLPDU is compared with the MIC obtained applying the AES-CCM* algorithm on the raw bytes of the DLPDU. The Network Trace Block keeps track of the Well-Known Key and the Network Key. The Network Key is obtained during the join process of a device.

Once authenticated, the Network Trace is updated with the last ASN used and with the packet timestamp. The Data DLPDUs are decoded on the NPDU layer, while the other types of DLPDUs are sent to the Fill Message block. Another issue involves the decryption of the NPDUs. To do the decryption, sniffers must hear the join process of the device, where the Session Keys provided by the NM are obtained. Without these keys the system is not able to decrypt the contents of the Security Layer messages. For Data DLPDUs, the payload contained in the Security Layer of the NPDU is decrypted, using the Join Key or the specific Device's Session Keys and Session Counters.

Once decrypted, the packet is decoded in the transport layer, where a TPDU is generated. The Network Trace interprets the commands contained in the TPDU in order to maintain an updated view of the network, with Network Keys, Sessions, Superframes, Links, Device's Timers, Services, and further information. A list of all decoded packets is generated in order to allow filtering of messages in future applications of the tool.

4.3 Topology and Routes

The information discovered and stored in Network Trace is used to build an updated view of the network topology and the routes used. Network neighbor's information is used to build the topology of the network. The routes used for packet propagation are obtained based on the graphs, superframes and routes configured on each device. A graph representing each route is built for further analysis.

4.4 Visualizer

The topology and the discovered routes are summarized by the Visualizer Block to be easily interpreted by the user. Representations such statistics, charts and graphs can be used for analysis. Information contained in the Network Trace about the devices and network also may be displayed.

5   Case Study

In order to evaluate the tool, we deployed a WH network in a laboratory environment. The network consisted of the following devices: a Network Manager, an Access Point and a Gateway (Emerson model 1420A), nine WH-compatible field devices developed in previous work [26] and a Wi-Analys Network Analyzer Sniffer, from Hart Communication Foundation. Fig. 6a shows the WH-compatible devices and Fig. 6b the sniffer.

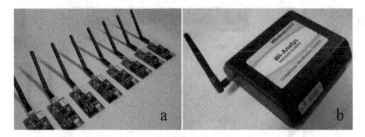

Fig. 6. WH compatible devices (a) and sniffer (b)

The data collected from sniffer was stored in a log file and later loaded in the tool. Packets were captured during a period of 120 minutes since network's birth. The sniffer was deployed close to the access point to get overall information of network. Fig. 7 shows a representation of the network.

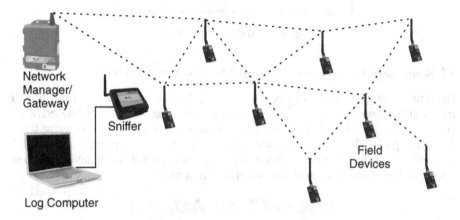

Fig. 7. Deployed network representation

The following subsections present analysis of the network behavior obtained with the captured packets. Before loading the file in the developed tool, we provided the Join Key (0x12345678000000000000000000000000) and Network ID (0001) of devices. The sensor devices publish their process variable each minute.

5.1 Network Topology Evaluation

The current topology of network is evaluated to find devices that may be bottlenecks for transferring data and devices with weak connections to neighbors. A graph is built showing discovered neighbors and the Received Signal Level (RSL) of packets overheard from neighbors. Fig. 8 shows the current graph when analysis reaches the end of log file. As observed, the connectivity of the network is high, as devices can hear almost all other neighbors. Blue circle represents the Access Point of the network.

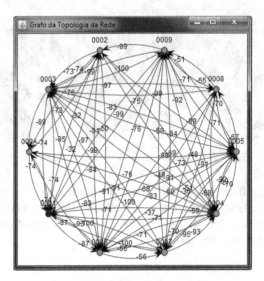

Fig. 8. Network topology graph

5.2 Routes used for Devices to Propagate Data to Access Point

The routes configured in the devices were used as basis to reconstruct information of graphs and paths of the network. Based on the information stored in the Network Trace, our tool has identified that the NM uses superframe routing. Superframe 0 has the uplink graph [3], used to forward data towards the access point. Superframe 1 contains the broadcast graph that is used by NM to send packets to all devices through a combination of source routing and superframe routing.

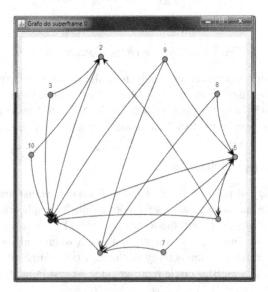

Fig. 9. Uplink graph contained in Superframe 0

6   Conclusion and Future Work

The use of wireless networks in industrial control and monitoring applications can present performance problems due to several factors. To track down such problems, it is necessary to inspect the network and nodes conditions after the deployment.

In this paper we present a software tool for inspection of routing in WH networks. Capture of information is done in a passive way by sniffers. The captured packets are used to build an overview of network topology and routes used in communications. Visualization of obtained information is done via graphs, charts and lists.

The study case has shown that tool can provide important information about the network conditions, and can help user to identify problems and understand the protocol and devices characteristics. User must be aware that packet loss caused by sniffers may affect the analysis.

On ongoing work, we are using this tool to analyze a WH deployment in an industrial application, to verify different aspects of network topology and routing strategies used in WH equipment. Information analyzed shall be used for improvements on devices and on Network Manager routing and scheduling algorithms, to better adjust the network performance for desired applications. The developing of enhanced algorithms for routing and scheduling in *Wireless*HART networks is still a necessity.

References

1. Tateson, J., Roadknight, C., Gonzalez, A., Khan, T., Fitz, S., Henning, I., Boyd, N., Vincent, C., Marshall, I.: Real World Issues in Deploying a Wireless Sensor Network for Oceanography. In: Proceedings of Workshop on Real-World Wireless Sensor Networks (REALWSN 2005), Stockholm (2005)
2. Ringwald, M., Römer, K.: Deployment of Sensor Networks: Problems and Passive Inspection. In: Proceedings of the 5th Workshop on Intelligent Solutions in Embedded Systems (WISES 2007), Madrid, pp. 180–193 (2007)
3. Han, S., Zhu, X., Mok, A.K., Chen, D., Nixon, M.: Reliable and Real-Time Communication in Industrial Wireless Mesh Networks. In: Proceedings of 17th IEEE Real-Time and Embedded Technology and Applications Symposium (RTAS 2011), Chicago, pp. 3–12 (2011)
4. HART Communication Foundation, http://www.hartcomm.org/protocol/wihart/wireless_technology.html (accessed September 2012)
5. Winter, J.M., Lima, C., Muller, I., Pereira, C.E., Netto, J.C.: WirelessHART Routing Analysis Software. In: Computing System Engineering Brazilian Symposium (SBESC 2011), Florianopolis, pp. 96–98 (2011)
6. Yu, D.: DiF: A Diagnosis Framework for Wireless Sensor Networks. In: IEEE Conference on Computer Communications (INFOCOM 2010), San Diego, pp. 1–5 (2010)
7. Han, S., Song, J., Zhu, X., Mok, A.K., Chen, D., Nixon, M., Pratt, W., Gondhalekar, V.: Wi-HTest: Compliance Test Suite for Diagnosing Devices in Real-Time WirelessHART Network. In: Real-Time and Embedded Technology and Applications Symposium (RTAS 2009), San Francisco, pp. 327–336 (2009)

8. Kim, A.N., Hekland, F., Petersen, S., Doyle, P.: When HART Goes Wireless: Understanding and Implementing the WirelessHART Standard. In: IEEE International Conference on Emerging Technologies and Factory Automation, Hamburg, pp. 899–907 (2008)

9. Song, J., Mok, A.K., Chen, D., Nixon, M., Blevins, T., Wojsznis, W.: Improving pid control with unreliable communications. In: ISA EXPO Technical Confererence, Houston (2006)

10. IEEE 802.11, http://grouper.ieee.org/groups/802/11/ (accessed July 2012)

11. Rappaport, T.S.: Wireless Communications – Principles & Practice. Prentice Hall Communications Engineering and Emerging Technologies Series, New York (1996)

12. Chen, D., Nixon, M., Mok, A.: WirelessHART: real-time mesh network for industrial automation. Springer, England (2010)

13. HART Communication Foundation, HCF SPEC 075, Rev. 1.1 (2008)

14. Simpson, W.: http://www.faqs.org/rfcs/rfc1549.html (accessed July 2012)

15. Dworkin, M.: Recommendation for Block Cipher Modes of Operation: The CCM Mode for Authentication and Confidentiality. National Institute of Standards and Technology. Special Publication 800-38C (2004)

16. HART Communication Foundation, HCF SPEC 085, Rev. 1.2. (2009)

17. Srinvasan, K., Kazandjieva, M.A., Jain, M., Kim, E., Levis, P.: SWAT: Enabling Wireless Network Measurements. In: ACM 8th Conference on Embedded Networked Systems (SENSYS 2008), Raleigh (2008)

18. Maerien, J., Agten, P., Huygens, C., Joosen, W.: FAMoS: A Flexible Active Monitoring Service for Wireless Sensor Networks. In: Göschka, K.M., Haridi, S. (eds.) DAIS 2012. LNCS, vol. 7272, pp. 104–117. Springer, Heidelberg (2012)

19. Rost, S., Balakrishnan, H.M.: A Health Monitoring System for Wireless Sensor Networks. In: Sensor and Ad Hoc Communications and Networks (SECON 2006), pp. 575–584 (2006)

20. Ramanathan, N., Kohler, E., Girod, L., Estrin, D.: Sympathy: a debugging system for sensor networks. In: IEEE 29th Annual International Conference on Local Computer Networks, Tampa, pp. 554–555 (2004)

21. Chen, B.-R., Peterson, G., Mainland, G., Welsh, M.: LiveNet: Using Passive Monitoring to Reconstruct Sensor Network Dynamics. In: Nikoletseas, S.E., Chlebus, B.S., Johnson, D.B., Krishnamachari, B. (eds.) DCOSS 2008. LNCS, vol. 5067, pp. 79–98. Springer, Heidelberg (2008)

22. Zeng, W., Chen, X., Kim, Y.A., Bu, Z., Wei, W., Wang, B., Shi, Z.J.: Delay monitoring for wireless sensor networks: An architecture using air sniffers. In: IEEE Conference on Military Communications (MILCOM 2009), Boston, pp. 1–8 (2009)

23. Depari, A., Ferrari, P., Flammini, A., Lancellotti, M., Marioli, D., Rinaldi, S., Sisinni, E.: Design and performance evaluation of a distributed WirelessHART sniffer based on IEEE1588. In: International Symposium on Precision Clock Synchronization for Measurement, Control and Communication (ISPCS 2009), Brescia, pp. 1–6 (2009)

24. Ban, S.J., Cho, H., Lee, C.W., Kim, S.W.: Implementation of IEEE 802.15.4 Packet Analyzer. In: International Conference on Computer, Electrical, and Systems Science, and Engineering (CESSE 2007), Bangkok, pp. 346–349 (2007)

25. Choong, L.: Multi-Channel IEEE 802.15.4 Packet Capture Using Software Defined Radio. M.S. thesis, UCLA (2009)

26. Muller, I., Pereira, C.E., Netto, J.C., Fabris, E.C., Algayer, R.: Development of WirelessHART Compatible Field Devices. In: IEEE Instrumentation and Measurement Technology Conference, Austin, pp. 1430–1434 (2010)

Automated Identification of Performance Bottleneck on Embedded Systems for Design Space Exploration

Yuki Ando[1], Seiya Shibata[1,*], Shinya Honda[1],
Hiroyuki Tomiyama[2], and Hiroaki Takada[1]

[1] Nagoya University, Nagoya, Japan
[2] Ritsumeikan University, Kusatsu, Japan

Abstract. Embedded systems usually have strict resource and performance constraints. Designers often need to improve the system design so that the system satisfies those constraints. In such case, performance bottlenecks should be identified and improved effectively. In this paper, we present a method to identify performance bottlenecks. Our method automatically identifies not only the bottlenecks but also a list of improvement rates of bottlenecks that is necessary for the system to satisfy design constraints. With the list of improvement rates, designers easily consider how to improve the bottlenecks. A case study on AES encryption and decryption application shows effectiveness of our method.

1   Introduction

As the functionality of embedded systems has increased, they are required more and more computation. Some processes representing the functions of the systems are implemented in dedicated hardware so that the system accelerates their computation. On the other hand, implementing processes in dedicated hardware causes to increase hardware area. For embedded systems, it is important to satisfy design constraints such as execution time and hardware area. So system designers are facing a problem that they have to efficiently find a system configuration satisfying the design constraints.

Figure 1 shows an example of design flow for embedded systems with dedicated hardware. It starts from changing software description to software/hardware (SW/HW) mixed description. Then, designers conduct exploration of SW/HW partitioning. During the exploration of SW/HW partitioning, system designers try to find a mapping that satisfies design constraints by changing the allocation of processes. In the past, design tools have been developed in order to efficiently explore SW/HW partitioning [1,2].

After the exploration of SW/HW partitioning, the designers have to check whether a mapping satisfies all design constraints because exploration of SW/HW partitioning may not find a mapping that satisfies the design constraints.

---

* Presently with NEC Corporation.

G. Schirner et al. (Eds.): IESS 2013, IFIP AICT 403, pp. 171–180, 2013.

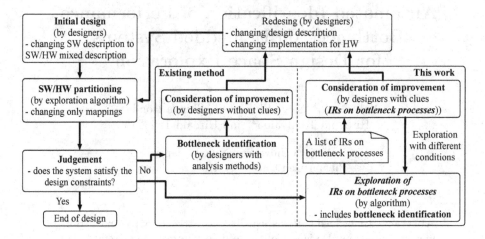

Fig. 1. Entire design flow

For example, a mapping satisfies design constraint of hardware area but may not satisfy that of execution time. From this mapping, changing an allocation of a process from SW to HW makes execution time faster. However, it brings bigger hardware area. As the result, new mapping satisfies design constraint of execution time but may not satisfy that of hardware area. Thus, exploration of SW/HW partitioning does not always find a mapping that satisfies all design constraints. In such case, designers need improve the design description.

There are two big problems to improve the design description. First problem is identification of bottlenecks on the system. In the existing design method, designers identify the bottlenecks using analysis tools. Fei et al. divided execution logs into particular behavior groups and analyze the behavior groups[3]. Valle et al. proposed a method to make logging of system performance easy[4]. Second problem is identification of improvement rates (IRs) of bottlenecks. With existing design methods, designers have to identify how much they have to improve bottlenecks to satisfy design constraints. Then, they consider how to change design description to improve the system performances. The existing design methods waste time of designers to improve design description.

In this paper, we propose a method to automatically identify not only bottlenecks but also a list of IRs of bottlenecks that are necessary to satisfy the design constraints. With our method, designers no longer identify how much they have to improve the bottlenecks because our method automatically takes care of that. It is ideal for designers to know the essential IRs on bottlenecks. In addition, our method lists up several candidates to improve the systems. Thus, our method brings shorter time to identify the IRs of bottlenecks, and designers can take more time to consider various ways to improve the system description.

Our main contribution is a method to explore the IRs on bottlenecks. In addition, our method explores IRs for not only execution time but also hardware area. A case study on AES shows the effectiveness of our method.

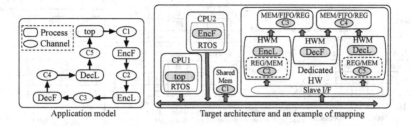

Fig. 2. An example of application model (AES) and target architecture

2   Application Model and Target Architecture

Fig.2 shows an example of application (AES encryption and decryption) model on left side. Application model describes a set of processes running concurrently and channels representing communications among processes. This kind of models is common for design tools such as ARTEMIS[5] and Metropolis[6].

Right side of Fig.2 depicts an example of our target architectures. It also shows an example of mappings (top and EncF are allocated to SW, and the others are allocated to HW) for AES encryption and decryption model. The figure shows typical architecture and mapping of system-on-a-chip. The processors (CPU) are assumed to be homogeneous, and the number of processors must be greater than or equal to one. Processors, dedicated hardware, and shared memory are connected through a standard on-chip bus. The processes allocated to SW are implemented onto processors as RTOS tasks. Those allocated to HW are implemented onto hardware modules (HWMs) in the dedicated hardware.

Memory is shared for communication among the processors (C1). For communication between the processors and hardware modules, memory (MEM) and the register (REG) are generated in HWMs (C2, C5). They are accessed from processors through a standard on-chip bus and the slave interface. HWMs can communicate with each other directly through the exclusionary FIFO, MEM, and REG (C3, C4). Thus, the architecture allows processors and hardware modules to communicate directly through a bus, memory, and the interfaces.

3   Exploration of Improvement Rate on Bottleneck Process

3.1   Definition of Bottleneck Process

In this paper, a process X is defined as a bottleneck process if reducing the execution time of process X shortens entire execution time of system without any change of mapping.

Figure 3 shows an example of bottleneck processes. The example has four processes. The original execution time of processes A, B, C, and D are 300, 400, 100, and 700, respectively. Processes A, B, C are mapped to a processor

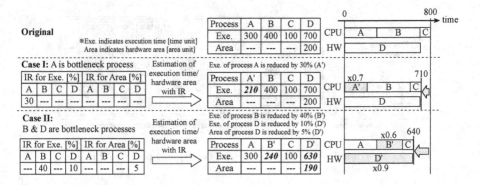

Fig. 3. An example of IRs and bottleneck processes.

(CPU) and process D is mapped to hardware module (HW). The original entire execution time is 800 as shown on the right side of the figure.

Case I shows that process A is a bottleneck process. The execution time of A is assumed to be 210 (A'), that is 70% of process A. The entire execution time of Case I is reduced to 710 because execution time of A' is applied. Reducing the execution time of process A causes to shorten the entire execution time. Therefore, process A is a bottleneck process under our definition.

With our definition, several processes may become bottleneck processes at the same time as shown Case II. The entire execution time also becomes shorter than original one when the execution time of process B and D are assumed to be 240 (B') and 630 (D'), respectively. Thus, processes B and D are bottlenecks.

3.2   Definition of Improvement Rate (IR)

IR indicates the ratio to shorten the execution time or to reduce the hardware area of process compared to original one. Examples of IR are also shown in Fig. 3. Each process has two types of IR, one for execution time and the other for hardware area. For example, original execution time and hardware area of process D are 700 and 200, respectively. In Case II, it has 10% of IR for execution time and 5% of IR for hardware area. Thus, execution time and hardware area of process D are assumed to be 630 and 190, respectively.

3.3   Exploration of the IRs on Bottleneck Processes

Under the definition of a bottleneck process and that of IR, estimating the entire execution time with IRs identifies bottleneck processes. If the entire execution time is reduced, processes that have IRs are bottlenecks. Thus, increasing the value of IRs unveils whether the processes are bottlenecks or not.

Fig. 4 shows the exploration flow of IRs on bottleneck processes. The inputs are a mapping to explore the IRs and design constraints of execution time and hardware area. The output is a set of IRs that satisfies the design constraints.

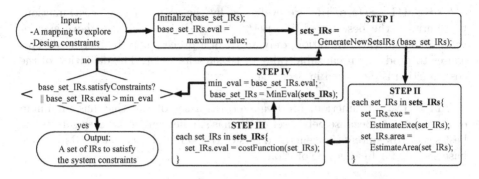

Fig. 4. Exploration flow of IRs for bottleneck processes

At the beginning, all IRs in a set of IRs (base_set_IRs) are initialized to 0% (Initialize). At the same time, evaluation value of base_set_IRs (base_set_IRs.eval) is initialized to maximum value. After the initialization, four steps are repeated. At step I, new sets of IRs are generated from base_set_IRs to increase values of IRs so that the input mapping satisfies the design constraints. At step II, execution time and hardware area are estimated with generated sets of IRs. At step III, all generated sets of IRs are evaluated by the cost function because increasing the same value of IR causes to produce unrealizable IR such as 100%. At step IV, the best set of IRs is selected for further exploration. The detail of each step is described end of this section. After step IV, if a set of IRs satisfies the design constraints, or there is no better set of IRs, the exploration ends.

After an exploration, designers get a mapping and its best set of IRs on bottleneck processes. The best set of IRs indicates how much bottleneck processes should be improved to satisfy the design constraints for the mapping. In addition, exploration on different mappings may bring better ones. Thus, designers can easily find the best mapping and its set of IRs on bottleneck processes among several pairs of them.

STEP I. From base_set_IRs, new sets of IRs are generated by a function GenerateNewSetsIRs. Only an IR in base_set_IRs is increased at once. Before the exploration, designers have to define static increasing number. Generating new sets of IRs on all IRs, the number of new sets is twice the number of processes in maximum.

STEP II. Execution time and hardware area are estimated for all sets of IRs in sets_IRs. Trace-based estimation tools [7,8] are assumed to be used to estimate the entire execution time with IRs. The tools usually take profiles of process execution time as input. For that, the tools can estimate the entire execution time with IRs by arranging the profiles of execution time. Hardware area is estimated by summation of the area of hardware modules. Area of hardware module is reduced when the hardware area is estimated with IRs.

STEP III. Sets of IRs are evaluated by the cost function (costFunction) to determine the best set of IRs. Better set of IR is assumed to have smaller value. Without this evaluation, only an IR of a process may be increased. This causes to produce unrealizable value of IR such as 100%. The definition of the cost function is described in Sect. 3.4.

STEP IV. A function, MinEval, returns a set of IRs that has minimum evaluated value. Because better set of IRs has smaller value, this step selects the best set of IRs among the generated sets of IRs. The selected set of IRs become base_set_IRs for further exploration.

3.4 Detail of Cost Function

In order to determine better sets of IRs, we propose a cost function (costFunction). First of all, the set of IRs should make a mapping satisfy the design constraints because this is the main purpose. So the cost function allows IRs to increase their values. Secondly, the set of IRs should not have impossible values of IRs such as 100%. So the cost function have to prevent that a set of IRs includes such impossible values. Thirdly, there may be some processes that are no longer improved. Such processes should not be listed to improve more. From these points, the cost function should have three features below. Note that smaller value is assumed to be better.

1. The value of cost function gets smaller (better) when the estimated execution time and hardware area close to the design constraints (the values of IRs get larger).
2. The value of cost function should be larger for large IRs to prevent impossible values of IRs.
3. Designers can set easiness of improvement on all processes separately.

For first feature, distance (dis) between estimated values and design constraints is used. For second feature, penalty ($penal$) depending on IRs is used. Third feature is handled by introducing values of easiness for processes.

There are three kind of parameters determined by designers before the exploration starts. Note that xxx should be either "exe" or "area" indicating execution time or hardware area, respectively.

- $target_{xxx}$: value of design constraints for exe/area
- $ease_{p\_xxx}$: value of easiness to improve process p for exe/area
- max_{xxx} : maximum value of exe/area

The inputs of the cost function are estimated values of execution time (est_{exe}) and hardware area (est_{area}), and a set of IRs ($rate_{p\_xxx}$). The cost function consists of distance (dis) and penalty ($penal$). It returns its value ($eval$) by (1).

$$eval = dis + penal \qquad (1)$$

From (2) to (4) show calculation of dis. Because our method deals with execution time and hardware area, distances for each design constraints (dis_{exe} and dis_{area}) are calculated as shown in (3) and (4).

$$dis = (dis_{exe} + dis_{area}) \, / \, 2 \tag{2}$$

$$dis_{xxx} = \begin{cases} 3 \times dif_{xxx} + 0.1 \; (dif_{xxx} > 0) \\ 0.001 \times dif_{xxx} \quad (others) \end{cases} \tag{3}$$

$$dif_{xxx} = est_{xxx} - target_{xxx} \tag{4}$$

The total penalty ($penal$) is given by (5). It is an average of penalties for execution time($penal_{exe}$) and hardware area ($penal_{area}$) given by (6). In the equation, $rate_{p\_exe}$ and $rate_{p\_area}$ indicate the IR of process $p \in P$ for execution time and hardware area, respectively. Note that P is a set of processes in the system. Standard value of easiness to improve process p ($ease_{p\_xxx}$) is assumed to be one. If it is bigger than one, it means that the process p is hard to improve, and vice versa. Values of easiness to improve process have to be determined by designers before the exploration starts.

$$penal = (penal_{exe} + penal_{area}) \, / \, 2 \tag{5}$$

$$penal_{xxx} = \left(\sum_{p \in P} (rate_{p\_xxx} * ease_{p\_xxx})^3 \right) / \, |P| \tag{6}$$

The coefficients in the cost function are calibrated with MPEG-4 decoder application that consists of 11 processes. We calibrated them on various combinations of design constraints, mappings and number of processors. Note that the easiness of improvement was set to one during the calibration.

4   A Case Study

This section shows a case study on AES encryption and decryption application (AES) in CHStone[9]. Before this study, we decided the aim to reduce hardware area while the execution time keeps the same. During the study, we improved the performance of AES twice along with the design flow shown in Fig. 1. The target architecture is Altera Stratix II FPGA [11] board which has a single soft core processor and dedicated hardware. Design constraints are execution time and hardware area (the number of look-up table (#LUTs)).

4.1   Initial Design of AES Encryption and Decryption

AES is written in C and the number of lines is 716. We divided AES description into five processes as shown in left side of Fig. 2 so that we can use our system-level design tool [10] and explore SW/HW partitioning. We just changed SW description to SW/HW mixed description. This design without any optimization is called initial design. In detail, the global arrays in C description are changed to shared-memory communication. Because the process named "top" is the sequencer of the application, it is not a target of improvement and exploration of SW/HW partitioning. EncF and EncL are the first half and last half of encryption, respectively. Also, DecF and DecL are the first half and last half of decryption, respectively. AES repeats encryption and decryption 10 blocks of data consisting of 16 integers for 100 times.

4.2   Improvement of Initial Design

We first explored SW/HW partitioning for initial design. As AES has four processes that can be allocated to SW and HW, so there are 16 mappings in total. We explored SW/HW partitioning by implementing all mappings onto the FPGA board with our tool. From this, we found 11 mappings that construct the trade-offs between execution time and hardware area. We also found that the shortest execution time and #LUTs were 1.31 seconds and 19,244, respectively.

In order to improve the design, we decided design constraints of 1.3 seconds for execution time and 18,000 for hardware area. For all processes, the easiness to improve process was set to one (default). We explored IRs for 11 mappings on trade-off with the design constraints. In this work, we used our own trace-based estimation tool [12] for exploration of IRs on bottleneck processes.

After the exploration, we had 11 sets of IRs (a set of IRs for each mapping). The best three results in terms of value calculated by the cost function are shown in Table 1. In the table, "Mapping", "IR for Exe." and "IR for Area" indicate allocation of processes, IRs for execution time and that for hardware area, respectively.

Table 1. Identified bottlenecks and IRs for initial design

ID	Mapping				IR for Exe. [%]]				IR for Area [%]			
	EncF	EncL	DecF	DecL	EncF	EncL	DecF	DecL	EncF	EncL	DecF	DecL
No.1	SW	HW	HW	HW	—	—	—	5	—	5	—	5
No.2	HW	SW	HW	25	—	15	5	—	—	—	—	
No.3	SW	SW	HW	—	40	15	5	—	—	—	—	

From the result of No.1, DecL was identified as a bottleneck for execution time. Its execution time had to be reduced 5% in order to satisfy the design constraints. So we considered how to improve its execution time with the result. Then, we decided to tune the design description because initial design was just changed to SW/HW mixed description from SW description. At redesign step, we reduced the number of memory accesses in DecL. We also unrolled the loop instructions in DecL because it was implemented on HW. After the redesign, we again explored SW/HW partitioning and found that mapping (No.1) has the execution time of 0.83 seconds and the hardware area of 16,573 in #LUTs. Thus, we could have a design that satisfied the design constraints.

4.3   Summary of Case Study to Improvement AES Application

As mentioned before, we improved AES twice along with the design flow shown in Fig. 1. The previous section shows the detail of first improvement of AES. In this section, we summarize our case study.

Table 2. Execution time (Exe.) and hardware area (Area) for designs

| Design | Allocation of process / Difference from Initial † | | | | Measured | |
	EncF	EncL	DecF	DecL	Exe. [sec]	Area [#LUTs]
Initial	HW	HW	HW	HW	1.31	19,244
Imp1	SW	HW	HW	HW / M, L	0.83	16,573
Imp2	HW / S	HW / S	HW	SW / M	1.29	12,501

†M: reducing memory accesses, L: loops are unrolled,S: reducing hardware area

Table 2 shows execution time and hardware area of three designs. Initial, Imp1 and Imp2 indicate initial design, first improved design and second improved design, respectively. After first improvement, we got a design named Imp1 that satisfied original design constraints (shorter than 1.3 seconds and less than 18,000 in #LUTs). The aim to improve AES was reducing hardware area while the execution time remains less than 1.3 seconds. As the execution time of Imp1 was 0.83 seconds, so we considered that sacrificing the execution time could reduce the hardware area.

We, once again, decided the design constraints of 1.3 seconds for execution time and 14,000 for hardware area. Then we explored SW/HW partitioning on Imp1. We, however, could not find any mapping satisfying new design constraints. Thus, we explored IRs on Imp1 design. With the results of exploration for IRs, we changed the synthesis option of hardware for processes EncF and EncL. The synthesis options are shown on Imp2 in Table 2. As a result, we got a design whose execution time and hardware area are 1.29 seconds and 12,501 in #LUTs that satisfied the design constraints.

This case study shows that we could improve AES by using only explored IRs. After the twice of improvements, hardware area was reduced 35% with shorter execution time compared to initial design. Therefore, IRs helped the designer to tune the description of application to satisfy design constraints.

5   Conclusion

We proposed a method to identify system bottlenecks and explore improvement rates of them for embedded systems. Because our method automatically identifies not only bottlenecks but also a list of improvement rates that is necessary to satisfy the design constraints, our method helps designers to improve the system without a time-consuming analysis. The case study on AES encryption and decryption application showed that our method surely identified system bottlenecks automatically. The designers efficiently consider how to improve the system with the list of improvement rates. Entire design time is shortened with our method. Therefore, our method is effective to improve the embedded systems.

Acknowledgment. This work was in part supported by STARC (Semiconductor Technology Academic Research Center).

References

1. Dömer, R., Gerstlauer, A., Peng, J., Shin, D., Cai, L., Yu, H., Abdi, S., Gajski, D.D.: System-on-Chip Environment: A SpecC-Based Framework for Heterogeneous MPSoC Design. EURASIP Journal on Embedded Systems (2008)
2. Ha, S., Kim, S., Lee, C., Yi, Y., Kwon, S., Joo, Y.P.: PeaCE: A Hardware-Software Codesign Environment for Multimedia Embedded Systems. ACM Trans. Design Automation of Electronic Systems (2007)
3. Gao, F., Sair, S.: Long term Performance Bottleneck Analysis and Prediction. In: International Conference on Computer Design, pp. 3–9 (2006)
4. Del Valle, P.G., Atienza, D., Magan, I., Flores, J.G., Perez, E.A., Mendias, J.M., Benini, L., Micheli, G.D.: A complete multi-processor system-on-chip FPGA-based emulation framework. In: International Conference on Very Large Scale Integration, pp. 140–145 (2006)
5. Pimentel, A.D.: The Artemis workbench for system-level performance evaluation of embedded systems. International Journal of Embedded Systems 3, 181–196 (2008)
6. Balarin, F., Watanabe, Y., Hsieh, H., Lavagno, L., Passerone, C., SangiovanniVincentelli, A.: Metoropolis: An Integrated Electronic System Design Environment. Computer (2003)
7. Ueda, K., Sakanushi, K., Takeuchi, K., Imai, M.: Architecture-level performance estimation method based on system-level profiling. In: Computers & Digital Techniques, pp. 12–19 (2005)
8. Wild, T., Herkersdorf, A., Lee, G.Y.: TAPES - Trace-based architecture performance evaluation with SystemC. Design Automation for Embedded Systems 10, 157–179 (2005)
9. Hara, Y., Tomiyama, H., Honda, S., Takada, H.: Proposal and Quantitative Analysis of the CHStone Benchmark Program Suite for Practical C-based High-level Synthesis. Journal of Information Processing 17, 242–254 (2009)
10. Shibata, S., Honda, S., Tomiyama, H., Takada, H.: Advanced SystemBuilder: A Tool Set for Multiprocessor Design Space Exploration. In: International SoC Design Conference, pp. 79–82 (2010)
11. Altera Corporation, http://www.altera.com/
12. Shibata, S., Ando, Y., Honda, S., Tomiyama, H., Takada, H.: A Fast Performance Estimation Framework for System-Level Design Space Exploration. IPSJ Transactions on System LSI Design Methodology 5, 44–55 (2012)

Compositional Timing Analysis of Real-Time Systems Based on Resource Segregation Abstraction[*]

Philipp Reinkemeier[1] and Ingo Stierand[2]

[1] OFFIS - Institute for Information Technology,
Oldenburg, Germany
philipp.reinkemeier@offis.de

[2] Carl von Ossietzky Universität Oldenburg,
Oldenburg, Germany
stierand@informatik.uni-oldenburg.de

Abstract. For most embedded safety-critical systems not only the functional correctness is of importance, but they must provide their services also in a timely manner. Therefore, it is important to have rigorous analysis techniques for determining timing properties of such systems. The ever increasing complexity of such real-time systems calls for compositional analysis techniques, where timing properties of local systems are composed to infer timing properties of the overall system. In analytical timing analysis approaches the dynamic timing behavior of a system is characterized by mathematical formulas abstracting from the state-dependent behavior of the system. While these approaches scale well and also support compositional reasoning, the results often exhibit large over-approximations. Our approach for compositional timing analysis is based on ω-regular languages, which can be employed in automata-based model-checking frameworks. To tackle the scalability problem due to state-space explosion, we present a technique to abstract an application by means of its resource demands. The technique allows to carry out an analysis independently for each application that shall be deployed on the same platform using its granted resource supply. Integration of the applications on the platform can then be analyzed based on the different resource supplies without considering details of the applications.

1 Introduction and Related Work

Developing safety-critical real-time systems is becoming increasingly complex as the number of functions realized by these systems grows. Additionally an increasing number of functions is realized in software, which is then integrated

[*] This work was partly supported by the Federal Ministry for Education and Research (BMBF) under support code 01IS11035M, 'Automotive, Railway and Avionics Multicore Systems (ARAMiS)', and by the German Research Council (DFG) as part of the Transregional Collaborative Research Center 'Automatic Verification and Analysis of Complex Systems' (SFB/TR 14 AVACS).

G. Schirner et al. (Eds.): IESS 2013, IFIP AICT 403, pp. 181–192, 2013.

on a common target platform in order to save costs. The integration on a common platform causes interferences between the different software-functions due to their shared resource usage. It is desirable to bound these interferences in a way to make guarantees about the timing behavior of the individual software-functions. A schedulability analysis delivers such bounds for interferences between software-tasks sharing a CPU by means of a scheduling strategy.

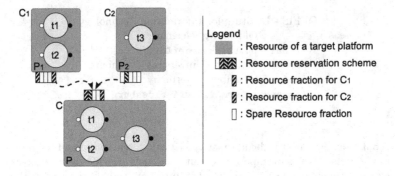

Fig. 1. Exemplary Integration Scenario using Resource Segregation

We present a compositional analysis framework using real-time interfaces based on ω-regular languages. Following the idea of interface-based design, components are described by interfaces and can be composed if their corresponding interfaces are compatible. The contribution of this work is a framework allowing to formally capture the resource demand of an interface, that we call segregation property. Compatibility of interfaces then can be reduced to compatibility of their segregation properties. Further a refinement relation is defined, which leads to a sufficient condition for compatibility of segregation properties. The framework can be used in (but is not restricted to) scenarios like the following: The bottom part of Fig. 1 shows a target platform that is envisioned by say an Original Equipment Manufacturer (OEM). It consists of a processing node (P). Suppose the OEM wants to implement two applications, components C_1 and C_2, on this architecture and delegates their actual implementation to two different suppliers. Both applications share the same resource of the target platform, i.e. tasks t_1, t_2 and t_3 are all executed on P after integration. Therefore, a resource reservation is assigned to each component, guaranteeing a certain amount of resource supply. Then the timing behavior of both components can be analyzed independently from each other based on their resource demands and the guaranteed resource supply. Verification of the successful integration of C_1 and C_2 on the platform then amounts to check whether the reserved resource supplies can be composed.

There have been considerable studies on compositional real-time scheduling frameworks [12,13,11,7,5]. These studies define interface theories for components abstracting the resource requirement of a component by means of demand functions [12,13], bounded-delay resource models [7], or periodic resource models [11,5]. Based on these theories the required resources of a component, captured by its interface, can for example be abstracted into a single task. This approach gives rise to hierarchical scheduling frameworks where interfaces propagate resource demands between different layers of the hierarchy. Our proposed resource segregation abstraction of a component is an extension of the real-time interfaces presented in [3]. Contrary to the aforementioned approaches, our real-time interfaces and resource segregation are based on ω-regular languages. That means, the approach can for example be employed in automata-based model-checking frameworks. In addition the results we present are not bound to specific task and resource models, like periodic or bounded delay.

Analytic methods provide efficient analysis by abstracting from concrete behavior. The drawback is that this typically leads to over-approximations of the analysis results. Computational methods on the other hand, such as model-checking for automata ([2,9,6]), typically provide the expressive power to model and analyze real-time systems without the need for approximate analysis methods. This flexibility comes with costs. Model-checking is computationally expensive, which often prevents analysis of larger systems. The contribution of this paper will help to reduce verification complexity for the application of computational methods.

The paper is structured as follows: Section 2 briefly introduces real-time interfaces presented in [3], where task executions are characterized by ω-regular languages over time slices occupied by the respective tasks. Section 3 provides the formalization of segregation properties for interfaces, which can be used to abstract from concrete behavior of an interface. We define refinement and composition operations on segregation properties that preserve schedulability of the composition of the associated interfaces. Section 4 shows that our approach is consistent with the (analytical) resource models of [11,5] by the definition of a translation. Section 5 discusses further work and concludes the paper.

2 Real-Time Interfaces

The resource segregation abstraction presented in this work is based on the real-time interfaces presented in [3]. Therefore, we briefly summarize the basic definitions. We assume a set of real-time components are to be executed on a set of resources such as processing nodes and communication channels. Each component consists of a set of tasks. A real-time interface of a component specifies the set of all its legal schedules when it is executed on the resources. For example, consider a component with two tasks 1 and 2, which are scheduled on a single resource in discrete slots of some fixed duration, like shown in Fig. 1 for component P_1. A schedule for this component can be described by an infinite word over the alphabet $0, 1, 2$. 0 means the resource is idle during the slot, and 1 and 2 means the corresponding task is running. The real-time interface of a component is an ω-language containing all legal schedules of the component. Therefore, an interface with a non-empty language contains at least one schedule and is said to be schedulable. Interfaces can be composed (intersection) to check whether two components together are schedulable.

Definition 1. *A real-time interface I is a tuple (L, T), where $T \subseteq \mathcal{T}$ is the set of tasks of the interface and $L \subseteq T^\omega$ is an ω-regular language denoting the set of legal schedules of I. The empty task 0 denoting an idle slot is part of every interface, i.e. $0 \in T$.*

The intuition of an interface is that it describes the set of schedules that satisfy the requirements of its component. An interface with an empty language is said to be not schedulable. Conversely, an interface with a non-empty language is said to be schedulable, as at least one legal schedule exists for the interface.

Example: Suppose that task t_1 in Fig. 1 is a periodic task t with period $p = 5$ and an execution time $e = 3$. The language of its interface I_1 can be described by the following regular expression: $L_{I_1} = 0^{<5}[t^3 \,|||\, 0^2]^\omega$, where $u \,|||\, v$ denotes all possible interleavings of the finite words u and v. That means, a schedule is legal for interface I_1, as long as it provides 3 slots during a time interval of 5.

Observe, that interface I_1 captures an assumption about the activation pattern of task t_1. The part $0^{<5}$ of the regular expression represents all possible phasings of the initial task activations. This correlates to the formalism of event streams, which is a well-known representation of task activation patterns in real-time systems (cf. [10]) by lower and upper arrival curves $\eta^-(\Delta t)$ and $\eta^+(\Delta t)$.

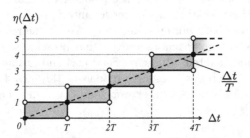

Fig. 2. Arrival curves of periodic events

Key to dealing with interfaces having different alphabets is the following projection operation: For alphabet T and language L of an interface I and $T' \subseteq T$, we consider its *projection* $pr_{T'}(L)$ to T', which is the unique extension of the function $T \rightarrow T'$ that is identity on the elements of T' and maps every element of $T \setminus T'$ to 0. We will also need the *inverse projection* $pr_{T''}^{-1}(L)$, for $T'' \supseteq T$, which is the language over T'' whose words projected to T belong to L.

Definition 2. *Given two interfaces $I_1 = (L_1, T_1)$ and $I_2 = (L_2, T_2)$ the parallel composition $I_1 \,\|\, I_2$ is the interface (L, T), where*

- *$T = T_1 \cup T_2$ and*
- *$L = pr_T^{-1}(L_1) \cap pr_T^{-1}(L_2)$*

The intuition of this definition is that a schedule is legal for $I_1 \parallel I_2$ if its restriction to T_2 is legal for I_2 and its restriction to T_1 is legal for I_1. That means tasks of an interface are allowed to run when the resource is idle in the other interface.

Definition 3. *Given two interfaces $I = (L, T)$ and $I' = (L', T')$, then I' refines I, $I' \preceq I$, if and only if:*

- *$T' \supseteq T$ and*
- *$pr_T(L') \subseteq L$*

The intuition of this definition is that all schedules legal in I' are (modulo projection) also legal schedules in I and I' is able to schedule more tasks from the set $T' \setminus T$ in the gaps left by schedules in I.

The following lemmas provide useful properties of the real-time interface framework.

Lemma 1. *Parallel composition of interfaces is associative and commutative.*

An associative and commutative composition operation guarantees that composable interfaces may be assembled together in any order. Therefore, real-interfaces support *incremental design*.

Lemma 2. *Refinement of interfaces is a partial order.*

As refinement is a partial order, it is ensured that: If interface $I' \preceq I$, then for any interface $I'' \preceq I'$ it holds that $I'' \preceq I$. That means interfaces can be refined iteratively.

Lemma 3. *Refinement is compositional. That means $I' \preceq I$ implies $I' \parallel J \preceq I \parallel J$.*

A compositional refinement allows to refine composable interfaces separately, while maintaining composability. Together with commutativity and associativity of the composition operator, we have that the real-time interfaces support *independent implementability*. Proofs for Lemma 1-3 are presented in [3].

3   Resource Segregation

While real-time interfaces are powerful enough to cope with complex designs and scenarios like depicted in Fig. 1, the refinement relation involves complex language inclusion checks. Moreover, the details of all components and their tasks must be known in order to compose them. Therefore, we introduce an abstraction for a real-time interface consisting of multiple tasks that we call *segregation property*. These segregation properties will be defined such that compositionality of segregation properties ensures compositionality of their interfaces, respectively. That means given two interfaces I_1 and I_2 and segregation properties B_{I_1} and B_{I_2}, we look for a composition operator $\parallel$ and a simple property φ, such that

$$B_{I_1} \parallel B_{I_2} \models \varphi \implies I_1 \parallel I_2 \text{ is schedulable}$$

3.1   Interface Composability

Recall, that an interface I describes a set of legal schedules. It represents for the activation patterns of its tasks a set of possible discrete slot allocations under which the tasks can be executed successfully. A segregation property B_I for an interface abstracts from the tasks of the interface, and only exposes a set of possible slots reservations for which the interface is schedulable. Note that a segregation property for an interface indeed may contain more available slots than are used by the respective interface.

Composition of the segregation properties B_{I_1} and B_{I_2} of interfaces I_1 and I_2 then combines non-conflicting slot reservations of B_{I_1} and B_{I_2}. The property φ states that at least one such non-conflicting slot reservation exists, i.e. the set of slot reservations defined by $B_{I_1} \parallel B_{I_2}$ is not empty.

We now define *slot reservation* and *segregation property* of an interface and define a composition operation. We use the composition operation on slot reservations to derive a composability condition for interfaces based on their segregation properties.

Definition 4. *A slot reservation B is an ω-regular language over $\{0,1\}$, $B \subseteq \{0,1\}^\omega$. Each ω-word $b \in B$ defines an infinite sequence of slots that are either available (0) or unavailable (1).*

We denote B_I a segregation property for interface I, if and only if for all $b \in B_I$ holds that I is schedulable for all its activation patterns using only the available slots defined in b.

Example: For task t_1 in the example above, B_{I_1} is a segregation property of I_1 if it contains for each sub-sequence of length 5 at least 3 available slots. A valid segregation property for I_1 is $B_{I_1} = \bigcup_{\sigma \in C_3^5} \sigma^\omega$, where C_3^5 denotes the set of finite words $\sigma = \sigma_1 \ldots \sigma_5$ over $\{0,1\}$ of length 5 obtained by combination of 3 symbols $\sigma_i = 0$ over 5 symbols and the remaining symbols are 1.

We define the parallel composition $B_1 \parallel B_2$ of slot reservations such that we select only those pairs $b_1 \in B_1, b_2 \in B_2$, where no slot is available (0) in both words, combining them into a single word $b \in B_1 \parallel B_2$, where slots are available that are available in either b_1 or b_2 and all other slots remain unavailable (1).

For convenience, we make use of the binary operators $\wedge$ and $\vee$ defined on elements of $\{0,1\}$ with their usual Boolean interpretations. We extend both operators to ω-regular words $b_i = b_{i_1} b_{i_2} \ldots \in \{0,1\}^\omega$, by their component-wise application: $b_1 \wedge b_2 = (b_{1_1} \wedge b_{2_1})(b_{1_2} \wedge b_{2_2}) \ldots$, and $\vee$ respectively.

Definition 5. *Given two slot reservations B_1 and B_2 the parallel composition $B_1 \parallel B_2$ is defined as:*

$$B_1 \parallel B_2 = \{b_1 \wedge b_2 | b_1 \in B_1, b_2 \in B_2 \text{ and } b_1 \vee b_2 = 1^\omega\}$$

Example: Fig. 3 depicts an illustration of the composition of the segregation property B_{I_1} of I_1 from the example above with another slot reservation $B_2 = [0^1 \mid\mid\mid 1^4]^\omega$.

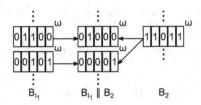

Fig. 3. Illustration of Slot Reservation Composition

The following lemma states the desired condition for composability of interfaces depending on their segregation properties:

Lemma 4. *Two interfaces I_1 and I_2 are composable and can be scheduled together if the parallel composition of their segregation properties is not empty, i.e. $B_{I_1} \parallel B_{I_2} \neq \emptyset$.*

Proof: As B_{I_1} is a segregation property for I_1 and B_{I_2} is a segregation property for I_2, I_1 is schedulable for all its activations patterns for *all* $b \in B_{I_1}$ and I_2 is schedulable for *all* $b \in B_{I_2}$, respectively. According to Definition 5 all words $b \in B_{I_1} \parallel B_{I_2}$ are sequences of slots such that there exists a pair $b_1 \in B_{I_1}, b_2 \in B_{I_2}$, where no slot is available in both words. Thus, interface I_1 can be scheduled using only the available slots in b that are also available in b_1, interface I_2 respectively. Consequently, it holds that each unavailable slot in $b_1 \in B_{I_1}$ is not used by I_1, and I_2 may schedule one of its tasks in these slots, if they are available in $b_2 \in B_{I_2}$. For interface I_2 the same argument applies. Thus, it follows that the language of $I_1 \parallel I_2$ is not empty, which according to Definition 1 means a legal schedule for $I_1 \parallel I_2$ exists. □

3.2 Refinement of Slot Reservations

Recall, that Definition 4 defines B_I to be a segregation property for interface I, if and only if I is schedulable for all its activation patterns *for every* $b \in B_I$. From this definition we conclude that given a segregation property B_I, *any subset* $B'_I \subseteq B_I$ is also a segregation property for interface I. Further, each $b = \sigma_1 \sigma_2 \ldots \in B_I$ defines a sequence of slots, where all slots $\sigma_i = 0$ are available to the interface. Obviously, if the interface is schedulable for $b \in B_I$, then it is also schedulable for b', where $b' = \sigma'_1 \sigma'_2 \ldots$ and $\sigma'_i = 0$ and $\sigma_i = 1$ for some i and $\sigma'_j = \sigma_j$ for all other slots $j \neq i$. In other words, we can always make more slots available to an interface without impact on its schedulability.

These observations give rise to a refinement relation on slot reservations. First, we define a partial order on ω-regular words over $\{0, 1\}$ as follows: Let be $b, b' \in \{0, 1\}^\omega$. We say $b' \leq b$ if and only if $\forall i \in \mathbb{N} : \sigma_{b'_i} = 1 \implies \sigma_{b_i} = 1$. That is, b' precedes b if all slots that are unavailable (1) in b' are also unavailable in b. Indeed b might contain additional unavailable slots that are available (0) in b'. In other words: Slots that are available in b are also available in b'. Obviously, a bottom element 0^ω and a top element 1^ω exist with regard to the partial order $\leq$. For any $b \in \{0, 1\}^\omega$ we have that $0^\omega \leq b \leq 1^\omega$.

We extend the relation on ω-regular words over $\{0,1\}$ to slot reservations (ω-regular languages over $\{0,1\}$) as follows:

Definition 6. *Given two slot reservations B' and B, then B' refines B, $B' \preceq B$, if and only if:*

$$\forall b' \in B' : \exists b \in B : b' \leq b$$

The refinement relation $\preceq$ on slot reservations is a pre-order, as mutual refinement not necessarily implies equivalence: $B \preceq B'$ and $B' \preceq B \not\Rightarrow B = B'$. Note, that this definition of refinement captures both observations: Given a segregation property B_I, any subset $B'_I \subseteq B_I$ is also a segregation property for I and it holds that $B'_I \preceq B_I$. Further, for a segregation property B_I, we can construct $B'_I \preceq B_I$ from B_I, where for some $b' \in B'_I$ we make more slots available, i.e. $\exists b \in B_I : b' \leq b$. Still B'_I is a segregation property for I. Thus, given a segregation property B_I for interface I, then any $B'_I \preceq B_I$ is also a segregation property for I.

However, B'_I may be an 'over-approximation' of B_I. Consider the segregation property B_I and a subset $B'_I \subset B_I$. As the interface I is schedulable for all words $b \in B_I$, we can understand B_I as a set of alternative slot reservations 'supported' by the interface I. Thus, this alternative is lost when eliminating a word from B_I in a subset $B'_I \subset B_I$. Now consider $B''_I \preceq B_I$ obtained by replacing some word $b \in B_I$ with a word $b'' \leq b$. The interface I is schedulable using only the available slots in b. b'' may be on over-approximation as more slots can be available in b'' that are not available in b. Both over-approximations of B_I lead to an increased probability of causing slot conflicts when composing them with another segregation property $B_{\tilde{I}}$. But If that composition is still not empty, I and $\tilde{I}$ are composable and can be scheduled together.

Example: Fig. 4 depicts an illustration of the preceding discussion on refinement applied on the segregation property B_{I_1} of I_1 from the example above.

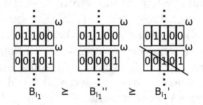

Fig. 4. Illustration of Segregation Property Refinement

The following lemma formalizes these observations and provides a sufficient condition for composability of interfaces (see Lemma 4):

Lemma 5. *Given two interfaces I_1 and I_2 and segregation properties B_{I_1} and B_{I_2}, respectively. Then for any two slot reservations $B'_{I_1} \preceq B_{I_1}$ and $B'_{I_2} \preceq B_{I_2}$ it holds that $B'_{I_1} \parallel B'_{I_2} \neq \emptyset \implies B_{I_1} \parallel B_{I_2} \neq \emptyset$.*

Proof: According to Definition 5 all words $b' \in B'_{I_1} \parallel B'_{I_2}$ are sequences of slots such that there exists a pair $b'_1 \in B'_{I_1}, b'_2 \in B'_{I_2}$, where no slot is available in both words. According to Definition 6 $b_1 \in B_{I_1}, b_2 \in B_{I_2}$ exist, where $b'_1 \leq b_1$ and $b'_2 \leq b_2$. Slots that are unavailable (1) in b'_1 are also unavailable in b_1. The same holds for b'_2 and b_2. It follows that b_1 and b_2 can be composed and $B_{I_1} \parallel B_{I_2}$ contains at least on element.   □

4   Periodic Resource Models and Resource Segregation

As discussed in Section 1, the idea of resource segregation and their exploitation in compositional analysis frameworks is not new. However to our best knowledge the principle has only been applied in frameworks that are based on analytical methods. For example the frameworks proposed by I. Lee et. al. [11,5] are based on the concepts of demand bound functions $dbf(\Delta)$ and supply bound functions $sbf(\Delta)$. The function $dbf(\Delta)$ characterizes the maximal processing demand of a real-time component within any interval of length Δ. The function $sbf(\Delta)$ characterizes the minimal processing power provided by the resource in any time interval of length Δ. The real-time component is considered to be schedulable, if $\forall \Delta : dbf(\Delta) \leq sbf(\Delta)$. Note, that the concept of service curves known from real-time calculus [4] is comparable with these frameworks, as described in [13]. In this section we discuss in more detail the relation of our approach with the frameworks presented in [11,5]. We will see that our approach is able to capture the models considered in these frameworks, and thus results established in these frameworks also apply in our setting.

Both frameworks are based on the concepts of demand bound functions and supply bound functions, where in [11] a *Periodic Resource Model* is presented and in [5] an *Explicit Deadline Periodic Resource Model* (EDP) is presented. Both models are used to create compositional hierarchical scheduling frameworks. In both frameworks a component is a set of tasks scheduled under a specific strategy. The total resource demand of a component to schedule all its tasks is expressed as a demand bound function $dbf(\Delta)$. The resource models are used to capture the amount of resource allocations of a partitioned resource, which is formally expressed as a supply bound function $sbf(\Delta)$. If a component is schedulable under the considered partitioned resource (defined by the resource model), i.e. $dbf(\Delta) \leq sbf(\Delta)$, then the resource model can be transformed into a task and components can be composed hierarchically. Thus, the composition problem is reduced to the abstraction problem.

The periodic resource model $\Gamma = (\Pi, \Theta)$ characterizes a partitioned resource that repetitively provides Θ units of resource with a repetition period Π. The EDP resource model $\Omega = (\Pi, \Theta, \Delta)$ is an extension of the periodic resource model. It characterizes a partitioned resource that repetitively supplies Θ units of resource within Δ time units, with Π the period of repetition. Keeping in mind the idea of transforming a resource model into a task at the next level of the hierarchy, the relation between both models becomes clear: A periodic resource model $\Gamma = (\Pi, \Theta)$ is the EDP model $\Omega = (\Pi, \Theta, \Pi)$ (cf. [5]). Therefore, in the following we focus on EDP resource models.

4.1   Real-Time Component Model

A real-time component is defined as $C = \langle\{C_1, \ldots, C_n\}, S\rangle$, where C_i is either another real-time component or a sporadic task. A sporadic task is defined by a tuple $\tau = (p, e, d)$, where p is a minimum separation time, e the execution time of the task and d a deadline relative to the release of task τ. It holds that $e \leq d \leq p$. The workload $C_1, \ldots, C_n$ is scheduled under strategy S that is either RM (rate monotonic), DM (deadline monotonic) or EDF (earliest deadline first). The *resource demand* of a component is then the collective resource demand of its tasks under its scheduler S. The *demand bound function* [8,1] $dbf_C(\Delta)$ characterizes the maximum resource demand for a task set in any given time interval of length Δ.

In our framework real-time components translate into interfaces, where each interface I is either a composition of interfaces $I = I_1 \parallel \ldots \parallel I_n$ or an 'atomic interface' in case of a single sporadic task. Given a task $t = (p, e, d)$, the language of the corresponding interface is $L_{I_t} = 0^{<p-1}[(t^e \parallel\!\parallel 0^{d-e})0^{p-d}]^\omega$, where $u \parallel\!\parallel v$ denotes all possible interleavings of the finite words u and v. Given a component $C = \langle\{C_1, \ldots, C_n\}, S\rangle$, then the condition $I_{C_1} \parallel \ldots \parallel I_{C_n} \neq \emptyset$ determines whether the component is schedulable at all under some scheduling strategy S. Now consider a fixed priority scheduling (FPS), say rate monotonic scheduling. The component is schedulable under FPS if and only if $I_{FPS} \preceq I_{C_1} \parallel \ldots \parallel I_{C_n}$. How to capture the scheduling of a task set under FPS in terms of an interface I_{FPS} is described in [3]. A segregation property $B_{I_{FPS}}$ of interface I_{FPS} characterizes the resource demands of $C = \langle\{C_1, \ldots, C_n\}, FPS\rangle$.

The resource demands of a component C, explicated by the demand bound function $dbf_C(\Delta)$ can be safely over-approximated by any function $f(\Delta)$, with $f(\Delta) \geq dbf_C(\Delta)$. For example in [11] a linear function $ldbf_C(\Delta)$ is given for EDF scheduling that provides an upper bound for $dbf_C(\Delta)$. In our framework over-approximations of the resource demands B_{I_C} of a component translate into refinements of B_{I_C}. As discussed in Section 3.2 any $B'_{I_C} \preceq B_{I_C}$ is also a segregation property for interface I_C, albeit a potential over-approximation of the resource demands defined by B_{I_C}.

4.2   Resource Model and Schedulability

Consider an explicit deadline periodic resource model $\Omega = (\Pi, \Theta, \Delta)$. It characterizes a partitioned resource that repetitively supplies Θ units of resource within Δ time units, with Π the period of repetition. The partitioned resource characterized by Ω, can also be characterized by the following slot reservation:

$$B_\Omega = 1^{\leq(\Pi-\Theta)}[(0^\Theta \parallel\!\parallel 1^{\Delta-\Theta})1^{\Pi-\Delta}]^\omega$$

The *resource supply* of a resource is the amount of provided resource allocations. Complementary to the demand bound function for components, the resource supply bound function $sfb_\Omega(\Delta)$ computes the minimum resource supply for Ω in a given time interval of length Δ.

The resource supply $sfb_\Omega(\Delta)$ can be safely under-approximated by any function $f(\Delta)$, with $f(\Delta) \leq sfb_\Omega(\Delta)$. Analogously, in our framework under-approximations of the resource supply are captured by the refinement relation. B''_Ω, with $B_\Omega \preceq B''_\Omega$, is a potential under-approximation of the resource supply of a resource.

In the context of EDP resource models, schedulability is defined for a real-time component $C = \langle \{C_1, \ldots, C_n\}, S \rangle$ using an EDP resource model Ω. Exact schedulability conditions are given for the scheduling strategies RM, DM and EDF. We will not go into the details of the theorems here and refer to [5] instead. Basically it must holds that $\forall \Delta : dfb_C(\Delta) \leq sfb_\Omega(\Delta)$. Schedulability of C under Ω can be formulated in our framework as refinement. Given the segregation property B_{I_C} and the resource supply B_Ω, then C is schedulable under Ω, if $B_\Omega \preceq B_{I_C}$. Sufficient conditions based on over-approximation of resource demands and under-approximation of resource supplies are induced by transitivity of the refinement relation. Given segregation property B_{I_C}, slot reservation B_Ω and $B'_{I_C} \preceq B_{I_C}$, and $B_\Omega \preceq B''_\Omega$, then $B''_\Omega \preceq B'_{I_C} \implies B_\Omega \preceq B_{I_C}$.

5 Conclusion

This paper proposes a formalization of *segregation properties* enabling compositional timing analysis based on ω-regular languages. By exploiting the formalism of real-time interfaces, segregation properties allow to abstract the concrete behavior of components, and provide conditions under which the composition of a set of components results in a schedulable system. The approach supports the verification process in two directions. Firstly, the abstraction helps to reduce verification complexity, which often prevents analysis of larger systems using model-checking techniques. Secondly, the approach subsumes well-known approaches in the domain of analytical resource models. This enables the elaboration of combined methods to further reduce analysis efforts.

While this initial approach supports only single resources, future work will allow for the expression of multiple resources. In this case, slot reservations do not argue over the alphabet $\{0, 1\}$, but over tuples $(r_1, ..., r_n)$ for n resources, where $r_i \in \{0, 1\}$. Indeed, this requires modified definitions of composition and refinement. A further extension of this approach will allow to support multiprocessor resources. In this case, segregation properties are no more defined over the alphabet $\{0, 1\}$, but for example over sets $\{0, 1, ..., m\}$ characterizing the number of available processing units of the resource.

References

1. Baruah, S., Rosier, L., Howell, R.: Algorithms and complexity concerning the preemptive scheduling of periodic, real-time tasks on one processor. Real-Time Systems 2, 301–324 (1990)
2. Basu, A., Bozga, M., Sifakis, J.: Modeling Heterogeneous Real-time Components in BIP. In: Proc. Conference on Software Engineering and Formal Methods, SEFM (2006)

3. Bhaduri, P., Stierand, I.: A proposal for real-time interfaces in speeds. In: Design, Automation Test in Europe Conference Exhibition (DATE), pp. 441–446 (March 2010)
4. Chakraborty, S., Kunzli, S., Thiele, L.: A general framework for analysing system properties in platform-based embedded system designs. In: Design, Automation and Test in Europe Conference and Exhibition (DATE), pp. 190–195. IEEE Computer Society (2003)
5. Easwaran, A., Anand, M., Lee, I.: Compositional analysis framework using edp resource models. In: Proceedings of the 28th IEEE International Real-Time Systems Symposium, RTSS 2007, pp. 129–138. IEEE Computer Society (2007)
6. Guan, N., Ekberg, P., Stigge, M., Yi, W.: Effective and Efficient Scheduling of Certifiable Mixed-Criticality Sporadic Task Systems. In: Proc. Real-Time Systems Symposium, RTSS (2011)
7. Henzinger, T., Matic, S.: An interface algebra for real-time components. In: Proceedings of the 12th IEEE Real-Time and Embedded Technology and Applications Symposium, RTAS 2006, pp. 253–266. IEEE Computer Society (2006)
8. Lehoczky, J.P., Sha, L., Ding, Y.: The rate monotonic scheduling algorithm: Exact characterization and average case behavior. In: IEEE Real-Time Systems Symposium, pp. 166–171. IEEE Computer Society (1989)
9. Perathoner, S., Lampka, K., Thiele, L.: Composing Heterogeneous Components for System-wide Performance Analysis. In: Design, Automation Test in Europe Conference Exhibition, DATE (2011)
10. Richter, K.: Compositional Scheduling Analysis Using Standard Event Models. Ph.D. thesis, Technical University of Braunschweig, Germany (2004)
11. Shin, I., Lee, I.: Periodic resource model for compositional real-time guarantees. In: Proceedings of the 24th IEEE International Real-Time Systems Symposium, RTSS 2003, pp. 2–13. IEEE Computer Society (2003)
12. Thiele, L., Wandeler, E., Stoimenov, N.: Real-time interfaces for composing real-time systems. In: Proceedings of the 6th ACM & IEEE International Conference on Embedded Software, EMSOFT 2006, pp. 34–43. ACM (2006)
13. Wandeler, E., Thiele, L.: Interface-based design of real-time systems with hierarchical scheduling. In: Proceedings of the 12th IEEE Real-Time and Embedded Technology and Applications Symposium, RTAS 2006, pp. 243–252. IEEE Computer Society (2006)

Towards Virtualization Concepts
for Novel Automotive HMI Systems

Simon Gansel[1], Stephan Schnitzer[2], Frank Dürr[2], Kurt Rothermel[2],
and Christian Maihöfer[1]

[1] System Architecture and Platforms Department
Daimler AG, Böblingen, Germany
firstname.lastname@daimler.com
[2] Institute of Parallel and Distributed Systems
University of Stuttgart, Germany
lastname@ipvs.uni-stuttgart.de

Abstract. Many innovations in the automotive industry are based on electronics and software, which has led to a steady increase of electronic control units (ECU) in cars. This brought up serious scalability and complexity issues in terms of cost, installation space, and energy consumption. In order to tackle these problems, there is a strong interest to consolidate ECUs using virtualization technologies. However, current efforts largely neglect legal constraints and certification issues and the resulting technical requirements.

In this paper, we focus on the consolidation of graphics hardware through virtualization, which received a lot of interest in the car industry due to the growing relevance of HMI systems such as head unit and instrument cluster in modern cars. First, we investigate relevant ISO standards and legal requirements and derive seven technical requirements for a virtualized automotive HMI system. Based on these requirements, we present the concept for a *Virtualized Automotive Graphics System* (*VAGS*) that allows for the consolidation of mixed-criticality graphics ECUs.

1   Introduction

Over the years, the automotive industry, which was mainly driven by hardware and mechanics in the past, has changed to an industry where about 90 % of all innovations are driven by electronics and software [3]. In current high-end cars, the IT hardware and software architecture is represented by more than 70 physically separated *electronic control units* (ECU), which are partitioned into different domains and connected via a network of different communication bus systems. To deploy new functionalities, the OEMs often add further ECUs to the vehicle. This trend of "new function, new ECU" has lead to serious scalability issues in terms of cost, installation space, and energy consumption. In order to deal with these problems and to stop this trend of adding further ECUs, there is a strong interest in the car industry to consolidate ECUs using virtualization technologies to share the same hardware between different components.

G. Schirner et al. (Eds.): IESS 2013, IFIP AICT 403, pp. 193–204, 2013.

In this paper, we focus on the consolidation of graphics hardware since it is of high relevance in modern cars. An increasing number of automotive functionalities and applications require highly sophisticated graphical representations in 2D or 3D based on hardware acceleration. For instance, the Head Unit (HU) uses displays integrated into the backside of the front seats and center console to display multimedia content; and displays connected to the Instrument Cluster (IC) show car specific information like current vehicle speed or warnings. Therefore, HU and IC are good candidates for hardware consolidation. Each virtualized ECU runs in a dedicated virtual machine (VM), and a virtual machine monitor (VMM) acts as middleware between VMs and hardware. Besides the already mentioned general benefits, the virtualization of IC and HU provides advantages such as the flexible placement of graphical output on previously separated displays, which is a matter of software implementation only. Moreover, virtualization enables OEMs to deploy custom applications inside a dedicated VM that is isolated from HU and IC.

This paper makes the following two contributions to enable the consolidation of graphics hardware in vehicular systems. First, we thoroughly *analyze relevant ISO standards and legal requirements* and derive *seven technical requirements for a virtualized automotive HMI system*. Such requirements have been largely neglected by current virtualization efforts, which did not target automotive systems with their specific requirements, in particular, with respect to safety. For OEMs, the certifiability of automotive system functionalities is highly relevant. According to [16, ISO 26262], for each functionality safety-criticality shall be identified and mapped to criticality-classes[1]. To fulfill the criticality-level, the severity and likelihood of failures must be determined using, for instance, *failure mode and effects analysis* (FMEA) [25]. Moreover, certifiability also applies to custom third-party applications. For instance, [12, ISO 15005] prohibits displaying movies to the driver while the vehicle is in motion. These specific regulations impose challenging technical requirements to virtualization.

As second contribution, we present a concept for a *Virtualized Automotive Graphics System* (*VAGS*). We elaborate on the challenges that are due to the identified requirements to consolidate mixed-criticality graphics ECUs as used, in particular, by the HU and IC. Although virtualization is a mature technology for general resources like CPU or main memory, existing concepts do neither provide sufficient isolation for accessing shared graphics hardware (GPU) and input devices (e.g., steering wheel buttons), nor do they provide sufficient isolation for implementing the flexible presentation of application windows. Our proposed architecture can be used as starting point for the future implementation of the specified components.

The rest of this paper is structured as follows. In the next section, we analyze automotive standards and guidelines and derive technical requirements. In Section 3, we present the concept for a *VAGS*. In Section 4, we briefly describe a

---

[1] [16, ISO 26262] specifies five safety requirement levels: Four ASIL (Automotive Safety Integrity Level) ranging from ASIL-A (low criticality) to ASIL-D (high criticality), and one no-criticality level QM (Quality Management).

first proof-of-concept implementation of our concepts. Finally, we discuss related work in Section 5 and conclude this paper with a summary and outlook onto future work in Section 6.

2   Requirements

In this section, we discuss requirements that are relevant for automotive HMI systems. Automotive application development is constrained by ISO standards, automotive design guidelines, legal requirements, and OEM specific demands. The design guidelines (e.g., [1, AAM 2006], [5, ESoP 2008], [18, JAMA 2004]) in the automotive domain are almost completely derived from the following ISO standards.

- [11, ISO 11428] Ergonomic requirements for the perception of visual danger signals.
- [12, ISO 15005] Requirements to prevent impairment of the safe and effective operation of the moving vehicle.
- [14, ISO 16951] Priority-based presentation of messages.
- [15, ISO 2575] Symbols for controls and indicators.
- [13, ISO 15408-2] Security in IT systems.
- [16, ISO 26262] Risk-based assessment of potentially hazardous operational situations and of safety measures.

In the following, we propose seven technical requirements for automotive HMI system. For each of them we added references to relevant sections of the mentioned ISO standards.

R1 – Input Event Handling

R1.1 – Restricted Access Control: For user input events *access control* is required and it shall not violate any of the following constraints [12, ISO 15005]. Applications using dialogues shall not require to use input devices in a way that demands removal of both hands from the steering wheel while driving (5.2.2.2.2). Additionally, exiting a dialog or an application shall always be possible (5.3.3.2.1) unless legally required or traffic-situation-relevant (5.3.3.2.3).

R1.2 – Restricted Processing Time: A *maximum processing time* for input event handling shall be met. For instance, response to tactile user inputs shall not exceed 250 ms (5.2.4.2.3).

R2 – Restricted Window Creation and Positioning

R2.1 – Restricted Visibility of Windows: Usually, graphical applications use API functions to change the *visibility of windows*, e.g., to create, hide, or position them. This functionality must be restricted, and functions not intended to be used by the driver must be inaccessible for him [12, ISO 15005] (5.2.2.2.4).

R2.2 – Priority-based Displaying of Windows: If multiple windows shall be displayed, the importance of each of them must be defined. Importance is represented by priorities, which can depend on safety requirements and software ergonomic aspects (5.2.4.2.4) that must be met by the system (5.2.4.3.3). Moreover, they can depend on urgency and criticality which have to be defined [14, ISO 16951] (3.5). Additionally, appropriate reactions (e.g., behavior in case of conflicts) shall be enforced [14, ISO 16951] (Annex B). Furthermore, country-specific legal requirements constrain the definition of the priorities, e.g., German law requires the constant visibility of the speedometer while the vehicle is in motion (StVZO §57 [19]). Additionally, visual information must be presented in a consistent way [12, ISO 15005] (5.3.2.2.1).

R2.3 – Timing Constraints: An automotive HMI system shall enable applications to provide important information to the driver within given *time constraints*. This means that windows showing information shall be visible within given time constraints [12, ISO 15005] (5.2.4.3.4). If applications require user interaction, e.g., if a user selects a radio channel, the flow of information must not adversely affect driving (5.2.4.2.1). Concretely, according to [1, AAM 2006] Section 2.1, each glance shall not exceed 2 seconds. Hence, any kind of animation shall not run longer than 2 seconds.

R3 – Trusted Channel

R3.1 – Integrity and Confidentiality: In environments where applications run inside VMs, communication is inevitable. This holds for communication that previously used dedicated communication hardware and is now replaced by software-based inter-VM communication. According to [13, ISO 15408-2], communication between applications and hardware must provide integrity and confidentiality, for both user data (14.5.8.2) and software components providing relevant functionality (17.1.5.3). All applications that need trusted communication shall be able to use it (17.1.5.2).

R3.2 – Authentication and Non-Repudiation: Identification shall be assured even between distinct systems (17.1.5.1), which also applies to inter-VM communication. A trusted channel also requires non-repudiation of origin (8.1.1 and 8.1.6.1-3) and receipt (8.2.1 and 8.2.6.1-3). This requires authentication and may also involve cryptographic key management (9.1.1) and key access (9.1.7.1).

R4 – Virtualized Graphics Rendering In our system, multiple VMs have shared access to a single GPU, and therefore the VMM has to provide isolation. That is, unintended interference between applications must not occur.

R4.1 – Priority Handling: Application windows must be assigned a priority which determines how GPU commands are processed [12, ISO 15005] (5.2.4.2.4 and 5.2.4.3.3), [13, ISO 15408-2] (15.2.5.1-2 and 15.2.6.1-2).

R4.2 – Rendering Time Constraints: Not only comparative requirements (like priorities) but also absolute timing requirements have to be fulfilled. A response to a drivers tactile input shall not exceed 250 ms [12, ISO 15005] (5.2.4.2.3). Similarly, emergency signals may require constant redraw rates to represent flashing lights [11, ISO 11428] (4.2.2). This requires appropriate CPU and GPU resources and imposes a minimum frame rate since the delay between two consecutive frames is constraint by an upper bound. The upper bound must be known to determine the effectiveness of safety-critical messages [14, ISO 16951] (Annex F) and also to allow for the definition of delays after which messages are displayed (Annex B).

R4.3 – GPU Resource Isolation: The GPU is a controlled resource according to [13, ISO 15408-2]. To prevent unintended interference, it must be possible to provide guarantees to certain applications that they are provided sufficient GPU resources such as processing time. Therefore, it must be possible to control which GPU resources individual windows, graphical applications, or VMs are allowed to use (15.3.6.1 and 15.3.7.1-2).

R5 – Reconfiguration of Policies A set of permissions that apply to user input events, application windows, and the related scheduling and isolation is called a *policy*. At each point in time, exactly one policy is active, though policies are dynamically switched during runtime depending on the system state.

R5.1 – Dynamic State Changes: In accordance to [12, ISO 15005], a *state change* happens either on user request or automatically by system-defined rules. A state can depend on a current vehicle condition like "vehicle is in motion" which could require the deactivation of applications that are not intended to be used by the driver while the vehicle is in motion (5.2.2.2.4). Otherwise, an automotive HMI system shall provide sufficient information and warnings to provide the driver with the intended purpose in a current state. For every state change, specified *deadlines* apply to determine a consistent and accurate transition between different states. The definition of states and system behavior is explained in more detail in [14, ISO 16951] (3.3 and Annex E).

R5.2 – Dynamic Policy Changes: Authorized software components shall be able to apply changes to policies during runtime. This includes granting and revoking permissions on both, currently active and currently inactive policies. As for R5.1, deadlines apply to dynamic policy changes. Where applicable and allowed, the driver shall be able to change the active policy to manipulate the flow of information (5.3.3.2.3).

R5.3 – Presentation Enforcement: The system-defined rules shall enforce the presentation of legally required messages and traffic-situation-relevant messages. Presentation requires that those messages are visible and perceivable, in particular, if state changes require driver attention [12, ISO 15005] (5.3.2.2.2). Furthermore, state-related information shall be displayed either continuously or upon request by the driver.

R6 – Certifiability For an OEM, certifiability is an essential part of the software development process, e.g., by using methods like FMEA [25]. The development process for certified software, in particular, for high criticality levels, is quite complex and expensive. A key indicator for complexity is the number of function points that correlates with the approximated number of software defects [3]. Hence, a system shall be developed with respect to an easy certification according to [16, ISO 26262].

R7 – System Monitoring System Monitoring puts the focus on logging, detecting, and reacting to events that possibly are relevant to provide safety.

R7.1 – Secure Boot: Derived from [13, ISO 15408-2], the system shall provide *secure boot* to ensure the integrity of the system. Compromising the system (14.6.9.1) or system devices or elements (14.6.9.2) by physical tampering shall be unambiguously detected.

R7.2 – Auditing: The *auditing* of all safety-critical related events shall be guaranteed to ensure traceability of system activities in an automotive HMI system that potentially violate safety or security. Therefore, direct hardware access must not be permitted to ensure that auditing cannot be bypassed. For a potential violation analysis, a fixed set of rules shall be defined for a basic threshold detection, [13, ISO 15408-2] (7.3.2). To indicate any potential violation of the system-defined rules, the monitoring of audited events shall also be based on a set of rules (7.3.8.1) that must be enforced by the system either as an accumulation or a combination of a subset of defined auditable events which are known to threat the system security (7.3.8.2). Similarly, all changes to policies initiated by applications shall be monitored and verified.

R7.3 – Supervision of Timing Requirements: It is a requirement to regulate the flow of information to ensure short and concise groups such that the driver can easily perceive the information with minimal distraction [12, ISO 15005] (5.2.4.2.1). Therefore, specified *time restrictions* need to be verified. This also includes the auditing of driver tactile input and system response time which shall not exceed 250 ms (5.2.4.2.3).

R7.4 – Detection of DoS Attacks: The occurrence of any event representing a significant threat such as a *DoS attack* shall be detectable by the system in real-time or during a post-collection batch-mode analysis [13, ISO 15408-2] (7.3.2).

R7.5 – Perception of Visual Signals: For the perception of visual danger signals, visibility properties like fractions of luminances [11, ISO 11428] (4.2.1.2) and colors of signal lights (4.3.2) have to be monitored. Monitoring is also required for certain safety-critical symbols defined in [15, ISO 2575].

R7.6 – Software Fault Tolerance: [13, ISO 15408-2] requires the detection of defined failures or service discontinuities and a recovery to return to a consistent and secure state (14.7.8.1) by using automated procedures (14.7.9.2). A list of potential failures and service discontinuities have to be supervised by a *watchdog* to detect entering of failure states. Furthermore, for a defined subset of functions that are required to complete successfully, failure scenarios shall be specified that ensure recovery (14.7.11.1).

R7.7 – System Integrity: In case of unrecoverable failures, the system shall be able to switch to *degraded operation mode* to preserve system integrity. A list of failure types shall be defined for which no disturbance of the operation of the system can take place [13, ISO 15408-2] (15.1.7.1). Moreover, the system shall ensure the operation of a set of capabilities for predefined failure types (15.1.6.1). This includes the handling of DoS attacks and detection of illegitimate policy changes. Some events have to be maintained in an internal representation to indicate if any violations take or took place. This includes the behavior of system activities for the identification of potential violations (7.3.10.2-3) like state changes (7.3.10.1).

3   Architecture

In this section, we briefly describe the architecture of a *Virtualized Automotive Graphics System* (*VAGS*) (cf. Fig. 1) that addresses the identified requirements.

Certifiability (R6) applies to the complete development process, all other requirements are represented by the functionalities of the components of our architecture. With respect to certifiability, we follow the approach of a microkernel-based VMM where drivers run in user space rather than kernel space. Therefore, the kernel code size is very small and easier to certify [3]. If driver code crashes, this does not affect the VMM. The *Virtualization Manager* runs in a dedicated VM and exclusively manages shared resources. It contains relevant drivers, e.g., for GPU and input devices. This ensures that access to all shared resources is controlled by a single trustworthy VM. Indirect hardware access by VMs facilitates Virtualized Graphics Rendering (R4) and System Monitoring (R7). Additionally, the Virtualization Manager contains multiple software components ensuring that every hardware access by VMs is in compliance with our requirements. Note that our architecture only shows four exemplarily VMs. However, we do not restrict the number of VMs. Therefore, it is possible to deploy additional VMs if needed. In order to access hardware, the HU and IC VMs communicate with the Virtualization Manager VM. For this bidirectional communication, a Trusted Channel (R3) is required to support secure communication between the different virtual machines. A trusted channel is provided by the cooperation of the *Isolated Communication Channel* and the *Authentication Manager*. The Isolated Communication Channel provides integrity and isolation for communication (R3.1) between applications and the Virtualization Manager. To initiate a connection, applications first have to provide valid credentials to the Authentication Manager, to guarantee non-repudiation of origin and receipt (R3.2). In particular, this is required for the communication between the graphical applications located on HU or IC and the virtualization manager, which needs to be trustworthy to ensure that the active policy is never violated.

Permission and Policy Management (R5) ensures that applications are getting their defined permissions to use functionalities or resources provided by

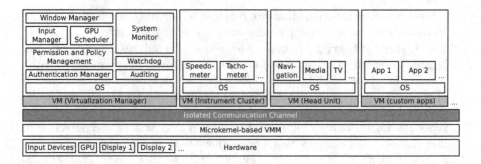

Fig. 1. Architecture

the Input Manager, Window Manager, or GPU Scheduler. Permissions are represented by the active policy, which depends on the current state (R5.1), e.g., "vehicle is parking" or "vehicle is in motion". The policy management is configured by rules that define transitions between policies performed whenever state changes (R5.2) in defined time constraints (R5.3).

The *Input Manager* performs Input Event Handling (R1) and is responsible for dispatching user input events to the intended applications (R1.1). Since the processing of user input is subject to time restrictions, a minimal delivery time for input events to the applications must be ensured (R1.2).

The *GPU Scheduler* is responsible for Virtualized Graphics Rendering (R4) according to drawing requirements and permissions of graphical applications. To this end, applications are assigned priorities that define the amount of dedicated GPU resources (R4.1). Besides priorities, according to (R4.2), deadlines apply to the graphical rendering of certain applications like the tachometer. The GPU scheduler, therefore, has to sequence graphics commands, schedule application requests and provide isolation between different contexts (R4.3).

The *Window Manager* provides the functionality for creating, positioning, and displaying windows of graphical applications. This represents a paradigm shift from fully user-defined window management to restricted window creation and positioning (R2). Applications with sufficient permissions interact with the Window Manager to create windows and to modify properties like size and position (R2.1). Moreover the Window Manager is responsible for correct window stacking (R2.2) and meeting rendering time requirements (R2.3).

In order to guarantee *Secure Boot* (R7.1), the integrity of code that is loaded must be verified, using, for instance, approaches described in [8]. The *Auditing* component (R7.2) traces all relevant system activities and interactions. The gathered traces can be used by the Watchdog and System Monitor components to detect inconsistencies (for R7.3 to R7.7). The *Watchdog* supervises relevant system functionalities and emits signals in case of system malfunctioning as required for R7.3 to R7.6. The *System Monitor* receives signals of detected system malfunctions from the Watchdog. Rules are used to configure its reaction on these signals.

4   Implementation

We have created a proof-of-concept implementation for the main parts of our proposed *VAGS* architecture. The implementation consists of a Window Manager using an hierarchical access control management for display areas and input events. It supports permission negotiation between different virtual machines and applications. The applications create, destroy and move their windows using a dedicated Window Manager API. Based on their permissions, applications are allowed to display their windows in dedicated display areas. Furthermore, each display area is mapped to a depth level representing the priority of the application. This prevents that application windows are overlapped by windows of applications with lower priority. The Window Manager has a dedicated compositing backend which is currently (as an intermediate step) based on X11 compositing.

Linux was used as operating system for the Virtualization Manager and the graphical applications. As a first step we used an x86 standard PC platform and created a set of automotive applications like speedometer and navigation software to demonstrate the feasibility of the concept.

For communication between applications located on different VMs, a transport layer has been implemented. The channels use a custom ring buffer implementation and shared memory to establish data transfer channels. These channels are used for forwarding graphics data like EGL, OpenGL ES 2.0, and API commands of the Window Manager, from the graphics applications to the Virtualization Manager. The management of shared memory is performed by a dedicated component in the Virtualization Manager. To allow applications on different VMs for initiating new connections, in each VM a management process performs the mapping of shared memory segments to applications. The Virtualization Manager performs simple scheduling using synchronization mechanisms of OpenGL ES 2.0.

5   Related Work

The concept of microkernel-based VMMs in virtualization is well known for many years. The focus on safety increased during the last few years, e.g., the NOVA microkernel [26]. Moreover, certifiability became more important, at least in case of the VMM [22].

A large number of work related to virtualization and graphics applications has been described in the literature. Due to space constraints, we only focus on windowing systems, GPU scheduling, and graphics forwarding in the following. According to [17], the X11 Windowing System does not provide security. Trusted X [4] has been proposed to provide security for the X Windowing System targeting the requirements in TCSEC B3 (superseded by [13, ISO 15408-2]) but has not been certified. To provide isolation, an untrusted X server and a window manager is deployed for each security level which impacts scalability. Therefore, mutual isolation of applications is practically impossible due to scalability issues. Nitpicker [7] is a GUI server with security mechanisms and protocols to provide secure and isolated user interaction using different operating systems. To achieve isolation between these OSes, Nitpicker uses the VMM L4/Fiasco [10]. The EROS Window System (EWS) [24] targets the protection of sensitive information and the enforcement of security policies by providing access control mechanisms and enforcing the user volition. A common denominator of Trusted X, Nitpicker, and EWS is that they only focus on security and thus do not comply with Input Event Handling (R1), Restricted Window Creation and Positioning (R2), and System Monitoring (R5). DOpE [6] is a window server that assures redrawing rates windows of real-time applications and provides a best-effort service for non-real-time applications. DOpE is based on L4/Fiasco [10] for isolation and IPC. However, policies are not enforced. Common to all these windowing systems is the fact that they do not support graphics hardware acceleration and do not provide any timing guarantees for rendering and displaying.

GERM [2] provides GPU resource management targeting fairness without addressing isolation or prioritization. Timegraph [21] enhances these concepts and provides priority-based scheduling of GPU command groups for DRI2. However, for the execution time of an GPU command group no upper bound can be guaranteed and the performance is heavily degraded. Additionally, due to latency induced by synchronous GPU operations, applications using the X Server and double buffering encounter additional problems addressed in [20]. However, the X Server itself does not provide sufficient isolation mechanisms and therefore cannot be used for an automotive HMI system.

VMGL [23] is an approach to transfer OpenGL commands from an OpenGL client to an OpenGL server using a TCP/IP connection. However, using TCP/IP causes significant latency and overhead. Blink [9] is a display system which focuses on the safe multiplexing of OpenGL programs in different VMs. Blink uses an OpenGL Client/Server to transmit the OpenGL commands and data via shared memory to a "Driver VM". The "Driver VM" is responsible for the execution of the OpenGL commands on the GPU. Blink proposes "BlinkGL" which increases performance, but requires applications to be modified.

6   Summary and Future Work

In this paper, we presented requirements for novel automotive HMI systems. From relevant ISO standards, we derived seven technical requirements for the physical consolidation of mixed-criticality graphical ECUs such as head unit and instrument cluster. Additionally we presented VAGS (Virtualized Automotive Graphics System), a novel automotive HMI concept which provides isolation between custom graphics applications running in dedicated VMs. Although these applications are not certified, a VAGS can guarantee that no unintended interference with certified OEM software can take place. We presented a suitable architecture and created a proof-of-concept implementation.

In future work we are going to improve graphics scheduling by using execution time prediction of graphics commands and by using a more suitable scheduling algorithm. Furthermore, we implement system monitoring, auditing, a watch-dog, and integrate authentication concepts. Since the current implementation is based on X11, which has a couple of drawbacks, we plan to switch to a native implementation tailored to embedded hardware. Finally, we evaluate and opti-mize the performance of our implementation depending on different application scenarios.

Acknowledgement. This paper has been supported in part by the ARAMiS (Automotive, Railway and Avionics Multicore Systems) project of the Ger-man Federal Ministry for Education and Research (BMBF) with funding ID 01IS11035.

References

[1] AAM: Statement of Principles, Criteria and Verification Procedures on Driver Interactions with Advanced In-Vehicle Information and Communication Systems. Alliance of Automotive Manufacturers (July 2006)

[2] Bautin, M., Dwarakinath, A., Chiueh, T.: Graphic engine resource management (2008)

[3] Ebert, C., Jones, C.: Embedded software: Facts, figures, and future. Com-puter 42(4), 42–52 (2009)

[4] Epstein, J., McHugh, J., Pascale, R., Orman, H., Benson, G., Martin, C., Marmor-Squires, A., Danner, B., Branstad, M.: A prototype b3 trusted x win-dow system. In: Proceedings of the 7th Annual Computer Security Applications Conference, pp. 44–55 (December 1991)

[5] ESOP: On safe and efficient in-vehicle information and communication systems: update of the European Statement of Principles on human-machine interface. Commission of the European Communities (2008)

[6] Feske, N., Hartig, H.: Dope – a window server for real-time and embedded sys-tems. In: Proceedings of the 24th IEEE Real-Time Systems Symposium, pp. 74–77 (December 2003)

[7] Feske, N., Helmuth, C.: A nitpicker's guide to a minimal-complexity secure gui. In: Proceedings of the 21st Computer Security Applications Conference, pp. 85–94 (December 2005)

[8] Gallery, E., Mitchell, C.J.: Trusted computing: Security and applications (May 2008)

[9] Hansen, J.G.: Blink: Advanced Display Multiplexing for Virtualized Applications. In: Proceedings of the 17th International Workshop on Network and Operating Systems Support for Digital Audio and Video (NOSSDAV), pp. 15–20 (2007)

[10] Hohmuth, M.: The Fiasco kernel: System Architecure. Technical report: TUD-FI02-06-Juli-2002 (2002)

[11] ISO 11428: Ergonomics – Visual danger signals – General requirements, design and testing. ISO, Geneva, Switzerland (December 1996)

[12] ISO 15005: Road vehicles – Ergonomic aspects of transport information and con-trol systems – Dialogue management principles and compliance procecdures. ISO, Geneva, Switzerland (July 2002)

[13] ISO 15408-2: Information technology – Security techniques – Evaluation criteria for IT security – Part 2: Security functional components. ISO, Geneva, Switzerland (August 2008)

[14] ISO 16951: Road vehicles – Ergonomic aspects of transport information and control systems (TICS) – Procedures for determining priority of on-board messages presented to drivers. ISO, Geneva, Switzerland (2004)

[15] ISO 2575: Road vehicles – Symbols for controls, indicators and tell-tales. ISO, Geneva, Switzerland (July 2010)

[16] ISO 26262: Road vehicles – Functional Safety. ISO, Geneva, Switzerland (November 2011)

[17] Epstein, J., Picciotto, J.: Trusting x: Issues in building trusted x window systems – or – what's not trusted about x. In: Proceedings of the 14th National Computer Security Conference, vol. 1. National Institute of Standards and Technology, National Computer Security Center (October 1991)

[18] JAMA: Guideline for In-vehicle Display Systems – Version 3.0. Japan Automobile Manufacturers Association (August 2004)

[19] Janker, H.: Straßenverkehrsrecht: StVG, StVO, StVZO, Fahrzeug-ZulassungsVO, Fahrerlaubnis-VO, Verkehrszeichen, Bußgeldkatalog. C.H. Beck (2011)

[20] Kato, S., Lakshmanan, K., Ishikawa, Y., Rajkumar, R.: Resource sharing in gpu-accelerated windowing systems. In: Real-Time and Embedded Technology and Applications Symposium (RTAS), 2011 17th IEEE. pp. 191–200 (April 2011)

[21] Kato, S., Lakshmanan, K., Rajkumar, R., Ishikawa, Y.: Timegraph: Gpu scheduling for real-time multi-tasking environments. In: Proceedings of USENIX Annual Technical Conference. USENIX Association, Berkeley (2011)

[22] Klein, G., Andronick, J., Elphinstone, K., Heiser, G., Cock, D., Derrin, P., Elkaduwe, D., Engelhardt, K., Kolanski, R., Norrish, M., Sewell, T., Tuch, H., Winwood, S.: seL4: Formal verification of an OS kernel. Communications of the ACM 53(6), 107–115 (June 2010)

[23] Lagar-Cavilla, H.A., Tolia, N., Satyanarayanan, M., de Lara, E.: VMM-independent graphics acceleration. In: Proceedings of the 3rd International Conference on Virtual Execution Environments, pp. 33–43. ACM, New York (2007)

[24] Shapiro, J.S., Vanderburgh, J., Northup, E., Chizmadia, D.: Design of the eros trusted window system. In: Proceedings of the 13th Conference on USENIX Security Symposium, vol. 13. USENIX Association, Berkeley (2004)

[25] Stamatis, D.: Failure Mode and Effect Analysis: FMEA from Theory to Execution. ASQ Quality Press (2003)

[26] Steinberg, U., Kauer, B.: Nova: a microhypervisor-based secure virtualization architecture. In: Proceedings of the 5th European Conference on Computer Systems, EuroSys 2010, pp. 209–222. ACM, New York (2010)

Exploiting Segregation in Bus-Based MPSoCs to Improve Scalability of Model-Checking-Based Performance Analysis for SDFAs

Maher Fakih[1], Kim Grüttner[1], Martin Fränzle[2], and Achim Rettberg[2]

[1] OFFIS – Institute for Information Technology, Germany
[2] Carl von Ossietzky Universität, Germany

Abstract. The timing predictability of embedded systems with hard real-time requirements is fundamental for guaranteeing their safe usage. With the emergence of multicore platforms this task becomes even more challenging, because of shared processing, communication and memory resources. Model-checking techniques are capable of verifying the performance properties of applications running on these platforms. Unfortunately, these techniques are not scalable when analyzing systems with large number of tasks and processing units. In this paper, a model-checking based approach that allows to guarantee timing bounds of multiple Synchronous Data Flow Applications (SDFA) running on shared-bus multicore architectures will be extended for a TDMA hypervisor architecture. We will improve the the number of SDFAs being analyzable by our model-checking approach by exploiting the temporal and spatial segregation properties of the TDMA architecture and demonstrate how this method can be applied.

1 Introduction

A look at the current development process of electronic systems in the automotive domain, shows that this development process is still based on the design of distributed single-core ECUs (Electronic Control Units), especially in the hard real-time domain (for safety-critical systems) with a single application running per ECU. Yet, because of the growing computational demand of real-time applications (in automotive, avionics, and multimedia), extending the design process for supporting multicore architectures becomes inevitable. Due to their significantly increased performance and Space Weight and Power (SWaP) reductions, multicores offer an appealing alternative to traditional architectures.

In "traditional" distributed systems, dedicated memory per ECU and predictable field-bus protocols are used. This allows temporal and spatial segregation and timing requirements can be verified using traditional static analysis techniques. In multicore systems, contention on shared resources such as buses and memories makes the static timing analysis of such platforms very hard. To enable the applicability of static analysis techniques in multicore systems, resource virtualization using a static time slot per application has been introduced [1]. Time slots are switched circularly by a resource manager or hypervisor. The hypervisor takes care of the temporal and spatial segregation. Each

G. Schirner et al. (Eds.): IESS 2013, IFIP AICT 403, pp. 205–217, 2013.

application can access all platform resources until its time slot is over. When switching to the next slot, the hypervisor takes care of storing the local state of all platform resources of the terminated slot and restores the local state of the next time slot to be activated. In this paper, we present a composable analysis that is capable to analyze real-time properties of SDFAs on multicore platforms using a shared-bus architecture and dedicated data and instruction memories per processing unit. When using the hypervisor architecture described above, composability can be exploited due to the guaranteed segregation properties.

Our method, allows a model-checking based performance analysis of multiple SDFAs running on a single multicore platform [2]. An SDFA consists of multiple actors that exchange information through tokens and follows the Synchronous Dataflow (SDF) [3] Model of Computation (MoC). SDFAs are represented as Synchronous Dataflow Graphs (SDFGs). Our multicore architecture consists of tiles, each of them has a processor core with its own instruction and data memory. Message passing of tokens is implemented through memory-mapped I/O on a shared memory connected to the tiles via shared bus architecture. The SDF semantics support the clean separation between task computation and communication times which enables the analysis of timing effects though shared memory accesses. The general idea is illustrated with the following example. Four SDFAs, each two of them are mapped onto a dedicated 2-tile platform, as shown on the left side of Fig. 1. Under this mapping all SDFAs meet their required deadlines. On the right side of Fig. 1 all four SDFAs have been integrated on a virtualized 2-tile platform, where every set of applications is statically mapped to a time slot (A, B to slot1 and C, D to slot2). Segregation is implemented through a hypervisor component which implements a TDMA protocol that manages the switching between time slots and guarantees that applications running in different time slots have exclusive access to each tile's processor and have their own private area in the tile's local memories as well as in the shared memory.

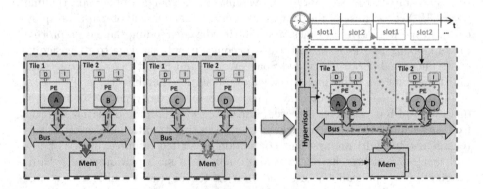

Fig. 1. Integrating four SDFAs on a 2-tile virtualized platform

In this paper, we improve the number of actors being analyzable by our model-checking approach [2] on a fixed number of tiles. This improvement benefits significantly from a composable analysis based on the temporal and spatial segregation properties of virtualized multicore platforms as described above. In Section 2, we discuss the related work addressing the performance analysis of synchronous dataflow graphs (SDFGs) on multicores. We extend our system model description for virtualized platforms in Section 3. In Section 4 we describe our compositional performance analysis for virtualized systems and evaluate its improvements with regard to scalability of our model-checking approach. The paper closes with a conclusion and gives an outlook on future work.

2   Related Work

2.1   Model-Checking

Lv et al. [4] presented an approach based on model-checking (UPPAAL) combined with abstract cache interpretation to estimate WCET of non-sharing code programs on a shared-bus multicore platform. Gustavsson et al. [5] moved further and tried to extend the former work [4] concentrating on modeling code sharing programs and enhancing the hardware architecture with additional data cache but without the consideration of bus contentions. In their work, they considered general tasks modeled at assembly level and analyzed these when mapped to an architecture where every core has its private L1 cache and all cores share an L2 cache without sharing a bus. Yet, the instruction level granularity of the modeled tasks lead to scalability problems even with a platform of four cores, on which four (very simple) tasks run and communicate through a shared buffer. Despite the advantage of the former two approaches being applicable to any code generated/written for any domain, the fine granularity of the code-level or instruction-level impedes the scalability of the model-checking technique. In [2], we intended to limit the application to an SDF MoC and limit the hardware architecture by removing caches, in order to reason about the scalability of a model-checking-based method for the performance analysis of SDFGs. We showed in [2] that our model-checking approach scales up to 36 actors mapped to 4-tiles and up to 96 actors on a 2-tiles platforms. In this paper, we intend to improve the number of actors being analyzable by our method on a fixed number of tiles (up to 4 tiles). In [6] an approach which combines model-checking with real-time analysis was presented to extend the scalability of worst-case response time analysis in multi-cores. Tasks are composed of superblocks where resource access phases can be identified. In this paper, we concentrate on SDF based applications with their specific properties and constraints. It is possible to use the abstraction techniques from [6] to analyze SDF applications. Dong et al. [7] presented a timed automata-based approach to verify the impact of execution platform and application mapping on the schedulability (meeting hard real-time requirements). The granularity of the application is considered at the task level. With tasks and processors having their own timed automata, the approach scales up to 103 tasks mapped to 3 cores. Yet, the communication model is missing in this approach.

2.2 Performance Analysis of SDFGs

Bhattacharyya et al. [3] proposed to analyze performance of a *single* SDFG mapped to a multi-processor system by decomposing it into a homogeneous SDFG (HSDFG). This could result in an exponential number of actors in the HSDFG compared to the SDFG. This in turn may lead to performance problems for the analysis methods. Ghamarian [8] presented novel methods to calculate performance metrics for single SDF applications which avoid translating SDFGs to HSDFGs. Nevertheless, resource sharing and other architecture properties were not considered. Moone [9] analyzed the mapping of SDFGs on a multiprocessor platform with limited resource sharing. The interconnect makes use of a network-on-chip that supports network connections with guaranteed communication services allowing them to easily derive conservatively estimated bounds on the performance metrics of SDFGs. Kumar [10] presented a probabilistic technique to estimate the performance of SDFGs sharing resources on a multi-processor system. Although this analysis was made taking into account the blocking time due to resource sharing, the estimation approach was aimed at analyzing soft real-time systems rather than those of hard real-time requirements. The work presented in [11] introduces an approach based on state-space exploration to verify the hard real-time performance of applications modeled with SDFGs that are mapped to a platform with shared resources. In contrast to this paper, it does however not consider a shared communication resource. Schabbir et al. [12] presented a design flow to generate multiprocessor platforms for multiple SDFGs. The performance analysis for hard real-time tasks is based on calculating the worst-case waiting time on resources as the sum of all tasks' execution times which can access this resource. This is a safe but obviously a very pessimistic approach. In [13] the composability of SDFGs applications on MPSoC platforms was analyzed. The resource manager proposed in their work, relies on run-time monitoring and intervenes when desired to achieve fairness between the SDFGs running. In difference to their work, we utilize a TDMA-based hypervisor which allows exclusive resource access for SDFGs assigned to time slots. Furthermore, in every time slot a model-checking-based method is utilized for the timing validation of multiple hard real-time SDFGs on a multi-core platform, considering the contention on a shared communication medium with flexible arbitration protocols such as First Come First Serve (FCFS).

3 System Model Definition

Definitions and terms of the system model are based on the X-Chart based synthesis process defined in [14]. We decided to use a formal notation (inspired from [3, 15]) to describe in an unambiguous way, the main modeling primitives and decisions of the synthesis process. This synthesis process takes as first input a set of behavior models, each implemented in the SDF MoC. The second input comprises resource constraints on the target architecture. The output is a model of performance (MoP) that serves as input for our performance analysis.

3.1 Model of Computation (MoC)

An SDF graph (SDFG) is a directed graph which typically consists of nodes (called actors) modeling functions/computations and arcs modeling the data flow. In SDFGs a static number of data samples (tokens) are consumed/produced each time an actor executes (fires). An actor can be a consumer, a producer or a transporter actor. We describe the formal semantics of SDFGs as follows:

Definition 1. *(Port) A Port is a tuple $P = (Dir, Rate)$ where $Dir \in \{I, O\}$ defines whether P is an input or an output port, and the function $Rate : P \to \mathbb{N}_{>0}$ assigns a rate to each port. This rate specifies the number of tokens consumed/produced by every port when the corresponding actor fires.*

Definition 2. *(Actor) An actor is a tuple $A = (\mathcal{P}, F)$ consisting of a finite set $\mathcal{P}$ of ports P, and F a label, representing the functionality of the actor.*

Definition 3. *(SDFG) An SDFG is a triple $SDFG = (\mathcal{A}, \mathcal{D}, T_s)$ consisting of a finite set $\mathcal{A}$ of actors A, a finite set $\mathcal{D}$ of dependency edges D, and a token size attribute T_s (in bits). An edge D is represented as a triple $D = (Src, Dst, Del)$ where the source (Src) of a dependency edge is an output port of some actor, the destination (Dst) is an input port of some actor, and $Del \in \mathbb{N}_0$ is the number of initial tokens (also called delay) of an edge. All ports of all actors are connected to exactly one edge, and all edges are connected to ports of some actor.*

Definition 4. *(Repetition vector) A repetition vector of an SDFG is defined as the vector specifying the number of times every actor in the SDFG has to be executed such that the initial state of the graph is obtained. Formally, a repetition vector of an SDFG is a function $\gamma : A \to \mathbb{N}_0$ so that for every edge $(p, q) \in \mathcal{D}$ from $a \in \mathcal{A}$ to $b \in \mathcal{A}$, $Rate(p) \times \gamma(a) = Rate(q) \times \gamma(b)$. A repetition vector γ is called non-trivial if and only if for all $a \in \mathcal{A} : \gamma(a) > 0$. In this paper, we use the term repetition vector to express the smallest non-trivial repetition vector.*

3.2 Model of Architecture (MoA)

Fig. 1 depicts our proposed platform architecture template. Each tile is made up of a processing element (PE) which has a configurable bus connection. A shared bus is used to connect the tiles to shared memory blocks. In addition, every PE has two local disjoint memories for instructions (IM)and data (DM). Furthermore, we assume that all tiles have the same bit-width as the bus and the architecture is fully synchronous using a single clock. This architecture enables the actors of SDFGs to communicate via buffers implemented in the shared memory. Only explicit communication (message passing) between actors will be visible on the interconnect and the shared memory. We assume constant access time for any memory block in the shared memory (as in [4]). Furthermore, we assume that bus block transfers are supported.

The hypervisor component implements global time slots on the platform using a TDMA protocol. Each time slot represents a subset (or all) of the platform resources to be used exclusively by the subset of SDFGs statically assigned to this slot. For this reason a shadow memories per slot for each local IM, DM and shared memory location is available to guarantee spatial segregation between different slots. The hypervisor has the role of switching cyclically between the slots, storing and restoring the local and global state through management of the different shadow memories. We describe our virtualized architecture model as follows:

Definition 5. *(Tile) A tile is a triple $T = (PE, i, M_p)$ with processing element $PE = (PE_{type}, f)$ where PE_{type} is the type of the processor and f is its clock frequency, $i \in \mathbb{N}_{>0}$ is the number of manageable slots and $M_p = ((m_{I_0} \ldots m_{I_{i-1}}), (m_{D_0} \ldots m_{D_{i-1}}))$ where $m_I, m_D \in \mathbb{N}_{>0}$ are the instruction and data memory sizes (in bits) respectively, and the index i represents the slot number of this memory. Total size of instruction and data memory is $i * m_X$ for $X \in D, I$.*

Definition 6. *(Execution Platform) An execution platform $EP = (H, \mathcal{T}, B, M_S)$ consists of a hypervisor component $H = (Sl, h)$ where Sl is the number of slots the hypervisor can handle, and h is the delay of switching from one slot to another, a finite set $\mathcal{T}$ of tiles $T_{H.Sl}$, a shared bus $B = (b_b, AP)$, where b_b is the bandwidth in bits/cycle and AP is the arbitration protocol (FCFS, TDMA, Round-Robin), and $M_S = (m_{s_0} \ldots m_{s_{H.Sl-1}})$ a shared memory where all slots have their own dedicated shared memory of the same size m_s in bits. Total size of the shared memory is $H.Sl * m_s$.*

Definition 7. *(Virtual Execution Platform) Let $\mathbf{Sl} := EP.H.Sl$ be the number of slots managed by the hypervisor. Then a virtual execution platform $VEP = (l, EP.\mathcal{T}, EP.B, EP.M_{S(0)})_0 \times \cdots \times (l, EP.\mathcal{T}, EP.B, EP.M_{S(Sl-1)})_{Sl-1}$ consists of the duration of each slot l, the tiles $\mathcal{T}$, the shared bus B and one shared memory partition $M_{S(j)}, 0 \leq j \leq EP.H.Sl - 1$ of EP. We define $VEP(i) = (l, \mathcal{T}, B, M_S)_i$ as the configuration of EP at the i-th time slot.*

3.3   System Synthesis

The system synthesis includes the definition of the Virtual Execution Platform, and the partitioning of SDFGs for different VEPs and the binding and scheduling of the SDFGs on the resources of their VEP. The mapping of the partitioned SDFGs on our VEP model is defined as follows:

Definition 8. *(Mapping) Let $\mathbf{Sl} := EP.H.Sl$ be the number of slots managed by the hypervisor. Then for every slot $0 \leq i \leq \mathbf{Sl} - 1$, let $\mathcal{A}_i$ be the set of actors and $\mathcal{D}_i$ the set of all edges of all SDFGs assigned to this slot. Then a mapping for each slot can be defined as a tuple $M_i = (\alpha_i, \beta_i)$ with*

1. *the function $\alpha_i : \mathcal{A}_i \to VEP(i).\mathcal{T}$ mapping every actor to a tile (multiple actors can be assigned to one tile)*
2. *the function $\beta_i : \mathcal{D}_i \to \bigcup_{VEP(i).\mathcal{T}} M_{p(i)} \cup VEP(i).M_S$ mapping every edge of the SDFG either to the slot's private memory of the tile or to the slot's shared memory partition.*

An edge mapped to a private or to the shared memory represents a consumer-producer FIFO buffer in an actual implementation [3]. The following three definitions allow us to express the scheduling behavior of multiple SDFGs mapped to the tiles of $VEP(i)$:

Definition 9. *(Static-order schedule) For an SDFG with repetition vector γ, a static-order schedule SO is an ordered list of the actors (to be executed on some tile), where every actor a is included in this list $\gamma(a)$ times.*

Definition 10. *(Scheduling Function) Let SO_i be the set of all SO schedules for all SDFGs considered in slot i. A scheduling function for slot i is a function $S_i : VEP(i).\mathcal{T} \to \mathbf{so}_i$, which assigns to every tile $t \in VEP(i).\mathcal{T}$ a subset $\mathbf{so}_i \subseteq SO_i$.*

Definition 11. *(Scheduler) A scheduler for a slot i is a triple $S_i = (\mathbf{so}_i, F, HS)$ where $\mathbf{so}_i \subseteq SO_i$ is the set of different SDFGs schedules assigned to one tile, F represents the functionality (code) of the scheduler and HS is the hierarchical scheduling, defining the order (priority) of execution of independent lists of different SDFGs assigned to one tile according to an arbitration strategy (Static-Order, Round-Robin, TDMA).*

We assume that all SDFGs running in the system are known at design time. Furthermore, while the actors execution order is fixed, the consumer-producer synchronization in each tile is performed at run-time depending on the buffer state [3]. A producer actor writes data into a FIFO buffer and blocks if that buffer is full, while a consumer actor blocks when the buffer is empty. An important performance metric of SDFG that will be evaluated in Section 5 is the *period*, defined in this paper as the time needed for one static order schedule of an SDFG to be completed.

3.4   Model of Performance (MoP)

In order to be able to verify that the performance of the SDFG stays within given bounds, we must keep track of all possible timing delays of all SDFGs per slot, with regard to the physical resources of the underlying multicore platform. To achieve this, a MoP is extracted from the synthesis process which includes only the SW/HW components where the timing delay is critical. From the hardware abstraction point of view, we consider a Transaction Level Model (TLM) [16] abstraction for the communication. This means that the application layer issues read/write transactions on the bus, abstracting from the communication protocol (see CAAM model [16]). After synthesis, the following system components can be annotated with execution times/delays: the *scheduler* that implements the static order schedule within an SDFG and the hierarchical scheduling across different SDFGs, the *actors*, the *tiles*, the *bus* and the *shared memories*. A new component (*communication driver*) is introduced into our system, which is responsible of implementing the communication between actors mapped to a tile with other components such as the private memory and the shared memory. In addition, when an actor blocks on a buffer, this driver implements a polling mechanism. If $\mathcal{A}_i$ is the set of actors, $\mathcal{S}_i$ the set of schedulers, $\mathcal{D}_i$ the set of edges, $\mathcal{C}_i$ the set of communication drivers, $VEP(i).B$ the bus, $VEP(i).M_S$ the set of shared memories, and $\bigcup_{VEP(i).\mathcal{T}} M_{p(i)}$ the set of private memories per slot, when considering the performance of the synthesized model, the following delay functions per slot i are defined:

- $\Delta_{A_i} : \mathcal{A}_i \times VEP(i).\mathcal{T} \to \mathbb{N}_{>0} \times \mathbb{N}_{>0}$ which provides an execution time interval $[BCET, WCET]$ for each actor representing the cycles needed to execute the actor behavior on the corresponding tile. This delay can be estimated using a static analyzer tool.
- $\Delta_{S_i} : \mathcal{S}_i \times VEP(i).\mathcal{T} \to \mathbb{N}_{>0} \times \mathbb{N}_{>0}$, $\Delta_{C_i} : \mathcal{C}_i \times VEP(i).\mathcal{T} \to \mathbb{N}_{>0} \times \mathbb{N}_{>0}$ assigns in analogy to Δ_{A_i} to every scheduler and communication driver a delay interval, which can be estimated using a static analyzer tool depending on the code of both components and the platform properties.
- $\Delta_{D_i} : \mathcal{D}_i \times \bigcup_{VEP(i).\mathcal{T}} M_{p(i)} \cup VEP(i).M_S \to \mathbb{N}_{>0}$ assigns to each communicating edge $d \in \mathcal{D}_i$ mapped to a communication primitive a delay which depends on the number and size of the tokens being transported on the edge and the bandwidth of the corresponding communication medium. We assume that the delay on the edge mapped to a private memory is included in the interval calculated by the static analyzer tool for the actors. Likewise, the shared memory access delay is included in the delay of the bus needed to serve a message passing communication.

Now, for each slot i we can abstractly represent every tile by the actors mapped to it, the scheduler, a communication driver, each with their delay as defined before, and its private memory. Each of the private memories in the tiles and the shared memories can be abstracted in a set of (private/shared) FIFO buffers with corresponding sizes depending on the rate of the edges mapped to them and the schedule (each edge is mapped to exactly one FIFO buffer). Note that although no delays are explicitly modeled on the private and shared buffers, these buffers are still considered in the MoP because of their effect on the synchronization which in turn affects the performance.

4 Compositional Performance Analysis Method

4.1 Model-Checking Based Performance Analysis within a Slot

The following method is used to analyze the performance of all SDFGs mapped to a single slot accessing a subset of the multicore's compute, memory and shared bus resources. The components of the MoP identified in the last Section can be formalized using the timed automata semantics of UPPAAL[1]. The composition can be described as follows:

System $=$ VirtualExecutionPlatform $||\ _{i=1}^{q}$ SDFG$_i$

SDFG$_i = {}_{j=1}^{r}$ Consumer$_j$ $||\ _{k=1}^{s}$ Producer$_k$ $||\ _{l=1}^{t}$ Transporter$_l$

VirtualExecutionPlatform$= {}_{m=1}^{u}$ Tile$_m$ $||$ Bus $||\ _{o=1}^{v}$SharedFIFO$_o$

Tile$_i=$ Scheduler$_i$ $||$ CommunicationDriver$_i$ $||\ _{p=1}^{w}$ PrivateFIFO$_p$

where $||$ means parallel composition of timed automata in UPPAAL, q is the number of SDFGs, r, s, t represent the number of actors (distinguished according to their type), u is the number of tiles, v is the number of shared FIFO, and w is the number of private FIFO buffers. In [2], we described the implementation and the interactions of timed-automata of different components of the MoP. In addition we illustrated, how performance metrics such as the Worst Case Period (WCP) can obtained with the help of UPPAAL model-checker. The evaluation in [2] showed that this method suffers from scalability limitations. E.g. up to 36 actors on a 4-tile platform and up to 96 actors on a 2-tile platform could be analyzed in a reasonable amount of time.

4.2 Performance Analysis across the Slots

With the proposed extension to our system model definition in Section 3, our approach in [2] can be used to obtain the WCP of multiple SDFGs per slot with the help of model-checking. In this subsection we describe how this WCP changes when considering other slots where different SDFGs are mapped. As described above, the hypervisor implements a temporal and spatial segregation between SDFGs of different slots. I.e. all SDFGs of a slot have exclusive access to the resources and no contention with other SDFGs from other slots can appear. Yet every SDFG in one slot can still have contention with other SDFGs mapped to the same slot. This contention and its effect can be analyzed using the model-checking method presented in the last Section 4.1 and in [2].

For the construction of the slots in the VEP, the length $VEP(i).l$ of every slot i is set to be equal to the maximum WCP of all SDFGs mapped to this slot. Since the hypervisor has the role to dispatch/suspend SDFGs in every slot, an execution platform dependent slot switching delay overhead $\mathbf{h} := EP.H.h$ is induced at the beginning of each slot. Assuming that SDFGs running in one slot are independent from those running in other slots, the following formula can be used to determine the WCP_{compos} of every SDFG after the composition:

$$WCP_{compos} = \sum_{i=0}^{\mathbf{Sl}} WCP_{max}(i) + (\mathbf{Sl} \times \mathbf{h}), \tag{1}$$

where $WCP_{max}(i)$ is the maximal WCP among the SDFGs running in slot i and $\mathbf{Sl} := EP.H.Sl$ is the total number of slots.

---

[1] UPPAAL 4.1.11 (rev. 5085), has been used in the experiments.

5 Evaluation

5.1 Performance Analysis

Suppose we have four SDFGs, each two of them are mapped onto a 2-tile platform (see Fig. 1). Now, we have the task to integrate both platforms on one multicore platform, such that they still meet their timing requirements. This is indeed, a typical use-case in many domains nowadays (automotive, avionics). The goal of this experiment, is to demonstrate how our proposed method can be applied to above use-case, and to show that in case the contention on the bus is high, partitioning induces only minor performance penalties.

Tab. 1 shows the parameters of the four artificial SDFGs, we constructed to examine the claim above. The actors' worst-case execution times were generated randomly (uniformly distributed) within a range of [5..500] cycles, and a timing requirement (WCP_{req}) was imposed on every SDFG. We have set the ports' rates deliberately high, in order to impose contention on the bus. High rates lead to longer communication time of the active actor, and this in turn leads to longer waiting time of other actors trying to access the bus. In addition, all edges of all SDFGs in all mappings were mapped to the shared memory in order to achieve a high contention on the bus. The bus has a bandwidth of 32 bits/cycle, a FCFS arbitration protocol and all tokens are of size 32 bits. Moreover, all SDFGs were scheduled according to a static order schedule.

First, we configured the timed automata templates to evaluate the mapping of the considered SDFGs, each pair on a 2-tile platform (see Fig. 1 left). The Worst-case Period (WCP_{isol}) values for every SDFG were calculated using the model-checking method as described in Section 4.1. Next, we integrated the four SDFGs and mapped them on a 2-tile platform but without the hypervisor component. Again, we utilize the model-checking based analysis to find the new WCP (WCP_{nocomp}) of every SDFG (see Tab. 1 (Exp. 2 tiles)). After that, we take use of the hypervisor extension, configuring two time slots. SDFGs A, B are assigned to $slot1$, and C, D are assigned to $slot2$ (see Fig. 1 right). The length of every slot is equivalent to the maximum WCP_{isol} (WCP_{max}) among the SDFGs

Table 1. Experiments Setup and Results, WCP in cycles

SDFGs Parameters			Exp. 2 tiles				Exp. 4 tiles	
Actors	Chan	Ports' Rate	WCP_{req}	WCP_{isol}	WCP_{nocomp}	WCP_{compos}	WCP_{isol}	WCP_{compos}
A	10	9	[1200,2400]	160000	54529	140863		135400	
B	10	9	[200,600]	160000	59895	117439	**145096**	171000	
C	10	9	[220,440]	160000	85001	141734		135400	
D	6	5	[100,200]	160000	44236	119466		69600	
E	10	9	[500,2000]					107850	**279050**
F	10	9	[300,600]					64500	
G	10	9	[700,1400]					66950	
H	6	5	[150,300]					37300	

assigned to this slot (slot1: 59895, slot2: 85001). The new WCPs (WCP_{compos}) are calculated according to Formula (1) assuming a hypervisor delay h of 100 cycles. The results depicted in Tab. 1 (Exp. 2 tiles), show that all SDFGs still respect their requirements, with a minor performance degradation of average 12.5% in the case of temporal and spatial segregation through the hypervisor.

5.2   Scalability

The model-checking method presented in [2] does not scale beyond 36 actors mapped to a 4-tile platform. In order to demonstrate the scalability improvement of our proposed extension, we consider the same set of artificial SDFGs presented above which have in total 36 actors, and another set of SDFGs (E, F, G and H) also having 36 actors (see Tab. 1). Every set was mapped on a 4-tile platform (without hypervisor) and both were first analyzed in isolation with the help of the model-checking method. After obtaining the WCP_{isol} of the single SDFGs in isolation (see Tab. 1: Exp. 4 tiles), we now map the 8 SDFGs onto a 4-tile platform with a hypervisor with two slots and a slot switching delay h of 100 cycles. SDFGs A, B, C, D were assigned to $slot1$ with the length 171000 cycles and E, F, G, H to $slot2$ having a length of 107850. Afterwise, we calculated the new WCP_{compos} of the single SDFGs according to (1) (see Tab. 1: Exp. 4 tiles). The results show that our composable analysis doubles the number of actors, which can be analyzed compared to [2] for this example, at the cost of performance degradation.

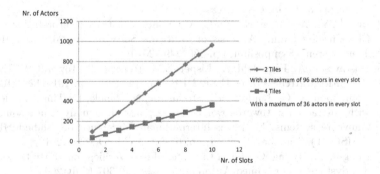

Fig. 2. Scalability Results

Clearly, we can now increase the number of SDFGs that can be analyzed by increasing the number of slots managed by the hypervisor. Fig. 2 shows that by 10 slots we could analyze up to 960 actors on a 2-tile platform and 360 actors on a 4-tile platform. Nevertheless, the designer should be acquainted with the fact that by increasing the number of slots the performance overhead of the single SDFG would be increased (for Exp. 4 tiles an average of 255%).

6 Conclusion

In this paper, we have presented a composable extension to our model-checking-based performance analysis method for the validation of hard real-time SDFGs mapped to a virtualized shared-bus multicore platform. Exploiting the temporal and spatial segregation properties of the hypervisor, significantly improves scalability depending on the number of slots (by ten slots) up to 360 actors mapped to 4-tile and up to 960 actors on a 2-tile platforms. Future work will address relaxing the MoC towards dynamic data flow graphs, and relaxing architecture constraints towards interrupts, cross-bar switches, and dedicated FIFO channels.

Acknowledgement. This paper has been partially supported by the MotorBrain ENIAC project under the grant (13N11480) of the German Federal Ministry of Research and Education (BMBF).

References

[1] Aeronautical Radio, I.: Arinc 653: Avionics application software standard interface. Technical report, ARINC, 2551 Riva Road Annapolis, MD 21401, U.S.A (2003)

[2] Fakih, M., Grüttner, K., Fränzle, M., Rettberg, A.: Towards performance analysis of SDFGs mapped to shared–bus architectures using model–checking. In: Proceedings of the Conference on Design, Automation and Test in Europe, DATE 2013, Leuven, Belgium, European Design and Automation Association (March 2013)

[3] Sriram, S., Bhattacharyya, S.S.: Embedded Multiprocessors: Scheduling and Synchronization, 1 edn. CRC Press (March 2000)

[4] Lv, M., Yi, W., Guan, N., Yu, G.: Combining Abstract Interpretation with Model Checking for Timing Analysis of Multicore Software. In: 2010 31st IEEE Real-Time Systems Symposium, pp. 339–349 (2010)

[5] Gustavsson, A., Ermedahl, A., Lisper, B., Pettersson, P.: Towards WCET Analysis of Multicore Architectures Using UPPAAL. In: 10th, pp. 101–112 (2011)

[6] Giannopoulou, G., Lampka, K., Stoimenov, N., Thiele, L.: Timed model checking with abstractions: Towards worst-case response time analysis in resource-sharing manycore systems. In: Proc. International Conference on Embedded Software (EMSOFT), Tampere, Finland, pp. 63–72. ACM (October 2012)

[7] Dong-il, C., Hyung, C., Jan, M.: System-Level Verification of Multi-Core Embedded Systems Using Timed-Automata, pp. 9302–9307 (July 2008)

[8] Ghamarian, A.: Timing Analysis of Synchronous Data Flow Graphs. PhD thesis, Eindhoven University of Technology (2008)

[9] Moonen, A.: Predictable Embedded Multiprocessor Architecture for Streaming Applications. PhD thesis, Eindhoven University of Technology (2009)

[10] Kumar, A.: Analysis, Design and Management of Multimedia Multiprocessor Systems. PhD thesis, Ph. D. thesis, Eindhoven University of Technology (2009)

[11] Yang, Y., Geilen, M., Basten, T., Stuijk, S., Corporaal, H.: Automated bottleneck-driven design-space exploration of media processing systems. In: Proceedings of the Conference on Design, Automation and Test in Europe, DATE 2010, Leuven, Belgium, pp. 1041–1046. European Design and Automation Association (2010)

[12] Shabbir, A., Kumar, A., Stuijk, S., Mesman, B., Corporaal, H.: CA-MPSoC: An Automated Design Flow for Predictable Multi-processor Architectures for Multiple Applications. Journal of Systems Architecture 56(7), 265–277 (2010)

[13] Kumar, A., Mesman, B., Theelen, B., Corporaal, H., Ha, Y.: Analyzing composability of applications on MPSoC platforms. J. Syst. Archit. 54(3-4) (March 2008)

[14] Gerstlauer, A., Haubelt, C., Pimentel, A., Stefanov, T., Gajski, D., Teich, J.: Electronic System-Level Synthesis Methodologies. IEEE Transactions on Computer-Aided Design of Integrated Circuits and Systems 28(10), 1517–1530 (2009)

[15] Stuijk, S.: Predictable Mapping of Streaming Applications on Multiprocessors, vol. 68. University Microfilms International, P. O. Box 1764, Ann Arbor, MI, 48106, USA (2007)

[16] Cai, L., Gajski, D.: Transaction Level Modeling: an Overview. In: First IEEE/ACM/IFIP International Conference on Hardware/Software Codesign and System Synthesis, pp. 19–24 (October 2003)

Formal Verification of Concurrent Embedded Software

Dirk Nowotka[1,*] and Johannes Traub[2]

[1] Department of Computer Science, Kiel University
dn@informatik.uni-kiel.de
[2] E/E- and Software-Technologies, Daimler AG
johannes.traub@daimler.com

Abstract. With the introduction of multicore hardware to embedded systems their vulnerability to race conditions has been drastically increased. Therefore, sufficient methods and techniques have to be developed in order to identify this kind of runtime errors. In this paper, we demonstrate an approach employing a formal technique in the verification process. We use MEMICS, which is a specialized constraint solver able to identify general runtime errors as well as race conditions. We show how this tool can be embedded into an existing software analysis tool chain. In particular, we describe the process of deriving the formal input model for the solver from C code. The advantage of using constraint solving techniques is that we can offer an entire trace leading to a race condition. The ongoing development of MEMICS is part of our work inside the ARAMiS project.

1 Introduction

One of the main goals of the ARAMiS project — "Automotive, Railway and Avionics Multicore Systems" — [BS] is to enhance on safety issues for multicore embedded technologies in vehicles. In terms of embedded systems a safety aspect is the assurance that the software running on them is free of any kind of runtime error, which they may suffer and fault from. Software can suffer from a lot of different runtime errors, like an arithmetic overflow, a division by zero, an index out of bound access, a null dereference, a race conditions and a stack overflow. A detailed list of runtime errors can be found in Table 1 in Section 3. The nastiest of these runtime errors are the race conditions, as they might only occur sporadically and are therefore very hard to detect or trace. With the current introduction of multicore hardware to embedded systems, their vulnerability to race conditions has increased drastically. To get this problem under control new tools and techniques are required.

In [NT12] we introduced the static software analysis tool MEMICS, which is able to detect race conditions as well as common runtime errors in C/C++ source code. Common static analysis tools like Astrée [CCF+05], Polyspace [pol], and Bauhaus [RVP06] are able to analyse large code fragments but do suffer from potential false positives which requires an extensive manual postprocessing of their results. MEMICS is based on constraint solving techniques which eliminate the problem of false positives. However, the complexity of constraint solving algorithms is very high which means that the

---

* This work has been supported by the BMBF grant 01IS110355.

G. Schirner et al. (Eds.): IESS 2013, IFIP AICT 403, pp. 218–227, 2013.

code fragments MEMICS can analyse are not too large. We believe that a combination of both approaches, approximative and precise techniques, together in one tool chain lead to a significant improvement of the analysis of concurrent code. In this paper we describe how MEMICS fits into a static analysis workflow. Moreover, we give a detailed description of the conversion of C code to the MEMICS input model.

Within the ARAMiS project there are two possible scenarios discussed, in which the MEMICS tool can be used to provide safety:

1. Migration to multicore hardware, and
2. Development for multicore hardware.

Both scenarios have the same origin. Lets assume an OEM has decided to replace the hardware of one of its ECU's — e.g. due to new features, optimized power consumption, or need for more performance — and the replacement hardware contains a multicore CPU, whereas the old one was a singlecore system. In this case the OEM has to decide, either to port the current software version to match all the new features of the multicore hardware or to entirely restart and build a new software from scratch. Still, no matter which of the two choices are picked, it is clear that the possibility of potential races has increased with the new hardware. Therefore MEMICS can be used to determine and eliminate races during the development process.

The MEMICS tool is described in Section 2, where we mainly focus on the MEMICS frontend. Section 3 provides current results of the MEMICS tool. In Section 4 we discuss the role and possible use cases of MEMICS inside the ARAMiS project. Finally we conclude our paper in Section 5 and give a perspective for the future.

2   The MEMICS Tool

In [NT12] we introduced MEMICS, while mainly focusing on the overall tool and the proof engine. The current paper is dedicated to the preprocessing engine in MEMICS, the MEMICS frontend, which is introduced in detail in Section 2.1. Figure 1 shows the architectural overview of MEMICS. The input to MEMICS is C/C++ source code, which in the first step is preprocessed in the MEMICS frontend and results in the MEMICS model. This model is then passed to the core of MEMICS, the actual proof engine, which checks if the model suffers from any runtime error.

2.1   The MEMICS Frontend

The MEMICS frontend describes the interface between the source input, which is C/C++ source code, and the MEMICS model. We decided to use the Low Level Virtual Machine (LLVM) [LA04] infrastructure as a base for this frontend, as it is currently one the most advanced and user friendly compiler framework. In the first step, the C/C++ sources get compiled using the CLANG [Fan10] compiler and are linked together using llvm-ld. The result is one bitcode file, which resides in the LLVM intermediate representation (IR) [Lat]. The LLVM IR is a combination of the LLVM language, which is based on the MIPS [Swe06] instruction set, and an unlimited set of virtual registers. In order to simplify and reduce the input problem, we can optionally run a Program Slicer

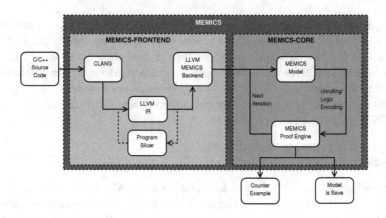

Fig. 1. An Overview of the MEMICS Architecture

[Wei81] directly on the LLVM IR. Due to the fact that this slice must not modify the overall behaviour of the program, we can only apply specific slicing techniques. The IR still features function- and variable-pointers as well as other specific types, which are not straight forward dealable by common verification techniques. So, instead of having to lower all the special features on our own, we decided to take advantage of the LLVM backend, which is generating plain machine code. Therefore, we derived the LLVM MEMICS backend from the MIPS backend and added some minor modifications to the instruction lowering. But instead of printing plain MIPS assembly code, the LLVM MEMICS backend creates the MEMICS intermediate representation, which is introduced in Section 2.2. Every machine instruction can be mapped one-by-one to a MEMICS instruction and every global variable is on the one hand applied to the MEMICS RAM and on the other hand assigned to the model.

Like almost any compiler infrastructure the LLVM MIPS backend supports three different relocation types [Lev99]: dynamic-no-pic, pic and static. Pic is short for "position independent code" and even allows the temporal storage of jump destinations into registers. Both, pic and dynamic-no-pic allow libraries to be fetched dynamically, which results in a smaller linked binary. Whereas in static relocation type all libraries are statically linked into the binary, which is therefore bigger. In the current development state our MEMICS intermediate representation requires absolute jump destinations, which forces us to either use dynamic-no-pic or static relocation type.

2.2 The MEMICS Intermediate Representation

The MEMICS intermediate representation (IR) or the MEMICS model is based on a combination of a finite state machine definition and the MIPS instruction set. An instruction inside the IR is defined as the 4-tuple:

$$< s_i, c, a, s'_i >, \text{where:}$$

s_i is the current program counter (PC), c is an optional condition (e.g. in a branch instruction), a is the actual MIPS instruction, and s'_i is the successor PC.

Figure 2 shows a small example of the conversion from C source code to the MEMICS IR. The source code shown in the first box is a simple function, which computes the division of the operands a and b. Compiling this code using CLANG results in the LLVM IR, which is shown in the second box of the figure. It is observable that the IR itself is already more like a machine language, compared to the actual source code. First of all local memory for the operands is allocated, which is afterwards assigned with the actual values of them. In the next step the values are read from the memory into the two virtual registers %0 and %1. Next the division itself takes place and finally the result is returned. The MEMICS IR, which is shown in the last box of Figure 2, is retrieved from the LLVM IR via the LLVM MEMICS backend. The result is even closer to the MIPS assembly language then the LLVM IR. The actual instruction has been embedded between the current program counter and the following program counter, which are both required in order to properly process the model. First of all in line 1 the local stack pointer gets allocated. In line 2 and 3 the operands - respectively the registers 4 and 5 - are stored in the local memory. Now, the actual division takes part in line 4, where the result is store in register lo and the remainder in register hi. In the next two instructions the result is assigned to the return value register 2 and the stack pointer gets freed. Finally the function returns to its caller, which is stored in the ra (return address) register.

2.3   The MEMICS Core

The MEMICS Core is the actual verification engine of the MEMICS tool, which checks if the MEMICS IR and its underlying C/C++ source code suffers from any runtime error or not. The verification process is based on Bounded Model Checking (BMC) [BCC+03]. Therefore, the MEMICS IR is unrolled step by step into a logic formula in Static Single Assignment (SSA) form [AWZ88, RWZ88] and then passed to the MEMICS Proof Engine. This proof engine is a self developed Interval Constraint Solver (ICS), based on the ideas from HySAT and its successor ISAT [FHT+07]. The main difference between an ICS and common SAT-/SMT-Solvers [MMZ+01, dMB09] - e.g. MiniSAT [ES03], Boolector [BB09], Z3 [dMB08] and many other - is, instead of dealing with fix-point variable decisions during the internal search procedure, variable ranges are deduced. Since the main purpose of our tool is software verification, it contains many special features regarding the analysis of software. For details on these features please refer to [NT12].

3   Results

In [NT12] we have tested MEMICS on an internal benchmark set, which contains different types of runtime errors, based on errors observed in real life. We used the Common Weakness Enumeration (CWE) [cwe] database to define the base classes for these errors. As the CWE gathers almost any kind of error, which is observable in a computer based environment, we do by far not match all error classes, but only show the most relevant ones for static software analysis. The result of these tests is shown in Table 1, where we have compared MEMICS with two analysis tools, CBMC [CKL04] and LLBMC [SFM10], which are also operating based on BMC.

C Code
| ```
int divide(int a, int b) {
    return (a / b);
}
``` |
| LLVM Intermediate Representation |
| ```
define i32 @divide(i32 %a, i32 %b) nounwind {
entry:
  %a.addr = alloca i32, align 4
  %b.addr = alloca i32, align 4
  store i32 %a, i32* %a.addr, align 4
  store i32 %b, i32* %b.addr, align 4
  %0 = load i32* %a.addr, align 4
  %1 = load i32* %b.addr, align 4
  %div = sdiv i32 %0, %1
  ret i32 %div
}
``` |
| MEMICS Intermediate Representation |
| ```
1: PC = 1 -> malloc(sp_reg' , 8) AND PC' = 2;
2: PC = 2 -> sw(4_reg, (memadr(sp_reg, 4) AND __clk__))
          AND PC' = 3;
3: PC = 3 -> sw(5_reg, (memadr(sp_reg, 0) AND __clk__))
          AND PC' = 4;
5: PC = 4 -> (lo_reg' = 4_reg / 5_reg)
          AND (hi_reg' = 4_reg % 5_reg)
          AND PC' = 5;
6: PC = 5 -> (2_reg'  = lo_reg)  AND PC' = 6;
7: PC = 6 -> free(sp_reg) AND PC' = 7;
8: PC = 7 -> PC' = ra_reg;
``` |

Fig. 2. From C Source Code via the LLVM IR to the MEMICS IR

With this results we have shown that our tool is already able to identify a lot of runtime errors, as well common sequential as difficult concurrent ones.

4 MEMICS and the ARAMiS Multicore Platform

As in the introduction already mentioned the main goal of ARAMiS is to provide a platform for multicore development. This platform should feature a seamless integration of the development tools along the development process. For this purpose one current development process is the creation of a global exchange format. This format should help all tools along the development process to intercommunicate with each other and pass on usable information or already computed results.

The MEMICS tool can intercommunicate and share information with common static analysis tools like Astrée, Polyspace, and others as well as race detection tools like
```

Bauhaus [RVP06] and others. Figure 3 illustrates the information sharing between those tools alongside the ARAMiS exchange format. The main idea behind the combination of these tools is to provide the best overall performance for all of them. Whereas tools like Astrée and Polyspace have the ability to handle large amounts of source code, they are based on abstract interpretation [CC77] and may therefore suffer from imprecision in the results. Bauhaus can also handle a lot of input in terms of source code, but it still suffers from false positives in the results, since it is working based on approximative techniques. On the other hand BMC tools like MEMICS are limited due to the state explosion problem, while offering enormous precision. In our case we even provide a direct counterexample leading to an error. In Section 4.1 and 4.2 we describe three different scenarios of possible tool intercommunication.

Table 1. Results of MEMICS compared to CBMC and LLBMC, where a ✓ represents a correct verification result, - a false one and o signals that the tool does not support the class of testcases

Class	Benchmark	CWE-ID	MEMICS	CBMC	LLBMC
Arithmetic	DivByZeroFloat	369	✓	✓	o
	DivByZeroInt	369	✓	✓	✓
	IntOver	190	✓	✓	✓
Memory	DoubleFree	415	✓	✓	✓
	InvalidFree	590	✓	✓	✓
	NullDereference	476	✓	✓	✓
	PointertToStack	465	✓	-	✓
	SizeOfOnPointers	467	✓	-	✓
	UseAfterFree	416	✓	-	✓
Pointer Arithmetic	Scaling	468	✓	-	✓
	Subtraction	469	✓	-	✓
Race Condition	LostUpdate	567[1]	✓	o	o
	MissingSynchronisation	820	✓	o	o
Synchronization	DeadLock	833	✓	o	o
	DoubleLock	667	✓	o	o

4.1   Combination: MEMICS ↔ Polyspace

The output of Polyspace is divided in three different groups: the green, orange and red results. A green result states the given property is free of faults, whereas a red one is an actual finding. All of the orange ones are not determinable and must therefore be manually reviewed. One can use MEMICS to check if the error is "real" or not. The definition of the check is acutally quite simple. Let us assume the indeterminable error is a potential division by zero occurring in the example function "divide" of Figure 2. In that case using the definition of the according MEMICS IR from Figure 2, the target-question MEMICS has to determine is:

$$PC == 4 \wedge 5\_reg == 0$$

---

[1] We did not find a straight forward ID for a lost update, but the example in this entry describes one.

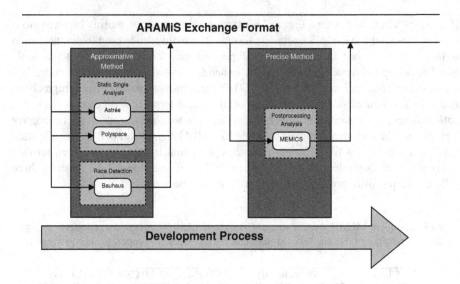

Fig. 3. ARAMiS Exchange Format: Intercommunication between Software Analysis Tools

4.2   Combination: Bauhaus ↔ MEMICS

In case of the Bauhaus race detector, two different scenarios can be considered. In the first case Bauhaus can just pass its common output as well as the system description - including the task definitions, their priorities and so on - to MEMICS in order to determine, which of the detected race pairs can really occur in the system. Such a race pair can either be a read operation from task A in conflict with a write operation from task B on the same shared resource or a write-write conflict between task A and B. So e.g. for a read/write conflict, given the read access occurs at PC = x, the write conflict occurs at PC = y and the resource is located at address z in the memory, the target-question for MEMICS is:

$$clk(load, z, A, PC = x) > clk(store, z, B, PC = y)$$

In the second case Bauhaus can use MEMICS to gather more information on the scheduling of tasks. With this help Bauhaus can reduce the set of potential race conditions. Let us assume that the initial program counter of task A is PC_taskA = x and for task B PC_taskB = y. The target-question for MEMICS, if e.g. the two tasks can start synchronously, is:

$$clk(PC\_taskA = x) == clk(PC\_taskB = y)$$

The MEMICS tool benefits from the first two scenarios described above, because adding a target-question to input of the MEMICS IR has almost the same impact as Program Slicing. It does not actually reduce the MEMICS IR, but reduces to search space only to the required behaviour, which is shown in Figure 4. This reduction can have a large impact on the overall time MEMICS requires to solve the input problem.

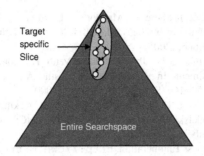

Fig. 4. MEMICS IR Slice: Searchspace Reduction to a specific Target

5 Conclusions and Future Work

In this paper we have described, how the software verification tool MEMICS maps C code to its input model. We have shown the advantages of using LLVM and that especially the LLVM Backend is the most suitable solution for our purpose. Moreover, we described the role of MEMICS inside a software analysis tool chain, in particular within the ARAMiS project. This gives our perspective in which cases MEMICS can enhance the development process.

Currently, we are running scalability tests of the MEMICS tool to test the limits of our approach and push those. Another ongoing work is to embed techniques like counterexample guided abstraction refinement (CEGAR) [CGJ+00] in order to improve on MEMICS efficiency. In terms of the ARAMiS project, we will use the exchange format, once it is available, for tying MEMICS into the tool chain. This will help us a lot in case of direct knowledge sharing with other tools like e.g. Bauhaus and Polyspace. The information we can retrieve from these tools is supposed to drastically reduce the size of the input in most cases.

References

[AWZ88] Alpern, B., Wegman, M.N., Zadeck, F.K.: Detecting equality of variables in pro-
         grams. In: Proceedings of the 15th ACM SIGPLAN-SIGACT Symposium on Prin-
         ciples of Programming Languages, pp. 1–11 (1988)
[BB09]   Brummayer, R., Biere, A.: Boolector: An Efficient SMT Solver for Bit-Vectors and
         Arrays. In: Kowalewski, S., Philippou, A. (eds.) TACAS 2009. LNCS, vol. 5505, pp.
         174–177. Springer, Heidelberg (2009)
[BCC+03] Biere, A., Cimatti, A., Clarke, E.M., Strichman, O., Zhu, Y.: Bounded Model Check-
         ing. Advances in Computers, vol. 58, pp. 117–148. Elsevier (2003)
[BS]   Becker, J., Sander, O.: Automotive, Railway and Avionics Multicore Systems -
         ARAMiS, http://www.projekt-aramis.de/
[CC77]   Cousot, P., Cousot, R.: Abstract interpretation: a unified lattice model for static anal-
         ysis of programs by construction or approximation of fixpoints. In: Proceedings of
         the 4th ACM SIGACT-SIGPLAN Symposium on Principles of Programming Lan-
         guages, POPL 1977, pp. 238–252. ACM, New York (1977)

[CCF+05] Cousot, P., Cousot, R., Feret, J., Mauborgne, L., Miné, A., Monniaux, D., Rival, X.:
          The ASTREÉ analyzer. In: Sagiv, M. (ed.) ESOP 2005. LNCS, vol. 3444, pp. 21–30.
          Springer, Heidelberg (2005)
[CGJ+00] Clarke, E., Grumberg, O., Jha, S., Lu, Y., Veith, H.: Counterexample-Guided Ab-
          straction Refinement. In: Emerson, E.A., Sistla, A.P. (eds.) CAV 2000. LNCS,
          vol. 1855, pp. 154–169. Springer, Heidelberg (2000)
[CKL04]   Clarke, E., Kroning, D., Lerda, F.: A Tool for Checking ANSI-C Programs. In:
          Jensen, K., Podelski, A. (eds.) TACAS 2004. LNCS, vol. 2988, pp. 168–176.
          Springer, Heidelberg (2004)
[cwe]   Common Weakness Enumeration, http://cwe.mitre.org
[dMB08]   de Moura, L., Bjørner, N.: Z3: An efficient SMT solver. In: Ramakrishnan, C.R.,
          Rehof, J. (eds.) TACAS 2008. LNCS, vol. 4963, pp. 337–340. Springer, Heidelberg
          (2008)
[dMB09]   de Moura, L., Bjørner, N.: Satisfiability Modulo Theories: An Appetizer. In: Oliveira,
          M.V.M., Woodcock, J. (eds.) SBMF 2009. LNCS, vol. 5902, pp. 23–36. Springer,
          Heidelberg (2009)
[ES03]   Eén, N., Sörensson, N.: An Extensible SAT-solver. In: Giunchiglia, E., Tacchella, A.
          (eds.) SAT 2003. LNCS, vol. 2919, pp. 502–518. Springer, Heidelberg (2004)
[Fan10]   Fandrey, D.: Clang/LLVM Maturity Report (June 2010),
          http://www.iwi.hs-karlsruhe.de
[FHT+07] Fränzle, M., Herde, C., Teige, T., Ratschan, S., Schubert, T.: Efficient solving of large
          non-linear arithmetic constraint systems with complex boolean structure. Journal on
          Satisfiability, Boolean Modeling and Computation 1, 209–236 (2007)
[LA04]   Lattner, C., Adve, V.: LLVM: A Compilation Framework for Lifelong Program Anal-
          ysis & Transformation. In: Proceedings of the 2004 International Symposium on
          Code Generation and Optimization (CGO 2004), Palo Alto, California (March 2004)
[Lat]   Lattner, C.: LLVM Language Reference Manual,
          http://llvm.org/docs/LangRef.html
[Lev99]   Levine, J.R.: Linkers and Loaders, 1st edn. Morgan Kaufmann Publishers Inc., San
          Francisco (1999)
[MMZ+01] Moskewicz, M.W., Madigan, C.F., Zhao, Y., Zhang, L., Malik, S.: Chaff: engineer-
          ing an efficient SAT solver. In: Proceedings of the 38th Annual Design Automation
          Conference, DAC 2001, pp. 530–535. ACM, New York (2001)
[NT12]   Nowotka, D., Traub, J.: MEMICS - Memory Interval Constrain Solving of (concur-
          rent) Machine Code. In: Plödereder, E., Dencker, P., Klenk, H., Keller, H.B., Spitzer,
          S. (eds.) Automotive - Safety & Security 2012: Sicherheit und Zuverlässigkeit für
          Automobile Informationstechnik. Lecture Notes in Informatics, vol. 210, pp. 69–83.
          Springer (2012)
[pol]   Polyspace, http://www.mathworks.com/products/polyspace
[RVP06]   Raza, A., Vogel, G., Plödereder, E.: Bauhaus – A Tool Suite for Program Analysis
          and Reverse Engineering. In: Pinho, L.M., González Harbour, M. (eds.) Ada-Europe
          2006. LNCS, vol. 4006, pp. 71–82. Springer, Heidelberg (2006)
[RWZ88]   Rosen, B.K., Wegman, M.N., Zadeck, F.K.: Global value numbers and redundant
          computations. In: Proceedings of the 15th ACM SIGPLAN-SIGACT Symposium
          on Principles of Programming Languages, pp. 12–27 (1988)
[SFM10]   Sinz, C., Falke, S., Merz, F.: A Precise Memory Model for Low-Level Bounded
          Model Checking. In: Proceedings of the 5th International Workshop on Systems
          Software Verification (SSV 2010), Vancouver, Canada (2010)

[Swe06] Sweetman, D.: See MIPS Run, 2nd edn. Morgan Kaufmann Publishers Inc., San Francisco (2006)

[Wei81] Weiser, M.: Program slicing. In: Proceedings of the 5th International Conference on Software Engineering, ICSE 1981, pp. 439–449. IEEE Press, Piscataway (1981)

On the Homogeneous Multiprocessor Virtual Machine Partitioning Problem

Stefan Groesbrink

Design of Distributed Embedded Systems, Heinz Nixdorf Institute
University of Paderborn
Fuerstenallee 11, 33102 Paderborn, Germany
s.groesbrink@upb.de, http://www.hni.uni-paderborn.de/

Abstract. This work addresses the partitioning of virtual machines with real-time requirements onto a multi-core platform. The partitioning is usually done manually through interactions between subsystem vendors and system designers. Such a proceeding is expensive, does not guarantee to find the best solution, and does not scale with regard to the upcoming higher complexity in terms of an increasing number of both virtual machines and processor cores. The partitioning problem is defined in a formal manner by the abstraction of computation time demand of virtual machines and computation time supply of a shared processor. The application of a branch-and-bound partitioning algorithm is proposed. Combined with a generation of a feasible schedule for the virtual machines mapped to a processor, it is guaranteed that the demand of a virtual machine is satisfied, even if independently developed virtual machines share a processor. The partitioning algorithm offers two optimization goals, required number of processors and the introduced optimization metric criticality distribution, a first step towards a partitioning that considers multiple criticality levels. The different outcomes of the two approaches are illustrated exemplarily.

1 Introduction

This work targets the hypervisor-based integration of multiple systems of mixed criticality levels on a multicore platform. System virtualization refers to the division of the resources of a computer system into multiple execution environments in order to share the hardware among multiple operating system instances. Each guest runs within a virtual machine—an isolated duplicate of the real machine. System virtualization is a promising software architecture to meet many of the requirements of complex embedded systems and cyber-physical systems, due to its capabilities such as resource partitioning, consolidation with maintained isolation, transparent use of multiple processor system-on-chips, and cross-platform portability.

The rise of multi-core platforms increases the interest in virtualization, since virtualization's architectural abstraction eases the migration to multi-core platforms [11]. The replacement of multiple hardware units by a single multi-core

G. Schirner et al. (Eds.): IESS 2013, IFIP AICT 403, pp. 228–237, 2013.

system has the potential to reduce size, weight, and power. The coexistence of mixed criticality levels has been identified as one of the core foundational concepts for cyber-physical systems [3]. System virtualization implies it in many cases, since the applicability of virtualization is limited significantly if the integration of systems of different criticality level is not allowed.

Contribution. This work addresses the partitioning of virtual machines with real-time requirements onto a multi-core platform. We define this design problem as the *homogeneous multiprocessor virtual machine partitioning problem* in a formal manner, specifying the computation time demand of virtual machines and the computation time supply of a shared processor. A mapping of a given set of virtual machines among a minimum number of required processors is achieved by a branch-and-bound algorithm, such that the capacity of any individual processor is not exceeded. This automated solution provides analytical correctness guarantees, which can be used in system certification. An introduced optimization metric is a first step towards a partitioning that considers multiple virtual machine criticality levels appropriately.

2   System Model

2.1   Task Model and Virtual Machine Model

According to the *periodic task model*, each periodic task τ_i is defined as a sequence of jobs and characterized by a period T_i, denoting the time interval between the activation times of consecutive jobs [16]. The worst-case execution time (WCET) C_i of a task represents an upper bound on the amount of time required to execute the task. The utilization $U(\tau_i)$ is defined as the ratio of WCET and period: $U(\tau_i) = C_i/T_i$. A criticality level χ is assigned to each task [24]. Only two criticality levels are assumed in this work, HI and LO.

A virtual machine V_k is modeled as a set of tasks and a scheduling algorithm A, which is applied by the guest operating system. A criticality level χ is assigned to each virtual machine. If a virtual machine's task set is characterized by multiple criticality levels, the highest criticality level determines the criticality of the virtual machine.

2.2   Multi-core and Virtual Processor

Target platform are homogeneous multi-core systems, consisting of m identical cores of equal computing power. This implies that each task has the same execution speed and utilization on each processor core. Assumed is in addition a shared memory architecture with a uniform memory access.

A virtual processor is a representation of the physical processor to the virtual machines. A dedicated virtual processor P_k^{virt} is created for each virtual machine V_k. It is in general slower than the physical processor core to allow a mapping of multiple virtual processors onto a single physical processor core. A virtual processor is modeled as a processor capacity reserve [18], a function $\Pi(t) \colon \mathbb{N} \mapsto \{0,1\}$ defined as follows:

$$\Pi(t) = \begin{cases} 0, & \text{resource not allocated} \\ 1, & \text{resource allocated} \end{cases} \tag{1}$$

The computation capacity of a physical processor core is partitioned into a set of reservations. Each reservation is characterized by a tuple (Q_k, Υ_k): in every period Υ_k, the reservation provides Q_k units of computation time. $\alpha_k = Q_k/\Upsilon_k$ denotes the bandwidth of the virtual processor.

The computational service provided by a virtual processor P_k^{virt} can be analyzed with its supply function $Z_k(t)$, as introduced by Mok et al. [19]. $Z_k(t)$ returns the minimum amount of computation time (worst-case) provided by the virtual processor in an arbitrary time interval of length $t \geq 0$:

$$Z_k(t) = \min_{t_0 \geq 0} \int_{t_0}^{t_0+t} \Pi(x)dx \ . \tag{2}$$

2.3   Notation

The symbols in this paper are therefore defined as follows:

1. $\tau_i = (C_i, T_i)$: task i with WCET C_i, period T_i, utilization $U(\tau_i) = C_i/T_i$
2. $P = \{P_1, P_2, ..., P_m\}$: set of processors $(m \geq 2)$
3. $V = \{V_1, V_2, ..., V_n\}$: set of virtual machines $(n \geq 2)$
4. $\tau_i \in V_k$: task τ_i is executed in V_k
5. $U(V_k) = \sum_{\tau_i \in V_k} U(\tau_i)$: utilization of V_k
6. $\chi(V_k) \in \{LO, HI\}$: criticality level of V_k
7. $P^{virt} = \{P_1^{virt}, P_2^{virt}, ..., P_n^{virt}\}$: virtual processors, V_k is mapped to P_k^{virt}
8. (Q_k, Υ_k) : resource reservation with bandwidth $\alpha_k = Q_k/\Upsilon_k$
9. $Z_k(t)$: minimum amount of computation time provided by P_k^{virt}
10. $\Gamma(P_i)$: subset of virtual processors allocated to P_i

All parameters of the system—number of processors and computing capacity, number of virtual machines and parameters of all virtual machines, number of tasks and parameters of all tasks—are a priori known.

3   The Homogeneous Multiprocessor Virtual Machine Partitioning Problem

The scheduling problem for system virtualization on multi-core platforms consists of two sub-problems:

(i) partitioning: mapping of the virtual machines to processor cores
(ii) uniprocessor hierarchical scheduling on each processor core

Sub-problem (ii) is well-understood and many solutions are available, e.g. [15]. This work focuses on sub-problem (i) and refer to it as the homogeneous multiprocessor virtual machine partitioning problem. More precisely, the virtual processors P^{virt} executing the virtual machines V have to be mapped to the physical processors P:

$$V \overset{f_1}{\mapsto} P^{virt} \overset{f_2}{\mapsto} P \ . \tag{3}$$

f_1 is a bijective function: each virtual machine V_k is mapped to a dedicated virtual processor P_k^{virt}. f_2 maps 0 to $n = |P^{virt}|$ virtual processors to each element of P. A solution to the problem is a partition Γ, defined as:

$$\Gamma = (\Gamma(P_1), \Gamma(P_2), ..., \Gamma(P_m)) \tag{4}$$

Such a mapping of virtual machines (equivalent to virtual processors) to physical processors is correct, if and only if the computation capacity requirements of all virtual processors are met; and by consequence the schedulability of the associated virtual machines is guaranteed.

The partitioning problem is equivalent to a bin-packing problem, as for example Baruah [2] has shown for the task partitioning problem by transformation from 3-Partition. The virtual machines are the objects to pack with size determined by their utilization factors. The bins are processors with a computation capacity value that is dependent on the applied virtual machine scheduler of this processor. The bin-packing problem is known to be intractable (NP-hard in the strong sense) [10] and the research focused on approximation algorithms [6].

4 Scheduling Scheme

It is an important observation that the hypervisor-based integration of independently developed and validated systems implies partitioned scheduling. As a coarse-grained approach, it consolidates entire software stacks including an operating system, resulting in scheduling decisions on two levels (hierarchical scheduling). The hypervisor schedules the virtual machines and the hosted guest operating systems schedule their tasks according to their own local scheduling policies. This is irreconcilable with a scheduling based on a global ready queue.

Virtual Machine Scheduling. In the context of this work, n virtual machines are statically assigned to $m < n$ processors. Although a dynamic mapping is conceptually and technically possible, a static solution eases certification significantly, due to the lower run-time complexity, the higher predictability, and the wider experience of system designer and certification authority with uniprocessor scheduling. Run-time scheduling can be performed efficiently in such systems and the overhead of a complex virtual machine scheduler is avoided.

For each processor, the virtual machine scheduling is implemented based on fixed time slices. Execution time windows within a repetitive major cycle are assigned to the virtual machines based on the required utilization and the maximum blackout time. As a formal model, the *Single Time Slot Periodic Partitions* model by Mok et al. [20] is applied. A resource partition is defined as N disjunct time intervals $\{(S_1, E_1), ..., (S_N, E_N)\}$ and a partition period $P_{partition}$, so that a virtual machine V_i is executed during intervals $(S_i + j \cdot P_{partition}, E_i + j \cdot P_{partition})$ with $j \geq 0$. Kerstan et al. [13] presented an approach to calculate such time intervals for virtual machines scheduled by either earliest deadline first (EDF) or rate-monotonic (RM), with $S_0 = 0$ and $S_i = E_{i-1}$:

$$E_i = \begin{cases} S_i + U(V_i) \cdot P_{partition} & \text{in case of EDF} \\ S_i + \frac{1}{U_{lub}^{RM}(V_i)} U(V_i) \cdot P_{partition} & \text{in case of RM} \end{cases}, \text{ with} \qquad (5)$$

$$U_{lub}^{RM}(V_i) = n_{tasks} \cdot (2^{\frac{1}{n_{tasks}}} - 1) \qquad (6)$$

In case of RM, a scaling relative to the least upper bound U_{lub}^{RM} is required. If the partition period is chosen as $P_{partition} = \gcd(\{T_k | \tau_k \in \bigcup_{i=1}^{n} V_i\})$, no deadline will be missed [13].

The virtual machine schedule is computed offline and stored in a dispatching table, similar to the cyclic executive scheduling approach [1]. The size of this table is bounded, since the schedule repeats itself after $P_{partition}$. Such a highly predictable and at design time analyzable scheduling scheme is the de facto standard for scheduling high-criticality workloads [21].

In the terms of the resource reservation model of the virtual processor, the bandwidth α_k of the virtual processor P_k^{virt} that executes virtual machine V_k is equal to $(E_k - S_k)/P_{partition}$, with $\Upsilon_k = P_{partition}$ and $Q_k = \alpha \cdot \Upsilon$. Note that this abstraction of the computation time demand of a virtual machine to a recurring time slot that is serviced by a virtual processor (Q_k, Υ_K) allows to regard the virtual machine as a periodic task and transforms the virtual machine partitioning problem to the task partitioning problem.

Task Scheduling. Any scheduling algorithm can be applied as task scheduler, as long as it allows to abstract the computation time requirements of the task set in terms of a demand-bound function $dbf(V_i, t)$, which bounds the computation time demand that the virtual machine could request to meet the timing requirements of its tasks within a specific time interval of length t [23]. As a task set cannot possibly be schedulable according to any algorithm if the total execution that is released in an interval and must also complete in that interval exceeds the available processing capacity, the processor load provides a simple necessary condition for taskset feasibility:
A virtual machine V_k, applying A as local scheduler and executed by a virtual processor P_k^{virt} characterized by the supply function Z_k, is schedulable if and only if $\forall\, t > 0 : dbf_A(V_k, t) \leq Z_k(t)$ (compare [23]).

5   Partitioning Algorithm

Common task set partitioning schemes apply Bin-Packing Heuristics or Integer-Linear-Programming (ILP) approaches in order to provide an efficient algorithm

[5][7]. In the context of this work, however, the number of virtual machines is comparatively small and the partitioning algorithm is to be run offline and does not have to be executed on the embedded processor. Therefore, the algorithm performs a systematic enumeration of all candidate solutions following the branch-and-bound paradigm [14]. The depth of the search tree is equal to the number of virtual machines n.

Two optimization goals are considered, according to which candidates are compared. Minimizing the number of processors is the basic optimization goal. In addition, the goal can be set to maximize the *CriticalityDistribution*, a metric defined as follows:

Definition. The *CriticalityDistribution* Z denotes for a partitioning Γ the distribution of the $n_{crit} \leq n$ HI-critical virtual machines among the m processors:

$$Z(\Gamma) = \frac{\sum_{i=1}^{m} \zeta(P_i)}{n_{crit}} \text{ , with} \tag{7}$$

$$\zeta(P_i) = \begin{cases} 1, & \text{if } \exists P_j^{virt} \in \Gamma(P_i)\colon \chi(V_j) = HI, \\ 0, & \text{otherwise.} \end{cases} \tag{8}$$

For example, assumed that $n_{crit} = 4$ and $m = 4$, Z equals 1 if there is at least one HI-critical virtual machine mapped to all processors; and Z equals 0.75 if one processor does not host a HI-critical virtual machine. This results, if the maximum number of processors is not limited, to a mapping of each cirtical virtual machine to a dedicated processor, which is potentially shared with LO-critical virtual machines, but not with other HI-critical virtual machines.

The motivation of the optimization goal criticality distribution is the *Criticality Inversion Problem*, defined by de Niz et al. [8]. Transferred to virtual machine scheduling, criticality inversion occurs if a HI-critical virtual machine overruns its execution time budget and is stopped to allow a LO-critical virtual machine to run, resulting in a deadline miss for a task of the HI-critical virtual machine. By definition of criticality, it is more appropriate to continue the execution of the HI-critical virtual machine, which can be done for highly utilized processors by stealing execution time from the budget of LO-critical virtual machines. It is in general easier to avoid criticality inversion, if virtual machines of differing criticality share a processor. If the number of virtual machines does not exceed the number of physical processors, all critical virtual machine are mapped to different physical processors. The partitioning algorithm either minimizes the number of processors or maximizes the criticality distribution, while minimizing the number of processors among partitions of same criticality distribution.

Before generating the search tree, the set of virtual machines V is sorted according to decreasing utilization. This is motivated by a pruning condition: if at some node, the bandwidth assigned to a processor is greater than 1, the computational capacity of the processor is overrun and the whole subtree can be pruned. Such a subtree pruning tends to occur earlier, if the virtual machines are ordered according to decreasing utilization.

We introduce that a virtual machine is termed to be *heavy*, if certification requires that this virtual machine is exclusively mapped to a dedicated processor or if other virtual machines can only be scheduled in background, i.e. the heavy virtual machine is executed immediately whenever it is has a computation demand. By consequence, a heavy virtual machine cannot be mapped to the same processor as other HI-critical virtual machines.

6   Example

The different outcome dependent on the optimization goal of the algorithm is illustrated with the examplary virtual machine set of Table 1. EDF is assumed for all virtual machines, so that a scaling is not required and $\alpha_k = U(V_k)$.

Table 1. Example: Set of Virtual Machines

	V_1	V_2	V_3	V_4	V_5	V_6	V_7	V_8	V_9	V_{10}
χ	LO	HI	LO	LO	HI	HI	HI	LO	LO	HI
U	0.6	0.5	0.5	0.3	0.25	0.2	0.2	0.2	0.2	0.15

Figure 1 depicts the virtual machine to processor mapping for three different goals, with a red virtual machine identifier denoting a HI-critical virtual machine. Subfigure (a) depicts the outcome for the optimization of the number of processors. The virtual machine set is not schedulable on less than four processors. The average utilization per processor is 0.775 and the criticality distribution Z is $3/5 = 0.6$. Subfigure (b) depicts the outcome for the optimization of the criticality distribution, however with a maximum number of $m_{max} = 4$ processors allowed. The allocation is therefore still characterized by the minimum number of processors. The criticality distribution Z improves to $4/5 = 0.8$. From a criticality point of view, this mapping is more suitable, since the options to avoid criticality inversion on processor P_3 are very limited in the first solution. Subfigure (c) depicts an unrestricted optimization of the criticality distribution, resulting in an additional processor. The optimal criticality distribution $Z = 1$ is achieved, however at the cost of exceeding the minimum number of processors, which leads to a decrease of the average utilization per processor to 0.62. The last mapping is the correct choice, if the five HI-critical virtual machines are heavy.

7   Related Work

The related problem of partitioning a periodic task set upon homogeneous multiprocessor platforms has been extensively studied, both theoretically and empirically [5][7]. Lopez et al. observed that ordering tasks according to decreasing utilization prior to the partitioning proves helpful [17], a technique applied in this work as well. Buttazzo et al. proposed a branch-and-bound algorithm for

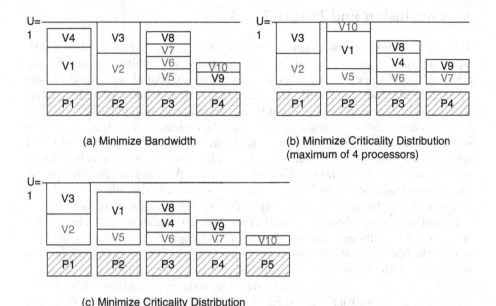

(a) Minimize Bandwidth

(b) Minimize Criticality Distribution
(maximum of 4 processors)

(c) Minimize Criticality Distribution

Fig. 1. Mappings for different Optimization Goals

partitioning a task set with precedence constraints, in order to minimize the required overall computational bandwidth [4]. Peng and Shin presented a branch-and-bound algorithm in order to partition a set of communicating tasks in a distributed system [22].

Kelly at al. proposed bin-packing algorithms for the partitioning of mixed-criticality real-time task sets [12]. Using a common mixed-criticality task model (characterized by an assignment of multiple WCET values, one per each criticality level in the system), they experimentally compare different kinds of task ordering according to utilization and criticality and observed that the latter solutions results in a higher percentage of finding a feasible schedule for a randomly generated task set.

Shin and Lee introduced a formal description of the component abstraction problem (abstract the real-time requirements of a component) and the component composition model (compose independently analyzed locally scheduled components into a global system)[23]. Easwaran et al. introduced compositional analysis techniques for automated scheduling of partitions and processes in the specific context of the ARINC-653 standard for distributed avionics systems [9], however, did not tackle the mapping of partions to processors. As required by the ARINC specification and as done in this work, a static partition schedule is generated at design time. Both the partitions and the tasks within the partitions are scheduled by a deadline-monotonic scheduler.

8   Conclusion and Future Work

This work defined the partitioning problem of mapping virtual machines with real-time constraints to a homogeneous multiprocessor architecture in a formal manner. This is the prerequisite for an algorithmic solution. Formal models were adapted to abstract and specify the computation time demand of a virtual machine and the computation time supply of a shared processor, in order to analytically evaluate whether it is guaranteed that the demand of a virtual machine is satisfied. The application of a branch-and-bound algorithm is proposed with two optimization metrics. A brief introduction on how to generate a feasible virtual machine schedule after the partitioning was given. A highly predictable and at design time analyzable scheduling scheme based on fixed time slices was chosen as this is the de facto standard for scheduling high-criticality systems.

Partitioning and schedule generation together guarantee that all virtual machines obtain a sufficient amount of computation capacity and obtain it in time, so that the hosted guest systems never miss a deadline. This automated solution provides analytical correctness guarantees, which can help with system certification. In contrast to a manual partitioning, it guarantees to find the optimal solution and scales well with regard to an increasing number of both virtual machines and processor cores. The optimization metric criticality distribution is a first step towards a partitioning that considers multiple criticality levels appropriately. The different outcomes of the two approaches were illustrated exemplarily.

The presented algorithm serves as a groundwork for a research of the partitioning problem. In particularly, we are going to include the overhead of virtual machine context switching, since it is for most real implementations extensive enough to not be neglected. The partitioning directly influences the virtual machine scheduling, which in turn heavily influences the number of virtual machine context switches. In addition, communication between virtual machines should be included, since the communication latency depends on the fact whether two virtual machines share a core or not. A further interesting question is whether a more detailled analysis of the timing characteristics of the virtual machines, in order to map guests with similar characteristics to the same processor, leads to better results.

Acknowledgments. This work was funded within the project ARAMiS by the German Federal Ministry for Education and Research with the funding IDs 01IS11035. The responsibility for the content remains with the authors.

References

1. Baker, T., Shaw, A.: The cyclic executive model and ada. Real-Time Systems (1989)
2. Baruah, S.: Task partitioning upon heterogeneous multiprocessor platforms. In: Real-Time and Embedded Technology and Applications Symposium (2004)
3. Baruah, S., Li, H., Stougie, L.: Towards the design of certifiable mixed-criticality systems. In: Real-Time and Embedded Technology and Applications Symposium (2010)

4. Buttazzo, G., Bini, E., Wu, Y.: Partitioning real-time applications over multi-core reservations. IEEE Transactions on Industrial Informatics 7, 302–315 (2011)
5. Carpenter, J., et al.: A categorization of real-time multiprocessor scheduling problems and algorithms. In: Handbook on Scheduling Algorithms, Methods, and Models (2004)
6. Coffman, E., Garey, M., Johnson, D.: Approximation algorithms for bin packing: a survey. In: Approximation Algorithms for NP-hard Problems, pp. 46–93 (1996)
7. Davis, R.I., Burns, A.: A survey of hard real-time scheduling for multiprocessor systems. ACM Computing Surveys (2010)
8. de Niz, D., et al.: On the scheduling of mixed-criticality real-time task sets. In: Real-Time Systems Symposium (2009)
9. Easwaran, A., et al.: A compositional scheduling framework for digital avionics systems. In: Real-Time Computing Systems and Applications (2009)
10. Garey, M., Johnson, D.: Computers and Intractability. W.H. Freman, New York (1979)
11. Intel Corporation (White paper): Applying multi-core and virtualization to industrial and safety-related applications (2009),
    http://download.intel.com/platforms/applied/indpc/321410.pdf
12. Kelly, O., Aydin, H., Zhao, B.: On partitioned scheduling of fixed-priority mixed-criticality task sets. In: IEEE 10th International Conference on Trust, Security and Privacy in Computing and Communications (2011)
13. Kerstan, T., Baldin, D., Groesbrink, S.: Full virtualization of real-time systems by temporal partitioning. In: Workshop on Operating Systems Platforms for Embedded Real-Time Applications (2010)
14. Land, A.H., Doig, A.G.: An automatic method of solving discrete programming problems. Econometrica 28(3), 497–520 (1960)
15. Lipari, G., Bini, E.: Resource partitioning among real-time applications. In: Euromicro Conference on Real-Time Systems (2003)
16. Liu, C.L., Layland, J.W.: Scheduling algorithms for multiprogramming in a hard-real-time environment. Journal of the ACM (1973)
17. Lopez, J., Garcia, M., Diaz, J., Garcia, D.: Utilization bounds for multiprocessor rate-monotonic systems. Real-Time Systems (2003)
18. Mercer, C., et al.: Processor capacity reserves: Operating system support for multimedia applications. In: Multimedia Computing and Systems (1994)
19. Mok, A., Feng, A.: Real-time virtual resource: A timely abstraction for embedded systems. In: Sangiovanni-Vincentelli, A.L., Sifakis, J. (eds.) EMSOFT 2002. LNCS, vol. 2491, pp. 182–196. Springer, Heidelberg (2002)
20. Mok, A., Feng, X., Chen, D.: Resource partition for real-time systems. In: Real-Time Technology and Applications Symposium (2001)
21. Mollison, M., et al.: Mixed-criticality real-time scheduling for multicore systems. In: International Conference on Computer and Information Technology (2010)
22. Peng, D., Shin, K.: Assignment and scheduling communicating periodic tasks in distributed real-time systems. IEEE Transactions on Software Engineering (1997)
23. Shin, I., Lee, I.: Compositional real-time scheduling framework with periodic model. ACM Transactions on Embedded Computing Systems 7 (2008)
24. Vestal, S.: Preemptive scheduling of multi-criticality systems with varying degrees of execution time assurance. In: Proc. of the Real-Time Systems Symposium (2007)

Fault-Tolerant Deployment of Real-Time Software in AUTOSAR ECU Networks

Kay Klobedanz[1], Jan Jatzkowski[1], Achim Rettberg[2], and Wolfgang Mueller[1]

[1] University of Paderborn/C-LAB, 33102 Paderborn, Germany
{kay.klobedanz,jan.jatzkowski,wolfgang.mueller}@c-lab.de
[2] Carl von Ossietzky University Oldenburg, 26129 Oldenburg, Germany
achim.rettberg@uni-oldenburg.de

Abstract. We present an approach for deployment of real-time software in ECU networks enabling AUTOSAR-based design of fault-tolerant automotive systems. Deployment of software in a safety-critical distributed system implies appropriate mapping and scheduling of tasks and messages to fulfill hard real-time constraints. Additional safety requirements like deterministic communication and redundancy must be fulfilled to guarantee fault tolerance and dependability. Our approach is built on AUTOSAR methodology and enables redundancy for compensation of ECU failures to increase fault tolerance. Based on AUTOSAR-compliant modeling of real-time software, our approach determines an initial deployment combined with reconfigurations for remaining nodes at design time. To enable redundancy options, we propose a reconfigurable ECU network topology. Furthermore, we present a concept to detect failed nodes and activate reconfigurations by means of AUTOSAR.

1 Introduction

Today's automotive vehicles provide numerous complex electronic features realized by means of distributed real-time systems with an increasing number of electronic control units (ECUs). Many of these systems implement safety-critical functions, which have to fulfill hard real-time constraints to guarantee dependable functionality. Furthermore, subsystems are often developed by different partners and suppliers and have to be integrated. To address these challenges, the AUTomotive Open System ARchitecture (AUTOSAR) development partnership was founded. It offers a standardization for the software architecture of ECUs and defines a methodology to support function-driven system design. Hereby, AUTOSAR helps to reduce development complexity and enables smooth integration of third party features and reuse of software and hardware components [1]. Figure 1 illustrates the AUTOSAR-based design flow steps and the resulting dependencies for the deployment of provided software components [2]. Deployment implies task mapping and bus mapping resulting in schedules affecting each other. The problem of mapping and scheduling tasks and messages in a distributed system is NP-hard [3]. Beside hard real-time constraints, safety-critical systems have to consider additional requirements to guarantee dependability. Hence, deterministic communication protocols and redundancy concepts

G. Schirner et al. (Eds.): IESS 2013, IFIP AICT 403, pp. 238–249, 2013.
© IFIP International Federation for Information Processing 2013

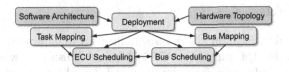

Fig. 1. System design flow steps and their dependencies [2]

shall be utilized to increase fault tolerance of such systems [4]. AUTOSAR supports FlexRay, which is the emerging communication standard for safety-critical automotive networks. It provides deterministic behavior, high bandwidth capacities, and redundant channels to increase fault tolerance. To further increase fault tolerance, node failures shall also be compensated by redundancy.

We present an approach for real-time software deployment built on AUTOSAR methodology to design fault-tolerant automotive systems. Our approach determines an initial deployment combined with necessary reconfigurations and task replications to compensate node failures. The determined deployment solution includes appropriate task and bus mappings resulting in corresponding schedules that fulfill hard real-time constraints (cf. Fig. 1). In addition, we propose a modified version of a reconfigurable ECU network topology presented in [5] to enable flexible task replication and offer the required redundancy. Regarding AUTOSAR, we propose a flexible Runnable-to-task mapping for fault-tolerant systems and present a concept for an AUTOSAR-compliant integration of our fault-tolerant approach: We propose an AUTOSAR Complex Device Driver (CDD) to detect failed nodes and initiate the appropriate reconfiguration.

The remainder of this paper is structured as follows. After related work and an introduction to AUTOSAR we present our proposal for a reconfigurable ECU network topology in Section 4. Section 5 describes our fault-tolerant deployment approach and applies it to a real-world application before we introduce a concept for AUTOSAR integration in Section 6. The article is closed by the conclusion.

2   Related Work

In general, scheduling of tasks and messages in distributed systems is addressed by several publications [6,7,8]. Other publications propose heuristics for the design of FlexRay systems [9,10,11]. In [12] strategies to improve fault tolerance of such systems are described. However, we propose an approach for fault-tolerant deployment of real-time software specific for AUTOSAR-based design flow. AUTOSAR divides task mapping into two steps: Mapping (i) software components (SWCs) encapsulating Runnables onto ECUs and (ii) Runnables to tasks that are scheduled by an OS. Since the number of tasks captured by AUTOSAR OS is limited, Runnable-to-task mapping is generally not trivial [13]. Although some approaches solve one [14] or even both [15] steps for an AUTOSAR-compliant mapping, to our knowledge, [16] is the only one considering this combined with fault tolerance. But unlike our approach, only a subset of the software requires hard real-time and each redundant Runnable is mapped to a separate task.

3   AUTOSAR

AUTOSAR provides a common software architecture and infrastructure for automotive systems. For this purpose, AUTOSAR distinguishes between *Application Layer* including hardware-independently modeled application software, *Runtime Environment (RTE)* implementing communication, and *Basic Software (BSW) Layer* providing hardware-dependent software, e.g. OS and bus drivers.

An Application Layer consists of *Software Components* (SWCs) encapsulating complete or partial functionality of application software [17]. Each Atomic-SWC has an internal behavior represented by a set of Runnables. "Atomic" means that this SWC must be entirely – i.e. all its Runnables – mapped to one ECU. Runnables model code and represent internal behavior. AUTOSAR provides RTE events, whose triggering is periodical or depends on communication activities. In response to these events, the RTE triggers Runnables, i.e. RTE events provide activation characteristics of Runnables. Based on RTE events, all Runnables assigned to an ECU are mapped to tasks scheduled by AUTOSAR OS. AUTOSAR *Timing Extensions* describe timing characteristics of a system related to the different views of AUTOSAR [18,19]. A timing description defines an expected timing behavior of timing events and timing event chains. Each event refers to a location of the AUTOSAR model where its occurrence is observed. An event chain is characterized by two events defining its beginning (stimulus) and end (response). Timing constraints are related to events or event chains. They define timing requirements which must be fulfilled by the system or timing guarantees that developers ensure regarding system behavior.

At Virtual Function Bus (VFB) level communication between SWCs is modeled by connected ports. We apply the Sender-Receiver paradigm in implicit mode, i.e. data elements are automatically read by the RTE before a Runnable is invoked and (different) data elements are automatically written after a Runnable has terminated [20]. AUTOSAR distinguishes *Inter-ECU* communication between two or more ECUs and *Intra-ECU* communication between Runnables on the same ECU [21]. For Inter-ECU communication, AUTOSAR supports the FlexRay protocol providing message transport in deterministic time slots [22]. FlexRay makes use of recurring communication cycles and is composed of a static and an optional dynamic segment. In the time-triggered static segment, a fixed and initially defined number of equally sized slots is statically assigned to one sender node. Changing this assignment requires a bus restart. Slot and frame size, cycle length, and several other parameters are defined by an initial setup of the FlexRay schedule. The payload segment of a FlexRay frame contains data in up to 127 2-byte words. Payload data can be divided into AUTOSAR *Protocol Data Units* (PDUs) composed of one or more words. Hence, different messages from one sender ECU can be combined by *frame packing*.

4   A Reconfigurable ECU Network Topology

To increase fault tolerance in an ECU network, node failures should be compensated by redundancy and software replication. In current distributed real-time

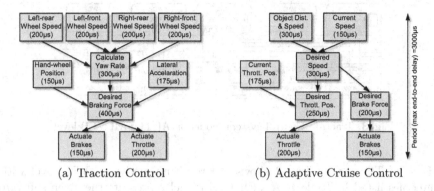

(a) Traction Control   (b) Adaptive Cruise Control

Fig. 2. Functional Components of a TC (a) and an ACC (b) system [11]

systems, failures of hardwired nodes cannot be compensated by software redundancy as connections to sensors and actuators get lost. We propose a modified network topology distinguishing two types of ECUs [5]: (i) *Peripheral interface nodes*, which are wired to sensors and actuators, and just read/write values from/to the bus and (ii) *functional nodes* hosting the functional software and communicating over the bus. Since peripheral interface nodes do not execute complex tasks, they only require low hardware capacities allowing cost-efficient hardware redundancy. Here, we focus on distributed functional ECUs that provide and receive data via communication bus and can therefore be utilized for redundancy and reconfiguration. In the following ECU refers to functional nodes.

5   Fault-Tolerant Deployment Approach

In this section we present our fault-tolerant deployment approach. It contains (i) initial definition and modeling of the given SW-architecture & HW-topology for interdependent (ii) Runnable & task mappings and (iii) bus mappings. For better traceability all steps of our approach are applied to a real-world application.

5.1   Modeling of Software Architecture

Figure 2 illustrates the functional components of a Traction Control (TC) and an Adaptive Cruise Control (ACC) system, shows data dependencies, and provides information about their timing properties [11]: worst-case execution times (WCETs) and periods. In AUTOSAR these components are modeled as SWCs, whose functional behavior is represented by Runnables. Putting each Runnable into a separate SWC enables mapping of each Runnable to an arbitrary ECU. Thus, we use Runnable-to-ECU and SWC-to-ECU mapping as synonyms. The set of Runnables is modeled as $\mathcal{R} = \{R_i(T_i, C_i, r_i, d_i, s_i, f_i) \mid 1 \leq i \leq n\}$. Each Runnable R_i is described by its period T_i, WCET C_i, release time r_i, deadline d_i, start time s_i, and finishing time f_i.

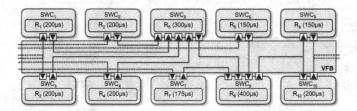

Fig. 3. Traction Control system model on AUTOSAR VFB level

For the TC system, Fig. 3 shows the resulting model on VFB level with Runnables listed in Table 1. A VFB level model represents the given software architecture with communication dependencies independent of the given hardware architecture and acts as input for the AUTOSAR-based system design. AUTOSAR Timing Extensions are used to annotate timing constraints for the model by means of events and event chains. Based on the event chain $R_1 \rightarrow R_5 \rightarrow R_8 \rightarrow R_{10}$ in Fig. 3, a maximum latency requirement defines that the delay between the input at R_1 (stimulus) and the output of R_{10} (response) must not exceed the given maximum end-to-end delay (period) of $3000\mu s$. Timing constraints are defined for each event chain. Dependencies between Runnables imply order and precedence constraints. Considering the maximum end-to-end delay for the event chains, we define an available execution interval $E_i = [r_i, d_i]$ for each Runnable R_i with release time:

$$r_i = \begin{cases} 0 & \text{, if } R_i \in \mathcal{R}_{\text{in}} \\ \max\{r_j + C_j \mid R_j \in \mathcal{R}_{\text{directPre}_i}\} & \text{, else.} \end{cases}$$

If a Runnable has no predecessors ($R_i \in \mathcal{R}_{\text{in}}$), the available execution interval of R_i starts at $r_i = 0$. Otherwise, r_i is calculated by means of r_j and C_j of the direct predecessors ($R_j \in \mathcal{R}_{\text{directPre}_i}$). The deadline of R_i is calculated as:

$$d_i = \begin{cases} \text{max end-to-end delay} & \text{, if } R_i \in \mathcal{R}_{\text{out}} \\ \min\{d_k - C_k \mid R_k \in \mathcal{R}_{\text{directSucc}_i}\} & \text{, else.} \end{cases}$$

If a Runnable has no successors ($R_i \in \mathcal{R}_{\text{out}}$), the available execution interval of R_i ends at $d_i =$ max end-to-end delay. Otherwise, d_i depends on r_k and C_k of the direct successors of R_i ($R_k \in \mathcal{R}_{\text{directSucc}_i}$). Table 1 summarizes the calculated available execution intervals E_i for the Runnables of the TC and ACC systems.

Table 1. Runnable properties for TC and ACC systems (values in μs)

R_i	||	TC System						||	ACC System							
	R_{1-4}	R_5	R_6	R_7	R_8	R_9	R_{10}	R_{11}	R_{12}	R_{13}	R_{14}	R_{15}	R_{16}	R_{17}	R_{18}
C_i	200	300	150	175	400	150	200	300	150	300	175	200	250	200	150
r_i	0	200	0	0	500	900	900	0	0	300	0	600	600	850	800
d_i	2100	2400	2400	2400	2800	3000	3000	2350	2350	2650	2550	2850	2800	3000	3000

Algorithm 1. INITIALMAPPING($\mathcal{R}, \mathcal{E}$)

Input: Runnables $\mathcal{R}$ and ECUs $\mathcal{E}$.
Output: RunnableMapping: M_{init} : $\mathcal{R} \mapsto \mathcal{E}$.
 1: SORTBYDEADLINEANDRELEASETIME($\mathcal{R}$)
 2: **for all** $R_i \in \mathcal{R}_{in}$ **do**
 3:     $\mathcal{E}_{tmp} \leftarrow$ GETFEASIBLEECUS($\mathcal{E}$)
 4:     ECU$_{tmp} \leftarrow$ GETEARLIESTFINISH($\mathcal{E}_{tmp}$)
 5:     MAPRUNNABLE(R_i, ECU$_{tmp}$)
 6: **end for**
 7: **for all** $R_i \in \mathcal{R} \setminus \mathcal{R}_{in}$ **do**
 8:     $\mathcal{E}_{tmp} \leftarrow$ GETFEASIBLEECUS($\mathcal{E}$)
 9:     ECU$_{tmp} \leftarrow$ GETMINIMUMDELAY($R_i, \mathcal{E}_{tmp}$)
10:     MAPRUNNABLE(R_i, ECU$_{tmp}$)
11: **end for**
12: **return** M_{init} : $\mathcal{R} \mapsto \mathcal{E}$

5.2 Runnable and Task Mapping

For a feasible SWC-to-ECU and Runnable-to-task mapping the properties of the ECUs have to be considered. The set of ECUs is $\mathcal{E} = \{ECU_j \mid 1 \leq j \leq m\}$. We consider a homogeneous network structure. Hence, the Runnable WCETs provided in Table 1 are valid for all ECUs. The objective of our approach is to determine a feasible combined solution for an initial software deployment and all necessary reconfigurations and task replications for the remaining nodes of the network in case of a node failure. Thus, each configuration has to fulfill the deadlines of all Runnables and the end-to-end delay constraints for all event chains. Therefore, our approach iteratively analyzes and reduces the resulting execution delay for each SWC-to-ECU mapping to finally ensure minimized end-to-end delays for all event chains. It starts with the initial mapping M_{init} described by peusdo-code in Alg. 1. The algorithm defines the mapping order of Runnables via sorting them by deadline and release time. Before each mapping a schedulability test has to determine the feasible ECUs in $\mathcal{E}$. Therefore, we propose our *Extended Response Time Analysis* for Rate (Deadline) Monotonic Scheduling which is a common approach for AUTOSAR OS:

$$X_i = (C_i + \delta_i) + \sum_{j=1}^{i-1} \left\lceil \frac{X_i}{T_j} \right\rceil C_j.$$

It combines the WCET C_i and the resulting communication delay δ_i to calculate the response time X_i for each Runnable R_i. The initial mapping begins with the Runnables $\mathcal{R}_{in}$, which have no precedence constraints, and maps them iteratively to the ECU hosting the last Runnable with the earliest finishing time. Thus, in a network with n ECUs, the first n Runnables will be mapped to empty ECUs. For Runnables with predecessors ($R \in \mathcal{R} \setminus \mathcal{R}_{in}$), Alg. 2 returns the ECU with the minimum execution delay. It determines the direct predecessors of R, their hosting ECUs $\mathcal{E}_{pre}$, and the last Runnables on these ECUs ($\mathcal{R}_{last}$). If

---

Algorithm 2. GETMINIMUMDELAY$(R, \mathcal{E})$

Input: A Runnable R and ECUs $\mathcal{E}$.
Output: ECU with minimum delay.
1: $\mathcal{R}_{\text{directPre}} \leftarrow$ GETDIRECTPREDECESSORS(R)
2: $\mathcal{E}_{\text{pre}} \leftarrow$ GETHOSTECUS$(\mathcal{R}_{\text{directPre}}, \mathcal{E})$
3: $\mathcal{R}_{\text{last}} \leftarrow$ GETLASTRUNNABLES$(\mathcal{E}_{\text{pre}})$
4: $\mathcal{R}_{\text{cap}} \leftarrow \mathcal{R}_{\text{last}} \cap \mathcal{R}_{\text{directPre}}$
5: **if** $\mathcal{R}_{\text{cap}} \neq \emptyset$ **then**
6:     ECU $\leftarrow$ GETHOSTECU(GETLATESTFINISH$(\mathcal{R}_{\text{cap}}), \mathcal{E})$
7: **else**
8:     ECU$_{\text{preMin}} \leftarrow$ GETEARLIESTFINISH$(\mathcal{E}_{\text{pre}})$
9:     **if** $\mathcal{E} \setminus \mathcal{E}_{\text{pre}} \neq \emptyset$ **then**
10:         ECU$_{\text{nonPreMin}} \leftarrow$ GETEARLIESTFINISH$(\mathcal{E} \setminus \mathcal{E}_{\text{pre}})$
11:         $\Delta \leftarrow$ DIFF$\langle$GETFINISHTIME(ECU$_{\text{preMin}}$), GETFINISHTIME(ECU$_{\text{nonPreMin}}$)$\rangle$
12:         **if** $\Delta >$ ComOverhead **then**
13:             ECU $\leftarrow$ ECU$_{\text{nonPreMin}}$
14:         **else**
15:             ECU $\leftarrow$ ECU$_{\text{preMin}}$
16:         **end if**
17:     **else**
18:         ECU $\leftarrow$ ECU$_{\text{preMin}}$
19:     **end if**
20: **end if**
21: **return** ECU

---

one or more of the direct predecessors of R are last Runnable(s), the algorithm maps R to the same ECU as the predecessor with the latest finishing time. This avoids additional Inter-ECU communication delay for the latest input of R. If there are Runnables mapped to $\mathcal{E}_{\text{pre}}$ after all direct predecessors, the Inter-ECU communication for input to R can take place during their execution. In this case the algorithm determines the ECU$_{\text{preMin}}$ with the earliest finishing time. If there are ECUs that do not host any of the direct predecessors of R, the one with the earliest finishing time (ECU$_{\text{nonPreMin}}$) is also considered. The algorithm compares the difference Δ between these finishing times to the communication overhead resulting by a mapping to ECU$_{\text{nonPreMin}}$. The communication overhead depends on the number of slots needed and on the slot size defined for bus communication (ref. Section 5.3). If the communication overhead is smaller than Δ, the algorithm returns ECU$_{\text{nonPreMin}}$, else it returns ECU$_{\text{preMin}}$. By means of Alg. 1 and Alg. 2 our approach determines a feasible initial mapping with minimized execution delays considering timing, order, and precedence constraints. In a network with n ECUs it has to perform n redundancy mappings. Alg. 3 calculates the redundancy mapping M$_{\text{red}}$ for a Runnable set to feasible remaining ECUs. Beside $\mathcal{R}_{\text{fail}}$ and $\mathcal{E}_{\text{rem}}$ it takes M$_{\text{init}}$ as an input, meaning that the set of Runnables initially mapped to $\mathcal{E}_{\text{rem}}$ is kept for each remaining ECU. This allows to combine Runnables on $\mathcal{E}_{\text{rem}}$ to tasks and the reuse of messages and slots in different reconfigurations. Similar to the initial mapping, the algorithm

Algorithm 3. REDUNDANCYMAPPING($\mathcal{R}_{\text{fail}}, \mathcal{E}_{\text{rem}}, M_{\text{init}}$)

Input: Runnables $\mathcal{R}_{\text{fail}}$, ECUs $\mathcal{E}_{\text{rem}}$, and Mapping M_{init}.
Output: RedundancyMapping: $M_{\text{red}} : \mathcal{R}_{\text{fail}} \mapsto \mathcal{E}_{\text{rem}}$.
1: $M_{\text{red}} \leftarrow M_{\text{init}}$
2: **for all** $R_i \in \mathcal{R}_{\text{fail}}$ **do**
3:     $\mathcal{E}_{\text{tmp}} \leftarrow$ GETFEASIBLEECUS($\mathcal{E}_{\text{rem}}$)
4:     ECU$_{\text{tmp}} \leftarrow$ GETECUMINE2E(R_i, $\mathcal{E}_{\text{tmp}}$, M_{red})
5:     $M_{\text{red}} \leftarrow M_{\text{red}} \cup$ MAPRUNNABLE(R_i, ECU$_{\text{tmp}}$)
6: **end for**
7: **return** $M_{\text{red}} : \mathcal{R}_{\text{fail}} \mapsto \mathcal{E}_{\text{rem}}$

---

iteratively inserts the Runnables from $\mathcal{R}_{\text{fail}}$. Hence, in each mapping step the redundancy mapping M_{red} is complemented by the currently performed mapping. In Alg. 4, for each assignment our approach determines the Runnable-to-ECU mapping resulting in the minimum overall end-to-end delay, i.e. longest end-to-end delay of all event chains. This algorithm checks each ECU$_i \in \mathcal{E}_{\text{rem}}$ based on their current mapping. It complements M_{cur} by inserting R preserving order and precedence constraints by means of deadlines and release times. This insertion results in Runnable shiftings and growing execution delays due to the constraints on one or more of the ECUs. The algorithm calculates the overall end-to-end delay for all event chains implied by M_i and stores it referencing to ECU$_i$. This results in a set of end-to-end delays (E2E): one for each Runnable-to-ECU mapping. Finally, Alg. 4 compares these values and returns the ECU with minimum overall end-to-end delay. Fig. 4 depicts Gantt Charts for the TC and ACC systems in a network with 3 ECUs. It shows how our SWC-to-ECU approach preserves the initial order of Runnables on remaining ECUs and inserts redundant Runnables. It also shows that our approach enables an efficient Runnable-to-task mapping to reduce the number of required tasks. For this purpose Runnables that are assigned to the same ECU and keep connected at each redundancy mapping, are encapsulated in one task. Summarized, this results in 13 tasks for the initial mapping and 18 tasks for the redundant Runnables. Although each redundant Runnable is mapped to a separate task, our approach also supports the encapsulation of redundant Runnables in one task.

Algorithm 4. GETECUMINE2E($R, \mathcal{E}, M_{cur}$)

Input: Runnable R, ECUs $\mathcal{E}$, and Mapping M_{cur}.
Output: ECU causing minimum overall E2E delay
1: **for all** ECU$_i \in \mathcal{E}$ **do**
2:     $M_i \leftarrow M_{\text{cur}} \cup$ MAPRUNNABLE(R, ECU$_i$)
3:     E2E$_{\text{ECU}_i} \leftarrow$ OVERALLE2EDELAY(M_i)
4:     E2E $\leftarrow$ E2E $\cup$ E2E$_{\text{ECU}_i}$
5: **end for**
6: ECU $\leftarrow$ ECUMINE2E(E2E)
7: **return** ECU

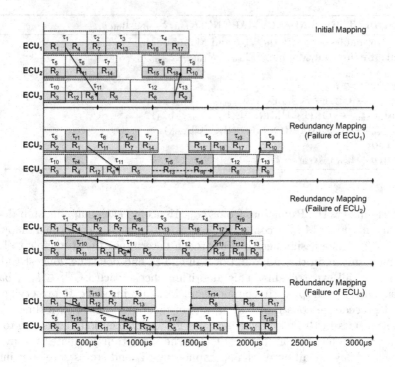

Fig. 4. Gantt Charts of Runnable and task mappings for TC and ACC systems

5.3 Communication and Bus Mapping

The number of Inter-ECU messages depends on the Runnable mappings; their size depends on the given software architecture. The message sizes of the TC and ACC systems are 10 to 22 *bits* [11] and require one or two words of a FlexRay frame. For each Inter-ECU message m_i, the Runnable mappings result in an available transmission interval $\text{Tx}_i = [f_{\text{send}}, s_{\text{recv}}]$. Thus, m_i may be transmitted in one slot θ of the slot set Θ_i in Tx_i. The number of slots in Θ_i depends on the slot size. Here, we consider a slot size of $\theta_{\text{size}} = 25\mu s$, i.e. up to 6 PDUs per frame. Alg. 5 describes our bus mapping approach. It adds the Inter-ECU messages $\mathcal{M}_{\text{M}_i}$ of all Runnable mappings to a common message set $\mathcal{M}$. For each message it determines the sender ECU and transmission interval per mapping and adds it to a common set Ω_{m_j}. Afterwards, it performs an assignment of slots to messages respectively sender ECUs. Therefore, all Inter-ECU messages $\mathcal{M}$ are considered. Analyzing all messages with the same sender ECU, the corresponding transmission intervals $\Omega_{\text{m}_i, \text{ECU}_j}$ get identified. Since the initial mapping is kept, Inter-ECU messages can be sent by the same ECU in one or more Runnable mappings (ref. Fig. 4). Thus, our approach reduces the number of needed slots for the ECU assignments. It compares the determined transmission intervals. For overlapping slots the first available common slot θ_{map} is assigned to the sender ECU for the transmission of m_i. Thus, the same message and slot is reused in

Algorithm 5. BUSMAPPING$(\Pi, \Theta, \mathcal{E})$

Input: RunnableMappings Π, Set of Slots Θ, and ECUs $\mathcal{E}$.
Output: BusMapping: $(\mathcal{M}, \mathcal{E}) \mapsto \Theta$
 1: **for all** $M_i \in \Pi$ **do**
 2:     $\mathcal{M}_{M_i} \leftarrow$ GETINTERECUMSGS(M_i)
 3:     $\mathcal{M} \leftarrow \mathcal{M} \cup \mathcal{M}_{M_i}$
 4:     **for all** $m_j \in \mathcal{M}_{M_i}$ **do**
 5:         $ECU_{send(M_i,m_j)} \leftarrow$ GETSENDERECU$(M_i, m_j, \mathcal{E})$
 6:         $\Theta_{m_j, ECU_{send(M_i,m_j)}} \leftarrow$ GETTXINTERVAL $(m_j, ECU_{send(M_i,m_j)})$
 7:         $\Omega_{m_j} \leftarrow \Omega_{m_j} \cup \Theta_{m_j, ECU_{send(M_i,m_j)}}$
 8:     **end for**
 9: **end for**
10: **for all** $m_i \in \mathcal{M}$ **do**
11:     $\mathcal{E}_{sender} \leftarrow$ GETSENDERECUS$(\Omega_{m_i}, \mathcal{E})$
12:     **for all** $ECU_j \in \mathcal{E}_{sender}$ **do**
13:         $\Omega_{m_i, ECU_j} \leftarrow$ GETTXINTERVALSFORSAMESENDER(Ω_{m_i}, ECU_j)
14:         $\theta_{map} \leftarrow$ GETFIRSTCOMMONANDAVAILABLESLOT(Ω_{m_i, ECU_j})
15:         MAPTOSLOT$((m_i, ECU_j), \theta_{map})$
16:     **end for**
17: **end for**
18: **return** $(\mathcal{M}, \mathcal{E}) \mapsto \Theta$

Table 2. Bus Mapping for Inter-ECU communication (excerpt)

Message	Sender: Transmission Interval (μs)	Slot (μs)
$R_1 \to R_5$	ECU_1:$[200, 500]$, $[200, 800]$, $[200, 1025]$	$[200, 225]$
	ECU_2:$[400, 700]$	$[400, 425]$
$R_2 \to R_5$	ECU_1:$[600, 800]$	$[600, 625]$
	ECU_2:$[200, 500]$, $[200, 700]$	$[225, 250]$
$R_4 \to R_5$	ECU_1:$[400, 500]$, $[400, 800]$, $[400, 1025]$	$[425, 450]$
$R_5 \to R_8$	ECU_2:$[1325, 1350]$	$[1325, 1350]$
$R_6 \to R_8$	ECU_2:$[850, 1350]$	$[1325, 1350]$

different reconfigurations. In non-overlapping intervals, m_i is mapped to the first available slot in each interval. It is also checked if the current message can be mapped to the same slot as one of the other messages by utilizing frame packing. Table 2 provides an excerpt of the determined bus mappings. It shows transmission intervals and assigned slots for messages per sender and gives examples for reuse and frame packing. Fig. 4 depicts the end-to-end delays for the event chain $R_1 \to R_{10}$ and shows that the end-to-end delay constraint is fulfilled for all mappings. The same holds for all other event chains.

6   Reconfiguration with AUTOSAR

Having a feasible AUTOSAR-compliant SWC-to-ECU and Runnable-to-task mapping, two challenges remain to solve by means of AUTOSAR: Detect a failed

ECU and activate the appropriate redundant tasks within the ECU network according to the fault-tolerant reconfiguration. While AUTOSAR specifies a BSW called Watchdog Manager to manage errors of BSW modules and SWCs running on an ECU, there is no explicit specification regarding detection of failed nodes within an ECU network. Therefore, we propose to extend AUTOSAR BSW by means of a Complex Device Driver (CDD, [23]). Using FlexRay-specific functionality provided by BSW of AUTOSAR Communication Stack, it can be monitored if valid frames are received. Combined with the static slot-to-sender assignment, each ECU can identify failed ECUs. When a failed ECU is detected, each remaining ECU has to activate its appropriate redundant tasks. For this purpose we propose using *Schedule Tables*: a statically defined activation mechanism provided by AUTOSAR OS for time-triggered tasks used with an OSEK Counter [13]. Here, we use the FlexRay clock to support synchronization of ScheduleTables running on different ECUs within a network. Note that tasks are only activated, i.e. tasks require an appropriate priority to ensure that they are scheduled in time. For each ECU we define one single ScheduleTable for each configuration of this ECU, i.e. a ScheduleTable activates only those tasks that are part of its corresponding configuration. Utilizing the different states that each ScheduleTable can enter – e.g. *RUNNING* and *STOPPED* – the ScheduleTable with the currently required configuration is RUNNING while all the others are STOPPED. Since in this paper we consider periodic tasks, ScheduleTables have repeating behavior, i.e. a RUNNING ScheduleTable is processed in a loop. Having an AUTOSAR-compliant concept to detect a failed ECU within a network and to manage different task activation patterns on an ECU, we need to combine these concepts. This can be done by using BSW Mode Manager. Defining one mode per configuration on a particular ECU, our CDD can request a mode switch when a failed ECU is detected. This mode switch enforces that the currently running ScheduleTable is STOPPED and, depending on the failed ECU, the appropriate ScheduleTable enters state RUNNING.

7   Conclusion

We presented an approach for fault-tolerant deployment of real-time software in AUTOSAR ECU networks and applied it to real-world applications. It offers methods for task and message mappings to determine an initial deployment combined with reconfigurations. To enable redundancy, we proposed a reconfigurable network topology. Finally, we introduced a CDD for detecting failed nodes and activation of reconfigurations.

Acknowledgements. This work was partly funded by the DFG SFB 614 and the German Ministry of Education and Research (BMBF) through the project SANITAS (01M3088I) and the ITEA2 projects VERDE (01S09012H), AMALTHEA (01IS11020J), and TIMMO-2-USE (01IS10034A).

References

1. Fennel, H., et al.: Achievements and exploitation of the AUTOSAR development partnership. In: Society of Automotive Engineers (SAE) Convergence (2006)
2. Scheickl, O., Rudorfer, M.: Automotive real time development using a timing-augmented autosar specification. In: Proceedings of the 4th European Congress on Embedded Real-Time Software, ERTS (2008)
3. Burns, A.: Scheduling hard real-time systems: A review (1991)
4. Paret, D.: Multiplexed Networks for Embedded Systems. Wiley (2007)
5. Klobedanz, K., et al.: An approach for self-reconfiguring and fault-tolerant distributed real-time systems. In: 3rd IEEE Workshop on Self-Organizing Real-Time Systems, SORT (2012)
6. Pop, P., et al.: Scheduling with optimized communication for time-triggered embedded systems. In: Proceedings of the 7th International Workshop on Hardware/Software Codesign, CODES (1999)
7. Pop, P., et al.: Bus access optimization for distributed embedded systems based on schedulability analysis. In: Proceedings of Design, Automation and Test in Europe, DATE (2000)
8. Eles, P., et al.: Scheduling with bus access optimization for distributed embedded systems. IEEE Trans. Very Large Scale Integr. Syst. 8(5) (2000)
9. Ding, S., et al.: A ga-based scheduling method for flexray systems. In: Proceedings of the 5th ACM International Conference on Embedded Software, EMSOFT (2005)
10. Ding, S., et al.: An effective ga-based scheduling algorithm for flexray systems. IEICE - Transactions on Information and Systems E91-D(8) (2008)
11. Kandasamy, N., et al.: Dependable communication synthesis for distributed embedded systems. In: International Conference on Computer Safety, Reliability and Security, SAFECOMP (2003)
12. Brendle, R., Streichert, T., Koch, D., Haubelt, C.D., Teich, J.: Dynamic reconfiguration of flexRay schedules for response time reduction in asynchronous fault-tolerant networks. In: Brinkschulte, U., Ungerer, T., Hochberger, C., Spallek, R.G. (eds.) ARCS 2008. LNCS, vol. 4934, pp. 117–129. Springer, Heidelberg (2008)
13. AUTOSAR: Specification of Operating System, Ver. 5.0.0 (2011)
14. Peng, W., et al.: Deployment optimization for autosar system configuration. In: 2nd International Conference on Computer Engineering and Technology, ICCET (2010)
15. Zhang, M., Gu, Z.: Optimization issues in mapping autosar components to distributed multithreaded implementations. In: 22nd IEEE International Symposium on Rapid System Prototyping, RSP (2011)
16. Kim, J., et al.: An autosar-compliant automotive platform for meeting reliability and timing constraints. In: Society of Automotive Engineers (SAE) World Congress and Exhibition (2011)
17. AUTOSAR: Software Component Template, Ver. 4.2.0 (2011)
18. AUTOSAR: Specification of Timing Extensions, Ver. 1.2.0 (2011)
19. Peraldi-Frati, M.A., et al.: Timing modeling with autosar - current state and future directions. In: Design, Automation, and Test in Europe Conference Exhibition, DATE (2012)
20. AUTOSAR: Specification of RTE, Ver. 3.2.0 (2011)
21. AUTOSAR: Specification of Communication, Ver. 4.2.0 (2011)
22. FlexRay Consortium: FlexRay Communications System Protocol Specification Ver. 2.1 (2005)
23. AUTOSAR: Technical Overview, Ver. 2.1.1 (2008)

Adaptive Total Bandwidth Server: Using Predictive Execution Time

Kiyofumi Tanaka

School of Information Science, Japan Advanced Institute of Science and Technology,
Asahidai 1-1, Nomi-city, Ishikawa, 923-1292 Japan
kiyofumi@jaist.ac.jp

Abstract. Along with the growing diversity and complexity of real-time embedded systems, it is becoming common that different types of tasks, periodic tasks and aperiodic tasks, reside in a system. In such systems, it is important that schedulability of periodic tasks is maintained and at the same time response times to aperiodic requests are short enough. Total Bandwidth Server (TBS) is one of convincing task scheduling algorithms for mixed task sets of periodic and aperiodic tasks. This paper proposes a method of using predictive execution times instead of worst-case execution times for deadline calculations in TBS to obtain shorter deadlines and reducing response times of aperiodic execution, while maintaining the schedulability of periodic tasks. From the evaluation by simulation, the proposed method combined with a resource reclaiming technique exhibits better average response times for aperiodic tasks, in case of a heavy load, by up to 39%.

Keywords: Real-time task scheduling, worst-case execution time, predictive execution time, total bandwidth server.

1 Introduction

Along with the growing diversity and complexity of embedded systems, it is becoming common that different types of tasks reside in a system. For example, control tasks that are required to completely meet real-time requirements (hard tasks) and user interface tasks that should give a certain level of response times but are not required to completely behave at real-time (soft tasks) would be mixed. To achieve real-time processing required in such a system, real-time scheduling algorithms that involve both hard and soft tasks and guarantee the schedulability of tasks (especially of hard tasks) must be used.

Hard tasks should be periodically invoked and be considered to spend their worst-case execution time (WCET), since the schedulability, that they satisfy their deadline requirements, must be confirmed in advance of system operation. On the other hand, soft tasks can run on aperiodic invocations because of inexact real-time requirements. There is a scheduling algorithm for such hard and soft tasks, Total Bandwidth Server (TBS) [1]. TBS has a merit that CPU utilization can be up to 100% while maintaining schedulability. This study explores algorithms based on TBS.

G. Schirner et al. (Eds.): IESS 2013, IFIP AICT 403, pp. 250–261, 2013.

Complexity of current processors and programs makes estimation of WCET difficult. For example, deep pipelining execution of machine instructions makes estimation of their execution times hard, or in a system with many tasks, whether each memory reference would hit in the cache memory or not is difficult to decide/predict [2]. In addition, the worst-case execution path in a program is almost impossible to trace since it includes many branches and loop structures, and all input patterns give a vast search range [3]. Consequently, WCET is obliged to be pessimistically estimated and leads to having a large gap with actual execution times. Due to this gap, it is difficult to obtain the best schedules by scheduling algorithms that use tasks' execution times.

In this research, it is taken into consideration that soft tasks are not required to completely satisfy the deadline constraints, and, instead of WCET, predictive execution time (PET) is introduced in the TBS-based scheduling algorithm, which aims to shorten response times of soft tasks.

2 Related Works

There are various scheduling algorithms proposed for task sets consisting of both periodic and aperiodic tasks. They are categorized to fixed-priority servers and dynamic-priority servers. Fixed-priority servers are based on rate monotonic (RM) scheduling [4], which has a merit that higher-priority tasks have lower jitters. As representative examples, Deferrable Server [5], Priority Exchange [5], Sporadic Server [6], and Slack Stealing [7] were proposed. On the other hand, dynamic-priority servers are based on earliest deadline first (EDF) scheduling [4], which provides a strong merit that CPU utilization can reach up to 100% while maintaining schedulability. Dynamic Priority Exchange [1], Dynamic Sporadic server [1], Total Bandwidth Server [1], Earliest Deadline Late Server [1], and Constant Bandwidth Server [8] are examples of dynamic-priority servers. The aim of these algorithms is to make response times of aperiodic requests shorter, while the effectiveness is obtained in exchange for their implementation complexity.

Total Bandwidth Server (TBS) provides good response times while leaving its implementation complexity moderate. It is assumed that hard tasks are invoked periodically and have their deadlines equal to the end of the period, and that soft tasks are invoked irregularly, but do not have their explicit deadline requirements in advance. When a soft task is invoked, tentative deadline is calculated and given to the task as:

$$d_k = max(r_k, d_{k-1}) + \frac{C_k}{U_s} \tag{1}$$

where k means kth instance of aperiodic tasks, r_k is the arrival time of the kth instance, d_{k-1} is the absolute deadline of the $k - 1$th (previous) instance, C_k is WCET of the kth instance, and U_s is the CPU utilization factor by the server which takes charge of execution of aperiodic tasks. The server is considered to occupy the U_s utilization factor and, every time an aperiodic request arrives, leads to give the instance the bandwidth of U_s. The term, $max(r_k, d_{k-1})$, prevents bandwidths of successive aperiodic instances from overlapping with each other. After an instance of an aperiodic task is given its deadline, all periodic and aperiodic tasks are scheduled by following EDF algorithm. By letting U_p be the CPU utilization factor by all hard periodic tasks, it was proved that a task set is schedulable if and only if $U_p + U_s \leq 1$ [1].

In TBS, overestimated WCET would make the deadline later than necessary by the formula (1). This might delay the execution of the aperiodic instance and cause long response time. The literature [10] showed the method, *resource reclaiming*, where deadline is recalculated by using actually elapsed execution time when the instance finishes, and the new deadline is used for the deadline calculation for subsequent aperiodic instances. By this method, the subsequent instances benefit from the earlier deadlines and their response times would be improved.

In the resource reclaiming, kth aperiodic instance is given deadline d'_k by:

$$d'_k = \overline{r}_k + \frac{C_k}{U_s} \tag{2}$$

$\overline{r}_k$ is the value calculated as:

$$\overline{r}_k = max(r_k, \overline{d}_{k-1}, f_{k-1}) \tag{3}$$

That is, the maximal value among the arrival time, the recalculated deadline of the previous instance and the finishing time of the previous instance is selected as the release time. When the $k-1$th aperiodic instance finishes, the deadline is recalculated by the following formula that includes the actual execution time, $\overline{C}_{k-1}$, of the instance, and is reflected in the formula (3), and then in the formula (2), for the subsequent task.

$$\overline{d}_{k-1} = \overline{r}_{k-1} + \frac{\overline{C}_{k-1}}{U_s} \tag{4}$$

There is another algorithm based on TBS. In the literature [11], Buttazzo, et al. proposed a method for firm (not hard) periodic and soft aperiodic tasks. Since firm deadline allows a task to be missed to some degree, the algorithm achieves shorter response times by skipping periodic executions at times and ensuring larger bandwidth for aperiodic tasks. This method aims to achieve short response times at the sacrifice of completeness of periodic instances. On the other hand, in this paper, a method of shortening response times of aperiodic instances while maintaining schedulability of periodic tasks is proposed.

3   The Adaptive Total Bandwidth Algorithm

As is the case with the total bandwidth server algorithm presented in the literature [1], this paper assumes that task sets consist of periodic tasks with hard deadlines and aperiodic tasks without explicit deadlines, where it is desirable that aperiodic execution finishes as early as possible. Since aperiodic tasks do not have deadline, it is not necessary to use WCET from a schedulability point of view. Although TBS dynamically gives tentative deadlines to aperiodic instances, missing the deadlines is not serious or catastrophic. Therefore, use of WCET for deadline calculation is not essential. Instead, shorter execution times can be assumed and used for the deadline calculation while maintaining schedulability of the whole task set. When the assumed execution times elapsed but the execution did not finish yet, the deadline only has to be recalculated by using longer execution times, for example, WCET. By this strategy, when aperiodic execution finishes in the assumed time, the corresponding short deadline and EDF algorithm can make the response time shorter.

3.1 Prediction of Execution Time (PET)

Generally, in real-time scheduling and its schedulability analysis, task execution is considered to spend worst-case execution time (WCET). In practice, task execution time is unknown beforehand and therefore WCET must be supposed to spend, especially in hard real-time systems. However, in most cases, actual execution time is shorter than WCET. Since WCET is pessimistically estimated, the difference between the actual execution time and WCET tends to be large.

As the impact of the difference, for example, when SJF (Shortest Job First) algorithm is applied based on WCETs, the average turnaround time would be worse than that of the same algorithm based on actual execution times, although this is an oracle with prior information. In Figure 1, (1) shows that WCETs of task A, task B and task C are 2, 3, and 4, respectively, and the execution order is A, B, and then C based on SJF. When this order is applied to actual executions where actual execution times are 2, 1, and 2 for task A, task B, and task C, respectively, the average turnaround time becomes 3.33 (Figure 1 (2)). On the other hand, if the actual execution times are known in advance and used in the algorithm, the average turnaround time will be 3 under SJF as shown in Figure 1 (3). Like this, decision based on WCETs is not necessarily the best.

For task sets consisting of both hard and soft tasks, although WCET must be assumed for execution of hard tasks, execution time shorter than WCET can be assumed for soft tasks since they can miss their deadline to some

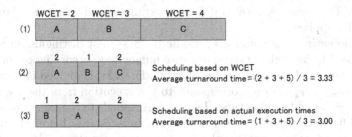

Fig. 1. Scheduling base on Shortest Job First

degree. Especially in the total bandwidth server environments, deadlines are not given to aperiodic tasks in advance. In run-time, (tentative) deadline is calculated using WCET and is assigned dynamically. If the deadline calculation for aperiodic tasks uses execution time shorter than WCET, earlier deadline can be obtained and therefore shorter response time can be expected. Assumption of shorter execution time can cause deadline misses. However, the deadline misses are not serious since the tasks are for soft real-time processing. After the misses, remaining execution has only to continue.

In this strategy, execution times should be predicted. There are various possible ways to obtain the predictive execution times (PET).

1. Random choice of execution times
2. Measurement in advance
3. Prediction using a history of execution

The above 1 has high possibility of choosing shorter times than actual execution times, and therefore would cause many deadline misses (although the misses are not serious). The next one seems effective but has a defect of not following the change of execution times when a task is executed many times in the system operation. The third one predicts execution times by an execution history of the same task and therefore can follow the fluctuation of execution times. The prediction method is not the most important essence of the proposed adaptive TBS. For the present, this paper uses the following prediction method which corresponds to the above 3.

$$C_{i_{PET_k}} = \alpha \times C_{i_{PET_{k-1}}} + (1 - \alpha) \times C_{i_{ET_{k-1}}}, \quad C_{i_{PET_0}} = C_{i_{WCET}} \qquad (5)$$

Here, $C_{i_{PET_k}}$ is PET for kth instance of an aperiodic task J_i. $C_{i_{ET_{k-1}}}$ is the execution time actually spent for the previous execution of the same task J_i. The initial value $C_{i_{PET_0}}$ is equal to WCET of the task, $C_{i_{WCET}}$. This formula calculates as the predictive execution time an weighted average of the previous PET and the previous actual execution time with the weighting coefficient α.

3.2   Definition of the Adaptive TB Server

In the adaptive TBS, an instance of an aperiodic task is divided into two sub instances. They are regarded as different instances, and then the original TBS is naturally applied.

In the following descriptions, aperiodic tasks are not distinguished and they are supposed to have global serial instance numbers, k, according to the request order. Execution of J_k, kth instance of aperiodic tasks, is divided into two parts, J_{PET_k} and J_{REST_k}. J_{PET_k} corresponds to the execution from the beginning of J_k to the predicted finishing time. J_{REST_k} corresponds to the execution from the predicted finishing time. If the execution of J_k finishes at or before the predicted time, J_{REST_k} does not exist. Let the worst case execution time of J_k be C_{WCET_k}, the predictive execution time of J_k be C_{PET_k}, and the execution time of J_{REST_k}

be $C_{REST_k} = C_{WCET_k} - C_{PET_k}$. When the kth aperiodic request arrives at the time $t = r_k$, two instances for the request are assigned deadlines as:

$$d_{PET_k} = max(r_k, d_{k-1}) + \frac{C_{PET_k}}{U_s} \tag{6}$$

$$d_{REST_k} = d_{PET_k} + \frac{C_{REST_k}}{U_s} \tag{7}$$

Deadline assignment in the original TBS was as:

$$d_k = max(r_k, d_{k-1}) + \frac{C_{WCET_k}}{U_s} \tag{8}$$

From $C_{REST_k} = C_{WCET_k} - C_{PET_k}$ and the formula (6), (7), and (8),

$$d_{REST_k} = max(r_k, d_{k-1}) + \frac{C_{PET_k}}{U_s} + \frac{C_{WCET_k} - C_{PET_k}}{U_s}$$

$$= max(r_k; d_{k-1}) + \frac{C_{WCET_k}}{U_s} \quad = \quad d_k$$

Therefore, two deadlines can be calculated by the formula (6) and (8) at the arrival time. The use of the formula (8) is more suitable than the formula (7) since the second term in the right expression is calculated with two constants and has only to be calculated once in advance of the system operation.

3.3   Example of Adaptive Total Bandwidth Server

In this section, an example of Adaptive TBS is shown. In Figure 2, (1) and (2) show scheduling results of the original and adaptive TBS, respectively. There are two periodic tasks, τ_1 and τ_2, and an aperiodic task request. The period of τ_1 is $T_1 = 4$, and its execution time $C_1 = 1$. τ_2 has the period $T_2 = 6$, and its execution time $C_2 = 3$. Therefore, the CPU utilization by the two periodic tasks is $U_p = 0.25 + 0.5 = 0.75$ and the CPU utilization by the aperiodic server is $U_s = 1 - U_p = 0.25$. The aperiodic request occurs at tick 3, and its WCET is supposed to be 3, while the predictive execution time and the actual execution time are 2. In the original TBS, the deadline of the aperiodic task is $d_{WCET} = 3 + 3/0.25 = 15$. Based on EDF algorithm, the aperiodic task starts execution at tick 5, and is suspended at tick 6 by τ_2. Then, after the execution of τ_1, the execution resumes at tick 10 and finishes at tick 11. Consequently, the response time becomes $11 - 3 = 8$. On the other hand, in the adaptive TBS, the two deadlines, $d_{PET} = 3 + 2/0.25 = 11$ and $d_{REST} = 11 + (3 - 2)/0.25 = 15$, are given. Based on EDF, the aperiodic task starts execution at tick 3 and finishes at tick 7, which gives the response time of $7 - 3 = 4$. In this example, the adaptive TBS shortens the response time by 4 ticks compared with the original TBS.

Suppose that the same task set is scheduled except that the actual execution time of the aperiodic task is 3 ticks. The adaptive TBS suspends the aperiodic execution at tick 7, resumes the execution at tick 11, and then finishes it at tick 12. Like this, even if the execution time is incorrectly predicted, the response time would be the same as or shorter than that in the original TBS.

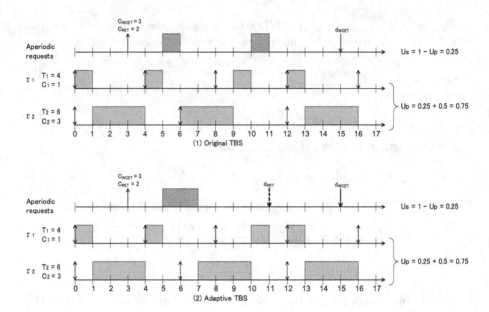

Fig. 2. Example of original and adaptive TBS

3.4 Adaptive Total Bandwidth Schedulability

After an aperiodic request is divided into two sub instances, the adaptive TBS behaves just as the original TBS, where the two sub instances can be considered to arrive at the same time. Obviously, from the formulas (6) and (7), the utilization by the two instances between $max(r_k, d_{k-1})$ and d_k is the same as that in the original TBS as follows.

$$U_{J_{PET_k}} = \frac{C_{PET_k}}{d_{PET_k} - max(r_k, d_{k-1})} = U_s, \quad U_{J_{REST_k}} = \frac{C_{REST_k}}{d_{REST_k} - d_{PET_k}} = U_s$$

Therefore, schedulability of the adaptive TBS leads to be the same as that of the original TBS presented in the literature [9].

3.5 Implementation Complexity

In the proposed algorithm, task execution is divided into two instances. However, operating systems should manage a task with a single information set, task control block. This is realized by re-setting up deadline and re-inserting the task in a ready queue when PET elapses and the task has not finished, which is the only difference from the original TBS. To find that execution reaches PET, the scheduler should be executed every tick timing. This is achieved by calling the scheduler when timer/tick interrupts occur, which is a natural procedure that operating systems usually follow. In addition, as described in the section 3.2, the value of the second term in the right side of the formula (8) should be statically computed and used when necessary to reduce the recalculation overheads.

3.6 Affinity with Resource Reclaiming

In the proposed adaptive TBS, when deadline is calculated for kth aperiodic request, d_{k-1} is needed. Since the previous ($k-1$th) aperiodic request is divided into two instances, the deadline for the second instance, that is $d_{REST_{k-1}}$, is used for the calculation. However, when the execution of the $k-1$th request finishes in its PET ($C_{PET_{k-1}}$), the second instance is not executed. In this case, instead of $d_{REST_{k-1}}$, $d_{PET_{k-1}}$ can be used to calculate the deadline for the kth task. This can be applied when the execution of the first instance of the $k-1$th aperiodic task finishes before the kth aperiodic task arrives. This is one of resource reclaiming methods.

A greedier method, resource reclaiming technique [10] described in the section 2, can be easily applied to the proposed adaptive TBS. When the execution of an aperiodic instance finishes, whether or not the execution is for the first or second instance after the task is divided, the deadline is recalculated by the formula (4), then the deadline is applied to the formula (3), and finally the following aperiodic instances can be given earlier deadlines by the formula (2).

In this paper, the former is called "simple resource reclaiming" and the latter "greedier resource reclaiming". In the evaluation section, these two resource reclaiming methods are combined with the proposed adaptive TBS.

4 Evaluation

4.1 Evaluation Methodology

In this section, simulation results of the proposed TBS are shown. In the evaluation, six methods, Original TBS, the original TBS with resource reclaiming described in the section 2 (Original TBS-95), the adaptive TBS without any resource reclaiming (ATBS w/o RR), the adaptive TBS with simple resource reclaiming described in the section 3.6 (ATBS w/ RR), the adaptive TBS with greedier resource reclaiming (ATBS-95), and the ideal TBS where execution times of instances are known (Oracle), are compared.

In the simulation, task sets consist of periodic tasks with the total CPU utilization (U_p) from 60% to 90% at intervals of 5% and aperiodic tasks with the total utilization from 0.5% to 2% in the observation period (100,000 ticks). The aperiodic server has the utilization $U_s = 1 - U_p$. For periodic tasks, their periods are decided by exponential distributions where the average value is 100 ticks. Their WCET and actual execution times are equal and obtained by exponential distributions with the average of 10 ticks. For aperiodic tasks, a task set is supposed to contain 1 to 4 different tasks. Each task in a set is invoked multiple times and the arrival times are decided by Poisson distributions with 1.25 per 1,000 ticks on average. The WCETs are decided by exponential distributions with the average of 8 ticks. Each task instance has its actual execution time decided by exponential distributions with the average of 4 ticks, under the condition that the upper bound is the corresponding WCET. For all aperiodic task sets, the average ratio of actual execution times to WCET was about 0.33.

For each U_p, all combinations of ten periodic task sets and ten aperiodic task sets (total 100 task sets) are simulated and the average value is shown. For the proposed methods, the weighting coefficient for PET calculation (α in the section 3.1) is 0.5.

4.2   Results

Figure 3 is the results where each task set contains only one aperiodic task. The utilization by the aperiodic task's execution is about 0.5%. In the figure, the horizontal axis indicates the CPU utilization by periodic tasks (U_p), and the vertical axis indicates the average response time of aperiodic task executions. Under 65%, the response times are almost the same for all the six methods. This is because the server utilization, $U_s = 1 - U_p$, is large enough to quickly serve the aperiodic requests. Over 70%, the differences gradually appear. When U_p is 90%, the response time of the original TBS is about 32 ticks, and that of the original TBS-95 is 28.5 ticks. On the other hand, ATBS w/o RR, ATBS w/ RR, and ATBS-95 exhibit the response times of 20.5, 18, and 17.5 ticks, respectively. In this evaluation, it is found that a method with deadline assignment based on PET (ATBS w/o RR) improves the response time by 36% compared to the original WCET-based method, and that a method with greedier resource reclaiming (ATBS-95) outperforms the original ATBS-95 by 39%. Consequently, the PET-based method exhibits better ability when it is applied with resource reclaiming.

Figure 4 is the results where four aperiodic tasks are included in the task sets. The utilization by the aperiodic tasks is about 2%. The trend is similar to Figure 3 except that the improvement by resource reclaiming is larger. This is because the higher aperiodic utilization leads to the situation where occurrences of aperiodic requests overlap with each other and the resource reclaiming is applied more frequently. The improvement of ATBS w/o RR to Original TBS is 13%, while ATBS-95 achieves more improvement over the original TBS-95, which is 22%.

The use of PET is discussed. The ratio of aperiodic executions that finished in PET was 56%. Table 1 is the average of the shortened deadline length for aperiodic instances that finished in their PET in the simulation of Figure 4. ("Shortened length" means how shorter the deadline is than that based on WCET.) The difference between ATBS w/o RR, ATBS w/ RR, and ATBS-95 does not exist, and therefore the table shows the ratio collectively. The larger U_p is, the longer the shortened length is. This is because larger U_p corresponds to smaller $U_s (= 1 - U_p)$, therefore the 2nd term of the right expression in the formula (1) would be larger and then the shortened length would be longer. Consequently, ATBS methods using PET provide larger improvements when the utilization by periodic tasks is high, in other words, when the capacity of the aperiodic server is small.

Next, effects of resource reclaiming are discussed. Table 2 shows ratios of resource reclaiming that actuallxy affected the deadline calculation of the succeeding tasks (that is, ratios of the cases that d_{k-1} is the maximum in the

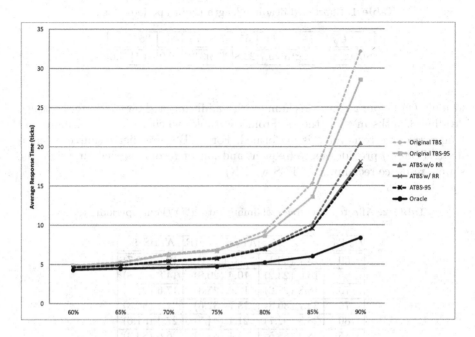

Fig. 3. Average response time (One aperiodic task)

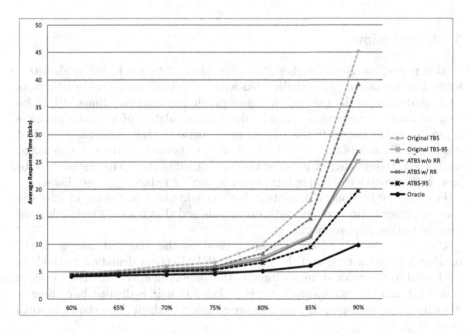

Fig. 4. Average response time (Four aperiodic tasks)

Table 1. Shortened deadline length (Four aperiodic tasks)

U_p (%)	60	65	70	75	80	85	90
Shortened length	19.7	22.8	26.5	31.8	40.0	54.1	84.6

formula (1) before resource reclaiming). In addition, it shows average shortened deadline lengths in parentheses. From the table, when U_p is larger, more and longer resource reclaiming is performed. For ATBS, greedier resource reclaiming (ATBS-95) provides more frequent and longer resource reclaiming than the simple resource reclaiming (ATBS w/ RR).

Table 2. Affected resource reclaiming ratio (%) (Four aperiodic tasks)

U_p (%)	TBS–95	ATBS w/ RR	ATBS–95
60	13.7 (20.1)	8.6 (18.1)	12.5 (19.7)
65	16.0 (23.2)	10.4 (20.8)	14.8 (22.8)
70	18.8 (28.2)	12.6 (25.3)	17.6 (27.7)
75	22.7 (36.8)	15.7 (32.6)	21.4 (36.3)
80	28.8 (52.7)	21.1 (44.5)	27.4 (51.6)
85	38.3 (85.5)	29.1 (68.9)	36.6 (83.3)
90	57.9 (299.1)	48.6 (252.9)	56.0 (297.4)

5   Conclusion

In this paper, for Total Bandwidth Server which is task scheduling algorithm for task sets consisting of periodic tasks with hard deadlines and aperiodic tasks without deadlines, the method that uses predictive execution times (PET) instead of worst-case execution times for deadline calculation of aperiodic instances is proposed. The use of PET is allowed since aperiodic tasks do not have explicit deadlines. The aim of the method is to shorten response times of aperiodic tasks, while the schedulability of periodic tasks is not influenced. The method can be used with resource reclaiming techniques to further reduce response times.

From the evaluation by simulation, it was confirmed that the use of PET can shorten response times of aperiodic executions and that resource reclaiming can provide further improvements.

Currently, obtaining PET is simply based on the weighted average of the previous execution time and the previous PET. Better calculation methods of PET need to be explored. In addition, in this paper, an aperiodic task execution is divided into two instances. There is a choice that it is divided into three or more instances and stepped deadlines are assigned to them. This choice is worth evaluating.

The evaluation in this paper used task sets that were generated based on probability distribution. To reflect actual situations where task execution times fluctuate, evaluation with actual program codes is desired. In addition, in the current evaluation, the greedier resource reclaiming exhibits better improvement than the simple resource reclaiming. However, considering the calculation overheads of reclaiming, the effects might be degraded. In such cases, the practicality of the simple resource reclaiming might emerge. In the future, evaluation with actual program codes and scheduling overheads should be performed.

References

1. Spuri, M., Buttazzo, G.C.: Efficient Aperiodic Service under Earliest Deadline First Scheduling. In: IEEE Real-Time Systems Symposium, pp. 2–11. IEEE Computer Society, San Juan (1994)
2. Lundqvist, T., Stenström, P.: Timing Anomalies in Dynamically Scheduled Microprocessors. In: IEEE Real-Time Systems Symposium, pp. 12–21. IEEE Computer Society, Phoenix (1999)
3. Wilhelm, R., Engblom, J., Ermedahl, A., Holsti, N., Thesing, S., Whalley, D., Bernat, G., Ferdinand, C., Heckmann, R., Mitra, T., Mueller, F., Puaut, I., Puschner, P., Staschulat, J., Stenström, P.: The Worst-Case Execution Time Problem – Overview of Methods and Survey of Tools. ACM Trans. on Embedded Computing Systems 7(3), 1–53 (2008)
4. Liu, C.L., Layland, J.W.: Scheduling Algorithms for Multiprogramming in a Hard-Real-Time Environment. Journal of the Association for Computing Machinery 20(1), 46–61 (1973)
5. Lehoczky, J.P., Sha, L., Strosnider, J.K.: Enhanced Aperiodic Responsiveness in Hard Real-Time Environments. In: IEEE Real-Time Systems Symposium, pp. 261–270. IEEE Computer Society, San Jose (1987)
6. Sprunt, B., Sha, L., Lehoczky, J.: Aperiodic Task Scheduling for Hard-Real-Time Systems. Journal of Real-Time Systems 1(1), 27–60 (1989)
7. Lehoczky, J.P., Ramos-Thue, S.: An Optimal Algorithm for Scheduling Soft-Aperiodic Tasks in Fixed-Priority Preemptive Systems. In: IEEE Real-Time Systems Symposium, pp. 110–123. IEEE Computer Society, Vienna (1992)
8. Abeni, L., Buttazzo, G.: Integrating Multimedia Applications in Hard Real-Time Systems. In: IEEE Real-Time Systems Symposium, pp. 4–13. IEEE Computer Society, Madrid (1998)
9. Spuri, M., Buttazzo, G.: Scheduling Aperiodic Tasks in Dynamic Priority Systems. Journal of Real-Time Systems 10(2), 179–210 (1996)
10. Spuri, M., Buttazzo, G., Sensini, F.: Robust Aperiodic Scheduling under Dynamic Priority Systems. In: IEEE Real-Time Systems Symposium, pp. 210–219. IEEE Computer Society, Pisa (1995)
11. Buttazzo, G.C., Caccamo, M.: Minimizing Aperiodic Response Times in a Firm Real-Time Environment. IEEE Trans. on Software Engineering 25(1), 22–32 (1999)

Real-Time Service-Oriented Architectures: A Data-Centric Implementation for Distributed and Heterogeneous Robotic System

Pekka Alho and Jouni Mattila

Tampere University of Technology, Dept. of Intelligent Hydraulics and Automation, Finland
{pekka.alho,jouni.mattila}@tut.fi

Abstract. Cyber-physical systems like networked robots have benefited from improvements in hardware processing power, and can facilitate modern component and service-based architectures that promote software reuse and bring higher-level functionality, improved integration capabilities, scalability and ease of development to the devices. However, these systems also have very specific requirements such as reliability, safety, and strict timeliness requirements set by the physical world, that must be addressed in the architecture.

This paper proposes a real-time capable service-oriented architecture, based on data-centric middleware and an open real-time operating system. A prototype implementation for a robotic remote handling scenario is used to test the approach. The architecture is evaluated on the basis of how well it fulfils the expectations given for the service-orientation, including: reusability, evolvability, interoperability and real-time performance. In one sentence, the goal is to evaluate the benefits of a data-centric approach to service-orientation in a performance-critical and distributed system.

Keywords: real-time, distributed, SOA, data-centric, middleware, robotics.

1 Introduction

Developing software for cyber-physical embedded systems such as networked robots is a demanding task, due to complex functionality that has to be realised in a distributed and heterogeneous computing environment which typically has requirements for real-time performance and fault tolerance. Many of the challenges in these systems are related to interoperability and growing scale. Typically a distributed control system will consist of several subsystems running on different platforms that produce and consume increasing amounts of data.

On a higher abstraction level, business processes are also becoming strongly networked to improve efficiency by automatically transferring data, task requests etc. between systems. This means that robotic systems must be integrated to operations management systems, open for external connections, and able to connect and cooperate with other machines. These requirements and challenges are not unique to robotics

G. Schirner et al. (Eds.): IESS 2013, IFIP AICT 403, pp. 262–271, 2013.

– other domains like industrial automation, mobile machines and telecommunication have very similar issues.

Service-oriented software engineering has evolved from component frameworks and object orientation to meet the demands of more open and networked environments. It promotes reuse by decomposing business processes into reusable core services. The main benefits of service-oriented architecture (SOA) include high level of decoupling – provided by the service model – and interoperability which enables service providers and consumers to exist on different platforms. Two major downsides typically associated with SOA are complexity of developing such a system and increased overhead caused by communication mechanisms [6]. The latter is also related to the lack of performance guarantees, and presents a major challenge especially for embedded systems. An SOA implementation for robotic system therefore needs to place heavy emphasis on solving this problem, which is one of the key design goals for the architecture presented in this paper.

Application of SOA design principles to real-time systems (RTSOA) is a research topic that has come up in the last decade, with research including experimental implementations [3], [9], [10] and related key features like service composition [2], [4]. However, most of the current RTSOA approaches are based on the existing message-based Web Service standards. Web services face challenges when used in embedded systems, as messages need to be serialized in real-time [2], and quality of service (QoS) must be managed at the transport layer. Other challenges include complexity of networking with HTTP, XML, and SOAP; constraints imposed by embedded system architecture; and verbosity of HTTP and XML.

We believe that the service-oriented approach may be beneficial for the development of cyber-physical systems, but there is a need to test out different implementation solutions that fulfil the specific limitations and requirements of the target domain, including reliable communications, limited resources, and deterministic behaviour. In this paper we present a data-centric approach to RTSOA and evaluate it by implementing the proposed reference architecture for a robotic remote handling scenario. Remote handling involves human operators remotely controlling robots that perform tasks like maintenance or construction in dangerous environments, so reliability and performance of the system are vital for successful task completion.

2   Real-Time Service Orientation for Robotic Systems

2.1   Design Goals

We see the following as the main design goals for the real-time service-oriented architecture:

- Promote software **reuse** by producing reusable and decoupled software modules.
- Enable **composing** a working system out of reusable and existing services.
- Improve **interoperability** of heterogeneous systems (platform & programming language independence).

- Ensure **evolvability** [8] in the future; the architecture should support changing requirements and operating environments during the system lifecycle.
- Deterministic **real-time performance,** despite dynamically changing environment.
- **Dependable and fault tolerant** operation.
- Improve **cost-efficiency & ease of development;** the implementation should be able to use off-the-shelf solutions for tools, software and hardware, instead of purpose-built applications and devices.

2.2   Reference Architecture

The reference architecture, introduced in [5], is a general proof-of-concept control system platform for machine automation as an alternative to proprietary and specialized solutions. The platform is based on the ideas of real-time service orientation, introduced previously in this section, and emphasizes integrability, interoperability, maintainability and heterogeneity. Service orientation allows software components to be published and located locally or over a network.

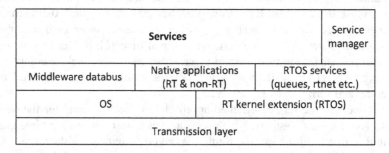

Fig. 1. Layered architectural view of the reference architecture

In section 3 we will describe the actual implementation of the reference architecture for a remote handling scenario. A high-level layered view of the reference architecture is shown in Fig. 1. Key concepts of the architecture are services, communication & information sharing mechanisms, composition, and fault-tolerance. These are described next.

2.3   Concurrency Model and Real-Time Performance

The choice of a concurrency model for the architecture directly affects decoupling of the modules and management of real-time constraints. Options for the concurrency model include processes, threads or call-back functions [1]. Each solution has its own pros and cons for ease of development and inter-process communication. For a service-based architecture, the process-based model (services as processes) makes most sense, as it is the most decoupled alternative. This decoupling provided by processes has benefits, including the possibility to more easily manage services at runtime and improved robustness.

A service can be defined as an independently developed, deployed, managed, and maintained software implementation that directly represents business tasks or devices.

A service can be defined by a verb which describes the function it implements, e.g. "generate a trajectory". Our implementation of services uses object orientation: service is an interface (virtual class) that has methods for starting, stopping, restarting etc. the service, which the service developer must implement. Services can use native applications and services provided by the operating system (e.g. APIs for communication).

2.4 Communication and Information Sharing

In order to communicate, components need some form of visibility or references between the communicating parties. However, this can lead to a tightly coupled system design that scales poorly. Examples of communication methods that impose coupling include sockets, remote method invocation and client-server model in general. A more decoupled solution is to use middleware based on the asynchronous publish/subscribe communication paradigm, which can be implemented as message-based like Java Message Service (JMS), or data-centric like Data Distribution Service (DDS)[1].

Another communication problem in distributed real-time systems is that networking can add unpredictable delays and unreliability to connections. Therefore we need to be able to set and monitor quality of service (QoS) parameters like reliability and how long the data is valid for each topic, so that the system can react appropriately if the QoS is compromised. QoS can be used to define if we want reliable sending (e.g. for commands) or just the most recent value as fast as possible (e.g. sensor measurements).

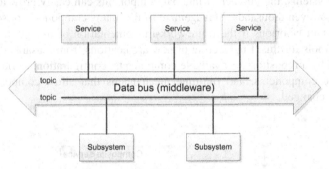

Fig. 2. Bus-based communication in SOA

The data-centric middleware can be used as a data bus between the services, as shown in Fig. 2: this is similar to the use of enterprise service bus (ESB) in enterprise SOAs. Another benefit of using a distributed middleware is a global data space where all data can be accessed; there is no central broker/repository that could act as a bottleneck or a single point of failure.

In an ideal situation we would have total location transparency for the services (no difference between accessing local and distributed services), but in order to achieve optimal real-time performance, the architecture uses separate communication methods

---

[1] A standard maintained by Object Management Group,
    http://portals.omg.org/dds/

for local and networked communications, termed local service bus and global service bus. The reference architecture itself is not committed to any specific communication standard, but the implementation uses DDS middleware and the communication mechanisms provided by the real-time operating system (RTOS) Xenomai[2].

Local connection of services as components and the use of DDS as a data-bus for distributed communications combine the strengths of component and service approaches, and provides optimal real-time performance in both cases. DDS can be used on low-end embedded systems to read and send sensor information, whereas XML-based solutions would be too heavy, and would necessitate a separate solution.

- Global service bus: DDS was chosen since it implements asynchronous data-centric publish/subscribe model and provides QoS management, making it suitable for cyber-physical systems, which place a heavy emphasis on sending and receiving data.
- Local service bus: services can use RTOS message queues (an asynchronous "mailbox") or shared memory for local real-time communication between two services. The queue-based local communication is similar to the component wiring approach used in component-based software engineering.

2.5   Composition

In complex systems, the number of internal components can easily grow to the range of hundreds or even thousands. Management of this many components or services can be complex and laborious if the framework-implementation of the architecture does not provide tools for this. Engineering of new applications from reusable components is supported by a repository of available components, configuration services to select and combine components, and run-time mechanisms that allow components to be dynamically changed.

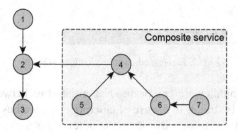

Fig. 3. Composite service (Key: circle denotes a service, arrow shows direction of data flow)

In the service-oriented architecture, higher level functionality can be implemented by creating composite services of the existing services, as shown in Fig. 3. Different means of implementing composition include programmatic, publish/subscribe, events

---

[2]   Real time Linux kernel extension and development framework,
      http://www.xenomai.org/

and orchestration engine. Since our reference architecture is based on the publish/subscribe model, this is a natural match for the composition mechanism, and enables flexible implementation of composite services. Services can be chained locally and globally to form new composite services. A single service can be part of multiple composite services and used by multiple other services, which can reduce the level of unnecessary redundancy in the system.

A repository provides a way to document and list available services or components. For SOAs this can be done by writing an interface description and saving it in the repository. Service registries, on the other hand, provide runtime information for finding and binding services. In our proposed data-centric approach, based on the use of a data bus, the middleware can handle registration of new publishers, and match subscribers to the provided data topics.

Service composition and management at runtime is handled dynamically through a local service manager, which controls spawning of new services. This makes it possible to modify a service and restart it on-the-fly, enabling faster deployment process by updating only related services, instead of having to recompile the whole system after every reconfiguration or update.

2.6   Fault Tolerance

Fault tolerance is a key requirement for the architecture, as many cyber-physical systems perform safety-critical tasks. A fault in the control system may endanger human lives (either directly or indirectly), cause operational downtime or damage the environment or equipment. Service-orientation can support error confinement with the modular architecture, based on the decoupling provided by the service model, although the system still needs to implement error detection and recovery.

Because of the decoupled design, developers cannot make the presumption that other services are always available, and must take the situation into account in their application code so that the service will react if a dependency goes down, e.g. because of failure or manual shutdown. The error handling approach based on decoupling is similar to the one used in the Erlang programming language, which can be summarized as "let it crash" [7]. In the event of an error, the process is terminated, presuming it is not an exception that can be handled. This forces other services to react and do error recovery, including entering their safe state. The architecture can still be prone to error propagation, so the services should be made fail-silent if possible, making it easier to detect faults.

In order to implement error detection, the system can use a service manager to detect crashed services based on heartbeat signals or monitoring the use of resources like CPU and memory. Unresponsive behaviour or unexpected increase in CPU usage for a service can indicate a fault in the service, and may endanger real-time performance of other services and cause unexpected and potentially dangerous behaviour. The service manager restarts the unresponsive service, which will put the system temporarily into a safe state by forcing other services to do error handling, according to the "let it fail" approach. Key principle is writing loosely coupled services, by forcing the developer to consider situations where the dependency services are not available or timing constraints are violated.

3 Implementation for a Remote Handling System

In order to test the proposed data-centric real-time approach to service-orientation, we implemented a remote handling control system (RHCS) for automated teleoperation of an industrial robot Comau SMART NM45-2.0, based on the reference architecture described in the previous section. A basic remote handling scenario consists of an operator using the web-server based Operation Management System (OMS) to send movement commands to the equipment controller. Virtual reality software (IHA3D) is used to visualize the position and movements of the robot.

Services deployed on the equipment controller for the remote handling system implementation are shown in Fig. 4. Service descriptions, real-time task priorities and execution periods are listed in Table 1.

Table 1. List of services used in the remote handling control system

Service name	Service description	Priority [0 .. 99]	Period [ms]
Trajectory-Generator	Generate a trajectory profile that the manipulator can follow from one point to another.	50	2
C4G	Interact with the low level control system of the manipulator.	91	2
C4GJoint-DataPub	Publish manipulator joint position data.	45	10
OmsCom	Read OMS commands and manipulator joint data; send commands to the trajectory generator to create new trajectories.	40	50
Measuring	Measure task execution time and jitter.	20	0.1

4 Evaluation of the Experiment

This section presents an evaluation of the problems and benefits of the proposed approach that could be observed with the implemented experimental system. The system is evaluated with the following criteria: reusability, interoperability, evolvability, real-time performance, fault tolerance, and ease of development. Dynamic composition performance depends greatly on the algorithm design [2] and it is not evaluated in this paper. Instead, a static composition is used.

Reused software includes TrajectoryGenerator service, C4G service and two subsystems (OMS and virtual reality). A service-based implementation avoids stovepipe system antipattern[3] as services are loosely coupled (no direct references to other services) and do not interfere with each other's namespaces etc., simplifying future reuse of services.

---

[3] http://sourcemaking.com/antipatterns/stovepipe-system

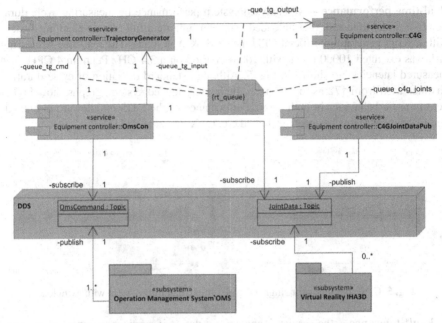

Fig. 4. Service deployment view for the system (Key: UML)

Interoperability of heterogeneous systems (machines and higher-level enterprise systems) is supported on any platform that has a compatible DDS implementation. DDS is available on several programming languages, therefore good programming language independence is provided. Interfaces to Web services, REST-based services and other communication platforms can be implemented with adapters.

Evolvability – the software must be able to accommodate new and changing requirements, including connections to unforeseen external sources. Ability to do this in the long term is especially important for industrial automation systems, because they have long expected lifetimes. This can be measured with evolvability, which describes the ability of software to accommodate future changes [8]. Performing a complete evolvability analysis is not reasonable in this context, so we focus on the changeability, extensibility and portability sub-characteristics:

- Changeability: Data typically has better consistency in the long run when compared to interfaces. However, if the data topics or queue configurations are changed or added, corresponding modifications must be implemented to both publishers and subscribers, but it is possible to provide extensions topics that provide the new or changed data, thus retaining compatibility with old implementations.
- Extensibility: New topics or functionality in the form of services can be added on-the-fly, without shutting down and recompiling the whole system. The run-time composition can be managed with the service manager, which can also be used to lazily launch necessary services (service chains).
- Portability is limited if RTOS-specific features like real-time queues are used.

Real-time performance – we analysed system performance by measuring cycle durations for a real-time task first unloaded and then running a full remote handling system with a script generating artificial CPU, network & disk loads. The real-time measuring task was executed 10000 times with 100 μs period on a 3.4 GHz Pentium 4 CPU. The measured latencies are shown in Fig. 5. Although standard deviation of cycle duration has increased from 172 ns to 410 ns in the heavily loaded system, graphs show highly deterministic behaviour in both cases. Performance of the DDS middleware in embedded real-time systems has been evaluated e.g. by Xiong et al. in [11].

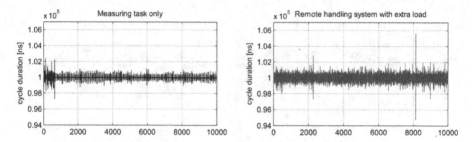

Fig. 5. Cycle durations for single task vs. remote handling system with extra load

Fault tolerance – the service manager can detect if services use more system resources than reserved at start-up, and force a restart. Other services need to react according to the "let it crash" error handling approach. After the services have been restarted, normal operation can be resumed if the fault was transient. A leaky bucket counter or an escalating retry timer can be used to distinguish transient faults from permanent ones.

An example case of error handling: the `TrajectoryGenerator` service is killed in the middle of running a trajectory to the `C4G` service, which controls the robot. `C4G` service detects that there is no new data available, and stops the movement of the robot, by ramping down the power in a controlled and safe fashion. Normal operation can be resumed when the `TrajectoryGenerator` is restarted.

Cost-efficiency & ease of development: the service-model is an intuitive approach for developers, as services can be interfaces to devices or related to tasks that must be accomplished. Linux-based development offers a variety of tools & drivers, reducing need for self-developed or proprietary choices. Communication configurations (for local queues) are currently hardcoded, so managing a large number of local communications becomes cumbersome, although the service manager can be used to start services. The local service communications should be standardized and details moved to external configuration files that could also be managed with tools to simplify management and reduce local coupling between services.

5   Conclusions

A dynamic module system based on services or components is necessary to manage complexity of embedded and distributed control systems. The module system should abstract the communications between modules, and provide tools for managing and deploying the configurations in order to improve software reusability and simplify development process, maintenance, and integration of new devices to the system.

In this paper we have presented our design concept for a service-based software architecture. Our proposed approach adapts the SOA paradigm with data-centric design, based on topic-based publish/subscribe middleware and RTOS. The experimental implementation of the architecture demonstrates integration of heterogeneous subsystems with the service-based control system through a scalable middleware-based data bus. The control system is based on an open RTOS and has deterministic real-time capabilities. Although all composition features in the prototype are not fully implemented, it provides contribution by testing the data-centric approach to implementing RTSOA.

References

1. Calisi, D., Censi, A., Iocchi, L., Nardi, D.: Design choices for modular and flexible robotic software development: the OpenRDK viewpoint. Journal of Software Engineering for Robotics 3(1), 13–27 (2012)
2. Tsai, W., Lee, Y.-H., Cao, Z., Chen, Y., Xiao, B.: RTSOA: Real-Time Service-Oriented Architecture. In: Proceedings of the 2nd IEEE International Symposium on Service-Oriented System Engineering (SOSE 2006), pp. 49–56. IEEE (2006)
3. Cucinotta, T., Mancina, A., Anastasi, G., Lipari, G., Mangeruca, L., Checcozzo, R., et al.: A Real-Time Service-Oriented Architecture for Industrial Automation. IEEE Transactions on Industrial Informatics 5(3), 267–277 (2009)
4. Moussa, H., Gao, T., Yen, I.-L., Bastani, F., Jeng, J.-J.: Toward effective service composition for real-time SOA-based systems. Service Oriented Computing and Applications 4(Special Issue: RTSOAA), 17–31 (2010)
5. Hahto, A., Rasi, T., Mattila, J., Koskimies, K.: Service-oriented architecture for embedded machine control. In: International Conference on Service-Oriented Computing and Applications. IEEE (2011)
6. Machado, A., Ferraz, C.: Guidelines for performance evaluation of web services. In: Proc. of the 11th Brazilian Symp. on Multimedia and the Web, WebMedia 2005, pp. 1–10. ACM (2005)
7. Armstrong, J.: Making reliable distributed systems in the presence of software errors. Dissertation. Royal Institute of Technology, Stockholm (2003)
8. Pei-Breivold, H., Crnkovic, I., Larsson, M.: A systematic review of software architecture evolution research. Inf. and Software Technol. 54(1), 16–40 (2012)
9. Panahi, M., Nie, W., Lin, K.-J.: A Framework for real-time service-oriented architecture. In: 2009 IEEE Conf. on Commerce and Enterp. Comput., pp. 460–467. IEEE (2009)
10. Garces-Erice, L.: Building an Enterprise Service Bus for Real-Time SOA: A Messaging Middleware Stack. In: 33rd Annual IEEE International Computer Software and Applications Conference, COMPSAC 2009, pp. 79–84. IEEE (2009)
11. Xiong, M., Parsons, J., Edmondson, J., Nguyen, H., Schmidt, D.C.: Evaluating the performance of publish/subscribe platforms for information management in distributed real-time and embedded systems (2011)

Contract-Based Compositional Scheduling Analysis for Evolving Systems*

Tayfun Gezgin[1], Stefan Henkler[1], Achim Rettberg[2], and Ingo Stierand[2]

[1] Institute for Information Technology (OFFIS)
[2] Carl von Ossietzky University Oldenburg

Abstract. The objective of this work is the analysis and verification of distributed real-time systems. Such systems have to work in a timely manner in order to deliver the desired services. We consider a system architecture with multiple computation resources. The aim is to work out a compositional state-based analysis technique to determine exact response times and to validate end-to-end deadlines. Further, we consider such systems in a larger context, where a set of systems work in a collaborative and distributed fashion. A major aspect of such collaborative systems is the dynamic evolution. New systems can participate, existing systems may leave because of failures, or properties may change. We use contracts to encapsulate systems which work in a collaborative manner. These contracts define sound timing bounds on services offered to the environment. When some systems evolve, only those parts which changed need to be re-validated.

Keywords: Compositional Analysis, Real-Time Systems, Scheduling Analysis, Model Checking, Abstraction Techniques.

1 Introduction

For safety-critical distributed systems it is crucial that they adhere to their specifications, as the violation of a requirement could lead to very high costs or even threats to human life. One crucial aspect for safety critical systems is that they have to work in a timely manner. Therefore, in order to develop safe and reliable systems, rigorous analysis techniques of timing-dependent behaviour are necessary. In literature, basically there are two approaches for scheduling analysis of distributed real-time systems. The classical approach is a holistic one, as it was worked out by e.g. Tindell and Clark [12]. Here, local analysis is performed evaluating fixed-point equations. The analysis is very fast and is able to handle large systems evaluating performance characteristics like time and memory

* This work was partly supported by European Commission funding the Large-scale integrating project (IP) proposal under ICT Call 7 (FP7-ICT-2011-7) Designing for Adaptability and evolutioN in System of systems Engineering (DANSE) (No. 287716), and by the German Research Council (DFG) as part of the Transregional Collaborative Research Center 'Automatic Verification and Analysis of Complex Systems' (SFB/TR 14 AVACS).

G. Schirner et al. (Eds.): IESS 2013, IFIP AICT 403, pp. 272–282, 2013.

consumption. Unfortunately, it delivers very pessimistic results when inter-ECU task dependencies exist. In [10] activation pattern for tasks are described by upper and lower arrival curves realizing a more *compositional* analysis method. Based on this work a compositional scheduling analysis tool, called SymTA/S, was created by SymtaVision. The concept has been developed by Kai Richter et.al. [8], and was improved and extended in several works, e.g. [9]. The main idea behind SymTa/S is to transform event streams whenever needed and to exploit classical scheduling algorithms for local analysis. This concept is very fast and is able to handle large systems, but typically yields pessimistic results.

The second approach is based on model checking, and has been illustrated for example in [5,4]. Here, all entities like tasks, processors, and schedulers are modeled in terms of timed automata. The advantage of this approach is that one gets exact solutions with respect to the modeled scheduling problem. As the state space of the analyzed system is preserved, checking complex characteristics like safety properties is possible. Unfortunately, the approach is not scalable, as the state space of the whole architecture is generated in one single step.

Our approach for scheduling analysis combines both analytical and model checking methods. Analogous to [5] we consider the full state space for analysis, where all inter-leavings and task dependencies are preserved. For this, the state space of the entire system architecture is constructed in a compositional manner. Based on the state space of a resource, response times are determined. Further, we propose a concept in order to handle timing properties of evolving systems. Evolving systems are such systems, where parts can change during run-time. Changes can occur due to failures and reconfigurations, or when new tasks are allocated to existing resources. When such a part of the system changes, it is desirable to only re-validate this part locally without the rest of the system.

Next, we present in Section 2 the foundation of our approach. In Section 3 we introduce operations on symbolic transition systems in order to realize our compositional analysis. In Section 3.3, we present our state-based analysis technique. The contract based approach for evolving systems is illustrated in Section 4, and finally we give a conclusion.

2   Fundamentals

In this work we consider system architectures consisting of sets of processing units (ECU). A set of tasks is allocated to each ECU. Our goal is to

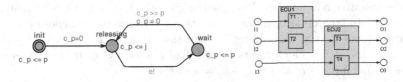

Fig. 1. Left: characterization of event streams; Right: example architecture

determine for each task corresponding response times, and whether all task deadlines and end-to-end deadlines are satisfied. More specific, a task is a tuple $\tau = (bcet, wcet, d, pr)$, where $bcet, wcet \in \mathbb{N}_{\geq 0}$ are the best and worst case execution times with respect to the allocated ECU with $bcet \leq wcet$, $d \in \mathbb{N}_{\geq 0}$ is its deadline determining the maximal allowed time frame from release time to task termination, and $pr \in \mathbb{N}_{\geq 0}$ is the fixed priority of the task. We will refer to the elements of a tasks by indexing, e.g. $bcet_\tau$ for task τ. The set of all tasks is called T. Independent tasks are triggered by events of a corresponding event stream (ES). An event stream $ES = (p, j)$ is characterized by a period p and a jitter j with $p, j \in \mathbb{N}_{\geq 0}$. Such streams can be characterized by upper and lower occurrence curves as introduced in the real-time calculus [11] or timed automata (introduced in the next section) like illustrated in the left part of Figure 1. In this work we will restrict to event streams where $j_\tau < p_\tau$ for all $\tau \in$ T. Also more general event streams with bursts would be possible. Automata for such event streams were presented in [6]. Task dependencies are captured by connecting corresponding tasks, like e.g. in Figure 1 where t_3 depends on t_2.

Each ECU in a system is modeled by the tuple $ecu = (\mathcal{T}, Sch, \mathcal{R}, \mathcal{S}, \mathcal{A})$. A mapping $\mathcal{T} : \mathsf{T} \to \mathbb{B}$ determines the set of tasks that are allocated to the ECU. For each ECU, a scheduling policy Sch is given. Three additional state dependent functions provide dynamic book keeping needed to perform scheduling analysis: (i) a ready map $\mathcal{R} : \mathsf{T} \to \mathbb{B}$ determines tasks, which are released but to which no computation time has been allocated up to now, (ii) a start delay map $\mathcal{S} : \mathsf{T} \to [t_1, t_2]$ with $t_1, t_2 \in \mathbb{N}_{>0}$ which determines the delay interval for a task getting from status *released* to *run*, and (iii) an active task map $\mathcal{A} : \mathsf{T} \to [t_1, t_2]$ with $t_1, t_2 \in \mathbb{N}_{>0}$ which determines the interruption times of tasks. This map is ordered and the first element determines the currently running task.

2.1   Timed Automata: Syntax and Semantics

Timed automata [1] are finite automata extended with a finite set of real-valued variables called clocks. Here, we define syntax and semantics of timed automata as employed by Uppaal. Uppaal adapts timed safety automata introduced in [7]. In such automata, progress is enforced by means of local invariants. States (or locations) may be associated with a timing constraint defining upper bounds on clocks. Let C be a set of clocks. A clock constraint is defined by the syntax $\varphi ::= c_1 \sim t \mid c_1 - c_2 \sim t \mid \varphi \wedge \varphi$, where $c_1, c_2 \in C$, $t \in \mathbb{Q}_{\geq 0}$ and $\sim \in \{\leq, <, =, > , \geq\}$. The set of all clock constraints over the set of clocks C is denoted by $\Phi(C)$. Valuation of a set of clocks C is a function $\nu : C \to \mathbb{R}_+$ assigning each clock in C a non-negative real number. We denote $\nu \models \varphi$ the fact that a clock constraint φ evaluates to true under the clock valuation ν. We use 0_C to denote the clock valuation $\{c \mapsto 0 \mid c \in C\}$, abbreviate the time shift by $\nu + d := \nu(c) + d$ for all $c \in C$, and define clock resets for a set of clocks $\varrho \subseteq C$ by $\nu[\varrho \mapsto 0]$ with $\nu[\varrho \mapsto 0](c) = 0$ if $c \in \varrho$, and $\nu[\varrho \mapsto 0] = \nu(c)$ else.

Definition 1 (Timed Automaton).
A Timed Automaton *(TA) is a tuple* $A = (L, l^0, \Sigma, C, R, I)$ *where*

- *L is a finite, non-empty set of locations, and $l^0 \in L$ is the initial location,*
- *Σ is a finite alphabet of channels, and C is a finite set of clocks,*
- *$R \subseteq L \times \Sigma \times \Phi(C) \times 2^C \times L$ is a set of transitions. A tuple $r = (l, \sigma, \varphi, \varrho, l')$ represents a transition from location l to location l' annotated with the action σ, constraint φ, and a set ϱ of clocks which are reset.*
- *$I : L \to \Phi(C)$ is a mapping which assigns an invariant to each location,*

The semantics of timed automata is given by timed transition systems.

Definition 2 (Timed Transition System).   *Let $A_i = (L_i, l_i^0, \Sigma_i, C_i, R_i, I_i)$ with $i \in \{1, ..., n\}$ be a network of timed automata with pairwise disjoint sets of clocks and alphabets. The semantics of such a network is defined in terms of a timed transition system $\mathcal{T}(A_1 \parallel ... \parallel A_n) = (Conf, Conf^0, C, \Sigma, \to)$, where*

- *$Conf = \{(l, \nu) \mid l \in L_1 \times ... \times L_n \wedge \nu \models \bigwedge_{j=1}^n I_j(l_j)\}$ is the set of configurations, and $Conf^0 = (l^0, 0_C)$, where $l^0 = (l_1^0, ..., l_n^0)$ is the initial location and 0_C is the initial clock valuation,*
- *$C = C_1 \cup ... \cup C_n$, $\Sigma = \Sigma_1 \cup ... \cup \Sigma_n$,*
- *$\to \subseteq Conf \times (\Sigma \cup \mathbb{R}_+) \times Conf$ is the transition relation. A transition $((l, \nu), \lambda, (l', \nu'))$, also denoted by $(l, \nu) \xrightarrow{\lambda} (l', \nu')$, has one of the following types.*
  - *A flow transition $(l, \nu) \xrightarrow{t} (l, \nu + t)$ with $t \in \mathbb{R}_+$ can occur, if $\nu + t \models \bigwedge_{j=1}^n I_j(l_j)$.*
  - *A discrete transition $(l, \nu) \xrightarrow{\lambda} (l', \nu')$ with $l' = l[l_i \to l_i']$ and $\lambda \in \Sigma$ can occur, if for some $i \in \{1, ..., n\}$ it holds that $(l_i, \lambda_i, \varphi_i, \varrho_i, l_i') \in R_i$, such that $\nu \models \varphi_i$, $\nu' = \nu[\varrho_i \mapsto 0]$ and $\nu' \models \bigwedge_{j=1}^n I_j(l_j')$.*

The function $l[l_i \to l_i']$ for a location vector $l = (l_1, ..., l_i, ..., l_n)$ represents the location vector $l = (l_1, ..., l_i', ...l_n)$. As the set of configurations is infinite, [1] gives a finite representation which is called region graph. In [2] a more efficient data structure called zone graph was presented. A zone represents the maximal set of clock valuations satisfying a corresponding clock constraint. Let $g \in \Phi(C)$ be a clock constraint, the induced set of clock valuations $D_g = \{\nu \mid \nu \models g\}$ is called a clock zone. Let $D^\uparrow = \{\nu + d \mid \nu \in D \wedge d \in \mathbb{R}_+\}$ and $D[\varrho \to 0] = \{\nu[\varrho \mapsto 0] \mid \nu \in D\}$. The finite representation of a timed automaton is given by a symbolic transition system.

Definition 3 (Symbolic Transition System).   *Let A be a network of timed automata with pairwise disjoint sets of clocks and alphabets. The symbolic transition system (zone graph) of A is a tuple $STS(A) = (S, S^0, \to)$ where*

- *$S = \{\langle l, D_\varphi \rangle \mid l \in L_1 \times ... \times L_n, \varphi \in \Phi(C)\}$ is the symbolic state set, and $S^0 = \langle l^0, 0_C \rangle$ is the initial state,*
- *$\to \subseteq S \times S$ is the symbolic transition relation with*
  - *$\langle l, D \rangle \to \langle l, D^\uparrow \cap D_{I(l)} \rangle$, where $I(l) = \bigwedge_{j=1}^n I_j(l_j)$*
  - *$\langle l, D \rangle \to \langle l', (D \cap D_{\varphi_i})[\varrho_i \to 0] \cap D_{I(l')} \rangle$ where $l' = l[l_i \to l_i']$, if there is a $i \in \{1, ..., n\}$ such that $(l_i, \lambda_i, \varphi_i, \varrho_i, l_i') \in R_i$.*

Note that for the general case some so called normalization operations on zones are necessary. If we build the symbolic transition system for an automaton containing clocks without a ceiling, i.e. some maximal reachable upper bound, it will lead to infinite sets of symbolic states. Nevertheless, for our cases the above definition will be sufficient as we always will have ceilings for all clocks. Please refer to [2] for more details on zone normalization operations.

3 Compositional Analysis

We build the state spaces - i.e. the symbolic transition systems (STS) - of each resource successively. These state spaces contain the response times of the allocated tasks. To construct the STS of a resource, besides the behaviour of the *scheduler* and characteristics of the allocated tasks, an *input STS* describing the activation times of the tasks is necessary. Generally, the inputs of the tasks are originated from different sources, such that multiple input STSs are given and we have first to build the product of these STS. As an example, consider Figure 1: to compute the STS of $ECU2$, we need the activation behaviour of task t_4, which is given by the event stream $I3$, while the input for t_3 is given by the output STS of resource $ECU1$. Further, the input STS of a resource can include behaviour which is not relevant for the computation of the resource STS. In the above example, to compute the STS of $ECU2$, only the part of the state space of $ECU1$ containing the behaviour of task t_2 is relevant. We can skip the part of the state space, in which detailed information about task t_1 is present.

In the following, we will first introduce both operations on STS, i.e. the abstraction operation in Section 3.1 and the product computation in Section 3.2. The construction of the STS of a resource is detailed in Section 3.3.

3.1 State Abstraction

In general, an abstraction function is defined as $\alpha : S \rightarrow S'$, where $S' \subseteq S$ for a state set S. In the context of scheduling analysis we will define in the following the state space of our considered problem domain. Then, we will introduce two specific abstraction functions, one operating on zones and one on locations. These two abstraction functions will then be combined and applied to our problem domain.

Considered State Space. To capture the initial non-determinism of the input event streams of n independent tasks of a ECU as defined in the previous section, the corresponding STS consists of 2^n locations. Let $L = \{0, (l^1), ... (l^n), (l^1, l^2), ..., (l^1, ..., l^n)\}$ be a set of discrete locations over index set $I = \{1, ..., n\}$. The location (l^i) indicates that an instance of task τ_i has already been released at least once. Analogously, location $(l^1, ..., l^n)$ indicates that all tasks have already been released at least once.

Besides the set of locations the considered state set is defined over clock valuations over a set of clocks C. For each *independent* task τ two types of clocks are needed, i.e. (i) clocks which trace the periodical activation of each task ($c_p(\tau)$ for task τ), and (ii) clocks which trace the time frame from releasing a task up to the finish of computation ($c_{active}(\tau)$). In order to capture overlapping task activations, i.e., where multiple *task instances* t_i of task τ may be active at the same time, multiple clocks $c_{active}(t_i)$ exist, one for each task instance. We need multiple clocks as we rely on using simple *clocks* in order to realize our scheduling analysis with preemption, i.e. we cannot change the derivative of a clock. Otherwise, we would have so called stopwatch automata where a stopwatch is used to track the allocated execution times of tasks. For this class of automata the reachability problem is known to be undecidable [3]. As we need to use one separate clock per task instance, we need to know a priory the maximal number of possible parallel activations of one task. For *dependent* tasks we need only the second class of clocks as we do not have to trace the activation times. For a task set T we will denote with $clk(\mathsf{T})$ the set of clocks of all tasks in T. As an example, consider the right part of Figure 1, where we have the periodical clocks $c_p(t_1), c_p(t_2), c_p(t_3)$, and allocated computation time clocks $c_{active}(t_1), c_{active}(t_2), c_{active}(t_3), c_{active}(t_4)$.

Abstraction on Zones. Let $C' \subseteq C$. For a constraint $g \in \Phi(C)$ let $g_{|C'}$ be the constraint, where all propositions containing clocks of the set $C \backslash C'$ are removed. Analogously, for a constraint $g \in \Phi(C')$ let $g_{|C}$ be the constraint extended with propositions containing clocks in $C \backslash C'$. The extension is defined in such a way, that it does not affect the original zone, i.e. $D_g = (D_{g|C})_{|C'}$ and the new constraints are of the form $0 \leq c \leq \infty$ forall $c \in C \backslash C'$. For example, consider the sets $C = \{c_1, c_2\}, C' = \{c_2\}$ and the constraint $g = c_1 - c_2 \leq 3 \wedge c_1 \leq 5 \wedge c_2 \leq 1$. Then $g_{|C'} = c_2 \leq 1$. Further, we have $(g_{|C'})_{|C} = c_2 \leq 1 \wedge 0 \leq c_1 \leq \infty$. For a zone $D = \{\nu \mid \nu \models g\}$ defined over C we define the zone projection operation $D_{|C'} = \{\nu \mid \nu \models g_{|C'}\}$ accordingly. Note that we have $D_g \subseteq D_{g|C'}$.

Abstraction on Locations. Let a set of locations L over index set I be given. For $I' \subseteq I$ let $\alpha_{I'}(L)$ be the set of locations over index set I', where locations with indexes not in I' are left out. For this, consider for example $I' = I \backslash \{i\}$. Then $\alpha_{I'}(l^1, ..., l^i, ..., l^n) = (l^0, ..., l^{i-1}, l^{i+1}, ..., l^n)$. As abbreviation we will directly use tasks instead of explicit indexes, e.g. $\alpha_{\{\tau_i, \tau_j\}} := \alpha_{i,j}$.

Abstraction on States of Symbolic Transition Systems. With the introduced abstraction functions on both clock zones and sets of locations we can now define the abstraction function which abstracts sets of states of a STS. Note that these states are tuple over locations and zones. Let $T \subseteq \mathsf{T}_e$, where T_e is the set of tasks allocated to ECU e. The abstraction function abstracts from the state set of the STS of ECU e to the parts where only information about a chosen sub-task set T is kept:

$$\alpha_T : \langle l, D \rangle \rightarrow \langle \alpha_T(l), D_{clk(T)} \rangle. \tag{1}$$

This abstraction function induces the following over-approximated STS:

Definition 4. *Let STS $A = (S, S_0, \rightarrow)$ be a STS over a task set T. The induced abstraction for $T \subseteq \mathsf{T}$ from α_T is the STS $A' = (S', S'_0, \rightarrow')$ with*

- *$S' = \alpha_T(S)$ is the induced set of abstract states, and $S'_0 = \alpha_T(S_0)$ is the initial abstract state,*
- *$\rightarrow' \subseteq S' \times S'$ the abstract transition relation, where $a \rightarrow' b$ iff there exists a $s_1 \in \alpha_T^{-1}(a)$ and $s_2 \in \alpha_T^{-1}(b)$ such that $s_1 \rightarrow s'_2$.*

Due to the definition of the transition relation it is obvious that this abstraction yields an over-approximation of the original STS.

3.2 Product Construction

Let $A_i = (S_i, S_i^0, \rightarrow_i)$ for $i = \{1, ..., n\}$ be a set of STSs over disjoint clock sets C_i and alphabets Σ_i. In the following, we define the product construction $A = A_1 \times ... \times A_n$, which is a STS over clock set $C = C_1 \cup ... \cup C_n$. For each created state of the product STS we need to keep track from which input states, i.e. states of the input STSs $A_1, ..., A_n$, it resulted. For this, we introduce for each A_i the function ξ_i that maps each product STS state to a state of A_i. The initial state of the product is given by

$$\langle l^0, 0_C \rangle = \langle (l_1^0, ..., l_n^0), 0_{C_1} \cup ... \cup 0_{C_n} \rangle \tag{2}$$

where $\langle l_i^0, 0_{C_i} \rangle$ is the initial state of A_i. Note that $\xi_i(\langle l^0, 0_C \rangle) = \langle l_i^0, 0_{C_i} \rangle$. The time successor $\langle l, D' \rangle$ of state $\langle l, D \rangle$ is then determined by

$$\langle l, D' \rangle = \langle l, D^\uparrow \cap D'_{1|C} \cap ... \cap D'_{n|C} \rangle \tag{3}$$

where $\xi_i(\langle l, D \rangle) = \langle l_i, D'_i \rangle$ for $i \in \{1, ..., n\}$ are the time successors of the input states. Note that the zones from all STSs are extended to the global clock set C.

Starting from the computed time successor, to compute all possible discrete steps in the product transition system, *each* outgoing transition from *each* STS is tried to be *fired*. In fact, this is also done in Definition 3: whenever the guards of a transition are fulfilled, a discrete transition is enabled and can be fired. This is the case, when the intersection of the zone induced by the guard and the current zone is not empty. The discrete successors of a state $\langle l, D \rangle$ of the product STS are given by the following set:

$$dSucc(\langle l, D \rangle) = \{\langle l[l_i \rightarrow l'_i], D' \rangle \mid \langle l_i, D_i \rangle \rightarrow \langle l'_i, D'_i \rangle \wedge D' \neq \emptyset\} \tag{4}$$

where $D' = (D \cap \rho^{-1}(D'_i)_{|C})[\rho(D'_i) \rightarrow 0] \cap D'_{i|C}$ and $\langle l_i, D_i \rangle = \xi_i(\langle l, D \rangle)$ for all $i \in \{1, ..., n\}$. The function $\rho(D)$ represents the set of clocks, which are reseted in the corresponding zone and $\rho^{-1}(D)$ represents the symbolic state *before* the reset operation of the corresponding transition has been performed. A discrete step is possible, if the resulting zone is not empty.

3.3 Resource Graph Computation

In this section we will illustrate the construction of the state space of a resource. Due to the limited page size we will only sketch the idea of our algorithm here. In the following we will use the functions $i.lb()$ and $i.ub()$ to access the lower and upper bound of an interval i.

Listing 1.1. Main code *computeResourceSTS(STS S_{in}, Configuration c_{in})*

```
set  Ψ(⟨l⁰,0_C⟩)  and  ξ.add(⟨l⁰,0_C⟩,⟨l⁰_in,0_{C_in}⟩)
while(  Ψ.size  > 0  )
    ⟨l,D⟩  =  Ψ.pop() ,  ⟨l_in,D_in⟩ = ξ(⟨l,D⟩)
        forall (edge_in ∈ outgoingEdges(⟨l_in,D_in⟩)): computeSuccessor (⟨l,D⟩,edge_in)
    checkDeadlines()
```

The main algorithm for the computation of a resource STS is illustrated in Listing 1.1. The input parameters are an *input STS S_{in}* describing the task activation times, and some configuration data such as the scheduling policy and informations about the allocated tasks. Analogous to the computation of the product, we need to keep track for each of the resource state, from which input state (i.e. state of the input transition system) it resulted. For this, we introduce the function ξ which maps each resource STS state to an input STS state.

The algorithm starts by creating the initial symbolic state $s_0 = \langle l^0, C_0 \rangle$ of the resource STS. This state is added to a set Ψ, which determines the states, for which successors have to be computed. The initial state $\langle l^0_{in}, 0_{C_{in}} \rangle$ of the input transition system is set as the corresponding input state of s_0.

The possible successors of a state $\langle l, D \rangle$ are determined by the successors of the corresponding input state $\xi(\langle l, D \rangle)$. The computation of the successors of a resource state proceeds analogous to the successor computation of the product STS introduced in the previous section. For this, the algorithm iterates through all outgoing transitions of the corresponding input state defining either the set of tasks, which can be released, or the (single) time successor, and builds a set of corresponding successors of the resource state. If $edge_{in}$ defines the time successor $\langle l_{in}, D_{in} \rangle$, we get the time successor of the current resource state $\langle l, D \rangle$ by computing $D^{\uparrow} \cap D_{in|C}$. If a task instance t is running in state $\langle l, D \rangle$, we further intersect the zone with the response time of the running task, i.e. $c_{active}(t) \leq wcet_t + interruptTimes_t.ub()$.

If else $edge_{in}$ defines a discrete successor which constitutes to a release of a new instance of task τ, we need to perform a case distinction: If there is no running task in the current resource state $\langle l, D \rangle$ (i.e. when the active task map $\mathcal{A}_l$ in location l is empty), we build the successor resource state $\langle l', D' \rangle$ by intersecting the current resource D with the zone of the successor of the corresponding input state. The active task map $\mathcal{A}_l$ then gets the entry $(t_\tau, [0, 0])$.

Else when we have a running task, we have to determine, whether this task can finish its computation before a new instance of the task determined by $edge_{in}$ can be released. This is done as follows.

1. If the running task t cannot terminate, i.e. $c_{active}(t).ub() < bcrt_t$, we try to release a new task instance as defined in the input STS state. For this, the intersection of the current resource state and the successor state of the corresponding input state is computed. Two cases can occur here:

    (a) If the intersection results in an empty zone, the discrete step cannot be taken and the next input edge is considered.

(b) Else, a new instance of task τ can be released. The active task map $\mathcal{A}_l$ gets the new entry $(t_\tau, [0,0])$. Then, the next running task wrt. the considered scheduling policy is determined. At least the new state is added to the graph and the set Ψ'.

2. If a running task t will terminate $(c_{active}(t).lb() == wcrt_t)$, its execution time is accumulated to all interrupted tasks by incrementing their interrupt times in the active task map $\mathcal{A}_l$. Then we determine the next running task according to the scheduling policy. If we move the task t from the ready map to the active map (i.e. a previously released task which did not get computation time so far), we have to store the time frame from release to start of t in order to correctly determine its allocated execution time. This time frame is given by clock $c_{active}(t)$ and is stored in the start delay map $\mathcal{S}$. Further, we have to reset $c_{active}(t)$ as no computation time has been allocated so far. At least, we are *recursing computeSuccessor*$(\langle l', D' \rangle, \tau)$.

If $c_{active}(t).ub() \geq bcrt_t \wedge c_{active}(t).lb() \leq wcrt_t$ then both 1) and 2) are executed in this order.

Each state which is generated in the *computeSuccessor* method is added to the set Ψ. For all newly generated states Ψ' we determine whether a deadline is violated as follows.

$$\forall \langle l, D \rangle \in \Psi', t \in \mathcal{A}_l \cup \mathcal{R}_l : \ D_t.ub() \leq d_t. \tag{5}$$

If Equation 5 is violated or no state is left in Ψ, the algorithm terminates.

4   Contract Based Analysis

Systems in our context may evolve. Such an evolution is illustrated in Figure 2. The system *System1* is first composed of two resources which deliver some service to its environment. After some time a reconfiguration of this system may occur. In Figure 2 the system is changed to a new decomposition structure

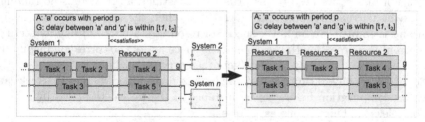

Fig. 2. Changing part of a system

consisting of three resources. Such reconfigurations would get necessary if for example some resources fail, loads of the tasks get larger, or new tasks are allocated to the system, such that new resources get necessary. If such systems are annotated by constraints determining the quality of the offered services, internal changes would not affect other systems, as these rely on the quality guarantees of the system. In the above example, a contract consisting of an assumption (A) and a guarantee (G) is annotated to the system. An assumption specifies how the context of the component, i.e. the environment from the point of view of the component, should behave. Only if the assumption is fulfilled, the component will behave as guaranteed. If now a change of a system occurs, we only need to check this part rather than all other systems. When a change occurs, we use the algorithm presented in Section 3.3 to re-validate the contract. This concept can be further extended to parts of Systems of Systems (SoS): if several systems cooperate in order reach some goals and to offer some services to their environment, these cooperating systems can again be annotated by such timing contracts. When a whole system is exchanged by another system in this part of the SoS, again only the STSs of the constituent systems of this part have to be build to re-validate the contract. As we do the analysis in a compositional manner, we further can reuse the STSs of these constituent systems, which are not affected by the changing system. This is for example the case, when they only deliver services to the changed systems and do not adhere on their services.

5   Conclusion and Future Work

In this work we presented a scheduling analysis technique for systems with multiple resources and potential preemptions of tasks. The state space of the entire system architecture is defined by symbolic transitions systems (STS) and is constructed in a compositional manner. For this, we introduced two operations on STSs, namely the product construction and the abstraction on parts of a STS. Further, we proposed a concept in order to handle timing properties of evolving systems. We proposed to encapsulate cooperating system by contracts, such that changes of such a part do not affect other systems. Currently, we are implementing our proposed concept. The implementation so far builds up the STS of the whole architecture and performs the response time analysis in a holistic manner. In future work we will validate our approach and compare it with related tools. We will investigate new abstraction techniques which will further boost the scalability of our approach.

References

1. Alur, R., Dill, D.L.: A theory of timed automata. Theor. Comput. Sci. 126(2), 183–235 (1994)
2. Bengtsson, J., Yi, W.: Timed automata: Semantics, algorithms and tools. In: Desel, J., Reisig, W., Rozenberg, G. (eds.) ACPN 2003. LNCS, vol. 3098, pp. 87–124. Springer, Heidelberg (2004)
3. Cassez, F., Larsen, K.: The Impressive Power of Stopwatches. In: Palamidessi, C. (ed.) CONCUR 2000. LNCS, vol. 1877, pp. 138–152. Springer, Heidelberg (2000)
4. David, A., Illum, J., Larsen, K.G., Skou, A.: Model-based framework for schedulability analysis using uppaal 4.1. In: Nicolescu, G., Mosterman, P.J. (eds.) Model-Based Design for Embedded Systems, pp. 93–119 (2009)

5. Fersman, E., Pettersson, P., Yi, W.: Timed automata with asynchronous processes: Schedulability and decidability. In: Katoen, J.-P., Stevens, P. (eds.) TACAS 2002. LNCS, vol. 2280, pp. 67–82. Springer, Heidelberg (2002)
6. Hendriks, M., Verhoef, M.: Timed automata based analysis of embedded system architectures. In: Parallel and Distributed Processing Symposium (April 2006)
7. Henzinger, T., Nicollin, X., Sifakis, J., Yovine, S.: Symbolic model checking for real-time systems. Information and Computation 111, 394–406 (1992)
8. Richter, K.: Compositional Scheduling Analysis Using Standard Event Models. PhD thesis, Technical University of Braunschweig, Braunschweig, Germany (2004)
9. Rox, J., Ernst, R.: Exploiting inter-event stream correlations between output event streams of non-preemptively scheduled tasks. In: Proceedings of the Conference on Design, Automation and Test in Europe, DATE, Leuven, Belgium (2010)
10. Thiele, L., Chakraborty, S., Gries, M., Maxiaguine, A., Greutert, J.: Embedded software in network processors - models and algorithms. In: Henzinger, T.A., Kirsch, C.M. (eds.) EMSOFT 2001. LNCS, vol. 2211, pp. 416–434. Springer, Heidelberg (2001)
11. Thiele, L., Chakraborty, S., Naedele, M.: Real-time calculus for scheduling hard real-time systems. In: IEEE International Symposium on Circuits and Systems (ISCAS), vol. 4, pp. 101–104 (2000)
12. Tindell, K., Clark, J.: Holistic schedulability analysis for distributed hard real-time systems. Microprocess. Microprogram. 40, 117–134 (1994)

Extending an IEEE 42010-Compliant Viewpoint-Based Engineering-Framework for Embedded Systems to Support Variant Management

André Heuer, Tobias Kaufmann, and Thorsten Weyer

paluno – The Ruhr Institute for Software Technology
University of Duisburg-Essen
Gerlingstr. 16
45127 Essen, Germany
{andre.heuer,tobias.kaufmann,thorsten.weyer}@paluno.uni-due.de

Abstract. The increasing complexity of today's embedded systems and the increasing demand for higher quality require a comprehensive engineering approach. The model-based engineering approach that has been developed in the project SPES 2020 (Software Platform Embedded Systems) is intended to comprehensively support the development of embedded systems in the future. The approach allows for specifying an embedded system from different viewpoints that are artefact-based and seamlessly integrated. It is compliant with the IEEE Std. 1471 for specifying viewpoints for architectural descriptions. However, the higher demand for individual embedded software necessitates the integration of variant management into the engineering process of an embedded system. A prerequisite for the seamless integration of variant management is the explicit consideration of variability. Variability allows for developing individual software based on a set of common core assets. Yet, variability is a crosscutting concern as it affects all related engineering disciplines and artefacts across the engineering process of an embedded system. Since the IEEE Std. 1471 does not support the documentation of crosscutting aspects, we apply the concept of perspectives to IEEE Std. 1471's successor (IEEE Std. 42010) in order to extend the SPES engineering approach to support continuous variant management.

1   Introduction

Embedded systems bear more and more functionality, must satisfy a growing number of crucial quality demands, and additionally have a higher degree of complexity and inter-system relationships. Key players of the German embedded systems community were involved in the project SPES 2020 (Software Platform Embedded Systems) which was a joined project funded by the German Federal Ministry of Education and Research[1]. SPES 2020 aimed at developing a model-based engineering approach that addresses the challenges mentioned above (cf. [4]).

---

[1] See http://spes2020.informatik.tu-muenchen.de/

G. Schirner et al. (Eds.): IESS 2013, IFIP AICT 403, pp. 283–292, 2013.

The project consortium represented important industrial domains in Germany: automation, automotive, avionics, energy, and healthcare. In the project, the partners from industry and academia jointly developed an artefact-centred, model-based engineering framework for embedded systems that is based on the IEEE Standard 1471 (cf. [9]). This framework is called the SPES Modelling Framework (or short: SPES MF). The SPES MF focusses on the software within an embedded system (cf. [10]) and allows for a seamless engineering of embedded systems, from the requirements to the technical architecture of the system under development (SUD) across multiple abstraction layers (cf. [4]).

Beside the need for seamless model-based engineering, there is a higher demand for the development of different variants of embedded systems. Variant management consists of activities to define variability, to manage variable artefacts, activities to resolve variability and to manage traceability information that are necessary to fulfil these activities (cf. [15]) in each step within the engineering process.

Thereby, variability is defined as the ability to adapt [17], i.e. a development artefact can exist in different shapes at the same time (cf. [15]). The current version of the SPES MF does not support the systematic consideration of variants. As a consequence, concepts and techniques are required for extending the SPES MF to support variant management in the engineering process of an embedded system. A prerequisite for that is the seamless consideration of variability across the engineering artefacts (cf. [3]).

Variability may cause crosscutting changes, for example, in the requirements and the architecture by adapting a system for a specific variant (cf. [14]). A new requirement may impose changes to the architecture. Thus, variability can be seen as a crosscutting concern. Since variability affects all existing viewpoints of the SPES MF, the SPES MF needs to be adapted to deal with such crosscutting concerns. In [10], perspectives are recommended to address crosscutting concerns. We define a Variability Perspective for SPES MF that supports the development of different variants of systems in a systematic and comprehensive way.

The paper is structured as follows: Section 2 describes the fundamentals for extending the SPES MF with respect to the consideration of variability in the different engineering artefacts. Section 3 describes our extension of the SPES MF to integrate the Variability Perspective in the SPES MF. Section 4 reviews the related work on integrating variability in architectural frameworks. Section 5 gives a conclusion and sketches the future research.

2   Fundamentals

In order to cope not only with the functionality and complexity of a single SUD but also with the variability of a number of similar embedded systems, this section describes the fundamentals to extend the SPES MF for supporting variant management.

2.1   Variant Management in the Engineering of Embedded Systems

Variability is defined as the ability to adapt. Thus, the variability of an embedded system is defined as the ability to adapt the system with regard to a specific context (e.g. context of use, cf. section 1).

It is widely accepted in industry and academia that variability should be documented explicitly in a variability model, which is already a well-proven paradigm in the software product line community (cf., e.g., [5], [12], [15]). This explicit documentation of variability is based on two ontological concepts and their relations. The *variability subject* is defined as a variable item of the real world or a variable property of such an item, e.g. the paint of a car (cf. [15]). The *variability object* is defined as a particular instance of a variability subject, e.g. red paint. A *variant* is a running system that is constituted of a selected set of variability objects. Consequently, in the engineering of variability-intensive embedded systems, *variant management* can be characterized as a process that complements the original engineering process (e.g. requirements engineering, architectural design) by systematically considering variants in each of the engineering disciplines. Performing continuous variant management additionally implies that the relationships of variants are seamlessly documented on a semantic level across the engineering process.

2.2   Viewpoint-Specifications Based on IEEE Std. 1471 and IEEE Std. 42010

The IEEE Std. 1471 [9] and its current successor IEEE Std. 42010 [10] introduce a conceptual framework for architectural descriptions (cf. section 1). The key concept of both frameworks is the *architectural viewpoint* (or short: *viewpoint*). To reduce the complexity, the architectural description of a system is typically divided into a number of interrelated views. A viewpoint can be characterized as a structured specification that supports the definition of such a *view* on the system. The specification of a viewpoint consists of the stakeholders' concerns (e.g. specifying the logical architecture) that are addressed by the view together with conventions for creating that view (e.g. the underlying ontology, the ontological relationships to other views, and rules for evaluating the quality of the corresponding views).

Beside the different interrelated views of a system, typically, a system architecture also bears certain crosscutting properties, i.e. properties that have an ontological grounding in each view or an ontological relationship to each one of the views. According to IEEE Std. 42010, architectural models can be shared across multiple views expressing the ontological relationships of the views. This is one possible implementation of the concept of *architectural perspectives* (or short: *perspectives*) introduced by ROZANSKI and WOODS in [16].

2.3   The SPES 2020 Modelling Framework

The SPES MF supports the development of embedded systems by focussing on the following principles (cf. [4]): *distinguishing between problem and solution, explicitly considering system decomposition, seamless model-based engineering, distinguishing between logical and technical solutions*, and *continuous engineering of crosscutting system properties*. These principles manifest themselves within the SPES MF in two orthogonal dimensions, the SPES viewpoints and the SPES abstraction layers.

The SPES MF Viewpoints. The different stakeholders (e.g. requirements engineers, functional analysts, solution architects) in the engineering process of an embedded system have different concerns. Based on the separation of concerns principle, the individual concerns of stakeholders are addressed by certain views that are, in accordance to IEEE Std. 1471, governed by viewpoints in the SPES MF. Each viewpoint addresses certain concerns in the engineering process of an embedded system. The SPES MF differentiates between the following four SPES viewpoints: the *SPES Requirements Viewpoint* addresses the structured documentation and analysis of requirements; the *SPES Functional Viewpoint* addresses the structured documentation and analysis of system functions; the *SPES Logical Viewpoint* addresses structured documentation and analysis of the logical solution, and the *SPES Technical Viewpoint* addresses the structured documentation and analysis of the technical solution.

The SPES MF Abstraction Layers. To reduce the complexity of the engineering process a coarse-grained engineering "problem" is decomposed into a number of fine-grained engineering problems following the strategy of *divide and conquer*, i.e. the composition of the fine-grained solutions is a solution for the coarse-grained engineering problem. Each time, a coarse-grained engineering subject is decomposed into a number of fine-grained engineering subjects; a new abstraction layer is created. Since the number of abstraction layers depends on the properties of the individual engineering context of an embedded system, the SPES MF does not define a certain number of abstraction layers. However the SPES MF provides the mechanism to create new abstraction layers that can be used by engineers to decompose the overall engineering problem to a level of granularity at which the complexity of the fine-grained systems is manageable without the need of performing another step of decomposition.

3   Integrating Variability in the SPES MF

To extend the SPES MF for supporting continuous variant management, firstly, the nature of variability is analysed. Secondly, a general concept for extending the SPES MF is defined and thirdly the specification of the Variability Perspective is presented.

3.1   An Insight into the Nature of Variability within the SPES MF Viewpoints

Variability can affect the SPES viewpoints in different ways. Within the SPES Requirements View the requirements of the SUD are specified by using different types of models (e.g. goal models, scenario models). For instance, requirements in terms of system goals (cf. e.g. [8]) are specifying the intention of the stakeholders with regard to the objectives, properties, or use of the system [8]. A variable goal thus represents an objective that may only apply in a specific usage context of the system. Goals can also be contradictory, for example, if a goal of a certain stakeholder excludes a goal of another stakeholder in a specific usage context of the system. In this situation, these two goals can never be included together in the same variant of a system. Thus, variability in goals may have its origin in variability concerning the stakeholders that have to be considered or in variable intentions of one stakeholder with respect to a different usage context.

In contrast to the Requirements View, the Technical View defines hardware components which implement specific functions or realize logical components. Variability on the Technical View could be embodied, for example, by different pins of hardware pieces, or by a different clock speed of a bus. It is obvious that the ontological meaning of variability in the Technical Viewpoint is different from the ontological meaning of variability in the Requirements Viewpoint. In the same way we come to the general conclusion that the ontological meaning of variability is different in all of the SPES viewpoints.

3.2   General Concept for Extending the SPES MF for Variant Management

A specific aspect where variability occurs, for instance, in the Requirements View of the SUD is on the ontological level that is different as a variable aspect in the Technical View (❶ in Fig. 1).Variability within the Requirements View can be modelled in an explicit *variability artefact* (i.e. variability model) with a precise ontological relationship to the *engineering artefacts* of the Requirements View (❷ in Fig. 1), whereas variability within the Technical Viewpoint can be documented in an explicit variability model that has a precise ontological relationships to the engineering artefacts of the Technical Viewpoint. This concept can also be applied to other viewpoints and results in distinct variability models for each of the SPES viewpoints.

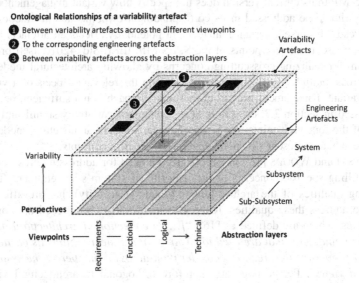

Fig. 1. Variability models in the different viewpoints and their relations

As already mentioned in Section 2.3, today's embedded software is engineered across different abstraction layers based on the SPES MF. Thus, most of the artefact types that are defined based on the underlying ontology of the viewpoints are used on each of the abstraction layers but with a different level of granularity of the engineering subject. On a subsystem layer in Fig. 1, for example, a component diagram models the structure of the SUD. On this level, an interface can be variable. However, on the sub-subsystem layer in Fig. 1, for example, the structure of the different components can also be modelled by a component diagram and interfaces can also be variable and both variable interfaces are related to each other. Additionally, the definition of a variability subject on a higher abstraction layer may lead to different alternatives that impose new variability objects representing different decompositions on a lower abstraction level. Thus, not only artefacts of different types, but also of the same type across different abstraction layers (❸ in Fig. 1) are affected.

The general concept of integrating variability in the SPES MF is also based on the empirical findings and conceptualizations of AMERICA ET AL. [1] as well as THIEL and HEIN [18]. AMERICA ET AL., argue to explicitly document the possible design decisions, by documenting viewpoint relevant variability. Furthermore, they argue that the explicit documentation of choices leads to an increased awareness of such choices, which in turn is beneficial for the stakeholder communication. THIEL and HEIN are interpreting variability as a kind of quality of the architecture of a system in terms of its configurability and modifiability. Variability is materialized in the artefacts by changes or adaptations of specific elements, e.g. interfaces.

3.3   Specifying Crosscutting Aspects Conform to IEEE Std. 42010

The SPES MF in its current version does not specify how variant management and thus variability should be addressed in its corresponding viewpoints and abstraction layers. As we already discussed, variant management potentially affects all artefacts and consequently crosscuts all viewpoints of the SPES MF. IEEE Std. 42010 itself provides a mechanism for realizing crosscutting concerns by allowing architectural models to be shared across multiple views and thereby focus on the relevant aspects of a view. Regarding variant management, we belief that this approach is not sufficient, because, as we discussed in section 3.2, the ontological meaning of variability significantly differs in each of the four viewpoints. As a consequence, a shared architectural model would need to be able to represent viewpoint-specific ontological concepts.

ROZANSKI and WOODS [16] also recognized a need for addressing crosscutting aspects fulfilling specific concerns of the majority of system's stakeholders. They are identifying qualities of the architecture (e.g. safety, security) that are affecting all views. To address these qualities, ROZANSKI and WOODS introduced the concept of perspectives, which are defined as [16]: "[...] *a collection of architectural activities, tactics, and guidelines that are used to ensure that a system exhibits its particular set of related properties that require consideration across a number of the system's architectural views*". Perspectives are therefore orthogonal to architectural views. In [16] a perspective specification template is proposed that addresses the quality properties in an IEEE Std. 42010 based specification.

3.4   Specification of the Variability Perspective for the SPES MF

Since variability can be regarded as a quality property and therefore as a crosscutting concern of a system architecture, we extend the SPES MF by following the approach that is described in Section 3.3. To that end we use the template proposed in [16] for specifying the architectural perspective. An excerpt from the specification of the Variability Perspective is shown in Table 1.

Table 1. Excerpt from the specification of the Variability Perspective

Section	Content
Applicability	Each SPES MF view is affected: • When applying the Variability Perspective to the Requirements View, it guides the requirements engineering process of the SUD so that the variability of the requirements can be considered systematically. • When applying the Variability Perspective to the Functional View, it guides the functional design for the SUD so that the variability of the system functions can be considered systematically. • When applying the Variability Perspective to the Logical View, it guides the design of the logical architecture of the SUD so that the variability within of the logical architecture can be considered systematically. • When applying the Variability Perspective to the Technical View, it guides the design of the technical architecture of the SUD so that variability of the technical architecture can be considered systematically. Each SPES MF abstraction layer is affected: • When applying the Variability Perspective to an abstraction layer, it guides the systematic engineering of the engineering subjects within that layer so that the variability can be considered across all views of the engineering subject.
Concerns	• *Variability:* the ability of the SUD to be adapted to a different context, e.g. context of usage, technological context, economical context, legal context or organizational context. • *Quality properties of variability:* correctness, completeness, consistent and traceable to its origin and to corresponding engineering artefacts.
Activities	*Steps for applying the Variability Perspective to the Requirements View:* • *Identification of variability in the requirements of the SUD:* This step aims at identifying variability in the requirements that is originated by variable context properties. • *Documentation of variability in the requirements of the SUD:* This step aims at documenting the variability in the requirements. • *Analysis of variability in the requirements of the SUD:* This step aims at analysing the variability in the requirements, e.g. with respect to correctness, completeness and consistency. • *Negotiation of variability in the requirements of the SUD:* This step aims at negotiating the variability in the requirements, with the stakeholders of the SUD. • *Validation of the variability in the requirements of the SUD:* This step aims at analysing the variability in the requirements, e.g. with respect to correctness, completeness and consistency. *Steps for applying the Variability Perspective to the Functional View:* • [...] *Steps for applying the Variability Perspective to the Logical View:* • [...] *Steps for applying the Variability Perspective to the Technical View:* • *Identification of variability in the technical architecture of the SUD:* This step aims at identifying variability in the technical architecture that is originated by, for example, variable technical resources (e.g. processors, communication infrastructure) as well as variable sensors or actuators).

Table 1. *(Continued)*

Architectural tactics	*Context Analysis and Documentation:* for structured analysis and documentation of the context properties that are the origin of variability • *Orthogonal Variability Modelling:* for explicit documentation of variability and its relationship to engineering artefacts • *Model Checking:* [...]
Problems and pitfalls	Problems and pitfalls that may arise: • The increasing complexity of variable artefacts that increases the effort to keep the engineering artefacts consistent. • Complex variability models tend to be ambiguous und confusing, for example, false optional features that are part of every product because of constraints. • [...]

4   Related Work

Today, multiple frameworks for designing a system's architecture exist. All these frameworks share the concept of multiple architectural views. In this context, cross-cutting concerns are often considered as quality or system properties or non-functional as well as quality requirements of a SUD, which need special consideration when crafting a system's architecture.

In terms of documenting a system's architecture the standards IEEE Std. 1471 [9] and its successor IEEE Std. 42010 [10] provide a conceptual framework for specifying viewpoints governing views (cf. section 2.2). Another approach for documenting a system's architectural views is proposed in "Views and Beyond" [7], which is compliant to IEEE Std. 1471 (cf. [6]).

ZACHMAN proposes a Framework [21], which makes use of six different architectural representations (viewpoints). This framework does not state how crosscutting concerns should be addressed in detail.

The Reference Model of Open Distributed Processing (RM-ODP) [11] proposes five viewpoints, focusing on particular concerns within a system. In addition a set of system properties are defined including quality of service, but it is not addressed how these properties should be encountered during system development.

The rational unified process (RUP) makes use of The 4 + 1 View Model of Architecture, which was introduced in [13]. In RUP four different kinds of non-functional requirements are distinguished, which are subject to an iterative, scenario-based process determining the key drivers of architectural elements. But no explicit guidelines are given how non-functional requirements should be addressed in the architectural design phase.

Attribute-Driven Design (ADD) [20] is a method that can be described as an approach for defining a software architecture based on the software's quality attribute requirements. Essentially, ADD promotes a recursive design process decomposing a SUD making use of the architectural tactics introduced in [2], resulting in views that are compliant to [7], and consequently explicitly address crosscutting concerns.

The TOGAF framework uses the iterative Architecture Development Method (ADM), which contains an analysis of changes etc. in terms of their cross architectural impact. In its current version [18], the TOGAF framework encourages the use of IEEE Std. 42010 in order to craft the necessary viewpoints and views.

ROZANSKI and WOODS [16] take the 4+1 View Model of Architecture as foundation and provide an IEEE Std. 42010 compliant viewpoint catalogue. The stakeholders' requirements as well as the architecture are subject to an iterative architecture definition process. But in contrast to RUP, crosscutting concerns are explicitly addressed in terms of perspectives.

As motivated in subsection 2.3, software intensive embedded systems need special consideration during their engineering. The domain independent model-based engineering methodology of SPES, takes these special needs and challenges into account. In doing so, the IEEE Std. 1471 based viewpoints of the SPES MF are explicitly tailored to the needs of the development of software intensive embedded systems. The above described frameworks are of a more general nature and are consequently not directly applicable in the context of such systems. As motivated in subsection 3.1, variability affects multiple viewpoints and their artefacts. Consequently, it is our firm belief that variability has to be addressed explicitly. Therefore we decided to apply the approach by ROZANSKI and WOODS to the SPES MF in order to address variability explicitly.

5   Conclusion

The specification of the Variability Perspective is an essential means for supporting the continuous variant management across the whole engineering process of embedded systems, which are based on the SPES MF. This is done by defining how to seamlessly integrate, among others, the identification, documentation and analysis of variability and its relationships to the underlying engineering artefacts across the viewpoints and abstraction layers of the SPES MF. In our future work we will apply the extension of the SPES MF for variant management to three industrial case studies (a driver assistance system for vehicles, a mission control software in unmanned aerial vehicles, and a desalination plant) to gain deeper insights concerning the applicability and usefulness for supporting the continuous variant management in the engineering processes of embedded systems.

Acknowledgement. This paper was partially funded by the BMBF project SPES 2020_XTCore under grant 01IS12005C and the DFG project KOPI grant PO 607/4-1.

References

1. America, P., Rommes, E., Obbink, H.: Multi-view variation modeling for scenario analysis. In: van der Linden, F.J. (ed.) PFE 2003. LNCS, vol. 3014, pp. 44–65. Springer, Heidelberg (2004)
2. Bass, L., Clements, P., Kazman, R.: Software Architecture in Practice. Addison-Wesley, Reading (2003)

3. Broy, M.: Outlook. In: Pohl, K., Hönninger, H., Achatz, R., Broy, M. (eds.) Model-Based Engineering of Embedded Systems – The SPES 2020 Methodology. Springer, Heidelberg (2012)
4. Broy, M., Damm, W., Henkler, S., Pohl, K., Vogelsang, A., Weyer, T.: Introduction to the SPES Modeling Framework. In: Pohl, K., Hönninger, H., Achatz, R., Broy, M. (eds.) Model-Based Engineering of Embedded Systems – The SPES 2020 Methodology. Springer, Heidelberg (2012)
5. Clements, P., Northrop, L.: Software Product Lines – Practices and Patterns. Addison-Wesley, Boston (2002)
6. Clements, P.: Comparing the SEI's Views and Beyond Approach for Documenting Software Architectures with ANSI-IEEE Std. 1471-2000. Technical Report, Software Engineering Institute, Carnegie Mellon University, CMU/SEI-2005-TN-017 (2005)
7. Clements, P.: Documenting software architectures: views and beyond. Addison-Wesley, Boston (2011)
8. Daun, M., Tenbergen, B., Weyer, T.: Requirements Viewpoint. In: Pohl, K., Hönninger, H., Achatz, R., Broy, M. (eds.) Model-Based Engineering of Embedded Systems – The SPES 2020 Methodology. Springer, Heidelberg (2012)
9. IEEE Recommended Practice for Architectural Description of Software Intensive Systems. IEEE Standard 1471-2000 (2000)
10. ISO/IEC/IEEE Systems and Software Engineering – Architecture description. ISO/IEC/IEEE Standard 42010:2011 (2011)
11. ITU-T X.903 | ISO/IEC 10746-3 Information Technology – Open Distributed Processing – Reference Model – Architecture.ISO/IEC Standard 10746-3 (2009)
12. Kang, K.C., Lee, J., Donohoe, P.: Feature-oriented product line engineering. IEEE Software 19(4), 58–65 (2002)
13. Kruchten, P.: The 4 + 1 View Model of architecture. IEEE Software 12(6), 42–50 (1995)
14. Noda, N., Kishi, T.: Aspect-Oriented Modeling for Variability Management. In: Proceedings of the 12th International Software Product Line Conference, pp. 213–222. IEEE Computer Society (2008)
15. Pohl, K., Böckle, G., van der Linden, F.: Software Product Line Engineering: Foundations, Principles and Techniques. Springer, Heidelberg (2005)
16. Rozanski, N., Woods, E.: Software Systems Architecture: Working With Stakeholders Using Viewpoints and Perspectives, 2nd edn. Addison-Wesley, Upper Saddle River (2012)
17. The ARTFL Project: Webster's Revised Unabridged Dictionary (1913+1828), http://machaut.uchicago.edu/?resource=Webster%27s&word=variability&use1913=on (accessed on December 19, 2012)
18. The Open Group: TOGAF Version 9.1. 10th new edn. Van Haren Publishing, Zaltbommel (2011)
19. Thiel, S., Hein, A.: Systematic integration of variability into product line architecture design. In: Chastek, G.J. (ed.) SPLC 2002. LNCS, vol. 2379, pp. 130–153. Springer, Heidelberg (2002)
20. Wojcik, R., Bachmann, F., Bass, L., Clements, P., Merson, P., Nord, R., Wood, W.: Attribute-Driven Design (ADD), Version 2.0. Technical Report, Software Engineering Institute, Carnegie Mellon University, CMU/SEI-2006-TR-023 (2006)
21. Zachman, J.A.: A Framework for Information Systems Architecture. IBM Systems Journal 26(3), 276–292 (1987)

Proteus Hypervisor:
Full Virtualization and Paravirtualization for Multi-core Embedded Systems

Katharina Gilles[1], Stefan Groesbrink[1], Daniel Baldin[1], and Timo Kerstan[2]

[1] Design of Distributed Embedded Systems, Heinz Nixdorf Institute,
Fuerstenallee 11, 33102 Paderborn, Germany
s.groesbrink@upb.de, dbaldin@upb.de, www.hni.uni-paderborn.de/
[2] dSPACE GmbH, Rathenaustrasse 26, 33102 Paderborn, Germany
tkerstan@dspace.de, www.dspace.de

Abstract. System virtualization's integration of multiple software stacks with maintained isolation on multi-core architectures has the potential to meet high functionality and reliability requirements in a resource efficient manner. Paravirtualization is the prevailing approach in the embedded domain. Its applicability is however limited, since not all operating systems can be ported to the paravirtualization application programming interface. Proteus is a multi-core hypervisor for PowerPC-based embedded systems, which supports both full virtualization and paravirtualization without relying on special hardware support. The hypervisor ensures spatial and temporal separation of the guest systems. The evaluation indicates a low memory footprint of 15 kilobytes and the configurability allows for an application-specific inclusion of components. The interrupt latencies and the execution times for hypercall handlers, emulation routines, and virtual machine context switches are analyzed.

1 Introduction and Related Work

System virtualization refers to the division of the hardware resources into multiple execution environments [21]. The hypervisor separates operating system (OS) and hardware in order to share the hardware among multiple OS instances. Each guest runs within a virtual machine (VM)—an isolated duplicate of the real machine (also referred to as partition). The consolidation of multiple systems with maintained separation is well-suited to build a system-of-systems. Independently developed software such as third party components, trusted (and potentially certified) legacy software, and newly developed application-specific software can be combined to implement the required functionality. The reusability of software components is increased, time-to-market and development costs can be reduced, the lifetime of certified software can be extended. The rise of multi-core processors is a major enabler for virtualization. The replacement of multiple hardware units by a single multi-core system has the potential to reduce size, weight, and power [19]. Virtualization's architectural abstraction eases the migration from

G. Schirner et al. (Eds.): IESS 2013, IFIP AICT 403, pp. 293–305, 2013.

single-core to multi-core platforms [11] and supports the creation of an unified software architecture for multiple hardware platforms.

Primary use cases for this technology are security for open systems and OS heterogeneity. First, if a system allows the user to add software, the isolation of potentially faulty or malicious software in a VM ensures against risks for the critical parts of the system. Second, multiple different OSs can be hosted to provide each subsystem a suitable interface. Industrial automation, medical, or mobile systems, for example, require often both a real-time operating system (RTOS) and a general purpose operating system (GPOS) [11]. The deterministic and highly efficient RTOS executes critical tasks such as the control of actuators or the cellular communication of a mobile device. The feature-rich GPOS supports the development of the graphical user interface. The integration of a legacy component may require a third OS.

Since system virtualization gained significant interest in the embedded real-time world, multiple vendors developed multi-core hypervisors for this domain, for example, Wind River's *Embedded Hypervisor*, LynuxWorks' *LynxSecure Hypervisor*, or Green Hills' *Integrity Multivisor*. See [7] for a recently published survey of both commercial and academic real-time virtualization solutions. In the academic world, Xi et al. developed a real-time scheduling framework for the hypervisor Xen [23], which supports PowerPC multi-core architectures. Xen relies on either paravirtualization [2] or on hardware assistance. Xen is not available for PowerPC without an additional hypervisor mode, although this is on the project's roadmap since 2006 [3]. XtratuM by Masmano et al. is a paravirtualization hypervisor implemented on PowerPC [17]. SParK by Ghaisas et al. is a hypervisor for PowerPC platforms without hardware assistance for virtualization [6]. However, their solution requires paravirtualization and does not support multi-core platforms. Closest to our work, Tavares et al. presented an embedded hypervisor for PowerPC 405, which supports full virtualization, but no multi-core architectures [22].

None of these hypervisors provides full virtualization on multi-core PowerPC platforms without hardware assistance. They rely on either paravirtualization or processor virtualization extensions. Examples for processors with hardware assistance for virtualization are Intel VT-x or AMD-V for x86 architectures. Virtualization support was added to the PowerPC architecture with instruction set architecture Power ISA Version 2.06 [9], is however only available for high performance processors. Typical platforms for embedded systems do not feature hardware assistance and many OSs cannot be paravirtualized for legal or technical reasons. By consequence, the applicability of existing PowerPC hypervisors is limited significantly.

We present the first real-time hypervisor for multi-core PowerPC platforms, which features both paravirtualization and full virtualization without relying on explicit hardware assistance for virtualization. Proteus ensures VM separation and is characterized by a bare-metal approach, a symmetric use of the processor cores, and a synchronization mechanism that does not rely on special hardware support. The evaluation shows a low memory and execution time overhead.

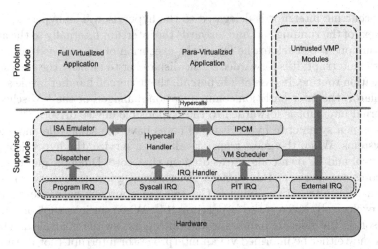

Fig. 1. Design of the Proteus Hypervisor [1]

2   Approach

In previous work, we developed a predecessor with the same name *Proteus*[1], a hypervisor for 32-bit single-core PowerPC architectures. In this work, we present a redesign for multi-core platforms.

2.1   Design

A *hosted* hypervisor runs on top of a host OS [21], which leaves resource management and scheduling at the mercy of this OS. Moreover, the entire system is exposed to the safety and security vulnerabilities of the underlying OS. A *bare-metal* hypervisor runs directly on top of the hardware, facilitating a more efficient virtualization solution. The amount of code executed in privileged mode is smaller compared to a hosted hypervisor, since only a (preferably thin) hypervisor and no OS is incorporated in the trusted computing base. The attack surface is reduced, both the overall security and the certifiability of functional safety are increased. Due to those performance and robustness advantages as well as the clearer and more scalable separation, the bare-metal approach is more appropriate for embedded systems and followed by our design.

The design of the Proteus hypervisor is depicted in Fig. 1. The PowerPC 405 [8] features two execution modes. In the *problem mode* for applications only a subset of the instruction set can be executed. In the more privileged *supervisor mode* for system software, full access to machine state and I/O devices is available via *privileged instructions*. Only the minimal set of components is executed in supervisor mode: interrupt and hypercall handlers, VM scheduler, and inter-partition communication manager (IPCM). All other components such as I/O device drivers are placed inside a separate partition (untrusted VMP modules) and executed in problem mode.

Any occurring interrupt is delegated to the hypervisor. The hypervisor saves the context of the running VM and forwards the interrupt internally to the appropriate component or back to the OS. If the execution of a privileged instruction caused the interrupt, it is forwarded to the dispatcher to identify the corresponding emulation routine. In case of a hypercall, the hypercall handler invokes either the emulator, the inter-partition communication manager, or the VM scheduler. An external interrupt is forwarded to the responsible device driver.

Proteus is a symmetric hypervisor: all cores have the same role and execute guest systems. When the guest traps or calls for a service, the hypervisor takes over control and its own code is executed on that core. Different guests on different cores can perform this context switch from guest to hypervisor at the same time. An alternative design is the *sidecore* approach with one dedicated core to exclusively execute the hypervisor [14]. When an interrupt occurs, the hypervisor on the sidecore handles it and no context switch is invoked. The hypervisor may either be informed via an interprocessor interrupt (not featured by the PowerPC 405) or a notification by the guest OS, which requires paravirtualization. To reconcile sidecore approach and full virtualization, a small fraction of the hypervisor could be executed on each core to forward interrupts. The guest OS could run unmodified, but each exception would involve a context switch and thereby a loss of the major benefit. If the sidecore is already serving the request of a guest, other guests have to wait, resulting in varying interrupt processing time, which is inappropriate for real-time systems. For these reasons, we decided in favor of a symmetric design.

2.2   Multi-core Processor Virtualization

The virtualization of the processing unit is the crucial part of a hypervisor. An instruction is called *sensitive* if it depends on or modifies the configuration of resources. According to a criteria defined by Popek and Goldberg, an instruction set is efficiently virtualizable, if the set of sensitive instructions is a subset of the set of privileged instructions [18]. The PowerPC fulfills this criteria and is fully virtualizable. In contrast for example to the x86 architecture, all sensitive instructions cause an exception (trap), if executed in problem mode.

Solely the hypervisor is executed in supervisor mode and the guests are executed in problem mode with no direct access to the machine state. This limitation of the guests' hardware access is mandatory in order to retain the hypervisor's control over the hardware and guarantee the separation between VMs. The PowerPC 405 does not provide explicit hardware support for virtualization such as an additional hypervisor execution mode. However, guest OSs rely themselves on an execution-mode differentiation. Therefore, the problem mode has to be subdivided into two logical execution modes: VM's privileged mode and VM's problem mode. By virtualizing the machine state register, the hypervisor creates the illusion that a guest OS is executed in supervisor mode, but runs it actually in problem mode. When a guest OS executes a privileged instruction in problem mode (e.g. an access to the machine state register) a trap is caused and the hypervisor executes the responsible emulation routine.

In a multi-core system, access to shared resources must be synchronized. A common solution are semaphores, accessed under mutual exclusion and assigned exclusively to one core at any time. The PowerPC 405 does not feature any hardware support to realize mutual exclusion in a multi-core architecture. Its instructions *lwarx* (load locked) and *stwcx* (store conditional) for atomic memory access do not work across multiple processor cores. Since interrupt disabling is as well not feasible for multi-core systems, Proteus implements a software semaphore solution: Leslie Lamport's Bakery Algorithm [15]. It does not require atomic operations such as test-and-set, satisfies FIFO fairness and excludes starvation, an advantage over Dijkstra's algorithm [4].

2.3   Full Virtualization and Paravirtualization

The capability to host unmodified OSs classifies hypervisors. In terms of *full virtualization*, unmodified guests can be hosted, whereas *paravirtualization* requires a porting of the guest OS to the hypervisor's paravirtualization application programming interface (API) [2]. The guest is aware of being executed within a VM and uses hypercalls to request hypervisor services, what can often be exploited to increase the performance [13]. The major drawback is the need to port an OS, which involves modifications of critical kernel parts. If legal or technical issues preclude this for an OS, it is not possible to host it. A specific advantage of paravirtualization for real-time systems is the possibility to apply dynamic real-time scheduling algorithms, which in general require a passing of scheduling information such as deadlines from guest OS to hypervisor.

Proteus supports both kinds because of those characteristics of the two approaches—paravirtualization's efficiency, but limited applicability on the one hand, full virtualization's support of non-modifiable guests on the other hand. If the modification of an OS is possible, the system designer decides whether the effort of paravirtualization is justified. The concurrent hosting of both paravirtualized and fully virtualized guests is possible without restriction. Proteus is designed for the co-hosting of GPOS and RTOS, and the natural approach is to host a paravirtualized RTOS and a fully virtualized GPOS. In addition, bare-metal applications without underlying OS can be hosted.

Each privileged instruction is associated with an emulating hypercall. Hypercalls are realized as system calls. A system call is identified as a hypercall, if it is executed in the VM's logical privileged mode. A paravirtualized OS can use hypercalls to communicate with other guests, call I/O functionality, pass scheduling information to the hypervisor, or yield the CPU.

2.4   Spatial and Temporal Separation

System virtualization for embedded real-time systems requires the guarantee of spatial and temporal separation of the guest systems. *Spatial separation* refers to the protection of the integrity of the memory space of both the hypervisor and the guests. Any possibility of a harmful activity going beyond the boundaries of a VM has to be eliminated. To achieve this, each VM operates in its own address space, which is statically mapped to a region of the shared memory. It is protected by the memory management unit (MMU) of the PowerPC 405. Communication between VMs is controlled by the IPCM. If the hypervisor authorizes the communication, it creates a shared-memory tunnel. Communication between VMs is mandatory, if formerly physically distributed systems that have to communicate with each other are consolidated.

Temporal separation is fulfilled, if all guest systems are executed in compliance with their timing requirements. A predictable, deterministic behavior of every single real-time guest has to be guaranteed. The worst-case execution times (WCET) of all routines are bounded and were analyzed (see section 3). These results make it possible to determine the WCET of a program that is executed on top of Proteus. System virtualization implies scheduling decisions on two levels. The hypervisor schedules the VMs and the guest OSs schedule their tasks according to their own scheduling policies. Proteus manages a global VM scheduling queue and each VM can be executed on each core. If this is undesired, a VM can be bound to one specific core or a subset of cores, for example to assign a core exclusively to a safety-critical guest [11]. If the number of VMs n_{guests} exceeds the number of processor cores n_{cores}, at each point in time, $n_{guests} - n_{cores}$ VMs are not executed. The cores have to be shared in a time-division multiplexing manner and the VM scheduling is implemented as a fixed time slice based approach. The guests' task sets have to be analyzed and execution time windows within a repetitive major cycle are assigned to the VMs based on the required utilization and execution frequency. This static scheduling approach is for example applied in the aerospace domain and part of the software specification *ARINC 653 (Avionics Application Standard Software Interface)*[20] for space and time partitioning in avionics real-time systems in the context of *Integrated Modular Avionics* [5]. See [12] for guidance of designing a schedule that allows all guests to meet their timing constraints. The scheduler can be replaced by implementing an interface.

3   Experimental Results

3.1   Evaluation Platform: IBM PowerPC 405

Target architecture of our implementation are platforms with multiple IBM PowerPC 405 cores [8], a 32-bit RISC core providing up to 400 MHz. It is designed for low-cost and low-power embedded systems and features separate instruction and data caches as well as a MMU with a software-managed TLB. Specifications and register-transfer level description are freely available to the research community. Due to the API compatibility within the PowerPC family, porting the results to other PowerPC processors should be fairly simple. In order to be able to evaluate the software with low effort on different hardware configurations, the evaluation platform is a software simulator for PowerPC multi-cores [10]. The *IBM PowerPC Multi-core Instruction Set Simulator* can optionally include peripheral devices (e.g. an UART) and provides an interface for external simulation environments. Many components of the simulated hardware can be configured, for example, the number of cores or cache sizes.

3.2 Memory Footprint

Dependent on the requirements of the actual system, Proteus can be configured. The workflow is based on the modification of a configuration file by the system designer. According to these specifications, the preprocessor manipulates the implementation files and removes unneeded code.

Figure 2 lists code and data size for the base functionality and the additionally required memory for different components, also depicted in a figure with a differentiation between text segment (executable instructions) and data segment (static variables). The hypervisor is written in C and assembly language. The efficiency of a hypervisor is highly dependent on the execution times of the interrupt handling. For this reason, most of the components called by those handlers and the handlers themselves are written in assembly language. All executables are generated with compiler optimization level 2 (option -O2 for the GNU C compiler), which focuses on the performance of the generated code and not primarily on the code size. The solely full virtualization supporting base requires a total of about 11 kilobytes. The addition of paravirtualization support accounts for less than 1 kilobyte.

The system designer can decide on enabling TLB virtualization (TLB V), device driver support, and inter-partition communication. *Innocuous register file mapping* (IRFM) is a performance boost for paravirtualized guests. By mapping a specific set of privileged registers into VM's memory space, no trap to the hypervisor is required to access these registers. *Previrtualization* (Pre V) is an approach to paravirtualize guests automatically [16]. The source code is analyzed at compile time in order to identify privileged instructions. At load time, the hypervisor replaces privileged instructions by hypercalls. If all features are enabled, the memory requirement of the hypervisor sums up to about 15 kilobytes.

Feature	Memory Footprint [bytes]			
	Assembler	C code	Data	Total
Base	2492	5732	2980	11204
ParaV	252	0	148	400
IRFM	292	476	0	768
PreV	0	256	0	256
TLB V	812	264	656	1732
Driver	0	648	12	660
IPCM	0	500	0	500
Total	3848	7876	3796	15520

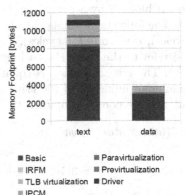

Fig. 2. Impact of Individual Components on Memory Footprint.

3.3   Execution Time Overhead

The following performance figures denote the worst-case execution time in case of enabled and hot instruction cache, resulting in a duration for each instruction fetch of one processor cycle, and a clock speed of 300 MHz.

Virtual Machine Context Switch. If multiple VMs share a core, switching between them involves the saving of the context of the preempted VM, the selection of the next VM and the resume of this VM, including the restoring of its context. Table 1 lists the execution times for a VM context switch. The overhead of accessing the semaphore that protects the ready queue accounts for a large part of the scheduling execution time.

Table 1. Execution Time of a Virtual Machine Context Switch (4 cores)

Routine	Execution time in ns (processor cycles)
VM Context Saving	450 (135)
VM Scheduling	2270 (681)
VM Resume	800 (240)
Total	3520 (1056)

Synchronized Shared Resource Access Routines. Figure 3 depicts the execution time of the subroutines of Bakery's Algorithm for synchronized shared resource access (semaphore operations $wait()$ and $signal()$). The execution time increases linearly with the number of cores, since the included execution of the function $mutex\_start()$ has to iterate over an array of length equal to the number of cores. The operation $wait()$ causes a blocking of the calling process, if the resource is not available. In case of four cores, the worst case occurs if the calling process is blocked by a process on each of the three other cores, as depicted in Fig. 4. The following formula calculates the worst-case waiting time. $wait\_short$ (14 cycles), $wait\_long$ (46 cycles), $signal\_short$ (15 cycles) and $signal\_long$ (54 cycles) refer to the shortest and longest paths through the routines wait() and signal(). The critical section is equal to $3 \cdot (wait\_long + mutex\_stop)$, which is the minimum influence of the critical section, since core 1 cannot perform the $signal()$ before core 4 completed the try to acquire the semaphore.

$$x = 3(mutex\_start + wait\_short + mutex\_stop + 3(wait\_long + mutex\_stop)$$
$$+ mutex\_start + signal\_long + mutex\_stop)$$
$$= 3(169 + 14 + 11 + 3(46 + 11) + 169 + 54 + 11) = 1797.$$

As a result, the worst-case waiting time for synchronized shared resource access sums up to 1797 processor cycles or 5990 ns.

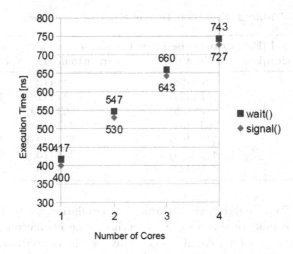

Fig. 3. Linear Dependency of Execution Time of Routines for Exclusive Resource Access on Number of Cores

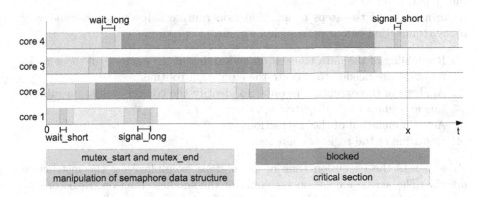

Fig. 4. Worst-case Waiting Time for Synchronized Shared Resource Access for 4 Cores

Interrupt Latency. Virtualization increases the interrupt latency. Any interrupt is first delivered to the hypervisor, analyzed and potentially forwarded back to the guest. For example, the additional latency of a programmable timer interrupt is 497 ns (149 processor cycles) and 337 ns (101 processor cycles) for a system call interrupt. To obtain the total interrupt latency, one has to add the interrupt latency of the guest OS. Timer interrupt handling takes longer, since the virtual interrupt timer has to be updated. Proteus omits the effort of saving the complete VM context by saving only the registers that are needed by the emulation routine. The implementation in assembly language uses the fewest possible number of registers.

Table 2. Execution Time of Emulation Routines

Privileged instruction	Execution time in ns (processor cycles)		
	Full virtualization	Paravirtualization	Speedup
rfi	527 (158)	410 (123)	28 %
wrteei	447 (134)	393 (118)	14 %
mtmsr	517 (155)	363 (109)	42 %
mtevpr	503 (151)	347 (104)	45 %
mtzpr	547 (164)	353 (106)	55 %
mfmsr	453 (136)	363 (109)	25 %
mfevpr	477 (143)	363 (109)	31 %

Emulation of Privileged Instructions. The emulation of privileged instructions is the core functionality of the hypervisor. The emulation service is requested via interrupt (full virtualization) or hypercall (paravirtualization). Table 2 lists the execution times of some exemplary emulation routines. Compared to full virtualization, paravirtualization speeds up the execution by 14% to 55%. The average speedup for all privileged instructions, not just the ones listed in this paper, is 39.25%.

An analysis of the steps of an emulation routine helps to understand why paravirtualization can achieve such a significant speedup:

1. Reenabling of the data translation and saving of the contents of those registers that are needed to execute the emulation routine.
2. Analysis of the exception in order to identify the correct emulation subroutine and jump to it (dispatching).
3. Actual emulation of the instruction.
4. Restoring of the register contents.

Table 3 lists the execution time of those steps exemplary for the instruction *mtevpr*. The actual emulation accounts for the smallest fraction. Register saving and restoring are expensive, however likewise for both full virtualization and paravirtualization. The performance gain of paravirtualization is based on the significantly lower overhead for identification of the cause of the exception

Table 3. Execution Time of Emulation Routine for *mtevpr*

Step of emulation routine	Execution time in ns (processor cycles)	
	Full virtualization	Paravirtualization
Save registers	137 (41)	137 (41)
Analysis and dispatch	220 (66)	73 (22)
Emulate	20 (6)	20 (6)
Restore registers	127 (38)	117 (35)
Total	503 (151)	347 (104)

and dispatching to the correct subroutine. In case of paravirtualization, only a register read-out is necessary in order to obtain the hypercall ID.

Hypercalls. A guest OS can request hypervisor services via the paravirtualization interface. The hypercall *vm_yield*, which voluntarily releases the core, has an execution time of 507 ns (152 processor cycles). By calling *sched_set_param*, the guest OS passes information to the hypervisor's scheduler. The execution time of this hypercall is 793 ns (238 processor cycles). The hypercall *create_comm_tunnel* requests the creation of a shared-memory tunnel for communication between itself and a second VM and is characterized by an execution time of 1027 ns (308 processor cycles). The hypercall *vm_yield* does not return to the VM and the execution time is measured until the start of the hypervisor's *schedule* routine. The other two hypercalls return to the VM and the execution time measurement is stopped when the calling VM resumes its execution.

4   Conclusion

Proteus is a hypervisor for embedded PowerPC multi-core platforms, which is able to host both paravirtualized and fully virtualized guest systems without hardware assistance for virtualization. It is a bare-metal hypervisor, characterized by a symmetric use of the processor cores. The synchronization mechanism for shared resource access does not rely on hardware support. This increases the execution time overhead, but extends the applicability of the hypervisor to shared-memory multiprocessor systems. The hypervisor ensures spatial and temporal separation among the guest systems.

Paravirtualization is due to efficiency advantages the prevailing virtualization approach in the embedded domain. Its applicability is however limited. For legal or technical reasons, not all operating systems can be ported to the paravirtualization interface. Proteus can host such operating systems nevertheless, based on full virtualization's execution of unmodified guests. Paravirtualized operating systems can use hypercalls to communicate with other guests, call I/O functionality, pass scheduling information to the hypervisor, or yield the CPU.

The evaluation highlighted the low memory requirement and the application-specific configurability. The memory footprint is 11 kilobytes for the base functionality and 15 kilobytes for a configuration with all functional features. The interrupt latencies and the execution times for synchronization primitives, hypercall handlers, emulation routines, and virtual machine context switch are all in the range of hundreds of processor cycles. The detailed WCET analysis of all routines make it possible to determine the WCET of a hosted application.

The Proteus Hypervisor is free software released under the GNU General Public License. The source code can be downloaded from https://orcos.cs.uni-paderborn.de/orcos/www .

References

1. Baldin, D., Kerstan, T.: Proteus, a Hybrid Virtualization Platform for Embedded Systems. In: Proc. of the International Embedded Systems Symposium (2009)
2. Barham, P., Dragovic, B., Fraser, K., Hand, S., Harris, T., Ho, A., Neugebauer, R., Pratt, I., Warfield, A.: Xen and the Art of Virtualization. In: Proc. of the 19th ACM Symposium on Operating Systems Principles (2003)
3. Blanchard, H., Xenidis, J.: Xen on PowerPC (January 2006), http://www.xen.org/files/xs0106_xen_on_powerpc.pdf
4. Dijkstra, E.W.: Solution of a problem in concurrent programming control. Communications of the ACM 8(9) (1965)
5. Garside, R., Pighetti, J.: Integrating modular avionics: A new role emerges. IEEE A & E Systems Magazine (2009)
6. Ghaisas, S., Karmakar, G., Shenai, D., Tirodkar, S., Ramamritham, K.: SParK: Safety Partition Kernel for Integrated Real-Time Systems. In: Sachs, K., Petrov, I., Guerrero, P. (eds.) Buchmann Festschrift. LNCS, vol. 6462, pp. 159–174. Springer, Heidelberg (2010)
7. Gu, Z., Zhao, Q.: A State-of-the-Art Survey on Real-Time Issues in Embedded Systems Virtualization. Journal of Software Engineering and Applications 5(4), 277–290 (2012)
8. IBM: PowerPC 405 Processor Core (2005), http://www-01.ibm.com/chips/techlib/techlib.nsf/products/PowerPC_405_Embedded_Cores
9. IBM: PowerPC ISA 2.06 Revision B (July 2010), https://www.power.org/documentation/power-isa-version-2-06-revision-b/
10. IBM Research: IBM PowerPC 4XX Instruction Set Simulator (ISS) (October 2012), https://www-01.ibm.com/chips/techlib/techlib.nsf/products/PowerPC_4XX_Instruction_Set_Simulator_(ISS)
11. Intel Corporation (White paper): Applying multi-core and virtualization to industrial and safety-related applications (2009), http://download.intel.com/platforms/applied/indpc/321410.pdf
12. Kerstan, T., Baldin, D., Groesbrink, S.: Full virtualization of real-time systems by temporal partitioning. In: Proc. of the 6th International Workshop on Operating Systems Platforms for Embedded Real-Time Applications (2010)
13. King, S., Dunlap, G., Chen, P.: Operating System Support for Virtual Machines. In: Proc. of the USENIX Annual Technical Conference (2003)
14. Kumar, S., Raj, H., Schwan, K., Ganev, I.: Re-architecting VMMs for Multicore Systems: The Sidecore Approach. In: Proc. of the Workshop on Interaction between Operating Systems and Computer Architecture (2007)
15. Lamport, L.: A new solution of Dijkstra's concurrent programming problem. Communications of the ACM 17, 453–455 (1974)
16. LeVasseur, J., Uhlig, V., Chapman, M., Chubb, P., Leslie, B., Heiser, G.: Pre-virtualization: Soft Layering for Virtual Machines. In: Proc. of the 13th Asia-Pacific Computer Systems Architecture Conference (2008)
17. Masmano, M., Ripoll, I., Crespo, A.: XtratuM: a Hypervisor for Safety Critical Embedded Systems. In: Proc. of the Eleventh Real-Time Linux Workshop (2009)
18. Popek, G.J., Goldberg, R.P.: Formal Requirements for Virtualizable Third Generation Architectures. Communications of the ACM 17(7), 412–421 (1974)
19. Prisaznuk, P.: Integrated Modular Avionics. In: Proc. of the IEEE National Aerospace and Electronics Conference (1992)

20. Prisaznuk, P.: ARINC 653 Role in Integrated Modular Avionics (IMA). In: Proc. of the 27th IEEEE Digital Avionics Systems Conference (2008)
21. Smith, J.E., Nair, R.: The Architecture of Virtual Machines. IEEE Computer (2005)
22. Tavares, A., Carvalho, A., Rodrigues, P., Garcia, P., Gomes, T., Cabral, J., Cardoso, P., Montenegro, S., Ekpanyapong, M.: A Customizable and ARINC 653 Quasi-compliant Hypervisor. In: Proc. of the IEEE International Conference on Industrial Technology (2012)
23. Xi, S., Wilson, J., Lu, C., Gill, C.: RT-Xen: Towards Real-time Hypervisor Scheduling in Xen. In: Proc. of the International Conference on Embedded Software (2011)

A Structural Parametric Binaural 3D Sound Implementation Using Open Hardware

Bruno Dal Bó Silva* and Marcelo Götz

Electrical Engineering Department
Federal University of Rio Grande do Sul - UFRGS, Porto Alegre, Brazil
bruno.silva@ims.ind.br, mgoetz@ece.ufrgs.br

Abstract. Most binaural 3D sound implementations use large databases with pre-recorded transfer functions, which are mostly prohibitive for real time embedded applications. This article focus on a parametric approach proposal, opening space for customizations and to add new processing blocks easily. In this work we show the feasibility of a parametric binaural architecture for dynamic sound localization in embedded platforms for mobile applications, ranging from multimedia and entertainment to hearing aid for individuals with visual disabilities. The complete solution, ranging from algorithms analysis and suiting, development using the Beagleboard platform for prototyping, and performance benchmarks, are presented.

Keywords: Binaural, Parametric, Beagleboard, Embedded, Digital Signal Processing.

1 Introduction

Virtual sound localization is an interesting feature for innumerous types of applications, ranging from multimedia and entertainment to hearing aid for individuals with visual disabilities. Binaural sound localization is a technique that uses single-channel input signal, and by proper manipulation, can produce two different signals (left and right) channels. By these means a human user might perceive the source located on a determined point in space.

Head-Related Transfer Function (HRTF), which is usually well known technique employed for binaural sound localization, is a hard problem and computational intensive task. Such systems, enabling a dynamic changing of azimuth angle, usually requires the usage of dedicated computing hardware (e.g.[1–3]). Nowadays execution platforms found in mobile devices usually offers a notable computation capacity for audio processing, which is usually promoted by the inclusion of a Digital Signal Processing (DSP) processor. However, HRTF related algorithms must be well designed for such platforms to take advantage of the available processing capacity.

---

* Currently with IMS Power Quality.

G. Schirner et al. (Eds.): IESS 2013, IFIP AICT 403, pp. 306–317, 2013.

In our work we aggregate various methods and models of parametric 3D binaural sound for dynamic sound localization, propose some algorithm suiting (specially for Interaural Level Difference - ILD filter) for embedded development, and validate them by prototyping using low-cost embedded hardware platform. In this work we present our first step towards a full-featured 3D binaural system, where we have implemented parametric DSP blocks on real-world hardware for feasibility evaluation.

The article is organized as follows. Firstly, in Sect. 2, we will introduce previous works on the field, followed by the models of our choice for embedded development and some considerations in Sect. 3. Then, the platform itself, technologic aspects and the employed algorithms adaptations are explained in Sect. 4. The experiment set-up including performance and localization quality results are shown in Sect. 5. Finally, Sect. 6 gives the summary, conclusions, and points out future work.

2 Related Work

Many previous researchers have invested on binaural sound localization. Two main areas of interest stand out: interpreting a dual-channel audio input so to discover the approximate position of the sound source (e.g. [4, 5]); and manipulation of a given single-channel input signal so to put it on a determined point in space as perceived by a human user. These two areas can be seen as the inverse of each-other, where the input of one is generally the output for the other. On this article we will explore the second field of research, knowing that much can be learned from the common physical principles involved.

Considering the problem of localizing a mono sound source for the human ear, we can still divide it in two great fronts: model-based and empiric localization. Many authors [1–3] rely on pre-recorded impulse-response databases and implement complex interpolations and predictive algorithms, varying from DSP-chip based algorithms to full-fledged System-on-Chip (SoC) solutions. Hyung Jung et al. [1] show a successful implementation of 5.1 surround sound system using hand-chosen responses, which works perfectly considering only 5 possible audio sources in space.

For more possible audio sources in a virtual space, almost infinite positions theoretically, we must have a rather large database of known responses and very complex interpolation algorithms, above all when considering as well the effects of elevation. Most of these systems rely on a public domain database of high-spatial-resolution HRTF [6]. Using such a database, implies storing it into the target execution platform.

We have relied on the second approach: a parametric model. For this we assume it is possible to approximate the physical response of the medium the sound is travelling in, the time and frequency response involved in the human shape (mainly the head and ears). We have searched successful models of such physical concepts, starting with [7], where Rayleigh gives us the prime of Psychoacoustics. Most of our model was inspired by the various works of Algazi, Brown and

Duda [8–13] ,who have much contributed to the field. Their models use simplistic filters perfectly suitable for low-cost and satisfying results. For pinna-related effects we have relied on the responses found in [14] and the spherical-model approximations given by [15].

3   Fundamentals

Most binaural 3D sound systems rely on a simple concept: the HRTF - Head Related Transfer Funcion. This macro-block represents the shaping suffered by the sound as it travels from source to the receiver's eardrums. The HRTF is usually divided in: ILD, ITD and PRTF, Interaural Level Difference, Interaural Time Difference and Pinna-Related Transfer Function respectively. We will disregard in this model the shoulder and torso effects, since they contribute mostly to elevation perception and our focus will be on azimuth. Fig. 1 shows the system's full conceptual block diagram.

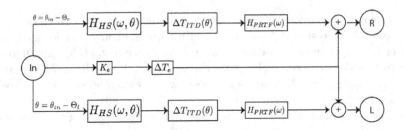

Fig. 1. Full localization model

3.1   ITD - Interaural Time Difference

ITD is conveyed by the difference in length of the paths to the left and right ears. This translates usually in a slight phase shift that is only perceivable for very low frequencies. By modelling the head as a sphere and considering the elevation angle ϕ to be always zero, that is, the sound source is always in the same plane the listener's ears, we have the following model from [15]:

$$DL = \begin{cases} DLD & , DLD < L \\ L + DLA & , DLD \geq L \end{cases} \quad DR = \begin{cases} DRD & , DRD < L \\ L + DRA & , DRD \geq L \end{cases} \quad (1)$$

where $\Delta D = DL - DR$ is the path difference, related to the ITD through the sound speed c. $ITD = \frac{\Delta D}{c}$. The geometric parameters are shown in Fig. 2.

The total ITD will be, then, discrete and taken in samples, according to the sampling frequency F_s. Both the linear and arc distances are solved using simple trigonometry and depend mostly on one parameter: the radius of the head, a_h.

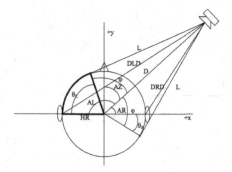

Fig. 2. ITD input parameters

3.2 ILD - Interaural Level Difference

ILD is given by the Head-Shadowing effect, studied and modelled by Rayleight [7] as the solution of the Helmoltz equation for a spherical head. Brown shows an approximate model by a minimum phase filter in [14], also found in [16]:

$$H_{HS}(\omega, \theta) = \frac{1 + j\frac{\alpha\omega}{2\omega_0}}{1 + j\frac{\omega}{2\omega_0}} \qquad (2)$$

where H_{HS} is the filter's frequency response, dependent on input azimuth angle θ, and α is given by:

$$\alpha(\theta) = \left(1 + \frac{\alpha_{min}}{2}\right) + \left(1 - \frac{\alpha_{min}}{2}\right) \cdot \cos\left(\pi\frac{\theta}{\theta_0}\right) \qquad (3)$$

The parameter θ_0 fixes the minimum gain angle (α_{min}). Brown suggest that θ_0 should be 150°, for maximum match with Rayleigh's model, but we've found that it creates discontinuity in the frequency spectrum that is perceived as a fast "warp" of the sound source, so we've preferred to make $\theta_0 = 180°$ without major losses to the original model. Then, by simple variable mapping we have the filter responses for the left and right ears defined by:

$$H_{HS}^l(\omega, \theta) = H_{HS}(\omega, \theta - \Theta_l) \qquad (4)$$
$$H_{HS}^r(\omega, \theta) = H_{HS}(\omega, \theta - \Theta_r) \qquad (5)$$

The ILD model result is shown in Fig. 3. We can see that it provides a valid approximation to Rayleigh's solution and at the same time allows a very simple digital filter implementation. Notice symmetrical responses to the ear's reference angle overlap.

3.3 PRTF - Pinna-Related Transfer Function

With the ILD and the ITD we have modelled the general sound waveshape arriving at the listener's ears. The two previous blocks cover most of the physical

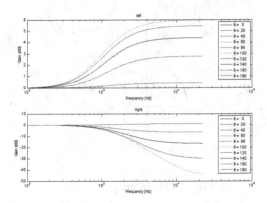

Fig. 3. ILD model result for left and right ears with $\theta = \{0, 180\}$

shaping, while the PRTF transforms the input wave even further, giving a more natural feeling to the user. We have used the models suggested in [14], which approximate the Pinna as a series of constructive and destructive interferences represented by notch and resonance filters. According to Spagnol et al., Pinna effects give many spectral cues to perceive elevation, we have found that adding their filter the azimuth plane ($\phi = 0$) we could create a rather superior localization feeling.

Spangol's general filter solutions are shown in Eq. 6 and 7. Table 1 shows the coefficients derived from the mentioned study, pointing the reflection (*refl*) and resonance (*res*) points with their central frequencies (f_C) and gain (G). The reflection coefficients will generate local minima in the frequency spectrum, whereas resonance frequencies will generate maxima, as it can be seen in Fig. 4.

$$H_{res}(Z) = \frac{V_0(1-h)(1-Z^{-2})}{1 + 2dhZ^{-1} + (2h-1)Z^{-2}} \tag{6}$$

$$H_{refl}(Z) = \frac{1 + (1+k)\frac{H_0}{2} + d(1-k)Z^{-1} + (-k - (1+k)\frac{H_0}{2})Z^{-2}}{1 + d(1-k)Z^{-1} - kZ^{-2}} \tag{7}$$

Table 1. PRTF filter coefficients

Singularity	Type	f_C [kHz]	G [dB]
1	res	4	5
2	res	12	5
3	refl	6	5
4	refl	9	5
5	refl	11	5

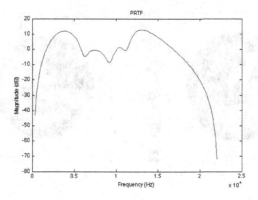

Fig. 4. PRTF filter result

3.4 RIR - Room Impulse Response

Considering the effects of the three previously mentioned models, we can achieve an acceptable result. But it suffers from lateralization, where the listener sometimes perceives the sound as coming from inside the head. The digitally processed waveshape does not have, yet, the necessary cues for proper localization. Brown suggests that a very simple RIR can make a difference [13]. As we can see in Fig. 1, there is a direct signal path that is not seen as dependent on the input angle θ. That is a simple echo. By simply adding to the resulting binaural signals the original mono input with delay and attenuation we can reduce lateralization by a considerable amount, increasing externalization. We have used a 15ms delay with 15dB attenuation.

3.5 System Response

The system's final response is shown in Fig. 5. The visual representation uses frequency as the radius, azimuth as argument and the system's output is color-coded in the z-axis. The polar plot clearly shows the different energy regions dependant on the azimuth and the reference angle – left or right ear. The distinctive "waves" are due to the Pinna effects, whereas the global energy difference is given by the Interaural Level Difference.

4 Development

Our main goal was to port the mentioned filters and models to an embedded platform. We have chosen the Beagleboard [17], a community-supported open hardware platform which uses Texas Instruments' DM3730, containing one ARM Cortex-A8 and one DSP C64x. Being derived from the OMAP platforms, this chipset allows real-world performance validation using embedded Linux relying on the two available cores: a General Purpose Processor (GPP) and a DSP

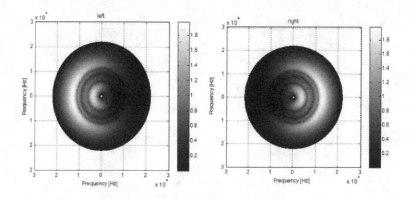

Fig. 5. System's final response in polar plot

Processor. We have loaded the Beagleboard with a custom lightweight Angstrom distribution built using Narcissus [18]. Narcissus also generates a full-featured development environment ready for cross-compiling.

The building environment has three standing points: `gcc-arm` generates an ARM-compatible linux ELF executable; `ti-cgt` generates DSP-compatible functions, bundled into a library file; then we call an external tool available for easy co-processing on this hybrid chips – C6RunLib. This tool, supported by Texas Instruments, relies on a kernel module called *dsplink* that handles communication between processors. C6RunLib acts as a linker, putting together the ARM code with the DSP library and adding necessary code for remote procedure calls. When a function that is run on the DSP side is called from within ARM code, *dsplink* is called and uses shared memory to actually have the function operated by the other core. We have not entered the details of C6RunLib's inner workings, but one important feature was missing: asynchronous cross-processor function calls were not available – we have solved this issue by letting the ARM-side thread hang while the DSP is busy operating the entry-point function.

The program consists of three main parts: User Interface, Audio Output and Signal Processing. The latter is done on the DSP core, while the others are performed by the GPP (ARM Processor). The User Interface allows the user to dynamically control the azimuth angle θ, azimuth automatic change rate, output volume, turn off the filters individually (so to benchmark localization quality easily without the need to rebuild the solution) and chose among three possible infinite loop audio inputs: noise, an A tone (440Hz) or a short phrase from Suzanne Vega's Tom's Diner (benchmark track suggested in [16] for its pure-voice contents). Audio Output and Signal Processing blocks require real time operation to operate smoothly and are detailed on Sect. 4.2.

4.1   Algorithm Suiting

The four filter blocks were implemented using digital filters with some help from TI's DSPLIB library[19] for better performance. Algorithm suiting for real time digital processing was the first step to take. The delay filters (ITD and RIR) are simple circular buffer filters, only the ITD has a variable delay given by the azimuth. PRTF is modelled by a fixed-point 16-tap truncated FIR filter calculated from Eq. 6 and 7 and using the coefficients from Table 1. Since PRTF is not sensible to azimuth changes, it is actually processed before we split the signal into two separate outputs, which is possible because all the filters are linear and the azimuth change is considerably slower than the system's response.

ILD algorithm is more complex because the filter's coefficients change with the azimuth. The minimum phase filter presented on Eq. 2 when sampled becomes:

$$H_{HS}(Z,\theta) = \frac{\left(\frac{\alpha(\theta)+\mu}{1+\mu}\right) + \left(\frac{\mu-\alpha(\theta)}{1+\mu}\right) Z^{-1}}{1 + \left(\frac{\mu-1}{1+\mu}\right) Z^{-1}} \tag{8}$$

where $\mu = \frac{\omega_0}{F_s} = \frac{c}{a_h \cdot F_s}$. By solving Eq. 8 symbolically on the time domain, being $h[n]$ the related impulse response at sample n we have the following generalization:

$$h[n] = \begin{cases} \frac{\alpha+\mu}{\mu+1} & , n = 0 \\ -\frac{2\mu(\alpha-1)}{(\mu+1)^2} & , n = 1 \\ h[n-1] \cdot \frac{(1-\mu)}{(\mu+1)} & , n > 1 \end{cases} \tag{9}$$

Using Eq. 9 the ILD is a time-variant fixed-point 16-tap FIR which is recalculated for every input buffer (given the azimuth has changed). On top of the presented model we have also added a low-pass filter to the input azimuth to avoid angle "leaps".

4.2   Prototyping System

As discussed in Sect. 4, we have to build blocks that rely on real time operation for our purposes. For audio output we have used Jack Audio Connection Kit [20], an open library made for this kind of processing. It interfaces with Advance Linux Sound Architecture (ALSA) and tries to guarantee audio transmission without over or underruns. Jack is called by instantiating a deamon that waits for a client to connect to its inputs and outputs. The client registers a callback function that has access to the deamon's buffers. In our application we have used 512 frames-long buffers at a 48kHz sampling frequency, meaning each buffer is valid for around 10ms, which is our processing deadline and output latency. We have not used Jack as the input source, instead the audio input is read from a file and kept in memory. To simulate real time audio capture, this memory area is used to feed new input every time the callback interrupt is called for new output, thus validating the real time premise.

The Jack callback function then signals another thread that sends the input signal to the DSP and receives back (always in a shared memory area) the processed response. All 512-samples buffers are signed with an incremental integer and constantly checked for skipped buffers, thus providing certainty that every input is processed and that every output is played back. Along with the signal buffers, the main application sends a structure containing the controllable parameters discussed previously. Fig. 6 illustrates the system's building blocks and their mutual operation. The left and right trunks operate both at application level (running on GPP) and are ruled by posix semaphores. The middle trunk operates inside Jack's callback function, which is triggered by the Jack daemon once the client is properly installed. The rightmost branch is the C6RunLib function that is processed on the DSP side, remembering that the Sync thread stays blocked during DSP operation.

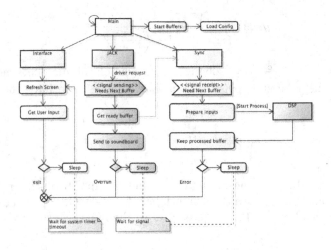

Fig. 6. System thread schema

Fig. 7 shows the function which is operated on the DSP, it follows almost exactly the flowchart presented previously. When done filtering the input signal, the function will sign the output buffers and return, letting the caller thread unblock and renders the newly processed buffers available for the next audio output callback. We have found that the very first call to a function running on the DSP side takes considerably longer than the subsequent ones because of the time needed to load the application code to the other processor. This task is masked by the facilities provided by C6RunLib but must be taken into account, otherwise the system will always shut down on the first buffer because of this latency and the fact that the callback function kills the program if an underrun is detected.

5   Experimental Results

We have tested the system's localization quality and perceived accuracy with a set of user trials. Three main set-ups were tested. One in which another person controls the azimuth freely and the subject must grade the localization feeling

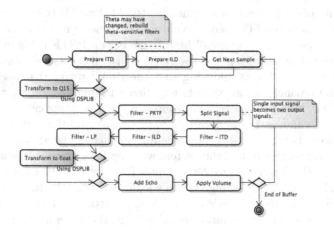

Fig. 7. Signal Processing Function

and try to point out where the sound is coming from. On another test subjects were free to change azimuth themselves. The grades being "Good", "Average" and "Poor". On a last test users were asked to point out where the sound source was in virtual space. The accuracy test is divided in two parts: guessing the azimuth angle of a "warping" sound source that instantly goes from one point to another and of a "moving" source which moves slowly until rest. In the accuracy test we have gathered mean and maximum perceived azimuth errors ϵ_μ and ϵ_M. All users were given the same test points set in random order.

We have noticed that most subjects feel a stronger localization when they have control over the azimuth, complying with the fact that a person with no sensing disabilities will rely on a sum of those to pinpoint an object on space, usually failing when depending solely on sound – create somewhat a placebo effect. When trying to point where the sound source is in a virtual space, users will always get the right quadrant if the sound source is "warping", but will generally fail to pinpoint angle giving $\epsilon_\mu = 43°$, $\epsilon_M = 70°$. When the subject is able to hear the virtual source moving to a resting position accuracy increases to as much as about 30 degrees without mistakes ($\epsilon_\mu = 21°$, $\epsilon_M = 30°$), totalling 12 clear zones in the azimuth plane.

The quality tests were also repeated three times for each of the available input samples. It was observed that the pure tone does not have enough spectral cues for localization and generates confusion most of the time. Noise is next on the list, but, for its high frequency components, it is still not as clear as it could be since the complex frequency response of the implemented system is on the lower side of the spectrum.

The mentioned accuracy results are valid for the third sample: human voice. Because of the short bandwidth and, some authors will argue, an inherent capability to localize voice this third input sample grades enormously better than the previous ones – which is largely consistent with the mathematical model. Lastly, fewer tests were run turning some filtering stages on and off so to observe the real necessity of each one. It was seen that the ITD and ILD work very closely together (although the ITD plays a void role with noise input, since phase cue is basically non-existent because of high frequencies). PRTF helps in fixing the sound source to the azimuth plane, the system without it was described as "noisy and confusing" by subjects, inducing that the PRTF wraps the spectrum to a more natural balance. Some subjects experienced lateralization when the RIR was turned off, losing completely the source in the virtual space.

As for performance, the system was built considering the fact it would not miss deadlines, so the described implementation was validated. We have tested some other parameters to test the system working under stress. It was observed that reducing the frame size to 256 samples (5ms deadline) would cause overruns depending on the operating system's load. For example, the system would run perfectly using its own video board and an attached USB keyboard, but would fail through an SSH connection. Although the same number of samples is processed per second, that is the sampling frequency remains unchanged, the cross-processor calls create noticeable overhead – a problem that could be approached by getting into the inner workings of C6RunLib.

Also, we have made it possible for the program to run fully on the GPP side, letting the DSP completely unused, and compared the CPU load reported by the operating system. When the filters are run by the second processor, the main CPU stays practically idle reporting in average 3% load. When running the complete system on the GPP side, the CPU goes almost to maximum load, floating most of the time around 97% . We were not able to sample the DSP load because the benchmarking functions provided by the libraries would crash the system. To give an approximation of DSP load, we have made the processing functions run redundantly n times, reaching overall failure at $n = 3$, so we estimate the DSP core load between 30% and 50% of its full capacity. The load tests were performed with a constantly changing azimuth, so the filter parameters would be constantly changing and we could observe the worst case scenario.

6   Conclusions

In this work we propose a full-featured 3D binaural system for sound localization. We successfully aggregated various methods and models of parametric 3D binaural, creating parametric DSP blocks. Furthermore, we have shown the feasibility by implementing and evaluating these blocks on a low-cost embedded platform. In our tests the azimuth angle was dynamically changed and clearly perceived by the user with enough accuracy, specially for human voice sound source.

Depending on the operating systems's load, some buffers overrun occurs, which decreases the output quality. This is caused probably by cross-processors calls, which relies on C6RunLib library. So, next steps in our work will be the C6RunLib internals analysis and propose some implementation solutions for this problem. We will also improve the model to consider elevation and more complex room responses.

References

1. Kim, H.J., Jee, D.G., Park, M.H., Yoon, B.S., Choi, S.I.: The real-time implementation of 3D sound system using DSP. In: IEEE 60th Vehicular Technology Conference, VTC2004-Fall, vol. 7, pp. 4798–4800 (September 2004)
2. Fohl, W., Reichardt, J., Kuhr, J.: A System-On-Chip Platform for HRTF-Based Realtime Spatial Audio Rendering With an Improved Realtime Filter Interpolation. International Journal on Advances in Intelligent Systems 4(3&4), 309–317 (2011)
3. Sakamoto, N., Kobayashi, W., Onoye, T., Shirakawa, I.: DSP Implementation of Low Computational 3D Sound Localization Algorithm. In: 2001 IEEE Workshop on Signal Processing Systems, pp. 109–116 (2001)
4. Raspaud, M., Viste, H., Evangelista, G.: Binaural Source Localization by Joint Estimation of ILD and ITD. IEEE Transactions on Audio, Speech, and Language Processing 18(1), 68–77 (2010)
5. Rodemann, T., Heckmann, M., Joublin, F., Goerick, C., Scholling, B.: Real-time Sound Localization With a Binaural Head-system Using a Biologically-inspired Cue-triple Mapping. In: 2006 IEEE/RSJ International Conference on Intelligent Robots and Systems, pp. 860–865 (October 2006)
6. Algazi, V.R., Duda, R.O., Thompson, D.M., Avendano, C.: The CIPIC HRTF Database. In: Proc. 2001 IEEE Workshop on Applications of Signal Processing to Audio and Acoustics (WASPAA 2001), New Paltz, NY, USA (October 2001)
7. Rayleigh, J.: The theory of sound. Number v. 1 in The Theory of Sound. Macmillan (1894)
8. Algazi, V.R., Dalton Jr., R.J., Duda, R.O., Thompson, D.M.: Motion-Tracked Binaural Sound for Personal Music Players. Audio Engineering Society Convention 119 (October 2005)
9. Algazi, V.R., Duda, R.O., Thompson, D.M., Avendano, C.: The Cipic HRTF Database. CIPIC U.C. Davis (2001)
10. Avendano, C., Algazi, V.R., Duda, R.O.: A Head-and-Torso Model for Low-Frequency Binaural Elevation Effects. In: IEEE Workshop on APplications of Signal Processing to Audio and Accoustics (1999)
11. Algazi, V.R., Avendano, C., Duda, R.O.: Estimation of a Spherical-Head Model from Anthropometry. National Science Foundation (2001)
12. Brown, C.P., Duda, R.O.: An Efficient HRTF Model For 3-D Sound. Master's thesis, University Of Mariyland, San Jose State University (1997)
13. Brown, C.P., Duda, R.O.: A Sructural Model for Binaural Sound Synthesis. IEE Transactions on Speech and Audio Processing 6 (1988)
14. Spagnol, S., Geronazzo, M., Avanzini, F.: Structural modeling of pinna-related transfer functions. In: Proc. Int. Conf. on Sound and Music Computing (2010)
15. Miller, J.D.: Modeling Interneural Time Difference Assuming a Spherical Head. Master's thesis, Stanford University (2001)
16. Zölzer, U., Amatriain, X.: DAFX: digital audio effects. Wiley (2002)
17. GolinHarris: Beagleboard.org (2011), http://beagleboard.org
18. Narcissus: Narcissus Angstrom Distribution, http://narcissus.angstrom-distribution.org/
19. TI: DSPLIB, http://processors.wiki.ti.com/index.php/DSPLIB
20. Davis, P.: Jack Audio Connection Kit, http://jackaudio.org/

Modeling Time-Triggered Ethernet in SystemC/TLM for Virtual Prototyping of Cyber-Physical Systems

Zhenkai Zhang and Xenofon Koutsoukos

Institute for Software Integrated Systems (ISIS)
Department of Electrical Engineering and Computer Science
Vanderbilt University
Nashville, TN, USA
{zhenkai.zhang,xenofon.koutsoukos}@vanderbilt.edu

Abstract. When designing cyber-physical systems (CPS), virtual prototyping can discover potential design flaws at early design stages to reduce the difficulties at the integration stage. CPS are typically complex real-time distributed systems which require networks with deterministic end-to-end latency and bounded jitter. Time-triggered Ethernet (TTEthernet) integrates time-triggered and event-triggered traffic, and has been used in many CPS domains, such as automotive, aerospace, and industrial process control. In this paper, a TTEthernet model in SystemC/TLM is developed to facilitate the design and integration of CPS. The model realizes all the necessary features of TTEthernet, and can be integrated with the hardware platform model for design space exploration. We validate the model by comparing latency and jitter with those obtained using a commercial software-based implementation. We also compare our model with the TTEthernet modeled in OMNeT++ INET framework. Our model provides startup and restart services that are necessary for maintaining synchronized operations in TTEthernet. We evaluate these services and also the efficiency of the simulation.

Keywords: TTEthernet, SystemC, TLM, Virtual Prototyping.

1 Introduction

Cyber-physical systems (CPS) are complex heterogeneous systems whose design flow includes three layers: the software layer, the network/platform layer, and the physical layer [1]. The interactions within and across these layers are complex. The physical layer interacts with the hardware platform through sensors and actuators. Embedded software runs on the hardware platform and communicates via a network to realize the desired functionalities. Due to the high degree of complexity, design flaws often appear at the integration stage. In order to discover potential design flaws at early stages, a virtual prototyping development approach is required.

In virtual prototyping of CPS, modeling the hardware platform in a System-Level Design Language (SLDL) is essential to quickly evaluate the interactions

G. Schirner et al. (Eds.): IESS 2013, IFIP AICT 403, pp. 318–330, 2013.

between the platform and the software layer and the physical layer at early design stages. Since CPS are typically distributed real-time systems, the network also plays an important role in design and integration.

In many CPS domains that require known and bounded network latency, such as automotive, aerospace, and industrial process control, time-triggered Ethernet (TTEthernet) has been used for real-time communication. Traditional Ethernet cannot be used, since it suffers from cumulative delay and jitter. TTEthernet integrates time-triggered traffic and event-triggered traffic together, and provides the capability for deterministic, synchronous, and lossless communication while supporting best-effort traffic service of Ethernet at the same time [2].

SystemC, which has become a *de facto* SLDL [3], is proposed to be one main part of virtual prototyping of CPS [4]. It allows system modeling and simulation at various levels of abstraction. In addition, the concept of transaction-level modeling (TLM) is adopted in SystemC to separate the computation and communication. A TLM communication structure abstracts away low-level communication details while keeping certain accuracy. Thus, both the software layer and the network/platform layer can be modeled in SystemC/TLM at early design stages making it suitable for virtual prototyping.

In this paper, we describe a TTEthernet model in SystemC/TLM for virtual prototyping in order to take into account the network effects in a CPS. The model in SystemC/TLM offers many advantages: (1) it is easy to acquire at early design stages; (2) it is scalable to a large number of nodes; (3) the model can be integrated with the hardware platform model in a straightforward manner; (4) it provides efficient and accurate simulation.

The main contribution of this work is a TTEthernet model in SystemC/TLM that realizes all the necessary features for facilitating the design and integration of CPS. The model is validated by comparing latency and jitter with those obtained using a commercial software-based implementation and the model in OMNeT++ INET framework [5]. The model is also evaluated for its startup and restart services and the simulation efficiency.

The rest of this paper is organized as follows: Section 2 gives the related work including TTEthernet and related modeling efforts. Section 3 describes the model in detail. Section 4 validates the model against a real implementation and the model in OMNeT++ INET framework and also evaluates the services in the model and the simulation efficiency. Section 5 concludes this paper.

2 Related Work

Time-triggered architecture (TTA) has been widely used in safety-critical CPS, which require reliable time-triggered communication systems, such as TTP/C, FlexRay, and TTEthernet [6]. Compared to the maximum bandwidth of TTP/C (25Mbit/s) and FlexRay (10Mbit/s), the bandwidth of TTEthernet can reach 100Mbit/s or even 1Gbit/s, making it very attractive in many CPS domains. As mentioned in [7], there are two versions of TTEthernet. The academic version uses preemption mechanism and only supports time-triggered (TT) and event-triggered (ET) traffic, while the industrial version uses non-preemptive integration of TT and ET and divides ET into rate-constrained and best-effort traffic classes. In [8], the academic version of TTEthernet is introduced to integrate TT and ET traffic together. In [9], an academic version of TTEthernet switch is developed which preempts ET message transmission when a TT message arrives to guarantee a constant transmission delay of TT messages caused by the switch regardless of the load of ET traffic on the network. In [10], a prototypical TTEthernet controller is described and implemented in an FPGA. TTTech Computertechnik AG company issued the TTEthernet specification in [11] and also developed industrial products [12]. Finally, the TTEthernet specification is standardized by SAE in [2].

Modeling TTEthernet has been used to simulate in-vehicle communication systems. In [5], an extension to the OMNeT++ INET framework is made to support simulation of TTEthernet. The model is based on standard Ethernet model in the INET framework. Although the evaluation shows the model is in good agreement with real implementation, the model does not consider different protocol state machines for different roles of synchronization, which results in some services of TTEthernet are simplified or not supported.

In order to support Ethernet networks in the system-level design in a SLDL, various models/approaches have been proposed. In [13], a half-duplex Ethernet based on CSMA/CD MAC protocol is simply modeled using SpecC and TLM techniques. In [14], an Ethernet interface in SystemC/TLM-2.0 is modeled for virtual platform or architectural exploration of Ethernet controllers. Another approach is to integrate network simulators with simulation kernels of SLDLs. In [15], the NS-2 network simulator is integrated into the SystemC/TLM design flow. The advantage of this approach is that network simulators have a good support for almost every commonly used network. However, such an approach requires the integration of two discrete-event simulation kernels, which can greatly reduce the simulation efficiency.

3   Modeling TTEthernet in SystemC/TLM

3.1   Framework

Our TTEthernet model in SystemC/TLM aims at facilitating the design and integration of the network/platform layer in a CPS, especially if the system is a distributed mixed time-triggered/event-triggered real-time system. As shown in Fig. 1, the network/platform layer consists of several computational nodes which communicate with each other through a TTEthernet network. The TTEthernet model includes two separate parts: the TTEthernet controller and the TTEthernet switch. The network is deployed in star topology or cascaded star topology which uses switches to integrate each star topology.

In each node of the system, a TTEthernet controller communicates with other designed hardware components through a memory-mapped bus. Standard TLM-2.0 sockets are used for this purpose. As a target of TLM, the TTEthernet

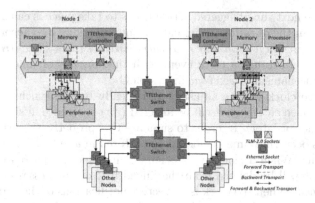

Fig. 1. Network/Platform Layer Design Using TTEthernet Model in SystemC/TLM

controller implements a blocking transport interface method for fast but loosely-timed simulation and non-blocking transport interface methods for slow but approximately-timed simulation.

In order to simulate the bidirectional communication link between two ports of the TTEthernet devices, a specific Ethernet socket is used to model the port. As the TLM-2.0 Ethernet socket introduced in [14], our Ethernet socket is a derived class from both initiator and target sockets of TLM-2.0. In order to distinguish different ports of a TTEthernet device, tagged initiator and target sockets are used as base classes of the Ethernet socket. For binding two Ethernet ports, bind() and operator() are overwritten to bind the initiator socket of each port to the target socket of the other port. For invoking transport interface methods, the operator→ distinguishes which socket of a port should be accessed according to the calling method. Since our TTEthernet model uses Ethernet rather than memory-mapped bus, interoperability is not concerned by introducing new transaction type for Ethernet which is similar to the TLM Ethernet payload type introduced in [14].

3.2   Clock Model

In TTEthernet, a synchronized global time is the base for all time-triggered operations. Each TTEthernet device (controller/switch) is driven by a clock having a clock drift. Thus, the clock synchronization service is crucial for the correct operation. In order to simulate its synchronization service, each TTEthernet device needs to have an independent clock with its own drift and offset. However, SystemC uses a discrete event simulation kernel which maintains a global time. If we simulate every tick of a clock with a drift, the simulation overhead will be too large, which can seriously slow down the simulation. Instead, we model the clock as follows: a random ppm value is assigned to each clock in the interval [-MAX_PPM, -MIN_PPM] ∪ [MIN_PPM, MAX_PPM]. According to the time-triggered schedule, the duration in clock ticks from the current time to the time when the next time-triggered action needs to take place is calculated. After that, we can get the duration in simulation time by taking into account its clock drift: $duration\,in\,simulation\,time = duration\,in\,clock\,ticks \times (tick\,time \pm drift)$, and then we can arrange a clock event with this amount of time by using the notification mechanism of sc_event in SystemC.

Because the clock will be adjusted periodically by the synchronization service, the arranged clock event will be affected (its occurrence in simulation time becomes sooner or later). In order to simulate this properly, the arranged clock event and its occurring time in clock ticks is stored in a linked list in an order of occurring time. When a clock event occurs or its time has passed due to clock adjustment, it will be deleted from the linked list and processes pending on it will be resumed. When the clock is corrected, notifications of the arranged clock events are canceled and new simulation times for the notifications of the events are recalculated based on the corrected clock.

A timer model is also built on the clock model, which uses the drift of the clock model to calculate the duration in simulation time and is used for timeout events. In contrast to clock events, timeout events are not affected by clock synchronization and only depend on how many ticks should pass before they occur.

3.3   TTEthernet Traffic Classes

TTEthernet supports three traffic classes: time-triggered (TT), rate-constrained (RC), and best-effort (BE). In order to recognize which traffic class a frame belongs to, either encoding it in the Ethernet MAC destination address or using EtherType field of the Ethernet frame header is feasible [2]. In our model, we employ the destination address divided into two parts to identify critical traffic (CT) including TT and RC. The first part (32 bits) of the destination address shows whether a frame belongs to CT by checking this part against the result of bitwise AND of CT marker and CT mask. The second part (16 bits) gives the CT ID which is used for further checking and scheduling.

TT messages are used for applications with strict requirements like deterministic end-to-end latency and bounded jitter. RC messages, compliant with ARINC 664 standard part 7, are used for applications with less strict requirements, for which sufficient bandwidth should be allocated. BE messages, using the remaining bandwidth of the network, form the standard Ethernet traffic which has no guarantee of delivery and transmission latency.

TTEthernet also has a transparent traffic used for its synchronization protocol. The synchronization message is called protocol control frame (PCF), and has three types: coldstart frames (CS) and coldstart acknowledgment frames (CA) are used for startup and restart services, and integration frames (IN) are used for synchronization service. In our model, the PCF traffic also uses the MAC destination address to encode its identity.

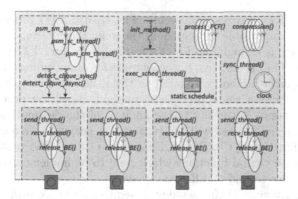

Fig. 2. TTEthernet Device Main Structure

3.4   TTEthernet Device

The TTEthernet controller and switch have several common functions/services.
We extract all the common ones, and implement them in a class named *tte_device*.
tte_device is the abstract base class of *tte_controller* and *tte_switch* which has pure
virtual functions that need to be implemented by *tte_controller* and *tte_switch*
to define different behaviors of these two different devices. Fig. 2 shows the main
SystemC processes in *tte_device*. There is an *init_method()* SystemC method
process which is sensitive to a power-on event and initializes the device. This is
used to model different power-on times given in a configuration file of different
devices. After power-on, startup service of TTEthernet will try to bring the
device into synchronized operation mode.

Ports: An Ethernet socket is used to realize the functions of Ethernet ports.
The TLM-2.0 transport interface methods are implemented to transmit standard
Ethernet frames. Ethernet socket has both blocking transport interface and non-
blocking transport interface. Due to the star or cascaded star network topology of
TTEthernet, the collision domain is segmented and only two TTEthernet devices
which are directly connected may contend for the use of the medium. We model
TTEthernet working in full-duplex mode so that collisions become impossible;
moreover, the non-preemptive integration of TT and ET is used that is compliant
with the products in [12]. Thus, the efficient blocking transport method becomes
accurate enough to model the communication between two TTEthernet devices.

Each TTEthernet device (controller/switch) can have several Ethernet ports
according to its configuration. For a controller, multiple ports represent redundancy which send the same frame in order to realize fault-tolerance. For a switch,
each port can be connected to a controller or a switch to create a separate
collision domain. Each port is associated with three dynamic thread processes
which are *send_thread()*, *recv_thread()*, and *release_ET()*. The *send_thread()* and
recv_thread() processes with the scheduler model the data link layer of TTEthernet, which uses TDMA MAC protocol. The *send_thread()* process is responsible
for starting a frame transmission, and is controlled by the scheduler process

and the *release_ET()* process via events. The *release_ET()* process knows the schedule and is responsible for signaling the *send_thread()* process to send an ET frame if there is enough gap for this frame before next TT frame dispatching time comes. The *recv_thread()* process waits for an incoming frame delivered by the *b_transport()* method registered to the Ethernet socket. When a frame is transmitted through the *b_transport()* method, it will be processed by the *recv_thread()* process. According to the analysis of the destination address, either a PCF handler process will be dynamically spawned, or one of the traffic processing functions (TT, RC, or BE) will be called. The traffic processing functions are pure virtual functions which need to be implemented by different TTEthernet device to realize different behaviors.

Scheduler: Every TTEthernet device sends packets according to a static schedule that relies on synchronized global time. The static schedule is generated by an off-line scheduling tool and used by the TTEthernet device through a configuration file. We use the off-line scheduling tool provided by TTTech [12], which guarantees two TT frames never contend for transmission.

The *exec_sched_thread()* process implements the function of the scheduler and is responsible for signaling the *send_thread()* processes of the ports to start a TT frame transmission according to the static schedule. It pends on a synchronization event occurring when the device enters the synchronized states, and starts executing the schedule when the event happens. If the device goes out of the synchronized states, it also signals the *exec_sched_thread()* process to stop executing the schedule. If the device is a synchronization master, the scheduler process also signals *send_thread()* processes to send out an integration PCF when PCF's dispatching time is reached (dispatching time is 0 in our model).

Protocol State Machine: Each TTEthernet device executes exactly one of the protocol state machines to maintain its role for synchronization, which are formulated in [2]. All TTEthernet devices can be classified into three different roles: synchronization masters (SMs), synchronization clients (SCs), and compression masters (CMs). Startup service of the protocol state machines tries to establish an initial synchronized global time to make devices operate in synchronized mode. When a device detects it is out of synchronization, restart service of the protocol state machines will try to resynchronize itself.

The model has three SystemC thread processes to realize different protocol state machines respectively, which are *psm_sm_thread()* for SM, *psm_sc_thread()* for SC, and *psm_cm_thread()* for CM, as shown in Fig. 2. Each state has its own *sc_event* object which is pended on by the state. If a state has a transition fired because of timeout, it also sets an event's notification by using the timer model, and pends on the event "OR" list of its own *sc_event* object and the timeout *sc_event* object. The *sc_event* object will be notified when any one of transitions of this state is enabled, and corresponding transition flag will be set showing the guard of this transition is met. By checking the flags in an order that is defined in [2], priorities of concurrent enabled transitions are enforced in the protocol state machines, which guarantees determinism. Since concurrent *sc_event* notifications will not queue up, events enabling concurrent transitions will not queue up during execution of the protocol state machines.

Clique detections are used in TTEthernet to detect clique scenarios where different synchronized time bases are formed in a synchronization domain. When cliques are detected, protocol state machines will try to reestablish synchronization. The *detect_clique_sync()* method process is responsible for synchronous clique detection and is sensitive to an event that will be notified when the acceptance window for receiving scheduled PCFs is closed. The *detect_clique_async()* method process is responsible for asynchronous clique detection and is sensitive to an event that will be notified when the acceptance window for receiving scheduled PCFs is closed in CMs or when the clock reaches the dispatching time in SMs or SCs.

Synchronization Service: When operating in synchronized mode, TTEthernet uses a two-step synchronization mechanism: SMs dispatch PCFs to CMs, and CMs calculate the global time from the PCFs (i.e. "compress") and dispatch "compressed" PCFs to SMs and SCs. SMs and SCs receive "compressed" PCFs and adjust their clocks to integrate into the synchronized time base.

When a PCF arrives, a dynamic PCF handler process (*process_PCF()*) will be spawned to cope with this PCF. Concurrent PCF handler processes may exist due to multiple PCFs arriving with small time difference. Permanence function [2] is used to reestablish the temporal order of the received PCFs. The *process_PCF()* implements the permanence function by using the timer model. By checking the PCFs, the process also enables some transitions whose guards only count on PCFs in the protocol state machines.

If the TTEthernet device is a CM, a dynamic compression process (*compression()*) may be spawned if there is no process handling corresponding integration cycle of the PCF. The integration cycle filed of a PCF shows which round of synchronization this PCF belongs to. Compression function [2] is used to collect PCFs having the same integration cycle number within a configurable interval and compress these PCFs for calculating the synchronized global time. The *compression()* also uses the timer model to realize all the time delays needed by its collection and delay phases.

When the acceptance window for receiving PCFs ends, the *sync_thread()* process will be resumed to calculate the clock correction from the PCFs that are in-schedule. After a fixed delay (at least greater than half of the acceptance window), the clock will be adjusted by the calculated correction value.

3.5   TTEthernet Controller and Switch

Both the TTEthernet controller and switch are derived from TTEthernet device, and implement the pure virtual functions to realize different behaviors of processing the traffic.

The TTEthernet controller also acts as a TLM-2.0 target which receives transactions containing Ethernet frames via a target socket. Extensions are made to the generic payload to show which traffic class the Ethernet frame belongs to. Each traffic class has its own transmission and reception buffers. In the case of a write command, the controller puts the extracted Ethernet frame into the corresponding traffic transmission buffer. When the controller receives a frame, it will signal the processor to read it via interrupt, and it puts the received frame into a transaction in response to a read command and sets the traffic class extension.

The TTEthernet switch uses critical traffic table and schedule table to route and forward CT (TT and RC) frames, and uses static/dynamic routing tables for BE frames. It also acts as a temporal firewall for TT traffic to segregate faulty controllers if they are babbling. For RC traffic, it uses token bucket algorithm to enforce a bandwidth allocation gap between two consecutive RC frames.

4   Experimental Results

In this section, we compare our TTEthernet model with the model in OMNeT++/INET framework [5] and a real TTEthernet implementation from TTTech for validation. We also evaluate the startup and restart services as well as the efficiency of the simulation.

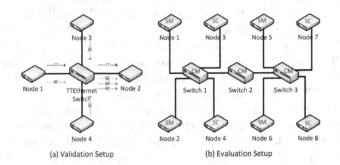

Fig. 3. Experiment Scenarios

4.1   Validation

We set up a star topology which has four nodes connected to a central TTEthernet switch with 100Mbit/s links as shown in Fig. 3 (a). Node 1 sends both TT traffic and BE traffic to Node 2, and both Node 3 as well as Node 4 send only BE traffic to Node 2. All the traffic goes through a TTEthernet switch. The communication period is 10ms, and the time slot is $200\mu s$. The maximum clock drift is set as 200ppm for the models. Node 1 sends a TT frame at 1ms offset of each period. The configuration files including their corresponding XML files for the nodes and switch are generated by the TTTech toolchain [12]. From the generated XML files, we extract parameters such as critical traffic table and schedule table to configure our model and the model in OMNeT++. In this setup, the switch dispatches the TT frame sent by Node 1 at 1.4ms offset of each period. The metrics we measure are average end-to-end latency and jitter of TT frames which are important factors for real-time communication systems. We measure these metrics for different TT frame sizes under full link utilization of BE traffic. Fig. 4 shows the results of our model in SystemC/TLM, the model in OMNeT++ INET framework, and the software stack implementation in Linux from TTTech [12].

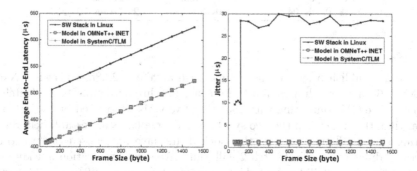

Fig. 4. Average End-to-End Latency and Jitter of Different Frame Sizes

From the figure we can see the model in SystemC/TLM and the model in OMNeT++ INET framework give very similar results. In [16], the method of measuring end-to-end latency of software-based implementation of TTEthernet is stated. According to [16], the measured latency gap ($90\mu s$) between frame size of 123 and 124 bytes of the software-based implementation is caused by the measuring port driver configuration. The measured jitter of the software-based implementation is bounded by $30\mu s$ [16]. The hardware-based implementations will bound the jitter more tightly [12].

4.2 Evaluation

We set up the network as shown in Fig. 3 (b) to evaluate the startup and restart services implemented in our model. In this cluster, Node 1, Node 2, Node 5, and Node6 are SMs; Switch 1, Switch 2, and Switch 3 are CMs; the rest are SCs. The integration cycle is 10ms, and the parameters are generated by the TTTech toolchain [12].

With different power-on times, we record the time when every powered device in the cluster enters its synchronized state in Tab. 1. Since different power-on times of Switch 2 may cause cliques in the cluster, we also record the time when every powered device is resynchronized back to its synchronized state due to clique detection and restart service. Since in this setup SCs only passively receive PCFs, we set the power-on times of them as 0s.

When every device approximately starts at the same time, the devices will be synchronized quickly which are shown in the first two cases. When the CMs are powered later than the SMs, the time when every one is synchronized will be delayed as shown in the third case. In the fourth case, Node 1, Node 2, and

Table 1. Startup and Restart Service Evaluation

N1 & N2 & N5 & N6	SW1 & SW2 & SW3	Sync	Resync
0s/0s/0s/0s	0s/0s/0s	29.834ms	-
0.1ms/1ms/0.5ms/1.2ms	1.1ms/0.8ms/1.5ms	30.845ms	-
2ms/4ms/8ms/6ms	30ms/10ms/40ms	79.856ms	-
0s/0s/0s/0s	0s/30ms/0s	38.677ms	-
0s/0s/0s/0s	0s/50s/0s	29.776ms	50.0256s

Switch 1 establish a synchronized time base at about 29.8ms; likewise, Node 5, Node 6, and Switch 3 establish the other synchronized time base. Switch 2 which is the CM connecting with the other two CMs is powered just a little bit later than the time when the two synchronized time bases are established. Since during this small time interval the clock drifts have not caused the two time bases to differ too much, Switch 2 will join in the synchronization quickly and the two time bases will be merged into one time base. In the fifth case, two separate synchronized time bases are established before Switch 2 is powered as well. However, this time Switch 2 is powered much later (about 49.07s) than the time when the two time bases are established. The clock drifts have caused the two subsets of devices not to be synchronized over subset boundaries. When Switch 2 is started, asynchronous clique detection and restart service implemented in our model result in a new synchronized global time, and at 50.0256s every device is synchronized.

Finally, we evaluate the scalability and simulation efficiency of our approach. We set up the evaluation using a central switch, and all the nodes are connected to the switch. The simulation time is 1000s, and increasingly add a pair of nodes into the network. Each pair of the nodes, such as Node 1 and Node 2, communicates with each other using TT, RC, and BE traffic. Each node sends out a TT frame, a RC frame, and a BE frame every 10ms. Thus, there are $300,000 \times number\ of\ nodes$ frames totally. The result is shown in Fig 5.

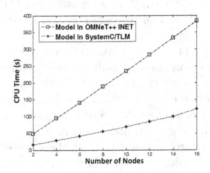

Fig. 5. Used CPU Time of Different Number of Nodes

From the results we can see the model in SystemC/TLM has good simulation efficiency when the number of nodes increases. The simulation speed of the model in OMNeT++ INET framework is also evaluated under the same computation environment (2.50GHz dual-core CPU and 6GB memory). We simulate the same topology and traffic by using the fastest mode in OMNeT++ to get rid of the influence of animation and text outputs.

5 Conclusions

Due to the complex interactions between different layers of a CPS, virtual prototyping has become an important approach to discover potential design flaws before the last integration stage. SystemC/TLM has been adopted for virtual prototyping because of its capability of modeling both the software layer and the network/platform layer of a CPS. TTEthernet has been used in many CPS domains and provides bounded end-to-end latency and jitter.

In order to take into account the network effects caused by TTEthernet when designing a CPS, a model in SystemC/TLM is proposed in this paper. The developed model considers all the necessary features of TTEthernet and can be integrated into the hardware platform model in a straightforward manner. We validate the model against the model in OMNeT++ INET framework and the software-based implementation from TTTech, and evaluate the startup and restart services which are used to maintain the synchronization by powering on the devices at different times.

The future work focuses on integrating this model into a mixed TT/ET distributed CPS simulation framework and using timed automata to verify this model.

Acknowledgments. This work has been partially supported by the National Science Foundation (CNS-1035655).

References

1. Sztipanovits, J., Koutsoukos, X.D., Karsai, G., Kottenstette, N., Antsaklis, P.J., Gupta, V., Goodwine, B., Baras, J.S., Wang, S.: Toward a Science of Cyber-Physical System Integration. Proceedings of the IEEE 100(1), 29–44 (2012)
2. SAE Standard AS 6802: Time-Triggered Ethernet (2011)
3. IEEE Standard 1666-2011: Standard SystemC Language Reference Manual (2011)
4. Müller, W., Becker, M., Elfeky, A., DiPasquale, A.: Virtual Prototyping of Cyber-Physical Systems. In: ASP-DAC 2012, pp. 219–226 (2012)
5. Steinbach, T., Kenfack, H.D., Korf, F., Schmidt, T.C.: An Extension of the OMNeT++ INET Framework for Simulating Real-time Ethernet with High Accuracy. In: SIMUTools 2011, pp. 375–382 (2011)
6. Kopetz, H., Bauer, G.: The Time-Triggered Architecture. Proceedings of the IEEE 91(1), 112–126 (2003)
7. Steiner, W., Bauer, G., Hall, B., Paulitsch, M.: Time-Triggered Ethernet: TTEthernet (November 2010)

8. Kopetz, H., Ademaj, A., Grillinger, P., Steinhammer, K.: The Time-Triggered Ethernet (TTE) Design. In: ISORC 2005 (2005)
9. Steinhammer, K., Grillinger, P., Ademaj, A., Kopetz, H.: A Time-Triggered Ethernet (TTE) Switch. In: DATE 2006, pp. 794–799 (2006)
10. Steinhammer, K., Ademaj, A.: Hardware Implementation of the Time-Triggered Ethernet Controller. In: IESS 2007, pp. 325–338 (2007)
11. Steiner, W.: TTEthernet Specification (2008)
12. TTTech Computertechnik AG: TTEthernet Products, http://www.tttech.com/en/products/ttethernet/
13. Banerjee, A., Gerstlauer, A.: Transaction Level Modeling of Best-Effort Channels for Networked Embedded Devices. In: Rettberg, A., Zanella, M.C., Amann, M., Keckeisen, M., Rammig, F.J. (eds.) IESS 2009. IFIP AICT, vol. 310, pp. 77–88. Springer, Heidelberg (2009)
14. GreenSocs Ltd: Ethernet Communication Protocol using TLM 2.0. (2010), http://www.greensocs.com
15. Bombieri, N., Fummi, F., Quaglia, D.: TLM/Network Design Space Exploration for Networked Embedded Systems. In: CODES+ISSS 2006, pp. 58–63 (2006)
16. Bartols, F., Steinbach, T., Korf, F., Schmidt, T.C.: Performance Analysis of Time-Triggered Ether-Networks Using Off-the-Shelf-Components. In: ISORCW 2011, pp. 49–56 (2011)

I/O Sharing in a Multi-core Kernel
for Mixed-Criticality Applications

Gang Li and Søren Top

Mads Clausen Institute for Product Innovation, University of Southern Denmark
{gangli,top}@mci.sdu.dk

Abstract. In a mixed-criticality system, applications with different safety criticality levels are usually required to be implemented upon one platform for several reasons(reducing hardware cost, space, power consumption). Partitioning technology is used to enable the integration of mixed-criticality applications with reduced certification cost. In the partitioning architecture of strong spatial and temporal isolation, fault propagation can be prevented among mixed-criticality applications (regarded as partitions). However, I/O sharing between partitions could be the path of fault propagation that hinders the partitioning. E.g. a crashed partition generates incorrect outputs to shared I/Os, which affects the functioning of another partition. This paper focuses on a message-based approach of I/O sharing in the HARTEX real-time kernel on a multi-core platform. Based on a simple multi-core partitioning architecture, a certifiable I/O sharing approach is implemented based on a safe message mechanism, in order to support the partitioning architecture, enable individual certification of mixed-criticality applications and thus achieve minimized total certification cost of the entire system.

Keywords: I/O sharing, multi-core systems, mixed-criticality, safety-critical real-time kernel, safe inter-core communication.

1 Introduction

A computer-based system in critical applications should guarantee to be safe, without making harm to humans or environment around, even in case of the corruption of some certain parts of safety-critical applications. In the real life, applications have different natural criticality levels. E.g. a KONE escalator [1] comprises a dual-channel safety-critical control logic system (an application) and non-safety-critical systems such as display. The criticality level of an application is defined as a Safety Integrity Level (SIL, a level of risk reduction) in the IEC 61508 [1], ranging from the least dependable SIL 1 to the most dependable SIL 4. The certification cost of an application with a SIL is in the direct proportion to the SIL since the development and certification of higher SIL applications has more rigorous requirements. When a system integrates different SIL applications

---

[1] http://www.kone.com

G. Schirner et al. (Eds.): IESS 2013, IFIP AICT 403, pp. 331–342, 2013.

on one platform with resources sharing(processor, memory or I/O) and no isolation mechanism is taken into account, all the applications have to be certified to the highest SIL, aiming at ensuring the dependability of the highest SIL applications. Otherwise, lower SIL applications with higher failure probability would corrupt higher SIL applications. The entire system being certified to the highest SIL definitely leads to unacceptable increase in the development and certification cost. The basic approach introduces partitioning between mixed-criticality applications in terms of logical and temporal behaviour, which can prevent the propagation of a number of faults between applications. Each application is presumed to reside on a partition in the system.

Besides the traditional partitioning approach (federated architecture), the ongoing partitioning trends are to share a processing element for different SIL applications, or implement them on individual cores on a multi-core platform or the combination of both, by using partitioning mechanisms that provides isolation between applications. E.g. ARINC651 [2] standards proposed Integrated Modular Avionics (IMA) architecture which enforces system-level spatial and temporal isolation to integrate mixed-criticality applications onto a processor. [3] implements mixed-criticality applications into different isolated cores on the trusted MPSoC platforms. Due to such partitioning mechanisms, different SIL applications on one processing element or platform can be certified individually according to their own SILs, and the total cost of development and certification is subsequently reduced. This is the exact objective of the ARTEMIS project Reduced Certification Costs Using Trusted Multi-core Platforms(RECOMP) [2].

Besides performing partitioning mechanisms regarding processors and memory, I/O partitioning is also a big challenging issue when I/Os have to be shared by mixed-criticality applications. Firstly, mixed-criticality applications are not completely isolated if partitions can operate on shared I/Os directly. Shared I/Os are usually related to the functions of both high SIL applications and low SIL applications. A low SIL application could fail and possibly masquerade as a high SIL application to perform incorrect input or output on its accessible I/Os, which therefore results in the failure of the high SIL application. Additionally, even if the low SIL application doesn't masquerade as the high SIL application, it also possibly puts I/Os out of operation and thus the high SIL application is unable to perform its critical operations. Secondly, even if each partition works well from its own point of view, the I/O operation could also fail. As seen in Fig.1, a safety-critical application (Partition 1) reaches the end point of its statically-allocated time slice and has to handover I/O resources to another partition when it's in the critical section of operating on the shared I/Os. This could be unacceptable for I/O operations. Furthermore, another application (Partition 2) takes the turn and possibly changes the I/O configuration or perform its desired operations on I/Os. In the next main frame (a periodical interval), Partition 1 obtains the turn again and continues to perform the rest of the operations. This raises the problem that Partition 2 maybe has modified the I/O configuration or has performed some input or output in the critical sec-

---

[2] http://www.recomp-project.eu

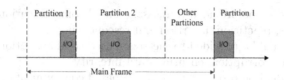

Fig. 1. Preempted I/O access by partitions

tion of Partition 1, which affects the functioning of I/O operations or disturbs the I/O operations (preempted I/O access) in Partition 1. This definitely makes Partition 1 non-functional.

In this paper, Section 2 discusses safety requirements of message-based I/O sharing approach on the basis of safety standards and our experiences. Section 3 introduces a simple multi-core partitioning architecture and then Section 3 investigates the design of message-based I/O sharing approach in our real-time kernel (HARTEX) [4]. Section 5 gives an example how this I/O sharing approach is used in an industrial safe stop component. Section 6 discusses related work and Section 7 concludes.

2   Safety Requirements

To enable the integration of mixed-criticality applications onto a multi-core platform, robust partitioning [5] is employed to provide an assurance of intended isolation of independent applications (partitions) implemented upon one platform. Regarding I/O sharing in the partitioning, informal requirements at the architectural level are proposed:

1. A partition must be unable to masquerade as another partition to operate on shared I/Os.
2. A partition must be unable to affect the shared I/O operations of another partition in terms of logical and temporal behaviour.
3. A partition must be unable to affect the logical and temporal behaviour of another partition through shared I/Os.
4. Any attempt of the incorrect access to I/Os must not lead to a unsafe state and can be detected and recognized, and results in a corresponding action to handle the violation.

Note that the second requirement enforces that a partition can't affect I/O operations of another partition, since the partition probably changes the I/O configuration without notifying another partition or disturbs the I/O operations. The third requires a partition to be isolated from another partition even if using shared I/Os.

Since message passing is used to transfer data between partitions inside one core or across multiple cores for I/O sharing, a set of safety requirements shall be proposed to ensure safe communication according to the safety standard IEC61508.

1. Protection shall be provided to message-based communication for detecting message loss, repetition, insertion and resequencing.
2. Protection shall be provided to message-based communication for detecting message data corruption, ensuring data integrity.
3. Protection shall be provided to message-based communication for detecting message transmission delay, ensuring temporal behaviour.
4. Protection shall be provided to message-based communication for detecting message masquerade, ensuring message correct identification recognition.
5. The message-based communication shall support mixed-criticality levels.
6. The message-based communication shall support the interaction across mixed-criticality partitions.
7. Any fault of message-based communication shall not leads to a unsafe state and can be handled after being detected.

The first to the fourth requirements ensures a safe message-based communication that is the base of the I/O sharing. The fifth one requires that different SIL communication services are provided to serve different SIL applications. The sixth one enables the communication between mixed-criticality partitions, which is required by the nature of applications. E.g. a high SIL control application needs to send control results to a low SIL display application.

3　System Design

To fulfill the requirements presented above and achieve an easier certification, one rule of thumb should be kept in our mind while designing the partitioning multi-core system architecture and I/O sharing in the HARTEX real-time kernel: simplification.

3.1　System Architecture

The proposed system architecture supports two levels of partitioning in the context of a configurable multi-core platform(e.g. System on Chip (SoC) platform): inter-core level and intra-core level as shown in Fig. 2. At the inter-core level, physical separation of processing cores is exploited to a great extent for core independence and isolation. Each core has a private memory(or a virtual private one), and the multi-core HARTEX kernel employs the asymmetric multi-processing (AMP) multikernel architecture proposed in [6]. This multi-core architecture proposed is similar to a federated architecture but residing on a chip, in order to achieve relatively effortlessly-certifiable partitioning and exploit the methodologies and frameworks used in distributed systems. Additionally, each core support intra-core partitioning similar to IMA if mixed-safety applications have to be allocated into one processing core. However, the intra-core partitioning is surely of more certification cost since it shares more resources and complicates the architecture of the kernel and hardware (involving Memory Management Unit or Memory Protection Unit). Therefore, partitions with different SILs are recommended to be allocated respectively into isolated cores at inter-core level. If the

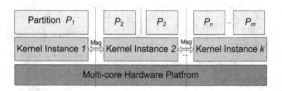

Fig. 2. System architecture

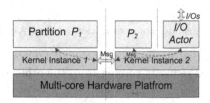

Fig. 3. I/O sharing approach

inter-core isolation can satisfy the system partitioning needs, intra-core isolation is no longer needed, avoiding the certification cost of intra-core isolation design. Therefore, the intra-core isolation mechanism is designed as a configurable component in the kernel. A violation handling mechanism of partitioning is required to process violations in a unified manner.

In this two-level partitioning architecture, I/O sharing among partitions can be addressed by a simple message-based approach, as shown in Fig.3. Each shared I/O has a dedicated actor that can perform all possible operations on the I/O. Tasks belonging to different partitions that require to share the I/O are no longer able to access the I/O directly. The I/O is only accessible to its hosted actor. The I/O with its actor works in an isolated partition and the other partitions can perform their desired operations on the I/O by sending a request via a safe message. The actor works as a server and processes all the requests buffered in a waiting queue when the actor partition gets its turn to run. All the execution of this approach is determined at the system integration time. This approach has two advantages. Firstly, less software has to be certified to the highest SIL among the mixed-criticality partitions. Each partition is isolated from the I/O partition and other partitions, so the low SIL partitions are just certified to their corresponding SILs. Of course, I/O actor has to be certified to the highest SIL, which is essentially inevitable. Secondly, this is a simpler solution for I/O sharing on a multi-core platform, comparing to multi-core mutual exclusion management. Therefore, it's easier to certify.

4   Kernel Design for I/O Sharing

I/O sharing in the HARTEX multikernel enforces the existence of a safe message passing manager and a certifiable I/O resource manager. A message across partitions has to be validated to a level of dependability by applying a set of

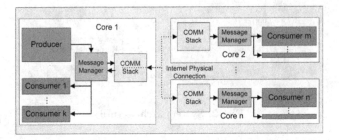

Fig. 4. Producer-consumer communication in the HARTEX multikernel

measures. The I/O sharing needs to abstract all I/O operations into a server model for message-based requests coming from the other partitions.

4.1 Safe Message Passing

Fig.4 presents the communication mechanism of the HARTEX multikernel in general. Each core has a message manager and a communication stack (COMM stack) for safe intra-core and inter-core communication. The message manager and the communication stack are dedicated to implement the safety layer and communication protocol respectively. The message manager takes the responsibility of managing messages and applying safety-related communication measures. If a message passing failure occurs, the message manager reports the failure to the Violation Manager in the HARTEX multikernel, which handles all kinds of violations in a unified manner. Additionally, the message manager pushes incoming requests of I/O sharing into I/O waiting queue. The communication stack is a typical layered network protocol for embedded systems, which takes care of message routing for intra-core and inter-core communication. It also provides timed-triggered communication that enables the communication subsystem to transfer a message at a specific time instance.

The communication process is fully controlled by the trusted kernel executing in the supervisor mode. The message manager provides a number of safety measures in the kernel space, listed in Table 1. A message can be configured to have several of these safety measures applied according to its SIL requirement. E.g. Cyclic Redundancy Check, Check Sum and Message Acceptance Filtering measures can be applied to one message, by putting these measures IDs into the message configuration. More safety-related measures can be added in the HARTEX multikernel. From Table 2, all the potential communication faults presented in IEC 61508 can be alleviated by the listed safety measures. Note that the pad in the table means all the measures labelled by pads should be applied together to cover this kind of faults.

4.2 I/O Sharing Management

In a multi-core system, some I/Os are dedicatedly connected to a specific core, but some can be connected to several cores (E.g. a LCD I/O interface connected

Table 1. safety communication measures in the HARTEX

Exploitation of interconnection hardware redundancy	Cyclic Redundancy Check
	Message via dual channels
Exploitation of time redundancy	Check sum
	Double-sending of a message
Other measures	Message Acceptance Filtering
	Message sequence index
	Timed Message Scheduling

Table 2. Communication faults are coved by specific safety measures

Failure types	Hardware redundancy	Time redundancy	Message filtering	Sequence index	Time-triggered scheduling
Repetitions				√	
Deletion				√	
Insertion				√	
Resequence				√	
Corruption	√	√			
Delay					√
Masquerade	•	•	•		

to multiple cores by a common bus). This raises issues from the multi-core point of view. Firstly, some dedicated resources possibly need to be accessed by the other cores. Secondly, multiple cores could use a shared exclusive resource concurrently. This contention can reduce system scalability and performance, since in the conventional way all the relevant states of a resource (E.g. free, being occupied) should be maintained for state consistency among all the cores. This complicated interaction causes the system to be of higher certification cost. Moreover, partitioning is not taken into account while sharing I/Os.

Our approach that improves the localizability of shared resources has been proposed. Each shared I/O is designed to form a partition on a specified core, and all the possible operations on the shared I/O are only performed by this partition. A client-server model for a shared I/O is introduced such that the operations on the I/O of all the other partitions (clients) are achieved by sending request messages to the specified I/O partition. An I/O actor (as a server) integrated with the resource manager on the host specified core receives request messages, validates the messages, performs corresponding operations on the shared resource, and optionally feedbacks operation results to the requesting cores. The I/O actor is isolated from the other partitions and the message-based requests are guaranteed by the mentioned safety measures applied in the mes-

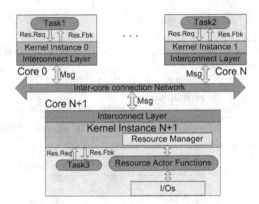

Fig. 5. Server-Client model of shared resource access mechanism

sages. Additionally, the upper limit of the number of requests from a partition in one Main Frame is predetermined in the actor partition as well as specific services of I/O operations that could be used by the partition. Fig. 5 illustrates that tasks on the same core or on different cores can send I/O requests to the resource server via the local message manager. The execution of the actor in the separation kernel is dependent on the allocated time slices of the actor partition.

This approach has several advantages. Firstly, the relevant states of shared resources are not necessary to be replicated among multiple cores. This approach directly facilitates higher system scalability and simplifies the system architecture. Secondly, an I/O resource accessible only to a core are enabled to be accessed by the other cores in a uniform manner by using this approach. Thirdly, the core-level subsystem with localized I/Os has less interference with the other cores logically besides the validated message requests, which facilitates the partitioning architecture. Therefore, the system abstraction model is more understandable and also easily analysed and certified. In the end, one crashed partition which could use a shared I/O is unable to affect the I/O resource utilization by the other cores, if the I/O actor partition works well and I/O message-based requests are well-validated. Tasks with different SILs are enabled to access the I/O without hindering the partitioning architecture, when the I/O actor is certified to the highest SIL of these tasks.

To achieve the server-client model of resource sharing, each I/O resource needs to be abstracted into an I/O actor model, which provides clients with all the operation functions. These functions are invoked by the resource manager according to the validated requests. E.g. a monitor can be simply abstracted into four functions: Monitor_config() function that can initialize and configure the monitor, Monitor_on() function that can turn on the monitor, Monitor_off() function that can turn off the monitor and Monitor_display() function that can display values on the monitor. Each function can get value parameters of a configurable size in the message-based request. All the functions corresponding to different operations have to take the I/O current configuration and states into consideration before executing its desired operations.

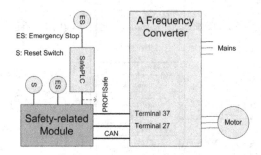

Fig. 6. A safety-related module for a frequncy converter

5   A Case Study: A Safety-Related Module for a Frequent Converter

There is a typical safety-critical application from industrial domain [7]: a safety-related module for a frequency converter used to control the speed of an electrical motor. E.g. controlling a rotating blade in a manufacturing machine. The failure of stopping the motor safely results in the harm to people or equipments. Therefore, a safety-related module implementing a safe stop is highly required. In Fig.6, the inputs of the safety-related module are a safe field bus (PROFISafe) and the local emergency stop button. In addition, a reset switch is used to recover the module into an initial state. According to standard IEC 61800-5-2, a safe stop can be ensured by two functions Safe Torque Off and Safe Stop 1. The safety function Safe Torque Off is achieved through the safety-related interface terminal 37 which can remove the power from electronics and afterwards the motor coasts. The Safe Stop 1 is to request an internal function of the frequency converter to ramp down the speed of the motor via the terminal 27. Both functions perform in conjunction to achieve a safe stop.

To achieve SIL 3 according to IEC 61508, 1oo2D structure [1] is selected for acquiring the hardware fault tolerance of 1, which has two redundant isolated channels with mutual diagnostics. An initial model of the safety-related model in a high abstraction level is proposed in Fig.7. The model only takes care of the high level components, their implementation in hardware or software, and the interaction. It's represented intuitively by the extended safety architecture taxonomy [7]. Black color represents components implemented in hardware and grey color means in software. Solid line represents safety-related components, dotted line represents diagnostics components and dashed line represents non-safety-related components.

As illustrated in Fig.7, only one multi-core chip comprising three isolated cores is used to implement the two safety-related channels and a non-safety-related channel respectively. Core 1 performs one safe-related channel and diagnostics, and similarly Core 2 performs the redundant safe-related channel and diagnostics. Core 3 executes the non-safety-related reset handler as well as the non-safety-related gateway. "A" in the grey dotted circle in the left are actuators

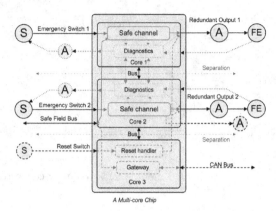

Fig. 7. A high-level abstraction model of a safety-related module for a frequncey converter on a multi-core chip

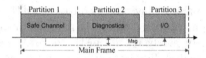

Fig. 8. I/O sharing in a safety-related module for a safe stop

that monitor their own emergency switches whether they are in the operational state or not, and "A" in the black line circle in the right are actuators that react to the external environment. Here we focus on the partitions on Core 1 as an example, aiming at investigating the sharing of the output port in the partitioning architecture. The safe-related channel (a component) can execute functional operations and the diagnostics component monitors the channels, sensors and actuators, which naturally constitutes two partitions. Both partitions share the redundant output 1 but have to be isolated. A fault taking place in the safe channel partition can not be propagated to the diagnostics partition, in order to avoid that the fault affects the judgement of the diagnostics partition and subsequently it is possibly undetectable.

In Fig.8, three partitions should be implemented upon Core 1: Safe Channel partition, Diagnostics partition and I/O partition. The Safe Channel partition performs the safety-related functions and sends safe messages to the Diagnostics and I/O partitions. The Diagnostics partition checks the correctness of the safe channel output, as well as the states of its objective sensor and actuator. If any fault takes place, the Diagnostics partition sends safe messages to the I/O partition to interact to the actuator, aiming at switching the system into a safe state in case of the fault. All the possible operations on the output 1 are abstracted into a well-defined model including the functional operations and handlers in case of different faults. This architecture to a great extent simplifies the development and certification of this case study.

6   Related Work

Exclusive shared I/O operations are usually executed under the protection of mutual exclusion management, which is widely used in real-time operating systems. However, the management of shared I/Os has to take into account the isolation in a partitioning architecture that comprises mixed-criticality applications. The traditional I/O sharing approach Time division multiple access (TDMA) to I/Os can not fulfil the isolation requirements between partitions since it only solves temporal isolation.

I/O virtualization is a new approach that ensures the division of I/O, where each virtual machine (partition) with its own system image instance can operate on I/Os independently. In the embedded system world, the XtratuM hypervisor is in charge of providing virtualization services to partitions, and all I/Os are virtualized as a secure I/O partition which can receive and handle I/O operation requests from the other partitions [8]. This is very similar to our separation kernel but still a little different. The XtratuM hypervisor is a virtualization layer that's prone to high-performance applications comparing to the HARTEX multikernel. The partition instance of the XtratuM can be a bare-machine application, a real-time operation system or a general-purpose operation system. The HARTEX multikernel focuses on fine-grained systems and its partition instance is a set of basic executable tasks. Therefore, the HARTEX multikernel leads to a small size of code (4300LOC) and simple architecture, and thus has less certification cost. It has advantages when it comes to small applications. Additionally, the HARTEX multikernel supports multi-core architecture with safe communication. A strongly partitioned real-time system in [9] proposes the Publish-Subscribe architecture in a microkernel for I/O sharing. Partition has the Pseudo-Device Driver to access the I/Os by sending requests to the microkernel. The microkernel layer has device queues to buffer requests, physical device drivers and a device scheduler to handle the requests. This benefits the system with high I/O bandwidth since I/Os can be operated in all authorized partitions. However, the approach results in poor portability and higher certification cost, due to the fact that, besides more complicated design, the code size of the kernel increases since the I/O drivers are added into the kernel and have to be certified together with the kernel. Once moving the kernel to another platform, the entire kernel has to be certified again with the drivers of the new platform, which is required by the safety standard IEC 61508, and thus leads to poor portability.

7   Conclusion

This paper targets simplification and reduced certification cost of mixed-criticality applications on a multi-core platform in the context of I/O sharing. This is a part of our deliverables for the RECOMP project. According to guidelines in the IEC 61508, this paper contributes a set of requirements to enable I/O sharing in a mixed-criticality system. Based on these requirements, a simplified partitioning multi-core architecture has been proposed with several advantages such as physical isolation between inter-core partitions, easy development and reduced certification. Furthermore, the safe message-based communication in the kernel can guarantee safe requests of accessing I/Os in the I/O partition with different levels of dependability in the kernel space. The simple I/O sharing approach has been fully explored to support mixed-criticality partitions without breaking the partitioning architecture. Therefore, a mixed-criticality system of isolated partitions that have to share I/Os can be allocated into one platform and partitions can be certified individually according to their own SILs and consequently the total certification cost is reduced. Since taking the overall consideration of hardware and software architecture, our I/O sharing approach in the context of partitioning systems is simple, flexible and certifiable.

References

1. Functional safety of electrical/electronic/programmable electronic safety related systems (2010)
2. Arinc specification 651: Design guidance for integrated modular avionics (1991)
3. Ernst, R.: Certificationn of trusted mpsoc platforms. In: 10th International Forum on Embedded MPSoC and Multi-core (2010)
4. Angelov, C.K., Ivanov, I.E., Burns, A.: Hartex: a safe real-time kernel for distributed computer control systems. Softw. Pract. Exper. 32, 209–232 (2002)
5. Integrated modular avionics (ima) development guidance and certification considerations (2005)
6. Baumann, A., Barham, P., Dagand, P.-E., Harris, T., Isaacs, R., Peter, S., Roscoe, T., Schüpbach, A., Singhania, A.: The multikernel: a new os architecture for scalable multicore systems. In: Proceedings of the ACM SIGOPS 22nd Symposium on Operating Systems Principles, SOSP 2009, pp. 29–44. ACM (New York (2009)
7. Berthing, J., Maier, T.: A taxonomy for modelling safety related architectures in compliance with functional safety requirements. In: Saglietti, F., Oster, N. (eds.) SAFECOMP 2007. LNCS, vol. 4680, pp. 505–517. Springer, Heidelberg (2007)
8. Masmano, M., Peiro, S., Sanchez, J., Simo, J., Crespo, A.: Io virtualisation in a partitioned system. In: Proceeding of the 6th Embedded Real Time Software and Systems Congress (2012)
9. Shah, R., Lee, Y.-H., Kim, D.Y.: Sharing I/O in strongly partitioned real-time systems. In: Wu, Z., Chen, C., Guo, M., Bu, J. (eds.) ICESS 2004. LNCS, vol. 3605, pp. 502–507. Springer, Heidelberg (2005)

Evaluating the Impact of Integrating a Security Module on the Real-Time Properties of a System*

Sunil Malipatlolla[1] and Ingo Stierand[2]

[1] OFFIS - Institute for Information Technology,
Oldenburg, Germany
sunil.malipatlolla@offis.de
[2] Carl von Ossietzky Universität Oldenburg,
Oldenburg, Germany
stierand@informatik.uni-oldenburg.de

Abstract. With a rise in the deployment of electronics in today's systems especially in automobiles, the task of securing them against various attacks has become a major challenge. In particular, the most vulnerable points are: (i) communication paths between the Electronic Control Units (ECUs) and between sensors & actuators and the ECU, (ii) remote software updates from the manufacturer and the in-field system. However, when including additional mechanisms to secure such systems, especially real-time systems, there will be a major impact on the real-time properties and on the overall performance of the system. Therefore, the goal of this work is to deploy a minimal security module in a target real-time system and to analyze its impact on the aforementioned properties of the system, while achieving the goals of secure communication and authentic system update. From this analysis, it has been observed that, with the integration of such a security module into the ECU, the response time of the system is strictly dependent on the utilized communication interface between the ECU processor and the security module. The analysis is performed utilizing the security module operating at different frequencies and communicating over two different interfaces i.e., Low-Pin-Count (LPC) bus and Memory-Mapped I/O (MMIO) method.

Keywords: Security, FPGA, Interfaces, Real-Time Systems.

1 Introduction and Related Work

Real-time applications such as railway signaling control and car-to-car communication are becoming increasingly important. However, such systems require high quality of security to assure the confidentiality and integrity of the information during their operation. For example, in a railway signaling control system, the

---

* This work was supported by the Federal Ministry for Education and Research (BMBF) under support code 01IS11035M, 'Automotive, Railway and Avionics Multicore Systems (ARAMiS).

control center must be provided with data about position and speed of the approaching train so that a command specifying which track to follow may be sent back. In such a case, it must be assured that the messages exchanged between the two parties are not intercepted and altered by a malicious entity to avoid possible accidents. Additionally, it is mandatory to confirm that the incoming data to the control center is in fact from the approaching train and not from an adversary. Similar requirements are needed in a car-to-car communication system. Thus, there is a need to integrate a security mechanism inside such systems to avoid possible attacks on them. Furthermore, above considered systems are highly safety relevant, thus the real-time properties typically play an important role in such systems. In general, the goal of a real-time system is to satisfy its real-time properties, such as meeting deadlines, in addition to guaranteeing functional correctness. This raises the question, what will be the impact on these properties of such a system when including, for example, security as an additional feature? To understand this, we integrate a minimal security module in the target real-time system and evaluate its impact on the real-time properties as a part of this work.

There exist some work in the literature which addresses the issue of including security mechanisms inside real-time applications. For example, Lin et al. [9] have extended the real-time schedulability algorithm Earliest Deadline First (EDF) with security awareness features to achieve a static schedulability driven security optimization in a real-time system. For this, they extended the EDF algorithm with a group-based security model to optimize the combined security value of selected security services while guaranteeing schedulability of the real-time tasks. In a group-based security model, security services are partitioned into several groups depending on the security type and their individual quality so that a combination of both results in a better quality of security. However, this approach had a major challenge as how to define a quality value for a certain security service and to compute the overhead due to those services. In another work, authors Marko et al. have designed and implemented a vehicular security module, which provides trusted computing [12] like features in a car [13]. This security module protects the in-vehicle ECUs and the communication between them, and is designed for a specific use in e-safety applications such as emergency breaking and emergency call. Further, the authors have given technical details about hardware design and prototypical implementation of the security module in addition to comparing its performance with existing similar security modules in the market. Additionally, the automotive industry consortium, autosar, specified a service, referred to as Crypto Service Manager (CSM), which provides a cryptographic functionality in an automobile, based on a software library or on a hardware module [2]. Though the CSM is a service based on a software library, it may be supported by cryptographic algorithms at the hardware level for securing the applications executing on the application layer. However, to the best of our knowledge, none of the aforementioned approaches addresses the issue of analyzing the impact on the real-time properties of a system when integrating a hardware security module inside it.

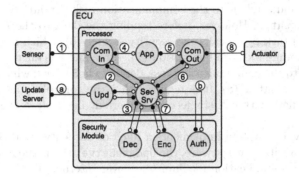

Fig. 1. System Scenario

The rest of the paper is organized as follows. Section 2 gives a detailed description of the system under consideration and its operation with the security module internals and the adversarial model. Section 3 evaluates the system operation with three different test scenarios, and presents the corresponding analysis results. Section 4 concludes the paper and gives some hints on future work.

2 System Specifications

2.1 System Model

The system under consideration is depicted in Figure 1. It comprises of a sensor, an actuator, an electronic control unit (ECU) with a processor & a security module, and an update server. The system realizes a simple real-time control application, where sensor data are processed by the control application in order to operate the plant due to an actuator. The concrete control application is not of interest in the context of this paper. It might represent the engine control of a car, or a driver assistant system such as an automatic breaking system (ABS).

The scenario depicted in Figure 1 consists of the following flow: Sensor periodically delivers data from the plant over the bus (1), which is in an encrypted form to avoid its interception and cloning by an attacker. The data is received by the input communication task ComIn, which is part of the operating system (OS). Each time the input communication task receives a packet, it calls the security service (SecSrv), which is also part of the OS, for decryption of the packet (2). The security service provides the hardware abstraction for security operations, and schedules service calls. The decryption call from the communication task is forwarded to the security module (3), which processes the packet data. The cryptographic operations of the security module modeled by Dec, Enc, and Auth are realized as hardware blocks. The decrypted data is sent back to the security service, which is in turn returned to the ComIn. Now the data is ready for transmission to the application (4), which is modeled by a single task App. The application task is activated by the incoming packet, and processes the sensor data. The controller implementation of the task calculates respective actuator data and sends it to the communication task `ComOut` (5) for transmission to the `Actuator`. However, before sending the data to the `Actuator`, the communication task again calls the security service (6), which in turn accesses the security module for data encryption (7). After `Enc` has encrypted the data, it is sent back to the communication task `ComOut` via `SecSrv`, which delivers the packet to the `Actuator` (8). It is required that the control application finishes the described flow within a single control period, i.e., before the next sensor data arrives.

Additionally, the system implements a function for software updates. To update the system with new software, the `UpdateServer` sends the data to the `Upd` task (a) via a communication medium (e.g., over Internet) to the outside. This received data must be authenticity verified and decrypted before loading it into the system. For this, the `Upd` forwards the data to the `SecSrv`, which utilizes the `Auth` block of the security module (b). Only after a successful authentication, the data is decrypted and loaded into the system else it is rejected.

The security module, integrated into the ECU, is a hardware module comprising of cryptographic hardware blocks for performing operations such as encryption, decryption, and authenticity verification. Though these operations are denoted as tasks in the system view, they are implemented as hardware blocks. Further, a controller (a state machine), a memory block, and an I/O interface are included inside the security module (not depicted in Figure 1). Whereas the controller executes the commands for the aforementioned cryptographic operations, the memory block acts as a data buffer. The commands arrive as requests form the `SecSrv` on the processor, and the responses from the security module are sent back. In essence, the `SecSrv` acts as a software abstraction of the hardware security module, for providing the required cryptographic operations to the executing tasks on the processor.

The security module is equipped with particular support for update functionality i.e., authenticity verification. In normal operation, the data is temporarily stored in the memory block of the security module to compare the attached Hash-based Message Authentication Code (HMAC) value by the update server with the computed HMAC value in the security module before decrypting and loading it. This kind of operation, where all update data is stored in memory of the security module, and authentication being applied at once on the data, is however not appropriate in the context of the considered real-time application. This is because, while the security module is performing authentication, other operations such as decryption of incoming sensor data or encryption of outgoing actuator data are blocked. Given this, large update data can block the device for a long time span, resulting in a violation of allowed delay by the control algorithm.

To avoid such a situation in the considered scenario, for authenticity verification, the HMAC is calculated in two steps. In the first step, a checksum of the update data is calculated using a public hash algorithm such as Secure Hash Algorithm (SHA-1). In the second step, the HMAC is computed on this checksum. The `Upd` task thus calculates and sends only the checksum of the data instead of whole data itself to the security module via `SecSrv`. Since the update process is not time critical, `Upd` task is executed with low priority, preventing any undesired interference with the real-time application. Therefore, only the interference for authentication of the single checksum has to be considered. However, since the update data being encrypted, `Upd` task needs to access the security module for its decryption. To this end, the data is split into packets and decrypted piece-wise. The impact of these operations has to be considered in the real-time analysis.

Another possibility to verify the authenticity of the update data would be to compute the HMAC iteratively within the security module. For this, the update data from the `Upd` task is sent to the security module in a block-by-block basis via the `SecSrv`. The computed HMAC on the received block is stored inside the memory block of the security module. Before sending the next block, the `SecSrv` checks for any pending requests for encryption or decryption operation from other high priority tasks. If there exists such a request, it is executed before sending the next block of data for HMAC computation. In order to handle this procedure, the security module should be equipped with an additional hardware block performing the scheduling of cryptographic operations. Further, the communication interface between the `SecSrv` and the security module has to be modified. Though, this method is currently not supported by our security module it is definitely a desired feature.

The goal of the security module is to provide a secure communication path between the sensor and the actuator and to provide authentic updates of the system. For this, the cryptographic blocks of the security module utilize standardized algorithms for providing the cryptographic operations such as encryption, decryption, hash computation, and HMAC generation & verification. Having said that, all the aforementioned cryptographic operations performed by the security module in the considered system utilize a single block cipher algorithm i.e., Advanced Encryption Standard (AES) as the base [10]. It is a symmetric key algorithm i.e., it utilizes a single secret key for both encryption and decryption operations. In addition to being standardized by National Institute for Standards and Technology (NIST), the AES-based security mechanisms consume very few computational resources, which is essential in resource constrained embedded systems.

2.2   Adversarial Model

To describe all possible attack points in the considered system, an adversarial model is formulated as depicted in Figure 2. The model highlights all the components (with a simplified ECU block) and the corresponding internal and external communication paths (i.e., numbered circles) of the original system (c.f. Figure 1). The adversary considered in the model is an active eavesdropper (c.f. Dolev-Yao Model [5]), i.e., someone who first taps the communication line to obtain messages and then tries everything in order to discover the plain text. In particular he is able to perform different types of attacks such as classical cryptanalysis and implementation attacks, as defined in taxonomy of cryptographic attacks by Popp in [11]. While classical cryptanalysis attacks include cloning by

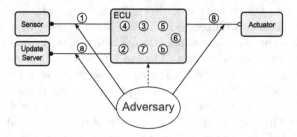

Fig. 2. Adversarial Model

interception, replay, and man-in-the-middle attacks, the implementation attacks include side-channel analysis, reverse engineering, and others.

For our analysis, we assume that the attacker is only able to perform classical cryptanalytic attacks on the external communication links (indicated by thick arrows coming from adversary) i.e., from sensor to ECU, ECU to actuator, and update server to ECU. In specific, under cloning by interception attack, the adversary is capable of reading the packets being sent to the ECU and store them for using during a replay attack. Whereas in a man-in-the-middle attack, the adversary can either pose as an ECU to authenticate himself to the update server or vice versa. In the former case, he would know the content of the update data and in the latter he may update the ECU with a malicious data to destroy the system. However, to protect the systems against the classical cryptanalytic attacks, strong encryption and authentication techniques need to be utilized. With reference to this, the security module in here provides techniques such as confidentiality, integrity, and authenticity which overcome these attacks. We rule out the possibility of attacker being eavesdropping the ECU's internal communication (indicated by a dotted arrow coming from adversary) because such an attack implies that the attacker is having a physical access to the ECU and thus control the running OS and the tasks themselves.

3   System Analysis

To analyze the impact of including the security feature on the real-time properties of the system, we consider three different test cases as detailed in the sequel. A brief description about the system set-up and the utilized tools is given before delving into the obtained results with the test cases.

The control application is executed with a frequency of 10 kHz, i.e., the Sensor sends each $100\,\mu s$ a data packet to the ECU. The update service is modeled as a sporadic application with typically very large time spans between individual invocations. All tasks of the processor are scheduled by a fixed priority scheduling scheme with preemption, where lower priority tasks can be interrupted by higher priority tasks. Furthermore, all tasks belonging to the OS (depicted by a dark gray shaded area of Figure 1) get higher priority than the application tasks. The priorities in descending order are ComIn, ComOut, SecSrv, App, and Upd.

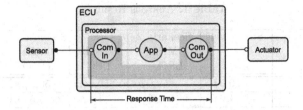

Fig. 3. Scenario 1 w/o security feature

The operations of the security module are not scheduled, and the module can be considered as a shared resource. The `SecSrv` task processes incoming security operation requests for the security module in first-in-first-out (FIFO) order.

For all test cases, the processor of the ECU is a 50MHz processor ($20\,ns$ cycle time) that is equipped with internal memory for storing data and code. Internal memory is accessed by reading and writing 16 Bit words within a single processor cycle. Communication between the ECU, the sensor, and the actuator is realized by a controller area network (CAN) bus. For simplicity, we assume that all data are transferred between the processor and the CAN bus interface via I/O registers of 16 bit width, and with a delay of four processor cycles. Communication over CAN is restricted to 64 Bit user data, and we assume that this is also the size of packets transmitted between the ECU and the sensor/actuator. In order to transmit 128 Bit data as required by the operation of the security module, each transmission consists of two packets. Receiving and transmitting data thus requires 16 Byte data transfer between the CAN bus controller and the processor, summing up to 64 processor cycles ($1.28\,\mu s$). Storing the packet into the OS internal memory costs additional $320\,ns$. Bus latencies are not further specified in our setting, as we concentrate on the timing of the ECU application.

The utilized AES algorithm inside the security module operates on 128 Bit blocks of input data at a time. Thus, all the blocks (`enc`, `dec`, and `Auth`) of the security module, operate on same data size because they utilize the same algorithm. The security module is implemented as a proof-of-concept on a Xilinx Virtex-5 Field Programmable Gate Array (FPGA) [7] platform. The individual cryptographic blocks of the security module are simulated and synthesized utilizing the device specific tools. Utilizing an operating frequency of 358 MHz for the FPGA, the execution time for each of encryption, decryption, and authentication operations is determined (by simulation) to be $46\,ns$ for a 128 Bit block of input data. The timing parameters for other operating frequencies of the security module are obtained by simple scaling. The utilized FPGA device supports storage in the form of block RAM with 36 kb size, which is large enough to be used as memory block of the security module.

We apply timing analysis in order to find the worst-case end-to-end response time of the control application, starting from the reception of sensor data up to the sending of actuator data (shown in Figure 3). Various static scheduling analysis tools are available for this task (e.g. [6,1]). The system however is sufficiently small for a more precise analysis based on real-time model-checking [4]. To this end,

Table 1. Analysis Results

Task	Scenario 1	Scenario 2 50MHz LPC	Scenario 3 50MHz LPC	Scenario 3 50MHz MMIO	Scenario 3 358MHz MMIO
App	$50.0\,\mu s$	$50.0\,\mu s$	$50.0\,\mu s$	$50.0\,\mu s$	$50.0\,\mu s$
ComIn	$1.6\,\mu s$	$1.6\,\mu s$	$1.6\,\mu s$	$1.6\,\mu s$	$1.6\,\mu s$
ComOut	$1.6\,\mu s$	$1.6\,\mu s$	$1.6\,\mu s$	$1.6\,\mu s$	$1.6\,\mu s$
SecSrv	—	$80\,ns$	$80\,ns$	$80\,ns$	$80\,ns$
Comm. CPU/SM	—	$1.46\,\mu s$	$1.46\,\mu s$	$400\,ns$	$200\,ns$
Dec	—	$358\,ns$	$358\,ns$	$358\,ns$	$46\,ns$
Enc	—	$358\,ns$	$358\,ns$	$358\,ns$	$46\,ns$
Auth	—	—	$358\,ns$	$358\,ns$	$46\,ns$
Response Time	$53.2\,\mu s$	$60.1\,\mu s$	$62.0\,\mu s$	$56.7\,\mu s$	$54.96\,\mu s$

the system is translated into a Uppaal model [3]. The worst-case response time is obtained by a binary search on the value range of respective model variable.

3.1   Target System without any Security Features

In the first scenario, which is shown in Figure 3, the communication tasks send the data directly to the control application and to the communication bus without encryption or decryption. The resulting end-to-end response time is shown in column "Scenario 1" of Table 1. As expected, the analysis shows that the execution times are simply summed up for the involved tasks since no further interferences occur in this simple setting. Indeed the situation would be different when multiple application tasks are executed on the same ECU, which would cause additional interferences.

3.2   Target System with Secure Communication Feature

In the second scenario, only the secure communication feature between the ECU and the sensor and the actuator is enabled. The update service however is switched off. This implies that the security module has to perform only encryption and decryption but no authentication. For this scenario, we assume that the security module communicates with the processor via a Low-Pin-Count (LPC) bus [8]. LPC is a 4 Bit wide serial bus defined with a clock rate of 33 MHz. According to the specification [8], the transfer of 128 Bit data plus 16 Bit command requires about $1.46\,\mu s$, when the bus operates with typical timing parameters. Each invocation of the SecSrv involves a transfer of the data to or from the security module, plus the execution time of the task of $80\,ns$ for internal copying operations. The security module operating at a clock rate of 50 MHz results in an individual execution time of $358\,ns$ for encryption and decryption (from simulation results). With this set-up, the timing analysis shows (column "Scenario 2" of Table 1), that enabling only the secure communication feature results in a significant raise in the response time of the system i.e., about 13% more than in the previous scenario.

3.3   Target System with Secure Communication and Secure Update Features

For the third scenario, both secure communication and authentic update features are enabled. This scenario has been analyzed with three different sets of timing parameters.

The first setting assumes the same parameters as for Scenario 2. Hence the security module operates at a clock rate of 50 MHz, and communicates with the processor via LPC. The results show a further raise in the end-to-end response time of the application because the update service might call the authentication service, which incurs an additional execution time to the pending encryption and decryption operations of the security module. Thus, it can be seen that the end-to-end response time is around 16% higher than in the first scenario.

For the second setting, we assume that the security module communicates with the processor via a Memory-Mapped I/O (MMIO) interface. Memory transfers are assumed to operate with 16 Bit words, and a delay of four processor cycles, resulting in transfer times of 80 ns. A transfer between the processor and the security module now sums up to 400 ns.

The final setting works with a very fast security module, and memory transfers only having two cycles delay. The security module operates at 358 MHz, which results in all cryptographic operations with 46 ns of execution time.

Surprisingly, the end-to-end response time in the second and the final setting has reduced and is only around 6.5% and 3.5% respectively. This implies that the type of communication interface between the processor and the security module has a significant impact on the resulting overall response time of the system.

In all settings, the software update function is assumed to perform the operations as discussed in Section 2. After calculating the checksum of the update data, task Upd sends an authentication request to SecSrv. When the authentication is successful (which is always true in the considered scenario), the task successively sends decryption requests for each packet of the update data, while waiting for the reply before sending a new request. The results shown in the table represent the worst-case behavior obtained with various values of the execution time (between 10 ns and 1 μs) needed by Upd between successive decryption requests. The impact of the operation of Upd remains rather small, which can be explained by the fact that the task is executed with low priority. However, the selection of the execution times was not exhaustive, and thus do not guarantee absence of race conditions. To enforce limited impact of the update function, the SecSrv should be modified by running with priority inheritance, where requests are executed with the same priority as the calling task. A more comprehensive analysis of this issue is subject of future work.

4   Conclusion

In this work, a real-time system integrated with a security module is analyzed to determine the impact of the latter on the worst-case response time of the system. For this, different communication interfaces such as LPC bus and MMIO method are utilized between the security module and the control unit processor of the system, for performing cryptographic operations such as encryption, decryption, and authentication. It is observed that the worst-case response time of the system is high for a slower interface (i.e., LPC) and decreases drastically for a faster interface (i.e., MMIO). Thus, when including a security mechanism in real-time systems it is necessary to consider about the type of communication interface being utilized. Though, the target system in here has a single ECU, a sensor, and an actuator, the typical systems have multiple such components which need a further investigation.

References

1. Anssi, S., Albers, K., Dörfel, M., Gérard, S.: chronVAL/chronSIM: A Tool Suite for Timing Verification of Automotive Applications. In: Proc. Embedded Real-Time Software and Systems, ERTS (2012)
2. Autosar Organization: Specification of Crypto Service Manager (2011), http://www.autosar.org/download/R4.0/AUTOSAR_SWS_CryptoServiceManager.pdf
3. Behrmann, G., David, A., Larsen, K.G.: A Tutorial on Uppaal 2004-11-17. Tech. rep. Aalborg University, Denmark (November 2004)
4. Dierks, H., Metzner, A., Stierand, I.: Efficient Model-Checking for Real-Time Task Networks. In: International Conference on Embedded Software and Systems, ICESS (2009)
5. Dolev, D., Yao, A.C.: On the security of public key protocols. Tech. rep. Stanford University, Stanford, CA, USA (1981)
6. Hamann, A., Jersak, M., Richter, K., Ernst, R.: A framework for modular analysis and exploration of heterogeneous embedded systems. Real-Time Systems 33(1-3), 101–137 (2006)
7. Inc., X.: Xilinx, http://www.xilinx.com/support/documentation/virtex-5.htm
8. Intel: Low Pin Count (LPC) Interface Specification. Intel Corp. (August 2002)
9. Lin, M., Xu, L., Yang, L., Qin, X., Zheng, N., Wu, Z., Qiu, M.: Static security optimization for real-time systems. IEEE Transactions on Industrial Informatics 5(1), 22–37 (2009)
10. National Institute of Standards and Technology (NIST): Advanced Encryption Standard (AES) (2001)
11. Popp, T.: An Introduction to Implementation Attacks and Countermeasures. In: Proceedings of IEEE/ACM International Conference on Formal Methods and Models for Co-Design (MEMOCODE 2009), pp. 108–115 (July 2009)
12. Trusted Computing Group, Inc.: Trusted Platform Module (TPM) specifications (2010), http://www.trustedcomputinggroup.org/resources/tpm_main_specification
13. Wolf, M., Gendrullis, T.: Design, implementation, and evaluation of a vehicular hardware security module. In: Kim, H. (ed.) ICISC 2011. LNCS, vol. 7259, pp. 302–318. Springer, Heidelberg (2012)

Author Index

Printed in the United States
By Bookmasters